Experiential Activities for

Teaching Multicultural Competence

in Counseling

Edited by
Mark Pope, Joseph S. Pangelinan, and Angela D. Coker

AMERICAN COUNSELING
ASSOCIATION
5999 Stevenson Avenue
Alexandria, VA 22304
www.counseling.org

Experiential Activities for
Teaching Multicultural Competence
in Counseling

10 9 8 7 6 5 4 3 2 1

American Counseling Association
5999 Stevenson Avenue
Alexandria, VA 22304

Director of Publications ▥ Carolyn C. Baker

Production Manager ▥ Bonny E. Gaston

Editorial Assistant ▥ Catherine A. Brumley

Copy Editor ▥ Kimberly Kinne

Cover and text design by Bonny E. Gaston

Library of Congress Cataloging-in-Publication Data

Experiential activities for teaching multicultural competence in counseling / edited by Mark Pope, Joseph S. Pangelinan, and Angela D. Coker.
    p. cm.
  Includes bibliographical references and index.
  ISBN 978-1-55620-284-1 (alk. paper)
1. Cross-cultural counseling.   2. Multiculturalism.   I. Pope, Mark, 1952–   II. Pangelinan, Joseph S.
III. Coker, Angela D.
  BF636.7.C76E95 2011
  158'.3071—dc22   2010043517

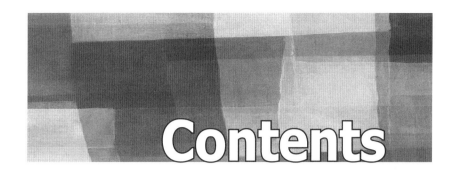
Contents

Activity handouts and PowerPoint presentations throughout the text are located on the enclosed CD-Rom.

Section 6
Oppression and Discrimination

Contents

Section 11
Socioeconomic Status and Social Class

Foreword

Patricia Arredondo

In the past 20 years, multicultural counseling classes have become staples in the majority of counselor training programs around the United States and, increasingly, in international classrooms as well. A new generation of scholars and practitioners has fueled the enthusiasm for teaching about multicultural topics and for creating innovative activities for bringing theories and concepts to life. *Experiential Activities for Teaching Multicultural Competence in Counseling* is an excellent resource for use in both multicultural counseling classes and other core classes in which infusion and reinforcement of cultural learning can readily occur. Multicultural advocates have always insisted on the relevance of cultural concepts in all counseling courses. Whether one is teaching family issues, group work, counseling theory, supervision, or, of course, practicum, the activities from this new text can serve to expand thinking and understanding about relevant cross-cultural perspectives and practices. In 1996, "Operationalization of the Multicultural Counseling Competencies" (Arredondo et al.) was published with the goal of providing behavioral examples to implement the landmark "Multicultural Counseling Competencies and Standards: A Call to the Profession" (Sue, Arredondo, & McDavis, 1992). It is gratifying to have a text that promotes the implementation of the multicultural counseling competencies.

Experiential Activities for Teaching Multicultural Competence in Counseling introduces a range of topics embedded in the multicultural counseling competencies. In the 11 sections and 121 chapters, professionals and graduate students provide alternative applications for personal and professional development. It has been well documented that lectures are only one modality for teaching; increasingly, it is experiential activities, both inside and outside of the classroom, that fortify the lessons to be learned. There are common themes across the different chapters. Among these is the emphasis on individuals' multidimensionality; respect of different worldviews; perspective taking; cross-cultural styles of learning, communicating, and responding to mental health interventions; identity development; and ecological considerations. After all, multicultural counseling models reinforce the interdependence of the individual, family, group, community, and nation. Context and culture count, and this principle is evident throughout the text.

The writers introduce activities that may have seemed dangerous or taboo 20 years ago. They address issues of socioeconomic classism, oppression, and discrimination, including White privilege, emotional discomfort in the context of counseling, and transgender identity. I particularly like the chapter addressing the use of proverbs and their culture-specific and cross-cultural applications and the chapter describing the use of cultural genograms.

The counseling profession has made great advances in the past 20 years, and the American Counseling Association has been instrumental in fostering the evolution of the multicultural counseling movement.

As Indira Ghandi stated, "You can't shake hands with a closed fist" (Simpson, 1988, p. 5). Mark Pope, Joseph S. Pangelinan, and Angela D. Coker have brought Ghandi's words to life.

References

Arredondo, P., Toporek, R., Brown, S. P., Jones, J., Locke, D., Sanchez, J., & Stadler, H. (1996). Operationalization of the multicultural counseling competencies. *Journal of Multicultural Counseling and Development, 24*, 42–78.

Simpson, J. B. (1988). *Simpson's contemporary quotations*. Boston, MA: Houghton Mifflin.

Sue, D. W., Arredondo, P., & McDavis, R. J. (1992). Multicultural counseling competencies and standards: A call to the profession. *Journal of Counseling & Development, 70*, 477–486.

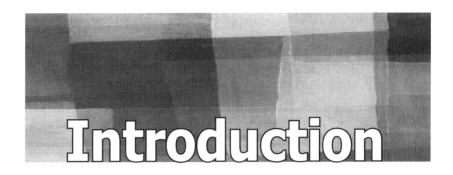

Introduction

We now live in diverse global village that has become increasingly more interconnected with each passing day. Understanding and appreciating this diversity is a key component of our work as counselors and counselor educators. Few among us would argue against the ethical premise that counselor education must be concerned with the development of the whole individual, which also includes culture and human diversity. The American Counseling Association's (ACA's) *Code of Ethics* (2005) includes the following statement on competence, which speaks to the issue of both professional ethics and human diversity:

> *C.2.a. Boundaries of Competence*. Counselors practice only within the boundaries of their competence, based on their education, training, supervised experience, state and national professional credentials, and appropriate professional experience. Counselors gain knowledge, personal awareness, sensitivity, and skills pertinent to working with a diverse client population.

When teaching multicultural counseling principles, it is generally viewed as best practice for faculty not only to devote whole courses to the issue of culture, but also to infuse cultural diversity throughout our profession's core curriculum. Faculty who have taught such classes have often found themselves adapting and using experiential activities as a means of increasing students' participation in the learning process. Often, such faculty have developed many of their activities in isolation and have shared these experiential activities only with other faculty who also share an interest in developing multicultural competence.

This book is primarily intended for newly minted counselor educators who are just beginning their academic careers and preparing to teach courses that are new to them or who are in the throes of developing or enhancing existing courses that may lack adequate cultural infusion. This book is also intended for seasoned counselor educators who are committed to implementing social and cultural foundations in any or all core content areas highlighted in the 2009 Council for Accreditation of Counseling and Related Educational Programs (CACREP) standards. This publication represents a collaborative effort to provide a central location of experiential activity resources for faculty wishing to implement consciousness-raising learning tools and strategies in the clinical training of counseling students.

The development of this book has been a two-year journey, starting with the collection of various activities from counselor education faculty across the country. We initially sent out a call for submissions to several counselor education Internet listservs (including CESNET) in addition to soliciting submissions at the annual ACA national conference. Immediately and over the course of a year and a half we received many responses and submissions from a diversity of practitioners and counselor educators. We are extremely proud of the collection presented in this volume.

We have tried to make this book very user-friendly, and so we have organized each activity (referred to as a "chapter") in several different ways that we hope will facilitate your use of these resources. First, this book is organized into 11 different sections that represent the primary subject matter that appears in both beginning and advanced multicultural counseling classes. This subject matter includes everything from introductory conversations about cultural diversity, definitions of *oppression* and *discrimination*, and components of becoming a culturally skilled counselor to considerations in counseling specific cultural groups (which includes considerations of race, sexual orientation, spirituality, and social class).

We developed a topical cross-index that provides a list of chapters that are cross-indexed by a more detailed list of topics and is divided into three parts: (a) chapters on topics related to the content and process of teaching multicultural counseling classes (including the use of popular culture/media, creative arts, personal narratives, and technology), (b) chapters on topics related to the various cultural groups, and (c) chapters infusing cultural diversity into core classes directly related to the CACREP standards.

These activities are fun and thought-provoking and are designed to stimulate critical consciousness in the areas of personal awareness, knowledge, and skills. They can be used in a stand-alone multicultural course or infused into career, research, family counseling, clinical and supervision training, group counseling, or human life span and development courses. Furthermore, a CD-ROM accompanies this volume that includes a compilation of all the group activities handouts shared in this book.

When an instructor selects and facilitates any experiential activity, we want to stress the importance of adhering to the use of safety guidelines and ethical diversity group work. An activity should not be used just to fill in an empty time slot. Group facilitators are responsible for determining the appropriateness and readiness of their class to engage in a particular activity. This determination includes making sure students are adequately prepared through prior class readings and/or class discussions. Group facilitators must also have sufficient training and experience in facilitating diversity work in addition to solid knowledge about group dynamics. Group facilitators must be responsible for clearly stating the purpose of the activity and how it ties into the overall objectives of the course. It is also important to set ground rules for participation (e.g., respect, appropriate use of language) in addition to determining clear procedures for handling any group conflict that may arise. For a detailed outline of diversity group work considerations, refer to the Association for Specialists in Group Work's (1998) Principles for Diversity-Competent Group Workers.

Finally, the three of us are grateful to the many talented authors who contributed to the development of this book. The contributing authors' biographies highlight their accomplishments and commitment as counselor educators. We appreciate their true scholarship, creativity, and willingness to allow us to highlight their work in this volume. We are proud to note that contributors to this book generously represent all five regions of the United States (i.e., North Atlantic, North Central, Southern, Rocky Mountain, and Western) highlighted by the Association for Counselor Education and Supervision (ACES). We are also grateful to Carolyn Baker of ACA for her guidance in the publication of this book, University of Missouri—St. Louis doctoral student David Hart for his graduate assistance, and Lynne McCarthy and Sue Cross for their administrative support. This book would not have come to fruition without your collective aid. We thank you!

We hope you find this publication a useful and valuable resource in your work as multicultural and social justice advocates. We are confident that you will find an activity that fits your needs within the content of your course. As you review and use this book, we welcome any comments or feedback you have regarding its contents. Please send all comments to Mark Pope at pope@umsl.edu.

—*Mark Pope, Joseph S. Pangelinan, and Angela D. Coker*

References

American Counseling Association. (2005). *ACA code of ethics*. Alexandria, VA: Author.
Association for Specialists in Group Work. (1998). *Principles for diversity-competent group workers*. Alexandria, VA: Author.

About the Editors

Mark Pope, Ed D, NCC, MCC, MAC, ACS, has been teaching multicultural counseling classes for over 20 years. He is currently professor and chair of the Division of Counseling and Family Therapy at the University of Missouri—Saint Louis. Dr. Pope is the author of 5 books, over 30 book chapters, over 40 journal articles, and over 100 professional presentations at the international, national, and state levels, and he has written extensively on various aspects of counseling, including the career development of ethnic, racial, and sexual minorities; violence in the schools; teaching career counseling; psychological testing; international issues in counseling; and the history of public policy issues in career counseling. His works have appeared as books, as conference presentations, and in such journals as the *Journal of Counseling & Development*, *The Career Development Quarterly*, *The Counseling Psychologist*, *The Family Journal*, and the *Journal of Multicultural Counseling and Development*. He has special expertise in Native American, Asian, and sexual minority cultures.

Dr. Pope has served as president of the ACA, National Career Development Association, and Association for Lesbian, Gay, Bisexual, and Transgender Issues in Counseling. He has been elected as a fellow of the ACA, American Psychological Association (APA), National Career Development Association, and Society of Counseling Psychology. He has also served as the editor of *The Career Development Quarterly* as well as on the editorial boards of several other professional journals.

Dr. Pope is an elder of St. Francis River Band of Cherokees and a senior trial judge in the Southeastern Cherokee Tribal Courts. He has worked with quite diverse populations, including individuals from a variety of cultures, races, ethnic groups, genders, and sexual orientations. Specifically, he has helped Native Americans who are both HIV+ and alcoholic, workers who are being laid off by their employer, heroin addicts on the southside of Chicago, psychiatrically hospitalized adolescents, people with AIDS and their partners, people who are abusing alcohol and other substances, same-sex and opposite-sex couples, and disadvantaged and ethnically diverse students. Dr. Pope has founded and designed the counseling programs for a variety of agencies, including high schools, colleges, and private counseling agencies, and he has been a career testing and planning consultant for a variety of profit and intentionally nonprofit corporations.

Dr. Pope also served as the director of psychological services for the American Indian AIDS Institute and the Native American AIDS Project in San Francisco.

Joseph S. Pangelinan, MS, NCC, LPC, is a doctoral student in the Division of Counseling and Family Therapy at the University of Missouri—Saint Louis. He was born and raised on Chuuk Island in the Micronesian region of the Pacific Ocean. In 1990, he completed his undergraduate studies at Benedictine College in Atchison, Kansas. After working in the field for two years, he matriculated in the counseling program at Southeast Missouri State University. While at Southeast Missouri State University, he completed all of his practicum and field experience hours at the Center for Health and Counseling, where he emphasized work with minority populations and international students. For his capstone master's thesis project, he did a comparative study on the psychological help-seeking behaviors of students from the United States and Turkey.

Upon graduation with a master's degree in counseling, Joe accepted a position with Bootheel Counseling Services in rural southeast Missouri, where he helped develop, market, and implement the Missouri Access/Crisis Response System. This effort involved working with individuals who are marginalized and not able to access mental health services because of geographic isolation, physical limitations, poverty, and social stigma.

In 1999, Joe moved to the Cottonwood Residential Treatment Center, a Missouri Department of Mental Health facility, to continue his work with children and adolescents who had been identified as mentally disordered or ill by the state. Three years later, Joe accepted a position at Logos School, where he remains.

In his current position, Joe works as a counselor and director of behavior intervention and field education. He provides individual and group counseling with student-clients who have been diagnosed with an emotional and often a learning disability. He also does treatment planning and consultation on difficult cases with teachers, parents, school districts, and other therapists. He trains and provides supervision to social work and counseling interns on best counseling practices with the students who have been identified with emotional and learning disabilities.

Joe has taught graduate counseling courses and presented programs at the local, regional, and national levels on multicultural issues, career development, crisis intervention, school counseling foundations, counseling practicum, and counseling field experience. He is a regular speaker on issues of cultural diversity at schools throughout the Saint Louis metropolitan region.

Angela D. Coker, PhD, LPC, NCC, is an assistant professor of counseling and family therapy at the University of Missouri—St. Louis. She is a licensed professional counselor in the state of Missouri and a national certified counselor. Born and raised in New York City, she received her BA in liberal arts from Brooklyn College, her MS in counselor education from the University of Wyoming, and her PhD in educational psychology and counseling from the Union Institute and University in Cincinnati, Ohio.

Dr. Coker has been teaching counselor education classes for over 10 years. She specializes in multicultural counseling, consultation, and advocacy. She is the author of several peer-reviewed journal articles and book chapters that address the intersections of race, gender, and class issues in counseling. Her particular area of research and clinical interest is in exploring the emotional and psychological needs of African American women. Her scholarly endeavors include an exploration of African American women's body image satisfaction, mental health perceptions and usage of counseling services, academic attainment, and workplace experiences. Dr. Coker has examined the developmental concerns and challenges of African American adolescent girls. She has also published on the importance of developing cultural competencies when conducting research with African American study participants.

Central to her academic inquiry is the question, How can counselor education and supervision be used to expand multicultural awareness, knowledge, and social advocacy? Dr. Coker is an active member of the ACA, Counselors for Social Justice, the Association for Counselor Education and Supervision, and Chi Sigma Iota. She is a community activist who has conducted numerous community outreach initiatives in the St. Louis metropolitan area. Her most recent outreach project included working with young homeless mothers.

About the Authors

Hector Y. Adames, PsyD, completed his graduate training in clinical psychology at Wright State University in Ohio and his clinical predoctoral internship at the Boston University School of Medicine's Center for Multicultural Mental Health. Currently, he is completing an APA-accredited postdoctoral residency in clinical neuropsychology. His research and clinical interests focus on multiculturalism, Latino/a psychology, and the intersection of neuropsychology, cultural competency, and professional training in psychology. He has received numerous awards, including the National Latino/a Psychological Association's 2006 Distinguished Student Service Award.

Dorienna M. Alfred, PhD, received her doctorate in counseling psychology from Indiana University and is a licensed psychologist in the state of Missouri. She currently practices in the area of college mental health at the University of Missouri Student Health Center in Columbia, Missouri. Her professional interests include health psychology, multicultural counseling and teaching competence, and Black liberation psychology research and practice.

Simone Alter-Muri, EdD, ATR-BC, LMHC, is founder, director, and professor of Art Therapy/ Art Education Programs at Springfield College in Springfield, Massachusetts. Dr. Alter-Muri has published, presented, and exhibited her art both nationally and internationally. In 2003 she received the title of Massachusetts Art Educator of the Year in Higher Education. Dr. Alter-Muri has been conducting on-going grant-funded research in gender issues and art development.

Sharon K. Anderson, PhD, is an associate professor of counseling and career development and director of graduate programs in the School of Education at Colorado State University. Her teaching and research focus on ethics and multicultural counseling. She is the author of several journal articles, book chapters, and two books, including a book titled *Explorations in Privilege, Oppression, and Diversity.*

Antonette Aragon, PhD, is an assistant professor in the School of Education at Colorado State University. Her research focuses on multicultural teacher education, antiracist multicultural education, and the examination of students who are marginalized. In particular she has studied Latina(o) students, social justice issues, students in poverty, and areas related to equity for all students. She was formerly a high school teacher in Loveland, Colorado, and a faculty member at Metropolitan State College of Denver. She deeply believes in education that fosters cultural competency aimed at building White teacher effectiveness to teach students who are racially, ethnically, linguistically, and socioeconomically different from themselves.

Jason Arnold, MS, is currently a fourth-year doctoral student in Counselor Education and Supervision at Southern Illinois University Carbondale (SIUC). He received his master's degree in community counseling from SIUC in 2005 and worked in outpatient mental health for a year before deciding to study for his PhD. He has been involved in teaching and supervising graduate students in their group facilitator training in the SIUC Counselor Education Program for the past four years.

Linda L. Autry, PhD, LPC-S, was a public school counselor for 13 years. She has an MEd in counseling from Tarleton State University and a PhD from Texas A & M—Corpus Christi. In addition, she is an LPC-S. She is currently a counselor educator at the University of Texas of the Permian Basin.

Debra Bergeron, PsyD, is a visiting assistant professor at Antioch University New England, where she received her doctorate in clinical psychology. Dr. Bergeron also holds a master's degree in expressive therapies from Lesley University and a bachelor's degree in art therapy from Mount Mary College. She is a licensed psychologist, licensed clinical mental health counselor, and a registered and board-certified art therapist.

Christine Suniti Bhat, PhD, is a counselor educator at Ohio University, with previous experience at California State University, Long Beach. She has over 20 years of international experience as an educator, counselor, and psychologist in diverse work environments, such as the Australian military, nonprofit agencies, schools, and universities in India, Australia, and the United States. Christine's recent publications have been in the areas of cyberbullying, race and racial identity in counseling supervision, and group counseling. As an Asian Indian Australian citizen working in the United States, she is on a journey of multicultural competence and enjoys the company of fellow travelers.

Edward J. Brantmeier, PhD, is an assistant professor in the School of Education at Colorado State University. He currently teaches multicultural education and foundations courses at the undergraduate and graduate levels. His research interests include the practical and theoretical braiding of multicultural education, of peace education, and of critical social theory within the context of teacher education and educational leadership; cross-cultural competence; intercultural peacebuilding; and cultural conflict and change.

Rebekah J. Byrd, MSEd, NCC, is currently a doctoral student at Old Dominion University. She has work experience in both school and mental health counseling, with recent work on a grant-funded resiliency and prevention program in a middle school setting. Her research interests include child and adolescent treatment, acute care, and social justice and advocacy work. She also serves as president of the Omega Delta chapter of Chi Sigma Iota International and is chair for the Human Rights and Social Justice Committee for the Virginia School Counseling Association.

Laura Lake Catterton is a graduate student in the counseling program at the University of North Texas, Denton. Prior to beginning graduate study, she taught art classes for elementary students and adults. Catterton is particularly interested in multicultural issues and expressive approaches to counseling, such as art and animal-assisted therapy.

Devika Dibya Choudhuri, PhD, NCC, LPC, ACS, was born in India and immigrated to the United States. Her clinical work has been in community and university settings with multicultural and international populations, and her research interests focus on multicultural issues in counseling pedagogy and supervision as well as the therapeutic use of culture in counseling. She is currently an associate professor of counseling at Eastern Michigan University.

Colleen M. Connolly, PhD, LPC, is an associate professor in the professional counseling program at Texas State University—San Marcos. She teaches in the marital, couple, and family emphasis and has research interests including strength and resilience in lesbian couples, developmental stressors in lesbian couples, created family, and feminist supervision.

Meg Connor, MA, LCMHC, adjunct faculty for clinical mental health counseling program at Antioch New England University, received a master's degree in counseling psychology from Antioch University New England and a bachelor's degree from the University of Massachusetts in Boston. A licensed clinical mental health counselor who is certified in EMDR II and MBTI, she maintains a full-time clinical practice at Monadnack Area Psychotherapy and Spiritual Services in Keene, New Hampshire, She specializes in the integration of psychotherapy and spirituality, women's issues, trauma, and career transitions.

Laurie M. Craigen, PhD, LPC, is an assistant professor in the Department of Educational Leadership and Counseling, Old Dominion University. She received her doctorate in philosophy in counselor education from the College of William and Mary in Williamsburg, Virginia. Her research interests include self-injury, eating disorders, prevention, and professional identity development. As a faculty member in the human services program, her teaching responsibilities include senior-level internship, interpersonal skills, addiction, and methods courses.

Cheryl Crippen, PhD, has a PhD in counseling from the University of New England, Australia, in which her dissertation focused on processes of cultural adaptation among intercultural parents. She has an MA in international relations and an MS in counseling psychology from California State University, Sacramento and Fullerton. Her research interests include cross-cultural counseling, intercultural families, and transcultural adoption. Her experience includes work in international education, cross-cultural training, and teaching at Makerere University in Kampala, Uganda. Currently, she is project director of the University of California, Irvine, Department of Psychiatry's Women and Children's Health and Well-Being Project.

Stephanie A. Crockett, MS Ed, is a doctoral student at Old Dominion University in the Department of Counseling. Her research interests include multicultural issues in career counseling, international student career development, and career issues and psychological distress associated with the college-to-work transition.

Michael D'Andrea, EdD, is a respected leader in the field of counseling, having published 6 books and over 200 book chapters, journal articles, and other scholarly works. He has also made over 250 professional presentations worldwide on various topics related to counseling, human development, and multicultural and social justice counseling. He has received several awards from the ACA as well as receiving fellow status with the APA in Division 17 (The Society for Counseling Psychol-ogy) and Division 45 (The Society for the Study of Ethnic Issues). In addition to his scholarly achievements, Dr. D'Andrea is widely known and respected for his work as a social justice advocate.

Judy Daniels, EdD, received her doctoral degree from Vanderbilt University in 1990. Since that time she has committed her career to being a counselor educator, theorist, researcher, and practitioner. In all of these professional capacities, Dr. Daniels has directed much time and energy to promoting multicultural and social justice counseling paradigms in the mental health professions. This effort has resulted in more than 75 publications and over 125 professional presentations at national and international counseling conventions, conferences, and workshops. Dr. Daniels is a fellow with the ACA and the recipient of several other professional awards and commendations.

Edward A. Delgado-Romero, PhD, is an associate professor and training director of the counseling psychology doctoral program of the University of Georgia. He is a fellow of the APA and the president-elect of the National Latina/o Psychological Association.

Cheryl Doby-Copeland, MPS, ATR-BC, LPC, is an art therapist/mental health specialist in the District of Columbia and is pursuing a doctorate in school psychology at Howard University. Cheryl served on the American Art Therapy Association (AATA) Board of Directors and is a past chairperson of the AATA Multicultural Committee. Cheryl developed and taught the social and cultural diversity course in George Washington University's Graduate Art Therapy Program. Her current research interests are the utility of drawing techniques in projective-expressive assessment as indicators of cognitive development and school-based parenting skills interventions to decrease school violence.

Peter C. Donnelly, PhD, is a visiting assistant professor at Rutgers University's Graduate School of Education. His research interests include examining multicultural counseling competency among counselors, identifying predictors of academic achievement among Black adolescents, and developing culturally relevant counseling interventions for working with at-risk youths. He has written and coauthored publications in this area.

Kylie P. Dotson-Blake, PhD, LPC, NCC, is an assistant professor in the College of Education, Department of Counselor and Adult Education, at East Carolina University. Her research interests and expertise include developing and evaluating culturally inclusive family-school-community partnerships, rural school counseling, and Latina/o family involvement in schools. Her current projects include designing and implementing international, interdisciplinary multicultural issues course opportunities for students using East Carolina University's Global Classroom technology.

Beth A. Durodoye, EdD, NCC, is a professor in the Department of Counseling at the University of Texas at San Antonio. She earned her master's degree in counseling from Marshall University and her EdD in counselor education from the University of Virginia. She is a former president of the Texas Association for Multicultural Counseling and Development. Her specialization is multicultural counseling, with scholarly interests centering on sociopolitical considerations that impact the mental health needs of diverse populations and international approaches to counseling.

Bengü Ergüner-Tekinalp, PhD, is an assistant professor in the Counselor Education Program at Drake University, Des Moines, Iowa. After completing her bachelor's and master's degrees in guidance and counseling at Middle East Technical University in Turkey, she moved to the United States to complete her doctoral degree in counselor education from Auburn University—Alabama. Her research interests are multicultural counseling, social justice and advocacy, school counselor roles and program effectiveness, and positive psychology.

Milton A. Fuentes, PsyD. Dr. Fuentes, a licensed psychologist, received his PsyD from the Graduate School of Applied and Professional Psychology, Rutgers University, in 1998. He is currently an associate professor of psychology and the director of the Latin American and Latino studies program at Montclair State University. He also established and directs the clinical and community studies laboratory in the Psychology Department.

Birmagidra M. Gainor, MEd, is a doctoral student in the counseling psychology program at the University of Georgia.

Michael Goh, PhD, is an associate professor, program coordinator, and training director in the counseling and student personnel psychology program at the University of Minnesota. Dr. Goh's teaching, research, and service are focused on improving access to mental health services for ethnically diverse, new immigrant, and international populations. His current research program includes cultural intelligence and cultural competence in mental health practice, multicultural master therapists, and help-seeking behaviors and attitudes across cultures and countries.

Andre Green, PhD, holds a BS degree in chemistry from Alabama State University, an MS degree in chemistry from Hampton University, and EdS and PhD degrees in curriculum and instruction, with a focus in science education, from Virginia Tech. His professional experience includes working in the Virginia public schools as a science and math teacher. He currently works as a science educator at the University of South Alabama in the College of Education.

Sally M. Hage, PhD, is an assistant professor of counseling psychology at the University at Albany, Department of Educational and Counseling Psychology, School of Education. She is a licensed mental health counselor who earned her doctorate at the University of Minnesota and an MDiv from the University of Notre Dame. Her research interests include online violence prevention and training, spirituality and counseling, ethics, prevention of interpersonal violence, and multicultural psychology. She has written extensively in the areas of prevention psychology, multicultural training, and spirituality and counseling.

Stephanie F. Hall, PhD, LPCC, is an assistant professor of psychological counseling at Monmouth University. She received her doctorate in counselor education from the University of New Orleans and is licensed as a professional counselor in Louisiana and Kentucky. Her research interests include: multicultural issues in counselor education and supervision, ethics and counselor competence, infusion of group work and multicultural concepts into the counselor education curriculum, the impact of mentoring on counselor educator identity development, and teaching preparation for graduates of counselor education doctoral programs.

Amney Harper, PhD, is an assistant professor in the Department of Professional Counseling at the University of Wisconsin Oshkosh. Dr. Harper completed her bachelor's degree in history and master's degree in community agency counseling at Ball State University. She then completed her doctoral degree in counselor education at Auburn University in Auburn, Alabama. Her research interests are LGBTQIQ populations (lesbian, gay, bisexual, transgender, queer, intersex, and questioning), social justice, multicultural counseling competency, feminist theory, racial identity, and existential theory.

David W. Hart, MS, is a doctoral student and research assistant at the University of Missouri—St. Louis and a part-time faculty member at Southwestern Illinois College. Hart completed his master's degree in counseling at California State University, Fullerton, where he received the Faculty Award for potential as a counselor. His research interests are in the clinical integration of spirituality and professional counseling, LGBTQI (lesbian, gay, bisexual, transgender, queer/questioning, intersex) identity development, and counseling the older adult client. Hart has a passion for promoting social justice through his clinical practice and scholarly research.

Danica G. Hays, PhD, LPC, NCC, is an assistant professor in the Department of Educational Leadership and Counseling at Old Dominion University. Her major research interests include qualitative methodology, assessment and diagnosis, trauma and gender issues, and multicultural and social justice concerns in counselor preparation and community mental health. Her primary teaching responsibilities are master's- and doctoral-level research methods courses, assessment, and doctoral supervision.

Liza Hecht, PsyD, is an adjunct faculty member at JFK University in the clinical psychology program. Dr. Hecht's areas of interest include multicultural issues, chemical dependency, behavioral health medicine, and psychological aspects of HIV.

Cheryl Holcomb-McCoy, PhD, is professor and director of the school counseling program in the School of Education at Johns Hopkins University (JHU). She joined the JHU School of Education in January 2009; before that, she held an associate professorship at the University of Maryland (1998-2008).

Dr. Holcomb-McCoy, a doctoral graduate of the University of North Carolina at Greensboro, is a specialist in school and multicultural counseling, and her research includes the development of instruments that measure school counselors' multicultural competence and self-efficacy. Since 1996, she has published or copublished over 50 refereed journal articles, books, book chapters, and reports. Among the recent grants and awards she has received is a $300,000 grant from the College Board (2006–2009) to direct a research project that examines the impact of school counseling activities on the college preparation of urban, low-income students. Dr. Holcomb-McCoy holds numerous leadership positions in various professional and academic organizations, including the American School Counselor Association. She serves on the editorial boards of several publications, including *Professional School Counseling, Counselor Education and Supervision,* and the *Journal for Specialists in Group Work.* In 2009, Dr. Holcomb-McCoy received the Counselors for Social Justice's Mary Smith Arnold Anti-Oppression Award.

Angela Rowe Holman, PhD, LPC, NCC, is an assistant professor in the College of Arts and Sciences, Department of Psychology and Counseling, at the University of North Carolina Pembroke and is a licensed professional counselor. Her areas of interest include college counseling, community agency counseling, peer supervision, gender and sexuality issues, and case conceptualization skills of counseling students.

Alicia M. Homrich, PhD, NCC, LPY, LMFT, is an associate professor and chair of the graduate studies in counseling program at Rollins College in Winter Park, Florida. In addition to her position as a counselor educator, Dr. Homrich is a licensed psychologist and a licensed marriage and family therapist. She is most interested in strengths and resiliency of counselors in training and uses a solution-oriented approach in counselor development and supervision. Dr. Homrich's specialization is family and relationship therapy, and she has developed a certificate program for the students in mental health counseling at Rollins College.

Monica Hunter, PhD, holds a BS degree in elementary education from Alabama State University, an MEd degree in school counseling from the University of South Alabama, and a PhD in counselor education and supervision from Auburn University. Her professional experience includes working in the public schools as a teacher, elementary school counselor, and secondary school counselor. She currently works as a counselor educator specializing in school counseling at the University of South Alabama in the College of Education.

Brian Hutchison, PhD, NCC, is an assistant professor in the Division of Counseling and Family Therapy at the University of Missouri—Saint Louis. He has authored or coauthored several book chapters, articles, and other materials on career theory and development and presented on these topics at numerous conferences and invited workshops. Dr. Hutchison has worked as a college career and school counselor. He is the past-president of the Pennsylvania Career Development Association as well as an active member of the National Career Development Association through its National Leadership Academy. Dr. Hutchison's research focuses on the impact of social class on counseling relationships, career development, and career planning behaviors. He has taught career and multicultural classes in a variety of settings for high school, undergraduate, and graduate students.

Arpana G. Inman, PhD, received her PhD in counseling psychology from Temple University. Currently, she is an associate professor in counseling psychology at Lehigh University. She has been teaching courses on diversity and multicultural perspectives since 2000 to a wide range of students in the field of education. Her areas of research include South Asian identity, Asian American coping and mental health, international counseling and psychology, and multicultural competencies in supervision and training.

Margo A. Jackson, PhD, is an associate professor in the Counseling Psychology Department, Division of Psychological and Educational Services, Graduate School of Education at Fordham University. She is president-elect-designate of the National Council of Counseling Psychology Training Programs. She earned her PhD in counseling psychology at Stanford University, EdM in counseling at the University of Buffalo, and BA in psychology and Spanish at the State University of New York at Binghamton. Her clinical, research, and teaching interests are in multicultural career counseling and psychotherapy training and supervision, and her focus is on examining methods to assess and constructively address hidden biases of counselors and educators.

Marty Jencius, PhD, earned his PhD in counselor education from the University of South Carolina. He is founder and list manager for CESNET-L, a listserv for counselor educators; cofounding editor of *The Journal of Technology in Counseling*, a Web-based, peer-reviewed journal; and founder of CounselorAudioSource.Net, a counseling podcast interview program. He is on the editorial board of the *International Journal for the Advancement of Counselling*. He has taught counseling in The Bahamas, Singapore, and Turkey.

Susan Kashubeck-West, PhD, received her PhD in counseling psychology from the Ohio State University. She has served on several journal editorial boards and has won several teaching awards. Her current research interests include multicultural issues, LGBT (lesbian, gay, bisexual, transgender) issues, body image, and eating disorders

Nathalie Kees, EdD, LPC, is an associate professor of counseling and career development in the School of Education at Colorado State University. Her teaching and research focus on individual and group counseling, spirituality and counseling, and diversity and gender issues in counseling. She has served as guest editor for special issues on women in counseling for the *Journal of Counseling & Development* and the *Journal for Specialists in Group Work*. She is coauthor of the book *Manager as Facilitator* and founder of ACA's Women's Interest Network. Dr. Kees has over 20 years of experience as a diversity trainer and advocate.

Julie Koch, PhD, is an assistant professor of counseling and counseling psychology at Oklahoma State University. She is a licensed K–12 school counselor in the states of Texas and Oklahoma. Her research interests involve immigrant and refugee children, LGBTQ (lesbian, gay, bisexual, transgender, queer/questioning) issues, counselor training, supervision and development, and ethics. She was a Monbusho Scholar and speaks Japanese.

Minsun Lee, MA, is a doctoral student in the Division of Counseling Psychology at the University at Albany, where she has taught an undergraduate diversity course. Her research interests include bicultural identity, therapy process, and color-blind racial ideology.

Matthew E. Lemberger, PhD, is an assistant professor and program coordinator of the school counseling track at the University of Missouri—Saint Louis. Dr. Lemberger specializes in issues related to school counseling, cultural issues in counseling, academic achievement and skill development, and individual psychology. As a former school counselor at both the elementary and secondary levels, he remains close to the schools by virtue of a number of grants that target the so-called achievement gap, especially in urban schools.

Joél Lewis, PhD, is an assistant professor in instructional design and development at the University of South Alabama. Her educational background includes a BS in human resource management and an MS and PhD in instructional design and development from the University of South Alabama. Her professional experience includes working as an instructional designer in various schools, businesses, and nonprofit organizations.

Jayne M. Lokken, PhD, earned her doctorate in counseling psychology from the University of North Dakota. She has been a licensed psychologist at Counseling and Psychological Services at St. Cloud State University for eight years and at the University of Wisconsin Oshkosh for five years prior to that. She is a generalist with special interest in multicultural/diversity issues, racial/cultural development, stress management, depression, anxiety, and a holistic approach to health. She is also very interested in college retention issues, career choice, and academic success. Her current research includes examining the impact of discrimination simulation exercises on reducing prejudice attitudes among college students and the relationship between attitudes toward group counseling, cultural identity, and help-seeking behaviors with American Indian students.

Imelda N. Lowe, PhD, is an assistant professor at the University of South Dakota. She has worked in the public schools for 13 years as a bilingual teacher and bilingual school counselor in Texas.

Her interests include play therapy, sandplay, Hispanic issues, and integration of expressive arts in the clinical supervision process.

Melissa Luke, PhD, LMHC, NCC, is an assistant professor and the coordinator of school counseling in the Counseling and Human Services Department at Syracuse University. Dr. Luke is a former teacher and school counselor, with a clinical focus in working with children and adolescents. Her scholarship interests include comprehensive developmental school counseling, counselor education and supervision pedagogy, and the training of school counselors to effectively meet the needs of historically marginalized children and adolescents.

Salvador Macias III, PhD, has been on the faculty of the University of South Carolina Sumter (a two-year regional campus) for 25 years. He received his undergraduate degree (biology and psychology) from the University of California, Riverside, and he earned his master's degree in general-experimental psychology and PhD in developmental psychology from Georgia State University. He is the past president of the South Carolina Psychological Association, has been elected to a three-year term as a member of APA's Committee for Psychology Teachers @ Community Colleges (one year as chair), and is a member of the National Latino Psychological Association. In addition, he has served as a reader for the Advanced Placement Psychology Exam.

Sukie Magraw, PhD, is the program director and a professor in the clinical psychology program at JFK University in Pleasant Hill, California. She teaches the first-year Integrated Professional Seminar, which includes three components: multicultural awareness, ethnographic practicum, and group process. Her areas of interest include feminist therapy, LGBT issues, alternative families, and multicultural training. She has a private practice in Berkeley, California.

Krista M. Malott, PhD, LPC, is an assistant professor in the Department of Education and Human Services at Villanova University. Her areas of instruction and research address work with diverse populations, specifically in regard to issues of power and oppression, work with immigrants, and ethnic identity development.

Mark D. Mason, **MEd,** is a doctoral student in the Division of Counseling Psychology at the University at Albany. He attended the University of Maryland for his MEd in counseling and personnel services, and he has taught courses such as the First Year Experience and Cultural Diversity at several universities. His research interests include deaf and hard of hearing populations and multicultural education.

William Maxon-Kann, **MEd,** is a doctoral student in the Counseling and Human Development Department at Kent State University. His program of study is in counselor education and supervision. He currently is affiliated with a private practice after several years in community mental health working with adults with a dual diagnosis of a mental health disorder and a substance use disorder. His scholarly interests include multicultural counseling, spirituality in counseling, and counseling transgender individuals and their families.

Paula S. McMillen, **PhD,** has both a PhD in clinical psychology and a master's degree in library science, a perfect combination to support her collaborative work in and passion for bibliotherapy. She has 10 years experience as an education librarian at Oregon State University and the University of Nevada, Las Vegas (UNLV). She has completed graduate-level coursework in children's and young adult literature and has taught a course titled Multicultural Children's Literature—a particular interest of hers—in a master's-level teacher education program. She is currently associate professor and education librarian at UNLV and a reviewer for the Children's Literature Comprehensive Database.

Kristin Meany-Walen, MA, LPC-I, NCC, is a doctoral student and assistant director of the Center for Play Therapy in the counseling program at the University of North Texas, Denton. Her teaching interests include play therapy, filial therapy, and counseling culturally diverse clients. Meany-Walen's clinical interests include children, families, and schools. Her research interests include play therapy, filial therapy, and counselor development.

Jill Miller, PsyD, is a psychological assistant and program director of PASSAGE program in the Center for the Vulnerable Child at Children's Hospital and Research Center Oakland. She is also an adjunct professor in the PsyD program, clinical psychology, at JFK University in Pleasant Hill, California. She currently teaches the first-year Integrated Professional Seminar, which includes three components: multicultural awareness, ethnographic practicum, and group process. Her areas of interest include family therapy, multiculturalism/sociocultural issues in the clinical psychology and health care settings, and social systems affecting children in foster care. In addition, Dr. Miller coorganized the Taskforce for Cultural Responsiveness and Accountability at Children's Hospital and Research Center Oakland, whose charge is to be aware of the impact of oppression, marginalization, and racism as it operates in their institution and the community at-large.

Annalise Millet is a doctoral student at Saint Louis University. She cotaught the course Foundations of Multicultural Counseling. She has been employed as graduate assistant for the past two years. This employment combines with her work at the Children's Advocacy Services of Greater Saint Louis with children who have experienced acute and complex trauma. In addition, Millet sees clients at the Center for Counseling and Family Therapy, which serves diverse populations in the Greater Saint Louis area.

Casey A. Barrio Minton, **PhD, NCC,** is an assistant professor of counseling in the counseling program at the University of North Texas, Denton. She teaches courses in multicultural counseling, assessment and diagnosis, community counseling, and crisis counseling. Dr. Barrio Minton's research interests include counselor preparation and crisis intervention.

Brian J. Mistler, PhD, received his MA in international conflict resolution from the University of Bradford in the U.K. and his PhD in counseling psychology from the University of Florida. Brian has received several grants and awards for cross-cultural trainings around the world, and in 2002 he was named an Ambassadorial Scholar by Rotary International. Dr. Mistler is currently on the staff of the Center for Counseling and Student Wellness at Hobart and William Smith Colleges in Geneva, NY. Current research interests include humor styles, tolerance for ambiguity, and methods of overcoming polarization.

Robin Moore-Chambers is a graduate from and an adjunct faculty at the University of Missouri—St. Louis in the Division of Counseling and Family Therapy where she teaches Foundations of Multicultural Counseling. She is an experienced workshop facilitator and has presented locally and nationally in areas of multicultural training. Although most of Moore-Chamber's background is in counseling, social work, and education, she is also an accomplished artist and musician and uses her creativity in workshops and classroom instruction. Her passion is social justice and intentional multicultural competence training. She believes that despite one's socialization and orientation in a sexist, racist, classist, and heterosexist society, there are yet opportunities for change. She encourages others to welcome the journey of multicultural development, self-searching, and awareness while on the path of healing and renewal as they learn to turn all kinds of stumbling blocks into stepping stones.

Kelly Most, MEd, is a licensed school counselor and is currently working on her PhD in counselor education and supervision from Kent State University. She has had the opportunity to lead diversity trainings in both school and clinical settings. Her research interests in counseling include multiculturalism, supervision, teaching, and technology. She is a part-time counseling instructor both in the traditional classroom and online.

Janice Munro, EdD, LPC, NCC, NCCH, is the assistant dean of education in the Division of Professional and School Counseling at Lindenwood University in St. Charles, Missouri.

Nancy Nishimura, EdD, NCC, teaches in a graduate counselor education program at the University of Memphis. Courses she teaches include Multicultural Counseling, Foundations of Counseling, Clinical Techniques, Spiritual Issues in Counseling, and Practicum Supervision. Her research interests include multiculturalism, multiracial persons, and spirituality.

Brigid M. Noonan, PhD, LMHC, NCC, ACS, is associate professor and chair in the Department of Counselor Education at Stetson University. She has over 18 years experience working with individuals, couples, and families while working for employee assistance programs, maintaining a private practice, and consulting for companies. Her areas of interest include addictive disorders, eating disorders, working with women, chronic illness and disability, advocacy within the counselor education field, working with diverse populations, and career development.

Martha S. Norton, MS, LMHC, earned her master's degree in counseling from the University of Vermont. She is a licensed senior staff counselor at the Student Counseling Services at Iowa State University. Her clinical interests are individuals with trauma, substance abuse assessment, eating disorders, family of origin, and cross-cultural issues. Her work has spanned a range of administrative focuses within the counseling center, including coordinating peer educations groups in topics such as diversity, career, and substance abuse prevention; and coordinating outreach, group services, and the substance abuse intervention and process addictions assessment services.

Anne M. Ober, PhD, LPC, is an assistant professor at Walsh University. She teaches the following courses: Social and Cultural Diversity, Introduction to Counseling, Research Methods and Program Evaluation, Lifespan Development, Advanced Abnormal Behavior, and Wellness. Her research interests include grief counseling and training, spirituality, multicultural counseling, and working with older adults. She has worked in college counseling and community mental health settings, working with individuals and couples as well as facilitating groups for older adults and people living with grief.

Derrick A. Paladino, PhD, LPC, NCC, is an assistant professor in the graduate studies in counseling program at Rollins College in Winter Park, Florida. Dr. Paladino is a licensed professional counselor and national certified counselor. His clinical interests lie in crisis/suicide assessment and intervention, college counseling, group counseling, and clinical supervision. Dr. Paladino's research interests fall in the areas of multiple heritage identity and acculturation, college student adjustment, counselor education and supervision, and crisis assessment and intervention.

Allison C. Paolini, MS, NCC, CFM, CPC, is a third-year doctoral candidate at the University of South Florida. She is obtaining her PhD in curriculum and instruction, with a concentration in counselor education, and her cognate is in marriage and family therapy. Paolini is a member of Chi Sigma Iota, American Association for Marriage and Family Therapy, ACA, and American School Counselor Association. She worked as an elementary school guidance counselor for two years and received the Russell C. Hill's Character Education Guidance Counselor of the Year Award in 2007. She is a national certified counselor, a certified family mediator, a parent coordinator, and a registered mental health counseling intern. Upon graduation, Paolini plans to become a professor and complete her clinical hours to become a licensed mental health counselor specializing in couples and family therapy

Tina R. Paone, PhD, NCC, NCSC, RPT-S, is an assistant professor and field placement coordinator for the school counseling program at Monmouth University. Dr. Paone is a registered play therapist supervisor (RPT-S) and has experience working with a diverse range of clients. Among her varying presentations, she has specifically focused on topics of group activity therapy, play therapy, and multicultural/diversity counseling.

Carol A. Parker, EdD, LPC, NCC, CSC, is an associate professor in the Department of Educational Leadership and Counseling at Sam Houston State University. Dr. Parker's research interests are leadership, issues of diversity and cultural competence, college admissions counseling, and service learning.

Agatha Parks-Savage, EdD, LPC, ACS, is an associate professor of counselor education and supervision at Regent University in Virginia Beach, Virginia. She has taught multiculturalism for eight years and has extensive clinical counseling experiences with culturally and clinically diverse populations. Her other interests include clinical counseling supervision, human sexuality, and research methods.

Shawn Patrick, **EdD, NCC, LPC,** is an assistant professor in the Professional Counseling Program at Texas State University—San Marcos.

She teaches in the marital, couple, and family emphasis and has interests in couples conflict reconciliation, new parent adjustment, and the use of narrative approaches in addressing privilege and culture. She is originally from St. Louis, Missouri.

Dale-Elizabeth Pehrsson, EdD, associate professor/chair of counselor education, University of Nevada—Las Vegas, is a counselor educator. Her expertise includes play, art, biblio, and story therapy. She has counseled children in schools, agencies, and private practice. She teaches master's/doctoral-level classes in social caring, multicultural competence, and diversity awareness. She advocates for competent graduate students preparation, especially in their work with clients experiencing international and immigration concerns. Her credentials include licensed professional counselor/supervisor, registered professional nurse, national certified counselor, approved clinical supervisor, distance credentialed counselor, and registered play therapist–supervisor. She is cofounder and clinical director of the Bibliotherapy Education Project.

Jacqueline Peila-Shuster, MEd, is an adjunct instructor in the Human Development and Family Studies Department and in the School of Education at Colorado State University. She is also working on her PhD in education and human resource studies, with emphases on counselor education and adult development. She completed her master's degree in counseling and career development at Colorado State in 2004 and was as an occupational therapist prior to that. Her areas of concentration include career counseling, adult development and aging, retirement, and strengths-based approaches to career and life planning.

Adelaida (Ade) Santana Pellicier, PhD, is tenured faculty and associate professor of educational psychology at Northern Arizona University. Dr. Pellicier has held multiple professional positions, including director of the Upward Bound Program at Kent State (13 years), elementary school teacher (4 years), and volunteer counselor (20+ years). Dr. Pellicier is a certified professional counselor, a volunteer school counselor at a local middle school, and a counselor educator.

Rosemary E. Phelps, PhD, is professor of counseling psychology and department head in the Department of Counseling and Human Development Services at the University of Georgia in Athens, Georgia. Dr. Phelps has built her career in higher education as a researcher, teacher, and supervisor. Her research focuses on diversity issues, mentoring, ethnic and racial diversity, and professional issues for students and faculty of color. She is the founder and director of the University of Georgia's Preparing Future Faculty in Psychology program. She has taught diversity courses throughout her career.

Yegan Pillay, PhD, PCC-S, is a counselor educator at Ohio University. He was previously the principal psychologist and the head of academic development in the Faculty of Military Science at the University of Stellenbosch in South Africa. His research and publication interests include diversity and social justice issues, identity development of racial and ethnic minorities, indigenous African psychotherapeutic interventions, and the use of narratives and stories as a therapeutic intervention strategy. He is registered with the Health Professionals Council of South Africa as a psychologist and is a professional clinical counselor with supervisor designation in the state of Ohio.

Tarrell Awe Agahe Portman, PhD, LMHC, NCC, is an assistant professor in the Division of Counseling, Rehabilitation and Student Development in the College of Education at the University of Iowa. She received her PhD from the University of Arkansas, Fayetteville, in May 1999. Dr. Portman has 15 years experience in K–12 public schools as a teacher and school counselor. She is a licensed mental health counselor. In April 2004, she was the first recipient of the ACA's Mary Smith Arnold Anti-Oppression Award for her work with social justice issues with elementary children.

Torey L. Portrie-Bethke, PhD, NCC, is an assistant professor in the counseling program at the University of North Texas. She teaches courses in parent and family counseling, group work, advanced skills, child and adolescent appraisal, and assessment and wellness. Her research interests include supervision and experiential counseling techniques.

Jordan S. Potash, MA, ATR-BC, LCAT, is an art therapist in Hong Kong and is pursuing a PhD in social work and social administration through the University of Hong Kong. His work has been focused on community development, adolescent concerns, cross-cultural relationships, and social change. He is a past chair of the Multicultural Committee of the American Art Therapy Association and a lecturer at both the George Washington University and the University of Hong Kong.

Bianca M. Puglia, PhD, LPC, is an assistant professor of counseling at Eastern Kentucky University. She is a national certified counselor and is licensed as a professional counselor in Louisiana. Her research interests include professional identity for counselors, disability identity development, and counselor preparation.

Michael S. Rankins, PhD, is an assistant professor of professional school counseling at Lindenwood University in St. Charles, Missouri.

Brooke Rawson is an advanced student at the University of Central Florida. Her research interests included cross-cultural communication and the application of Gestalt techniques as part of the development of cultural competence. She is working toward her bachelor's and soon her master's degree. She works as a guardian ad litem, helping abused and neglected children, and also works as a substitute teacher.

Mark C. Rehfuss, PhD, LPC, ACS, is an associate professor of counselor education and supervision at Regent University in Virginia Beach, Virginia. He has taught multiculturalism for four years and works clinically with diverse populations of adults. He appreciates the intersection of spirituality and culture that can often happen within counseling sessions. His other interests include career counseling, human sexuality, and supervision.

Kate Davis Rogers, MA, LPAT, LPCC, is an art therapist (LPAT, ATR-BC) and counselor (LPCC) who has worked with people for over 25 years. She found teaching multiculturalism at the graduate level one of the most delightful experiences of her life. She has worked with people of all ages in a variety of settings and with a variety of issues. Having worked with people from Australia

(Aborigines) to rural New Mexico (Native Americans) to Minneapolis to Africa, she has found people to be endlessly fascinating and creative in their search for more joy and love in their lives.

Carmen F. Salazar, PhD, NCC, is a counselor educator who regularly teaches master's- and doctoral-level classes in multicultural counseling, and she is committed to infusing multiculturalism and diversity in the other courses she teaches. She is editor of a book describing how diversity can be infused into group leadership, *Group Work Experts Share Their Favorite Multicultural Activities: A Guide to Diversity-Competent Choosing, Planning, Conducting, and Processing*, published by the Association for Specialists in Group Work. She serves on the editorial boards of the *Journal for Social Action in Counseling and Psychology* and the *Journal for Specialists in Group Work.*

Varunee Faii Sangganjanavanich, PhD, NCC, ACS, is an assistant professor in the Department of Counseling and Educational Psychology at Texas A&M University—Corpus Christi. She previously served as a counselor for the Gender Reassignment Institute in Bangkok, Thailand. She has extensive clinical and scholarly experience with transgender individuals, especially with ones who have undergone or plan to undergo gender reassignment surgery. Her work in this area has also included providing sexuality counseling for the partners and family members of transgender individuals.

Angela Schubert, MEd, LPC, is a doctoral candidate and mentor program coordinator at the University of Missouri—Saint Louis. Schubert's research interests are in elderly sexual development, sexual freedom and expression in nursing homes, and sexuality issues among individuals with eating disorders. She is also the Missouri state chair for the American Association of Sexuality Educators, Counselors, and Therapists.

Erin M. Schwartz, MEd, is a doctoral student in the counseling psychology program of the University of Georgia. She received a bachelor of arts degree in psychology from Wake Forest University and a master of education degree in community counseling from the University of Georgia.

Ellen L. Short, PhD, is currently an assistant professor at Long Island University in the Department of Human Development and Leadership, Counseling Programs, School of Education. She received her MA in counseling psychology from Northwestern University and her PhD in counseling psychology from New York University. Her areas of specialization in teaching, scholarly research, and publishing are group dynamics focusing on race, ethnicity, gender, and culture; HIV, substance use/abuse, and high-risk behaviors among heterosexual populations (dissertation); and multicultural assessment of intelligence tests. She is the coauthor of *Racial and Cultural Dynamics in Group and Organizational Life.*

April Sikes, PhD, LPC, NCC, is an assistant professor in counselor education and is program director of school counseling at Southern Arkansas University. Her research interests include school counseling, substance abuse, child abuse and neglect, and ethical and legal issues in counseling. She has presented and copresented at national, regional, and state conferences on a variety of subjects, including play therapy in elementary and middle school settings, child abuse and neglect, ethical and legal issues in school counseling, and adolescent dating violence. She is an active member of several professional organizations, including the American School Counselor Association and the ACA. She is also an editorial review board member for the *Journal of School Counseling* and the *Journal of Humanistic Counseling.*

Hemla D. Singaravelu, PhD, is a licensed professional counselor and associate professor in the Department of Counseling and Family Therapy at Saint Louis University (SLU). She was the co-chair and director of the master's program. Prior to teaching at SLU, she served as an assistant professor at Southwest Missouri State University and coordinator of Career and Mentor Programs at Fitchburg State College in Massachusetts. She received her doctorate in educational psychology-counselor education from Southern Illinois University at Carbondale, specializing in career development and multicultural/diversity counseling. She has been an editorial board member for the *Journal* *of Counseling & Development* and *The Career Development Quarterly*. Her research interests and publications are in multicultural counseling issues, career development of diverse populations, and international students. She recently published the book *A Handbook for Counseling International Students in the United States*. She was born and raised in Malaysia.

Anneliese A. Singh, PhD, LPC, NCC, is on the editorial board of the *Journal for Specialists in Group Work* and has published on feminist group work interventions with survivors of trauma. She has extensively presented and published on issues affecting LGBTQ youths in schools, LGB people of color, transgender concerns in counseling, and social justice issues in counselor training. She has designed, implemented, and evaluated groups for women, Asian American/Pacific Islanders, people of color, and LGBTQ people in high school and college settings. Dr. Singh has also run theoretically based violence prevention groups in middle schools

Allison L. Smith, PhD, NCC, ACS, is an assistant professor at Antioch University New England. She teaches in the Clinical Mental Health Program within the Applied Psychology Department.

Sherri Snyder-Roche, MA, LMHC, ATR, has been a practicing psychotherapist for 24 years. She established a private practice in 2000 in integrated psychotherapy. She feels honored to have worked with a wide variety of populations, and from each she has learned tremendously and has developed immense respect for individuals' challenges and courage. She has worked with deaf, deaf and blind, developmentally challenged, and physically challenged people; trauma survivors; victims of domestic violence; wheel-chair bound people; cancer survivors; children, teenagers, and adults; individuals with addictions; individuals who suffer from eating disorders; Spanish speaking people; Vietnamese people; and gays and lesbians. She is immensely grateful to all the individuals who have shared their stories and opened their hearts.

Michael Starkey, MA, is a PhD candidate in the counseling and student personnel psychology program at the University of Minnesota. His

research interests include multicultural counseling and psychotherapy, existential counseling and psychotherapy, and therapist development.

Rose M. Stark-Rose, PhD, earned her doctorate in counseling psychology from the University of Wisconsin—Milwaukee. She is a licensed psychologist and faculty member in Counseling and Psychological Services at St. Cloud State University. Her clinical interests are working with individuals with eating disorders, career counseling, and counseling domestic and international students of color. Her current research includes examining the impact of discrimination simulation exercises on reducing prejudice attitudes among college students, content analysis of group counseling articles with U.S. racial minorities, and the relationship between attitudes toward group counseling, cultural identity, and help-seeking behaviors with American Indian students.

Mei Tang, PhD, is an associate professor of counseling in the Human Services Division and is director of the counseling program at the University of Cincinnati. She graduated from University of Wisconsin—Milwaukee in 1996. Dr. Tang's research areas include career development and assessment, acculturation/cultural identity of ethnic minorities, counseling school-age population, and cross-cultural issues in counseling.

Chippewa M. Thomas, **PhD, LPC, NCC,** is an assistant professor in the Department of Special Education, Rehabilitation, Counseling/School Psychology at Auburn University who, as a counselor educator, prepares master's-level counseling students to work in the mental health work force. She holds a master of education in community mental health counseling and a bachelor's degree in psychology. She was born in Tanzania, East Africa, reared in Los Angeles, California, and now resides in Opelika, Alabama.

Rebecca Toporek, PhD, is the coordinator of Career Counseling Specialization and associate professor in the Department of Counseling at San Francisco State University. She has published numerous articles on career counseling and on multicultural and social justice competence, and she has co-edited two books on multicultural counseling and social justice. She has received awards from the National Career

Development Association, the Association of Multicultural Counseling and Development, Counselors for Social Justice, and the Section for Vocational Psychology of the Society for Counseling Psychology.

Gina C. Torino, PhD, is a postdoctoral fellow at the Sarah Lawrence College Counseling Center and an adjunct instructor at Manhattan College. Her research interests include racial-cultural competence development, women and leadership, facilitating difficult dialogues on race in classroom settings, and gender microaggressions

Ling-Hsuan Tung, MA, is a psychology intern at the Center for Multicultural Training in Psychology at Boston University School of Medicine/Boston Medical Center and a doctoral candidate in counseling psychology at the University of Minnesota. Her outpatient placement is at South Cove (Asian) Community Health Center, where she provides bilingual (Mandarin/English) counseling to people of all ages. Her inpatient placement is at Lemuel Shattuck Hospital, where she delivers services in psychotherapy, psychological testing, and forensic psychology to adults with severe and persistent mental illness. Her research interests include multicultural issues, cross-cultural counseling, international psychology, immigration/acculturation, forgiveness, and positive psychology.

Mary E. Walker, PhD, is a retired public school art teacher. She has an MS in counseling from Houston Graduate School of Theology and a PhD from Texas A&M—Corpus Christi. She currently provides counseling through a local church.

Cheryl B. Warner, PhD, is an assistant professor in leadership, counselor education, human and organizational development at Clemson University, Clemson, South Carolina. Dr. Warner teaches the following courses: Multicultural Counseling, Beginning Counseling Skills, Advanced Counseling Skills and Techniques, Psychodiagnostics, and Group Counseling. Her research interests are in the areas of multicultural counseling competency, cultural identity development in African American youths, and multicultural clinical supervision and professional development. Dr. Warner has presented on these topics at national and regional conferences.

Anne M. Warren, MEd, ATRL-BL, is an art psychotherapist working with Native American children, adolescents, and adults in a Northern Wisconsin Native American community clinic. Anne holds master's degrees in art therapy and education. She is a licensed, board-certified art psychotherapist and professional counselor and is a certified Waldorf teacher.

Anna M. Williams-Viviani, BA, NCC, LCPC, ACS, is a doctoral student in counselor education and supervision at the University of Iowa with 10 years clinical experience as a master's-level community counselor. She taught an undergraduate course at Bradley University in Peoria, Illinois, and has presented at state, regional, and national conferences. Most recently she copresented at the North Central American Counselor Education and Supervision conference in Indianapolis on "Counselors-in-Training Perspective of Supervision in Sexual Abuse Populations." She has published in the *Journal of School Counseling* on self-mutilation. Research interests include violence against women, trauma-related grief, practice issues, and counselor preparation.

Carlotta J. Willis, EdD, NCC, ACS, professor and program director for the clinical mental health counseling program at Antioch University New England, received a doctorate in counseling psychology from the University of Massachusetts in Amherst, a master's degree in movement psychotherapy from Lesley College, and a bachelor's degree in theatre from Northwestern University. A licensed psychologist, certified Laban Movement analyst, certified psychomotor therapist (Espenak), nationally certified counselor, and approved clinical supervisor, she has also been the alumni career consultant for Antioch University New England. She is interested in multicultural counseling, Spanish language, and creative approaches to career development and counselor education.

Rebecca A. Willow, EdD, NCC, LPC, holds a doctoral degree in counselor education and supervision from Duquesne University in Pittsburgh, Pennsylvania. She is a nationally certified counselor, a licensed professional counselor, and a certified secondary guidance counselor in the state of Pennsylvania. She is an associate professor in Gannon University's community counseling program, where she teaches the Multicultural Issues in Counseling course. Her primary area of scholarship is multicultural counseling and education, particularly race relations. Other areas of interest are spirituality, existentialism, bereavement, counselor education, and supervision. Her greatest passion is raising her 9-year-old daughter, Alayna Michelle.

Ariel Winston, MS, is from Richmond, Virginia. She has a bachelor's degree in psychology from the University of Virginia, a master of science degree in school guidance and counseling from Longwood University, and is a doctoral student in the counselor education and practice program at Georgia State University.

Kayoko Yokoyama, PhD, is an associate professor in the clinical psychology program at JFK University in Pleasant Hill, California. She teaches the first-year Integrated Professional Seminar, which includes three components: multicultural awareness, ethnographic practicum, and group process, as well as courses on Asian American psychology and psychology of women. She has worked at university counseling centers in New York, Arizona, and California and has specialized training in eating disorders and body image. Her areas of interest include feminist therapy, multicultural training, body image, and Asian American issues. She has a private practice in Albany, California.

Adam Zagelbaum, **PhD, NCC,** is an assistant professor at Sonoma State University within the Department of Counseling's School Counseling/ Pupil Personnel Services track. He obtained his doctorate from Ball State University's counseling psychology program, along with certification as a school counselor. He has experience as both a school and community counselor within several different settings, including the school system of Trinidad and Tobago, the correctional facilities and alternative schools of Wisconsin, children's centers within the southern Mississippi region, and various university counseling centers.

Suzanne Zilber, PhD, is a counseling psychologist who earned her doctorate at Ohio State University. She has been a licensed psychologist for 17 years. Dr. Zilber is owner of Catalyst Counseling in Ames, Iowa, and specializes in the treatment of eating disorders; sexual trauma in childhood; gay, lesbian, and bisexual and multicultural issues; career exploration; and accidents and disasters. In addition, she has provided organizational consultation and trainings to nonprofit organizations.

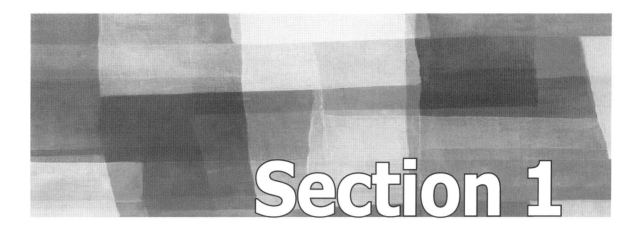

Section 1

Introduction to Multicultural Counseling

Activities in this first section are designed to help students examine concepts of bias, discrimination, and oppression. Activities in this section are also designed to begin scholarly dialogue about the ways in which culture can influence people's lives and their interactions with others. These activities can be used in a variety of core counseling courses in addition to introductory multicultural counseling courses. These activities can also serve as ice-breakers or getting-to-know-you exercises intended to increase student discussion and classroom interaction.

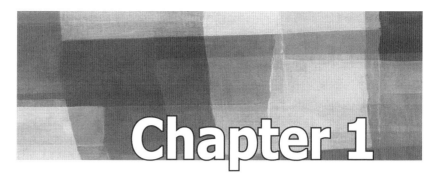

Fallout Shelter

Jason Arnold

Topics: Introduction to Multicultural Counseling
Culturally Skilled Counselor
Human Growth and Development
Career Development
Group Work

Purposes: Awareness of biases and the influences on personal choices is the focus of this activity. Participants in this activity discuss biases that they may not initially be aware of. This activity also enhances group understanding of how personal biases can affect an individual's career decision making and development.

Learning Objectives: Participants will (a) be able to recognize underlying biases or perceptions they have concerning roles and job stereotypes and (b) understand how personal biases and diversity affect the workplace.

Target Population: This activity is appropriate for both undergraduate and graduate students. This population can be of any discipline or major area of study. In addition, this type of activity can be carried out in either a classroom or a psychoeducational group format.

Group Size: The fallout shelter activity can be used in a group of any size. For smaller groups between three and seven participants, a single group can be used to carry out the activity. For those classes or groups that consist of eight or more members, the class or group can be divided up into smaller groups of participants.

Time Required: 40 minutes

Setting: This activity can be carried out in many types of settings, including classrooms, seminars, and psychoeducational groups in counseling or career development centers at colleges or universities. The room for this activity should be of a size that can accommodate the size of the group or class. The activity does not require a high level of movement, with the exception of potential small-group work (i.e., dividing the group into dyads or triads if your class or group is a very large size). Seating arrangements for the activity should be in a circle so that the teachers or group facilitators as well as the students or group members can see and hear one another. If the group is large, the instructors or group facilitators can divide up the class or group into smaller groups to ease and facilitate communication. If this is done, it is helpful to keep the smaller groups seated in the circle format.

Materials: Handout 1.1 ("Fallout Shelter"), a large pad of paper, a whiteboard or blackboard, and markers

Instructions for Conducting Activity

Before starting the activity, remind the class or groups to be respectful as they will be hearing many different opinions and that this is okay. Have the class or group arrange their chairs in a circle so that the members are able to face each other. If the class is larger than seven people, the instructor or group facilitator may wish to divide the class into smaller groups in order to be able to manage communication.

After everyone in the class or group is seated, the instructor or group facilitator will pass out the "Fallout Shelter" handout. After everyone has a copy, the instructor or group facilitator will read the vignette at the top of the handout and, when finished, will check the group(s) for understanding. Each individual member will take a minute or two to check off or circle the eight people on the list that he or she would like to include in fallout shelter.

When they are finished, if a single group is being used in the activity, the group leader will assist the group in coming to a consensus as to which of the eight individuals on their handout should be included in the shelter. The group facilitator will use a large tablet or pad or, if a whiteboard or chalkboard is available, will write eight spaces on the board, one space for each individual who will be put in the fallout shelter. As the group comes to a consensus on a person on the list, the group facilitator will write that person's name down on the pad or board until all eight spaces have been filled.

During this decision-making process, the group leader will assist in helping the group come to a decision as to who they want to include in the shelter. The key is to help negotiate differences of opinion by using core basic helping skills (e.g., paraphrasing, summarizing, reframing, reflection of meaning and belief, basic attending) that can allow members to state their opinions and understand that differences of opinion are acceptable. Reflection of feeling and advanced empathy can be used; however, this is not a counseling or psychotherapy exercise so it may not be appropriate to use this particular skill set with this population. If the instructor does need to use these techniques, he or she should do so sparingly.

After the eight-person list is completed, the instructor or group facilitator should explore why specific individuals on the list were not included on the list of those who were to go into the shelter. This investigation is particularly helpful in exploring biases that individuals may have about specific careers. For example, if the group does not include the minister, the instructor or facilitator may choose to explore why. Example questions might include the following: Is this a bias regarding a religious tradition or faith? Or is this a reflection of a stereotype that group members hold about the ministerial profession? Also, the instructor or facilitator should be aware of wording used when discussing the individuals on the list. The list of individuals does not indicate sex, race, or background status, which can allow for biases to emerge during the activity. If a member indicates the sex, race, or background status of an individual on the list, the instructor or group facilitator should put forth a question discussing the assumption being made by the individual or group. If the class or group is large, use of smaller groups can be helpful in managing the communication of the group.

When the activity is completed, the facilitator should take some time in the remaining moments of the activity to assist in the processing of the activity with the students or group members. This technique will help group members make sense of what they have experienced. Questions can include the following:

1. How did you decide who would be included in the shelter?
2. What was it like making this decision?
3. What was it like to hear other differences of opinion?
4. How can personal biases affect a person's career decision making?
5. How can personal biases impact the workplace?

Handout: Handout 1.1: Fallout Shelter

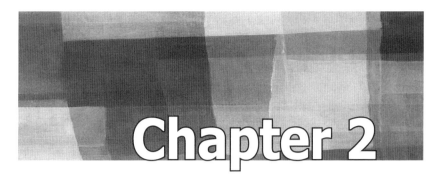

Chapter 2
Top 20 Multicultural Counselors

Edward A. Delgado-Romero and Birmagidra M. Gainor

Topics: Introduction to Multicultural Counseling
Oppression and Discrimination
Professional Identity and Ethical Practice
Research and Program Evaluation

Purposes: The purposes of this activity are to (a) emphasize and highlight the research contributions of multicultural counselors and (b) understand the lived experiences of multicultural counselors.

Learning Objectives: As a result of this activity, students will be able to

- identify prominent multicultural scholars and their contributions to the field,
- determine what research issues multicultural scholars have highlighted and addressed,
- understand the barriers that multicultural scholars have overcome, and
- appreciate the professional and personal struggles of multicultural scholars.

Target Population: This activity is designed for students in a multicultural counseling course at any level. This exercise could also be used in an introductory class to emphasize multicultural issues or in a research class to explicitly include multicultural issues.

Group Size: Individual or group presentations, depending on overall class size

Time Required: 15–30 minutes for each presentation

Setting: Regular classroom setting

Materials: Ideally these presentations are presented via PowerPoint presentations.

CACREP Standards Addressed: K.1.a (Professional Identity), K.2.b (Social and Cultural Diversity), K.8.a. (Research and Program Evaluation)

Instructions for Conducting Activity

Before class, the instructor prepares a list of 20 prominent multicultural scholars whose work covers a broad range of topics (ideally reflecting diverse topics, per the class syllabus). The list included as a handout is not static; instructors should prepare updated lists each semester incorporating new scholars and upcoming research. Presentations are scheduled throughout the semester to coincide with the topic of the course on a given day. For example, on a day when African American issues in counseling are discussed, then the instructor assigns a prominent scholar on African American issues (e.g., Janet Helms). Students are instructed to present a brief overview of the research, practice, and service contributions of the scholar. Whenever possible they will highlight publicly available personal information that sheds light on the work of the scholar (e.g., Helms, 2001). Students are encouraged to use information from the Internet or request copies of keynote or award acceptance speeches to supplement their presentations. The instructor of the course should present the first scholar in order to set an example of how to make an effective presentation.

Then the student nominates a second scholar who is not on the top 20 list whom the student feels is making significant contributions to multicultural research, practice, or service. No scholar can be presented twice during the semester. Generally, I assign established scholars as the top 20 and encourage the students to find emerging scholars to present as their nominations. For example, over the last two years the scholars (and the topic of the day) I have assigned have included the following: Patricia Arredondo (Latino/a issues), Allen Ivey (multicultural counseling competencies), Courtland Lee (African American males), Thomas Parham (psychological nigrescence), Mark Pope (Native American issues, gay and lesbian career development), Gargi Roysircar-Sodowsky (acculturation of Asian Americans), Rebecca Toporek (social justice and multicultural supervision and training), and Joe White (history of multicultural counseling).

Throughout the semester, I make sure that my students note both themes in the scholars' research or life stories as well as institutions that have been important in the development of multicultural counseling research and practice. For example, when discussing service one can discuss the pioneering presidencies of Patricia Arredondo and Mark Pope of the American Counseling Association. Likewise, students can learn about the key roles scholars have played as journal editors (e.g., Roysircar-Sodowsky and the *Journal of Multicultural Counseling and Development*) and outside of academia (e.g., the work of private practitioners, such as Melba Vasquez). It is also interesting to note the working and mentoring relationships between scholars (e.g., Parham was a student of Helms) and those scholars whose work represents a wide range of personal and professional interests (e.g., Pope in his work with LGBT [lesbian, gay, bisexual, transgender], Native American, and career issues). In addition, students should take note of research that scholars engaged in that changed the direction of multiculturalism in the field of counseling (e.g., the multicultural counseling competencies).

Students often feel overwhelmed when looking at the curriculum vitae of a multicultural scholar like Michael D'Andrea and may feel discouraged about ever making an impact in the field. However, after reading D'Andrea's (1999) narrative, students can understand his personal and professional development and the basis of his work. I find this exercise to be informative and enlightening for the students, but most of all this exercise helps to humanize multicultural scholars, which provides a context for their work while emphasizing the scholarly contributions that have been made. An added side benefit is that after using this exercise for several years, students have gone out and met, and in some cases worked with, the very people they presented.

Handout: Handout 2.1: Sample Top 20 Multicultural Scholars List

References

D'Andrea, M. (1999). The evolution and transformation of a White racist: A personal narrative. *Journal of Counseling & Development, 77*, 38–42.

Helms, J. E. (2001). Life questions. In J. G. Ponterotto, J. M. Casas, L. A. Suzuki, & C. M. Alexander (Eds.), *Handbook of multicultural counseling* (2nd ed., pp. 22–29). Thousand Oaks, CA: Sage.

Additional Readings

Arredondo, P. (2002). Mujeres Latinas—santas y marquesas. *Cultural Diversity and Ethnic Minority Psychology, 8*, 1-12.

Goldberger, N., Clinchy, B., Belenky, M., & Tarule, J. (1987). Women's ways of knowing: On gaining a voice. In P. Sharer & C. Hendrick (Eds.), *Sex and gender* (pp. 201–228). Thousand Oaks, CA: Sage.

Introduction to Multicultural Counseling

Lee, C. C. (2005). Reflections of a multicultural road warrior. In R. K. Conyne & F. Bemak (Eds.), *Journeys to professional excellence: Lessons from leading counselor educators and practitioners* (pp. 155–167). Alexandria, VA: American Counseling Association.

Pope, M. (2005). Crashing through the "lavender ceiling" in the leadership of the counseling professions. In J. M. Croteau, J. S. Lark, M. A. Lidderdale, & Y. B. Chung (Eds.), *Deconstructing heterosexism in the counseling professions: A narrative approach* (pp. 121–128). Thousand Oaks, CA: Sage.

Santiago-Rivera, A. L. (2009). Allen Ivey: Pioneer in counseling theory and practice, and crusader for multiculturalism and social justice. *The Counseling Psychologist, 37*, 67–92.

Sue, D., & Sue, D. (1995). Asian Americans. In S. Vacc, S. DeVaney, & J. Wittmer (Eds.), *Experiencing and counseling multicultural and diverse populations* (3rd ed., pp. 63–89). Philadelphia, PA: Accelerated Development.

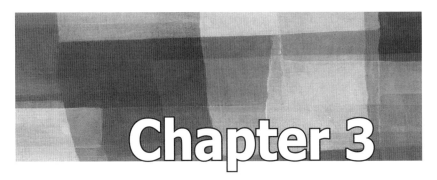

Chapter 3

Privilege Step Forward

Monica Hunter, Andre Green, and Joél Lewis

Topics: Introduction to Multicultural Counseling
Cultural Identity Development
Culturally Skilled Counselor

Purposes: The purpose of this activity is to provide an opportunity for students to understand issues related to discrimination, oppression, and power that affect individuals from other cultural groups.

Learning Objectives: As a result of this activity, students will be able to

- understand the concept of White privilege,
- compare and contrast the daily impact of White privilege on other cultural groups,
- develop an understanding of overt and covert examples of discrimination, and
- develop an empathic understanding of other cultural groups' experiences.

Target Population: During the first half of the semester, for graduate counseling students in multicultural counseling courses

Group Size: This activity can be used with small or large groups

Time Required: Approximately 45 minutes

Setting: This activity can be done in a room in which students have space to move for the first part of the lesson and a desk at which small groups can meet and write.

Materials: Paper and pens or pencils

Instructions for Conducting Activity

Begin by asking students if they think that White privilege exists.

In an open space, have students stand in a horizontal line all at the same point. Explain that you are going to read statements, and, in general, if the statement applies to them they should take one step forward (if your class does not have any minority students, then assign a few of your students to think from the minority worldview).

Read the following statements:

1. I can, if I wish, arrange to be in the company of people of my race most of the time.
2. I can go shopping alone most of the time, pretty well assured that I will not be followed or harassed.

3. I can be sure that my children will be given curricular materials that testify to the existence of their race.
4. I can go into a grocery store and count on finding the staple foods that fit my cultural traditions, into a hairdresser's shop and find someone who can cut my hair.
5. I can be pretty sure that if I ask to talk to the "person in charge," I will be facing a person of my race.
6. I can easily buy posters, postcards, picture books, greeting cards, dolls, toys, and children's magazines featuring people of my race.
7. If I declare there is a racial issue at hand or there isn't a racial issue at hand, my race will lend me more credibility for either position than a person of color would have.
8. I am not made acutely aware that my shape, bearing, or body odor will be taken as a reflection on my race.
9. I can choose public accommodation without fearing that people of my race cannot get in or will be mistreated in the places I have chosen.
10. I can be sure that if I need legal or medical help, my race will not work against me.

Ask your students to look at one another and see which students are ahead and which students are behind. Explain this is the very nature of the impact of oppression and power in our society: The dominant culture moves ahead as other minority groups are left behind. Share with them Peggy McIntosh's (1989) work on White privilege.

Place students into small groups. Explain that privilege exists in other ways in our society. Each group will create a new list of privilege. Think of the assigned minority group's worldview. They will construct their own list of privilege explaining their daily experiences. They can use the format and style that Peggy McIntosh used for White privilege. Assign the students to the following groups (provide them a sheet on which to write their list): Size/Weight Privilege, Sexual Orientation Privilege, Socioeconomic (SES) Privilege, and Physical Ability Privilege.

You can provide your students the following example:

SES Privilege: I can be sure that my children will receive a quality education based on the amount of money I can pay for private education or the neighborhood I live in for a quality public school.
Size/Weight Privilege: I can be sure to not pay a higher price for an airplane ticket based on my size.

Have students share their lists with the class. Encourage the other students to think of additional items to add to other groups' lists.

References

McIntosh, P. (1989, July/August). White privilege: Unpacking the invisible knapsack. *Peace and Freedom*, 8–10.

Additional Readings

Sue, D., & Sue, D. (2008). *Counseling the culturally diverse: Theory and practice* (5th ed.). New York, NY: Wiley.

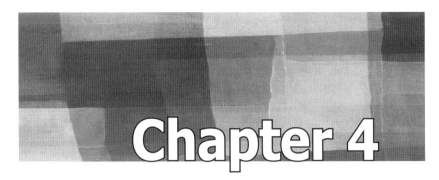

Chapter 4
Multicultural Bingo

Monica Hunter, Joél Lewis, and Andre Green

Topics: Introduction to Multicultural Counseling
Definitions of Cultural Diversity
Culturally Skilled Counselor

Purposes: The purposes of this activity are to provide an opportunity for students to get to know each other through an ice breaker and for students to begin to understand possible barriers to help seeking when a client is of a culture different from their own.

Learning Objectives: As a result of this activity, students will be able to

- compare and contrast various cultural experiences,
- understand the impact of cultural experiences in cross-cultural counseling, and
- develop an empathic understanding of the client's perspective on seeking counseling.

Target Population: First class session during the semester for graduate counseling students in multicultural counseling courses

Group Size: This activity can be used with small or large groups.

Time Required: Approximately 20 minutes

Setting: This activity can be done in basically any room in which students can get up and move around.

Materials: Two sets of "Similar Cultural Experiences" handouts (see Handouts 4.1 and 4.2), pens or pencils, timer

Instructions for Conducting Activity

Begin by telling students, "We are going to play a game to have a chance to get to know each other." Explain that you are going to pass out a sheet of paper faced down and they are not going to turn it over until you say "Begin." Tell them they are going to find on the other side of the paper various experiences. They must get up and circulate around the room to find other students who have had these experiences. If they find another student with the experiences, they need to get that student to sign their sheet. When you say "Time!" they must all stop obtaining signatures and go back to their seats. The objective of the game is for students to circulate around the room to talk to their classmates and find out more about them. The person with the most signatures wins (an option is for the instructor to give a little prize for the most signatures).

Pass out the first "Similar Cultural Experiences" handout (Handout 4.1) faced down to each student. Once you have given each student a sheet, tell the students "Begin!" Allow enough time for the students to be able to circulate around the room to talk with their classmates. Encourage them to get up and talk to students they may not know. Allow 3-5 minutes before calling "Time!"

Have the students sit down and count up the number of signatures on their sheets. Find out which student has the most signatures; for example, ask, "Who has more than 10 signatures?" Ask the student who has the most signatures to tell you the names under the different categories. Use this as a time for discussion; for example, for the category "Attended college outside the state of our school," have the students raise their hands to tell about the college they attended and in which state. For the category "Have children," the instructor can ask students how many children they have, ages, names, and so forth. The point is to get students to start to elaborate on their experiences.

Tell them you are going to have them try the activity again to get a chance to know each other a little more. If they came close to winning last time, they may have a chance now. Follow the same procedure of passing out the paper face down, being sure students don't turn it over. This time you are passing out the second "Similar Cultural Experiences" handout (Handout 4.2). This handout has experiences that may be viewed negatively by others. Once every student has a sheet, say "Begin!" Only allow students to turn the sheets over and then call "Time!" **Caution**: Be sure no one gets an opportunity to begin circulating and sharing information.

As students begin looking at the handout sheet, help them start to process it by initiating an honest discussion, asking them the following questions:

1. What are you thinking as you look at this sheet?
2. What is the difference between this sheet and the first sheet? Students may say this sheet has personal information. Explain the first sheet contained personal information as well; give the example of the category "Christian."
3. Would you feel comfortable telling others the information on the second handout?

Even though we may share similar experiences on the second sheet, explain the societal stigma and judgment associated with items on the second handout. Explain that the clients we help as counselors come to us with various experiences and oftentimes come during a crisis in their lives. If clients' lives were perfect then they wouldn't have a need to see us. Have students explain from the client's perspective their fears of entering the counseling relationship and sharing personal information. Ask your students how willing they would be with opening and sharing all the skeletons in their closets by discussing their personal experiences with a stranger. Share with your students how the literature has revealed that minority clients may not seek counseling and, if they do, may terminate early. Begin discussing with students possible barriers to cross-cultural counseling.

End the icebreaker by explaining to students that they should always humble themselves in understanding their clients' perspectives. They should listen empathically as clients share their story with them.

Handouts: Handout 4.1: Similar Cultural Experiences #1 (can be adapted according to students)
Handout 4.2: Similar Cultural Experiences #2 (can be adapted according to students)

Additional Readings

Constantine, M. G., & Sue, D. W. (2005). *Strategies for building multicultural competence in mental health and educational settings.* Hoboken, NJ: Wiley.
Sue, D., & Sue, D. (2008). *Counseling the culturally diverse: Theory and practice* (5th ed.). New York, NY: Wiley.

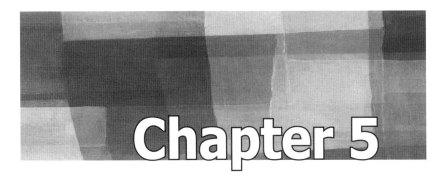

Chapter 5

Diversity:
Passive Tolerance Vs. Active Insistence[1]

Salvador Macias III

Topics: Introduction to Multicultural Counseling
Barriers to Effective Cross-Cultural Counseling
Oppression and Discrimination
Group Work
Creative Arts

Purposes: The purpose of this activity is to have participants model a process of selecting "neighbors" according to certain "rules." By moving about the classroom according to simple decision parameters, they will see patterns both of segregation and integration develop from seemingly innocent decisions.

Learning Objectives: Participants will learn from a clear demonstration that exclusion and isolation result from decisions that, though they may not be intended to generate segregation, necessarily lead to it because they maintain a passive tolerance. And, on the other hand, participants will also learn that a pattern of inclusion and integration is only possible if there is an active desire to maintain it.

Target Population: This activity works well with undergraduates, graduate students in their first or second year, and gatherings of nonprofessionals, and it also works well as a teaching demonstration for professionals and more advanced graduate students.

Group Size: A class of about 20 to 40 works best; classes smaller than 20 will not generate a sufficient number of possible seating arrangements, and groups too large are unwieldy to manage.

Time Required: As a demonstration it can be managed in about 15 to 20 minutes, but with lively discussion and as a starting point for a lecture on population patterns, it can easily be used to cover a typical 50-minute class.

Setting: A typical classroom with desks in rows and columns works best. The students need to be able to move about and exchange seats readily, and this is not easily accommodated in seminar rooms in which students sit around a common table, in theater-style seating, or in standard lecture halls with fixed, room-length counter tables that function as writing surfaces.

---

[1]This activity was inspired by a computer program described by Rauch (2002), and a version of this activity was presented at the 2008 meeting of the American Psychological Association by the author (Macias, 2008).

Materials

1. Five-inch square pieces of paper of two different colors, such that half the class will receive one color, the rest the other color.
2. Overhead transparency and three sheets with grid marking, each square symbolizing one desk, made up to match the geometric pattern of desks in the class. That is, if the desks are arranged in a 5 × 5 pattern, the grids should have squares in a 5 × 5 pattern.
3. Two markers, one in each color of the pieces of paper. (Note, in the absence of an overhead transparency, a chalkboard or a dry-erase board will suffice, but I recommend drawing all the grids on the board before class begins.)

Instructions for Conducting Activity

Ask the participants to arrange themselves in the classroom such that there are no empty desks among them. Distribute the colored pieces of paper in a haphazard order, one per student. Draw the resulting color distribution on the overhead. I have found it easiest if the participants, in turn, call out their color and I mark my grid accordingly (see Figure 5.1 for sample random distribution).

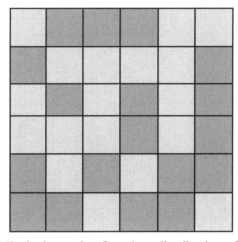

Figure 5.1. Typical sample of random distribution of class seating.

Once the pieces of paper are distributed, the class is ready for the first "rule" of relocation. Ask the participants to look at the pieces of papers held by their neighbors; their neighbors are to their front, behind, left, and right. If at least two have the same color as they do, they should remain where they are and do nothing. If fewer than two neighbors share their color, they should raise their hand (with the paper in it) and change seats with someone who has the other color. After these changes take place, ask the class, again, to look to their neighbors to check to see if one half of them now share their color of paper. If not, the same procedure should be followed (i.e., raise their hands, change seats, and so forth) When there are no more moves necessary or possible (it may be that one or two participants will be seated such that the rules are violated, but they may not be able to move because their colleagues with the other color are all seated according to the rule), ask them once again to call out their colors so that you can draw them into the second grid (see Figure 5.2 for sample distribution).

At this point it is relatively easy to guide the class in a discussion (see the following section for recommendations regarding the lecture and conversation issues of relevance). After the discussion, the second rule should be introduced. Beginning from the seats they now occupy, ask the participants to seek at least one neighbor who has a piece of paper opposite in color to theirs. As before, they should examine their neighbor's papers and raise their hands if they do not have at least one neighbor with a different color. Also as before, this may take two or three iterations. When complete, again draw this new distribution on the third grid (see Figure 5.3).

The first (i.e., random) filled-in grid will show a mixed up-order. Some colors will be bunched together, but just as likely there will be much mixing. The second grid (according to the rule such that at

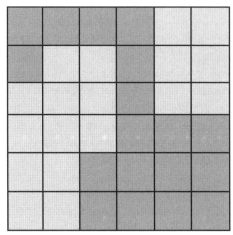

Figure 5.2. Sample distribution when half of neighbors share the same color card.

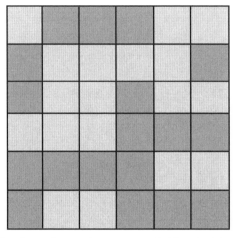

Figure 5.3. Sample distribution when at least one neighbor holds a card of the opposite color.

least one-half the neighbors hold the same color) will show a very strong segregation pattern that will have very little mixing. The grid can easily be compared with typical cities with ethnically pure neighborhoods, isolated enclaves of one ethnicity surrounded by another, and so forth. After the first rule has been implemented, I recommend a short discussion. For example, this rule did not require segregation. If people followed this rule in choosing where to live, where to work, where to sit in a restaurant, and so forth, no one would accuse them of being racist. Such people would happily accept neighbors who are different from themselves; they just do not want to be "alone." Thus, the point is made that a passive attitude (which tolerates separation) does not, nor can it, result in diversity; rather, as this activity demonstrates, it creates the opposite—separation and isolation.

The second rule is only a mild insistence for inclusion—just one of four neighbors is required to be different. Yet this rule results in an impressive amount (though not perfect) of mixing in the participants. Again, the point should be made that this diversity can only result from an active insistence.

Additional Discussion Points

It should be noted that this demonstration begins with the premise that diversity is desirable and that it is our joint responsibility to work toward a society that respects and seeks inclusion. Because this premise may not be so obvious to our students, a certain amount of preparation may be necessary to create a working philosophy for this value system.

Many people already understand the principle of diversity and recognize the importance of an inclusive community—inclusion in the classroom, churches, the workplace, neighborhoods, and so forth. In addition, they easily understand when told that the world, by and large, is not inclusive, and that we all have responsibilities to work for positive change. What many people often do not understand is their (and our) own complicity; that we contribute to and are often responsible for separation and isolation in ways we do not recognize in our daily lives. To be more specific, failure to be active in insisting on diversity is tantamount to a passive tolerance of exclusion and segregation.

Most students are open to the ideas presented and demonstrated in this activity but often do not see a connection to situations that achieve real-life status. As it happens, I am familiar with a real statewide organization that experienced the unintentional segregation that Figure 5.2 demonstrates (see Handout 5.1). That is, by using a passive approach to diversity, this organization generated a Whites-only steering committee for their annual convention simply by failing to insist on inclusion. The story depicted in Handout 5.1 offers a clear demonstration of the dangers of a passive approach and generates the impact that only a true narrative can.

In addition, an easy demonstration of this very point may well exist in many classrooms where one may wish to use this demonstration. If the gathering is multiethnic, it is likely that the seating choices evidenced by members of the audience (e.g., students on the first day of class) represent a noninclusive seating arrangement. In any case, it isn't difficult to suggest situations from our everyday lives that make this point and to discuss potential irony in the behavior of people who supposedly value diversity.

Handout: Handout 5.1: Diversity Story: Passive Tolerance = Exclusion

References

Macias, S., III. (2008, August). Diversity: Passive tolerance vs. active insistence. In S. Macias (Chair), *Teaching take-outs symposium with diversity activities.* Symposium conducted at the annual convention of the American Psychological Association, Boston, MA.

Rauch, J. (2002, April). Seeing around corners. *Atlantic Monthly, 289,* 35–48.

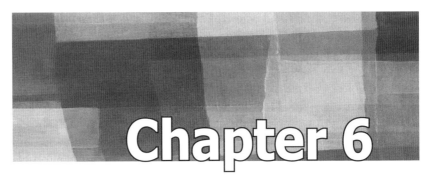

Chapter 6
Imagine

Yegan Pillay and Christine Suniti Bhat

Topics: Introduction to Multicultural Counseling
Definitions of Cultural Diversity
Barriers to Effective Cross-Cultural Counseling
Cultural Identity Development
Oppression and Discrimination
Culturally Skilled Counselor
Group Work
Multiple Identities/Biracial, Multiracial

Purposes: Prejudice, bias, and stereotypes occur insidiously and are often outside the awareness of individuals. The purpose of this activity is to provide an opportunity for the participants to empathically understand individuals who are marginalized in society and to recognize how the participants themselves may inadvertently contribute to the status quo. This activity is aimed at expanding multicultural counseling competencies as it relates to awareness, knowledge, and skills.

Learning Objectives:

- Participants will explore a baseline definition of *diversity* and will be actively involved in reformulating this definition throughout the session or sessions.
- Participants will explore self-identity and the influences of identity formation.
- Participants will become aware of their prejudices, biases, and stereotypes regarding individuals who may be different from themselves with respect to race, ethnicity, gender, socioeconomic status (SES), sexual orientation, abilities, religious/spiritual beliefs, and so forth.
- Participants will enhance their awareness of how individuals who are marginalized in society by virtue of their race, ethnicity, gender, SES, sexual orientation, abilities, or religious and spiritual beliefs may self-identify.
- Participants will imaginatively transpose themselves temporarily into the phenomenological world of individuals who are marginalized in society because of race, ethnicity, gender, SES, sexual orientation, abilities, or religious/spiritual beliefs with the goal of giving them the opportunity to empathically understand the everyday reality of an individual who is marginalized.

Target Population: This activity is suitable for students in various disciplines, including counselor education. It is a versatile for all types of diversity-related training.

Group Size: Initial didactic component lends itself to larger groups. The large group is then broken up in smaller groups of approximately 6-10 participants.

Time: Approximately 90–120 minutes

Setting: A regular classroom that allows for the seating to be rearranged for small-group discussion

Materials: Handouts 6.1 and 6.2; pencils; clipboard; and a flipchart or large writing surface, such as a chalkboard or whiteboard

Instructions for Conducting the Activity

There are three phases in this activity: (a) introduction (icebreaker), (b) working stage, and (c) processing stage. The instructor should begin by telling the participants, "Today you are going to participate in an activity that will initially require you to read a few questions and write a few short responses. You will then have an opportunity to share your responses with others in the group. Please note that there are no wrong or right answers, and every opinion is valued and respected. Participation is strongly encouraged."

Phase One: Introduction (Icebreaker)

1. Pass out the clipboard with Handout 6.1. Facilitator should read the instruction to participants: "Complete Items 1 and 2 of the handout. Please note that you will be sharing your responses with other members of the group. You have 10 minutes to complete this section. Please place your pencils down when you are finished."
2. When all participants are finished, have the participants introduce themselves by their first and last names (if this is the first time that they are meeting) and have them share their cultural heritage. Generally individuals enjoy sharing aspects of their heritage; therefore, this is a safe icebreaker. On a page of the flipchart or a section of the writing board, the cofacilitator records all the responses related to heritage.
3. Once everyone has had a chance to share his or her heritage (including the facilitator's), responses to Item 2 of Handout 6.1 (the "I am . . ." sentence) are shared and then recorded on another page or section of the writing board.
4. Finally, responses to Item 3 are shared and noted. If there are obvious omissions regarding diversity, encourage the group by stating, "Is there anything else that anyone would like to add?" If there are no further responses you may stop at this point (you will return to this exercise at the end).

Phase Two: Working

1. Facilitator should say, "We all have this wonderful ability to use our imagination. In this next activity you will have the opportunity to use the gift of your imagination. In this handout that I am passing out, read the different hypothetical scenarios and circle only one that you feel most comfortable imagining yourself being the person depicted in the scenario. You will have approximately 5 minutes for this activity. You will be invited to share your selection with the group."
2. Pass out Handout 6.2. When it is evident that all the participants have made a selection, the facilitator should solicit feedback from the group as to which selections were made. For example, the facilitator may ask, "Who chose being confined to a wheelchair?" and "Who imagined to be of a different race/ethnic group?" and so forth. The facilitator should begin with what may be the least threatening. The wheelchair scenario is the one that participants tend to be most willing to begin sharing. The facilitator then should seek volunteers in the group who would be willing to share. The following facilitator prompts may encourage sharing:

   - "Describe what it's like to be confined to a wheelchair." The purpose of this prompt is to explore how the participant imagined experiencing and sharing the reality of an individual who may be differently abled.

- "Can you describe your day from the time that you got up this morning to this moment?" The purpose of this prompt is to raise awareness and promote an empathic understanding in the participant of the day-to-day experiences of individuals who are marginalized in society by virtue of their minority status.
- "What are some of the assumptions that are made about you? The objective here is to explore prejudices, biases, and stereotypes. Through sharing from the perspective of the "other," the participant may indirectly be able to tap into his or her own prejudices, biases, and stereotypes.
- "The 'I am . . .' sentence that you shared earlier, is it the same or is it different?" If the response is "it is different," the follow-up questions may be, "How is it different?" In the initial response most individuals tend to provide some superficial adjectives, such as "tired," "hard working," and so forth (see Tatum, 2003). It has been observed that when participants take on the role of the marginalized person, their "I am" statements become less superficial and more akin to the responses that one may receive from an individual who is on the margins in society, for example, "I am frustrated," "I am scared," or "I am angry."

When the discussion on the one topic has been saturated, the facilitators should then solicit input from other group members, such as "Who chose being of a different race or ethnicity, sexual orientation, class status, gender, or religion?" The facilitator may creatively use similar prompts as above.

Phase III: Processing

1. Invite participants to share their broad experiences with the activity, for example, "You are no longer the imagined person—you are now yourself. Share with the group your general reactions (emotions, thoughts, and behavior) to imagining being someone who is different with respect to race, ethnicity, gender, SES, sexual orientation, abilities, or religious/spiritual beliefs."
2. Ask participants to share what they learned about individuals who are different with respect to race, ethnicity, gender, SES, sexual orientation, abilities, or religious/spiritual beliefs.
3. As participants, "What did you learn about yourself through this experience as you imagined yourself to be in the shoes of the person that you chose? Share with the group only that which you feel comfortable sharing."
4. Ask what was the easiest aspect of this activity.
5. Ask what was the most challenging aspect of the activity.
6. Ask participants, "How do you see your role when you observe others in your circle (your friends, peers, or family members) use derogatory words when talking about individuals who are different with respect to race, ethnicity, gender, SES, sexual orientation, abilities, or religious/spiritual beliefs?"
7. The facilitator should then ask the group members, "Does anyone have any more words to add to our diversity list?" If there are obvious omissions, the facilitator may say, "Does language fit? What about social class? What about country of origin?"

Handouts: Handout 6.1: Personal Definitions of Diversity
   Handout 6.2: Diversity Simulation Exercise

References

Tatum, B. D. (2003). *"Why are all the Black kids sitting together in the cafeteria?" and other conversations about race*. New York, NY: Basic Books.

Introduction to Multicultural Counseling

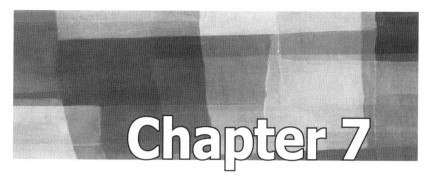

Chapter 7

Multicultural Simulation Project (MSP)

Robin Moore-Chambers

Topics: Introduction to Multicultural Counseling
Definitions of Cultural Diversity
Oppression and Discrimination

Purposes: The purpose of this activity is to provide students opportunities to participate in a simulation of historical and structural biases in America based on various topics of difference, including ethnicity, religion, gender, sexual orientation, education, social class, and abilities.

Learning Objectives: As a result of this activity, students will (a) assess their own personal awareness and biases in their perception and behavior toward others, (b) better understand the concept of privilege and doors of opportunities open to some and not to others, (c) have a better understanding of historical structural boundaries that divide people, (d) develop a sensitive understanding of broad definitions of culture and the concerns and worldview of minority populations beyond ethnic identification, and (e) develop multicultural competencies in counseling diverse populations.

Target Population: Graduate-level college students

Group Size: Preferably at least 15 participants and as many as 30

Time Required: Approximately 120 minutes

Setting: Most appropriate in a classroom with individual desks or tables that can be grouped into three sections.

Materials: Brown paper bag, colored markers, paper, tablecloth, scissors, balloons, adhesive tape, stapler, colored paper, some sort of snacks, napkins, cups, beverage of choice, trash container, well-sharpened pencils, dull-sharpened pencils, broken pencils, strings, music (preferably soft rock or relaxation music), dry-erase board, dry-erase pens, and a bell or whistle.

Instructions for Conducting the Activity

This activity is a simulation project in which the instructor sets up the room as a microcosm of cultural and class differences, accentuating boundaries and divisions with intentional privileges for some and oppressive conditions for others. The activity is more useful when presented on the first or second day of class when students have not had opportunities to get to know the teaching style of the instructor.

Prior to the start of class, the instructor divides the classroom into three sections: Group A, Group B, and Group C. The instructor should write "GROUP A" in bold, black, uppercase letters on a poster board and tape it on the wall or dry-erase board in the center of the wall or board. The Group A area should encompass the majority of space in the classroom (at least 85%) and should be clearly sectioned off with visible boundaries (e.g., chair or table barricade). Despite class size, there should be more chairs than needed for this group. The instructor will place a sign on the wall next to the extra chairs that reads, "DO NOT TOUCH: PROPERTY OF GROUP A." Inflated balloons should be taped on the wall or chairs (be creative). More than enough newly sharpened pencils are placed all around Group A's seating area (and in the surplus area of extra seats). This part of the room should be decorated festively. Set up a table with a tablecloth and refreshments. Another table should have the majority of the supplies on it. Music should be playing softly. (Most classrooms are Internet accessible for this task.)

The instructor should write "Group b" with a black marker on a sign that is placed on the wall in the middle of the seating area. Section off Group B's area to include at least 10% of the classroom, with clear boundaries marked. The ideal group size should be six, with four chairs available. Three pieces of colored paper should be provided on the desks. At least two of the pieces should be crumbled up then smoothed out. Three (barely sharpened pencils) are provided.

For the Group C area, the instructor should write "group c" in lowercase letters with a light-colored marker. The area for Group C should be sectioned off in the farthest corner of the classroom. The trash container should also be in this area in close proximity to participants' seating area. The ideal group size should be four, with two chairs available. Two pieces of dark-colored paper are supplied for this group. Ball up one sheet and put it on the floor in the seating area. Split or tear the other two pieces and put them on one of the tables in the seating area. If it is possible to adjust the lighting in the classroom and to draw the blinds or lower the shades, do so to make this section of the room as dark and gloomy as possible.

Cut colored paper into small pieces that match the number of students in the class. Write either "A," "B," or "C" on them, fold them, and put them into the brown paper bag. Despite the size of the class, Group A should always have the largest number of group members, Group B should have no more than five members, and Group C should have no more than three.

Specific Instructor Guidelines

1. The instructor stands at the door and holds the bag open for students to take a number as they walk into the classroom. As they enter, the instructor says, "Welcome! Please go to the area of the room with the letter that matches the letter you were given." Particularly to Group C, the instructor says, "Please go to the section of the room with the alphabet that matches the number you chose." Although the instructor is kind to all the students, she or he is extra nice and supportive to Group A members by saying, "Oh you're in Group A! Right over there (pointing), I knew you were a Group A person! And there are refreshments in your area; please help yourself to the refreshments!" As Groups B and C realize there are less seats than the number of group members, the instructor repeatedly reminds them not to take chairs from the overflow in Group A. After all students are seated, the instructor states that she or he has directions for each group and someone from the group should read the instructions to the rest of the group. The instructor takes Group A's instructions to them (enough for each of them) and states that someone from Groups B and C should come and get their instructions (one sheet for Group B and one for Group C), which are put on a desk at the front of the room. All three groups are given three separate sets of instructions (see Handouts 7.1, 7.2, and 7.3).

2. The instructor completely caters to Group A in every way and continually tells them that she or he is there to serve them. A person in Group A is asked to read the guidelines to the group, and the instructor offers to help them with their project and commends them as they follow their instructions. Group A is reminded that refreshments are provided and makes condescending statements about Groups B and C, such as the following: "You don't have to share with them—it's not your fault they are over there"; "I hope they don't try to take your extra chairs—those are there for

you in case you need them"; and "People should just be happy with what they have and not be jealous—they should learn to follow the rules."

3. The instructor monitors Groups B and C closely, does not make eye contact with them, and largely ignores them. If GroupsB or C members attempt to take an extra chair from Group A's overflow, the instructor reminds them that they are breaking the rules, causing their entire group to lose points—that they are stealing and causing trouble. If Group B or C members ask if they can have a chair from Group A's overflow, make sure that you are not making eye contact with them and say, "You will all have to share and get along."

4. After 15 minutes have passed, ask Group A if they are finished. If they haven't, give them more time. After they have completed their assignment, ring the bell or whistle one time. Show excitement about the construction Group A has made, clap, and ask the class to join you in clapping for Group A's accomplishments that day: They worked hard, didn't complain, and finished the task that was put before them. Do not make any references to Group B or C. Tell the class that the activity is over and ask them to help you rearrange the seating area to a circle for discussion. Allow a 5-min break and offer refreshments to the entire class.

Discussion

The instructor begins the discussion by thanking everyone for participating, considering the uncomfortable nature of the setting and format. First, ask someone from Group A to read their instructions aloud. Then ask for someone from Groups B and C to read their instructions aloud. (Up until this point the groups did not know there were different rules for each group.) Second, ask students to give their overall impressions of their guidelines and exercise. The instructor must not immediately begin to divulge the rationale and explanations for the room set-up but should allow students to share their thoughts about their experience. Be aware that experiential exercises like this one—although a simulation—have the potential to stir strong emotions. After about 15 minutes of discussion, use a dry-erase marker to draw three sections on the board labeled Group A, Group B, and Group C. Say that you would like for the class to tell you who they think fits in the three group categories. Ask students to consider broad definitions of group identities in America. Welcome discussions of their individual group dynamics.

Interpretation and Rationale

Group A. The space allocated, celebration, decoration, refreshments, extra chairs, and catering represent unearned privileges and assets for dominant groups in America. Groups that typically fit into this group are European/White Americans and White males. Other groups that students may include (and are allowed) are areas where privilege is applied, such as the educated, rich, and famous; Christians; heterosexuals; and able-bodied.

Group B. The smaller space, set boundaries, incomplete and misleading directions, assumptions of cheating, lowercase letters used in the sign, fewer and unequal supplies, and fewer chairs represent historical and structural discrimination and bias toward ethnic minority groups and other marginalized groups, such as blue-collar workers, non-Christians, the middle class, and women.

Group C. The smaller space than Groups A and B, location of the space in a corner (preferably close to a trash container), lower lights, confusing instructions, lowercase letters used in the sign, less and torn supplies, and application of fault and blame for identity represent the historical homophobic and heterosexist discrimination and bias toward lesbian, gay, bisexual, and transgender (LGBT) populations in America. Other groups that students might include are homeless and poverty populations, gender variant, and individuals who have limited physical abilities. (Ask participants to give a rationale for selecting certain groups for Group A, B, and C.)

Questions for Discussion

1. What were your overall impressions of the room set up?
2. What were your feelings when you realized that Group A received privileges and Groups B and C did not?

3. How did it feel to be in the privileged group or nonprivileged groups?
4. What was your initial impression of the privileged group's space, surplus chairs, service from the instructor, refreshments, and so forth?
5. What were your group's specific dynamics?
6. How did your group members interact with each other, knowing that you were purposely denied privileges while Group A not only had certain advantages but also had a surplus of privileges?

Note: If either group helped another group, ask them to explain their intentions. If no one from Group A reached out to share with Group B or C, ask them questions pertaining to their intentions and motives.

Handouts: Handout 7.1: Group A Instructions
Handout 7.2: Group B Directions/Rules
Handout 7.3: Group C Rules

Additional Readings

McIntosh, P. (1989, July/August). White privilege: Unpacking the invisible knapsack. *Peace and Freedom*, 8–10. Retrieved from http://mmcisaac.faculty.asu.edu/emc598ge/Unpacking.html
Ore, T. (2006). *The social construction of difference and inequality.* New York, NY: McGraw Hill.
Sue, D.W., & Sue, D. (2008). *Counseling the culturally diverse: Theory and practice.* Hoboken, NJ: Wiley.

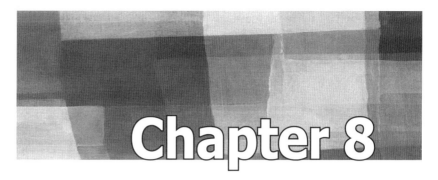

Chapter 8

Take a Stand: Which Side Are You On?

Mark Pope

Topics: Introduction to Multicultural Counseling
Definitions of Cultural Diversity
Oppression and Discrimination
Dimensions of Worldviews
Human Growth and Development

Purposes: This activity is designed to enable students to understand that human beings have a variety of attributes, behaviors, and beliefs, and rarely does everyone agree or have the same attribute. It is a particularly effective activity to conduct early in the development of a classroom's culture as it aids in the development of the tolerance and acceptance of others' attributes, behaviors, and beliefs.

Learning Objectives: After the activity, participants will (a) understand that not everyone has the same worldview that they do, (b) develop increased tolerance and acceptance of others, and (c) learn more about the other students in their class.

Target Population: Undergraduate or graduate students in counseling, education, psychology, or social work

Group Size: 15–30 participants optimally, but really unlimited

Time Required: 30–50 minutes

Setting: Classroom setting with large space at the front of the room.

Materials: Whiteboard/chalkboard or flipchart

Instructions for Conducting Activity

1. The instructor will first read to the class the instructions at the top of the handout "Take a Stand" (see Handout 8.1): "I ask that all participants please stand and come to the front of the room. Participants should move to a place along a continuum between the designated opposite sides of the room according to their responses on each of the items."
2. Once students have chosen their positions, ask them to look at where their classmates have placed themselves on the continuum and if there is anyone's position that surprises, confuses, or especially pleases them.

3. At the end when all the items have been presented, process their feelings and reactions to the exercise. Following are some issues to guide your processing:

- What did it feel like to commit to these positions or categories?
- How did you feel when you belonged to a "minority" opinion or group? Did it matter if you had control of the issue (an opinion) or had no control (eye color)?
- Which issues were more sensitive, and how did that influence your "stand"?

Handout: Handout 8.1: Take a Stand

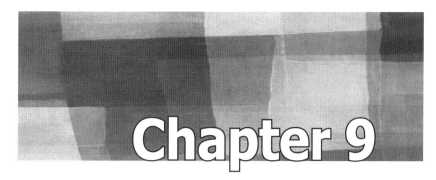

Chapter 9
"I'm Different, You're Different, We're the Same!"

April Sikes

Topics: Introduction to Multicultural Counseling
Barriers to Effective Cross-Cultural Counseling
Culturally Skilled Counselor
Professional Identity and Ethical Practice

Purposes: The purpose of this icebreaker is to help students introduce themselves and get to know each other in a safe environment. This activity aims to provide students with an opportunity to recognize, accept, and appreciate individual differences.

Learning Objectives: As a result of this activity, students will

- gain knowledge about invisible cultural diversity,
- develop an awareness of individual differences and uniqueness, and
- recognize and appreciate racial, cultural, and ethnic diversity.

Target Population: Undergraduate and graduate students in counseling-related professions may benefit from this activity.

Group Size: 10 to 20 participants

Time Required: 30 minutes

Setting: Medium- to large-size classroom (enough room for participants to move throughout the room easily and safely)

Materials: One worksheet (Handout 9.1) and one pencil or pen per student

Instructions for Conducting Activity

1. Welcome students.
2. Present the words *uniqueness* and *cultural diversity*. Ask the class to define both terms.
3. Provide the class with a definition for *uniqueness* and *cultural diversity*. Define *uniqueness* as "The state or quality of being different or one-of-a-kind. There is no one on this earth exactly like you." Define *cultural diversity* as "The differences, including language, customs, dress, and religious beliefs, that exist among various culture groups."
4. Distribute the "I'm Different, You're Different, We're the Same!" handout.

5. Inform the students they will walk around the classroom looking for others who have the same personal characteristics listed on the worksheet. They will walk up to one student at a time, introduce themselves, pick one characteristic on the worksheet, and ask if he or she has the same characteristic. For example, a student will ask another student if English is his or her primary language. If so, the student will write the student's name in the box with English as primary language listed.
6. The students will complete the activity until all students have introduced themselves and filled in a characteristic box. Allow at least 15 minutes for this portion of the activity.
7. Ask for volunteers to share a few of their characteristics and what they learned about some of their classmates.
8. Discuss activity through debriefing/processing questions. Some of these questions might include the following:

   a. How are you different from your classmates? How are you the same?
   b. How do differences and similarities help in developing relationships? Working with others?
   c. As an advocate in your field, how can you promote cultural diversity?
   d. What did you learn from this activity?
   e. How will you apply this information when working with future clients?

Handout: Handout 9.1: "I'm Different, You're Different, We're the Same!"

Additional Readings

Duffey, J. (2005). *Henry's helpful hints: Classroom guidance diversity*. Lesson presented at the meeting of the 2005 Georgia School Counselors Association Annual Conference, Atlanta, GA.

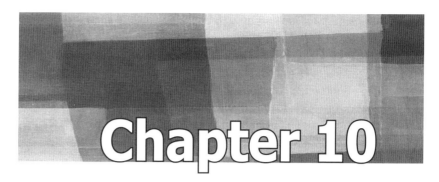

Chapter 10
Creating a Safe Space for Cross-Cultural Training

Hemla D. Singaravelu and Annalise Millet

Topics: Introduction to Multicultural Counseling
Counseling Lesbian, Gay, Bisexual, Transgender (LGBT), and Other Sexual Minority Clients
Helping Relationships

Purposes: This activity aims to provide a safe space for participants to discuss highly charged issues like racism, homophobia, sexism, and so forth. Some typical problems that can arise through these discussions include misunderstandings attributable to unclear communication, participants feeling left out if no one responds to their comments, and students feeling disrespected in an environment that should foster safety and value. The development of group norms, or rules of behavior, by participants is central to creating a safe and open environment, thus allowing participants to generate questions as well as share experiences and ideas without fear of being chastised. These group norms also allow the instructor to feel a level of comfort to raise controversial topics for discussion.

Learning Objectives: Upon completion of this activity, participants will have

- developed a list of acceptable norms or "rules" of behavior to foster an open and collaborative environment,
- developed a sense of clarity about the importance of their point of view in discussion, and
- demonstrated a climate of respect among participants and between the instructor and students.

Target Population: Participants in cross-cultural training programs and counseling students

Group Size: 5–25

Time Required: 35–40 minutes

Setting: Classrooms or discussion rooms with chairs arranged in a semicircle or participants facing each other.

Materials: Chalkboard, dry-erase board, or flipchart.

Instructions for Conducting Activity

1. Instructor will start this activity by stating that topics discussed in the room have the potential to create conflict among participants. Each participant has her or his own set of values and beliefs that can clash with another participant. In order to create a safe zone for discussion of sensitized

topics, it might be helpful to create some *dos* or *don'ts* for all to feel safe enough to express their lived experience and ideas.

2. "What are some guidelines or rules we can create in here to allow each person to feel safe enough to express his or her views?"

3. It is important that the participants, themselves, develop these norms so that they feel some level of comfort, responsibility, and control of their space and can then express and explore ideas freely.

4. The instructor can offer suggestions of some possible group norms if participants are struggling. For example, confidentiality, nonjudgmental comments, use of "I" statements when speaking, and so forth.

5. Participants will define and develop the limits of these norms as well agree to the proposed ideals. This process creates a space in which the students hold each other accountable to this working document.

6. Once everyone has created and written the list of norms generated, the instructor will ask if all participants are in agreement with the norms.

7. Participants are told that this list is a working document and that future adjustments can be made to the list of norms.

8. Participant will be responsible for adhering to the norms they developed.

Additional Readings

Myers, S., & Anderson, C. (2008). *The fundamentals of small group communication.* New York, NY: Sage.

Sue, D. W., & Sue, D. (2005). *Counseling the culturally diverse: Theory and practice.* New York, NY: Wiley.

Yalom, I., & Leszcz, M. (2005). *Theory and practice of group psychotherapy.* New York, NY: Basic Books.

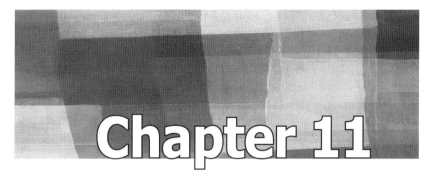

Chapter 11
Multicultural Panel and Discussion

Ariel Winston

Topics: Introduction to Multicultural Counseling
Definitions of Cultural Diversity
Cultural Identity Development
Multiple Identities/Biracial, Multiracial

Purpose: This activity aims to provide participants with personal experiences from individuals of different cultures. It promotes dialogue among the guests and the participants and allows for personal reflection.

Learning Objectives: As a result of this activity, students will

- have an individual with whom to connect an experience,
- have the opportunity to ask questions that could be seen as inappropriate in an alternative setting, and
- be able to discuss issues of race, gender, sexual orientation, and capability.

Target Population: Individuals who would like to become more culturally competent

Group Size: Any size

Time Required: 1–2 hours, depending on size of panel

Setting: Classroom in which a panel can be organized in the front of the classroom during the first section and space to break up into small groups during the second section

Materials: Individuals who ascribe to different groups (African American, White, Asian, Hispanic, Native American, mixed background, homosexual, disabled, and so forth) who are willing to discuss life as it relates to race, classification, or ability. Individuals should be independent of the class and open to answering questions concerning their social classification(s).

Instructions for Conducting Activity

This activity includes two sections. Participants should be encouraged to speak their minds and to ask questions that are personally relevant. In order to ensure the safety of the panelist(s) and classroom participants, the facilitator should explain the understanding of confidentiality to everyone involved. The classroom should be seen as a safe place for dialogue. Facilitators should also make themselves available for conversations afterward, in case anyone has any unresolved issues or feelings to discuss.

The first section will be in lecture or panel format. A speaker or speakers from different groups (Black, White, Hispanic, Asian, Native American, mixed culture, disabled, homosexual, women, and so forth) will join the class to share some of their life experiences. These individuals should be independent of the class and open to answer questions concerning their social classification(s). (Depending on time constrictions, speakers can be used individually. For example, if the focus of the week is Asian clients, you may choose to use solely an Asian guest speaker.) Students will be allowed to ask questions. A key highlighted feature is the White guest speaker. Often multicultural classes focus on the experiences of minority individuals, but by including and discussing White culture, students who are minority can also learn about the other.

After the speaker has finished and left, the second section will include small-group discussion based on the information learned from speakers. This is the time for processing and reflecting on what was heard. Students will break up into small groups. (If the class size is too small to divide into groups, an open class discussion should take place.) Students will be required to actively participate in discussions.

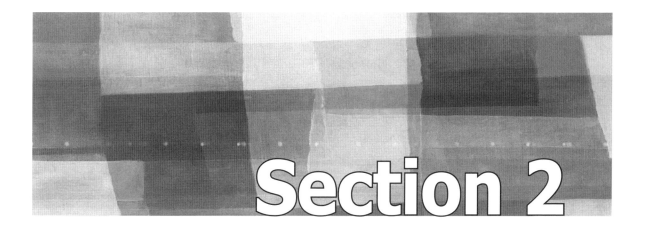

Section 2

Definitions of Cultural Diversity

The group activities in this section are designed to assist counselors-in-training in constructing and understanding definitions of cultural diversity. These class exercises vary in scope and content and are intended to help counselors-in-training examine, talk about, and enhance their cultural vocabulary. Students have opportunities to examine their own social identities as well as the cultural identities of others. These experiential activities can be used in any core counseling course as a means of infusing social and cultural awareness.

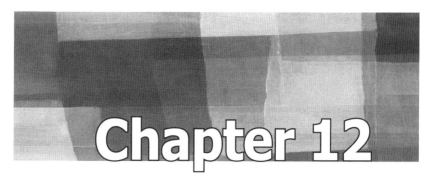

Chapter 12

An Introduction to the Discussion of Race: Why Are Counselors Comfortable Using a Color-Blind Approach?

Antonette Aragon, Nathalie Kees, Jacqueline Peila-Shuster,
Sharon K. Anderson, and Edward J. Brantmeier

Topics: Multiple Identities/Biracial/Multiracial
Culturally Skilled Counselor
Oppression and Discrimination
Cultural Identity Development
Definitions of Cultural Diversity

Purpose: Rationale—When working with counselors and students, it is a common belief that we must look beyond the color of one's skin. It seems comfortable to believe that a color-blind approach is easy to use when working with students. Yet when we ignore a person's racial background, we ignore who they are. Counselors who are White may ignore their own racial identity because they are part of the dominant White culture. As part of the dominant White culture in America, there are systems of privilege at work that provide advantages to the dominant White cultural and structural group. At the same time, students of color are asked to close off their racial identity and are excluded from the power differentials within systems of privilege that White cultural groups experience. Therefore, it is only when students feel a connection with their counselors or teachers—when students believe they are recognized, respected, and valued—that counselors and educators are in a position to make a positive difference in students' lives.

The purpose of the activity is to introduce a discussion about how a color-blind approach is unconsciously chosen because it is easy to ignore someone's race. When we ignore a person's racial background, we ignore who they are. The activity compels one to examine how structural aspects of racism promote inequity.

Learning Objectives: As a result of this activity, participants will be able to (a) deconstruct how the identification of race is easily ignored; (b) critically examine how a color-blind approach is often chosen because of one's own privileged White cultural position; (c) reflect on power, privilege, and dominance in a broader U.S. society; and (d) define how race is a social construction of U.S. society.

Target Population: Graduate students in the fields of counseling, psychology, social work, and the helping professions in general.

Group Size: 10–70 participants

Time Required: 60–90 minutes

Setting: A classroom setting

Materials: Whiteboard or large pad of paper, markers, paper, pens/pencils, handout with six squares identified by particular characteristics, and video titled *Race: The Power of An Illusion, Vol. 1*.

Instructions for Conducting Activity

1. Ask students if they agree with a color-blind perspective and why; record their responses on a whiteboard or large pad of paper.
2. Provide a sheet of paper that has six squares on it with one of the following written in each square: Race/Ethnicity, Religion, Language, Core Values, Family, and Personal Belongings.
3. Ask students to write a little bit about each in the boxes. For example, write your race/ethnicity in the Race/Ethnicity box, "English" in the language box, "honesty and respect" under Core Values, and so forth.
4. Tell the students the following hypothetical situation: "A regime is taking over, and it is necessary to give up one of these boxes and to cross it out."
5. Ask students to discuss with a partner sitting next to them why they chose to cross the box off.
6. Continue to ask students to cross out boxes and after each time of asking them to cross the box out, ask that they discuss with their partner why they chose that box. Continue doing this until there are only two boxes left.
7. When two boxes are left, ask the students as a group to vote to see who got rid of what.
8. In the times that I have conducted this activity, the majority of students almost always cross out race first. This will be a good time in the activity to have a discussion about how you cannot get rid of race, yet that is what we ask our students of color to do every day they walk in our offices or classrooms.
9. Have a quick discussion to find out why they think the majority of them crossed out race first.

Process Questions

- After the quick discussion above, show students the following quote and have a discussion about it: "Colorblind discourse asserts that any consideration of race is itself racist. It protects racism by making it invisible" (Kandaswamy, 2007). Connect this quote to their answers related to using a color-blind perspective in their practice that they shared at the beginning of the class.
- Why is it difficult to discuss race as a topic?
- What are fundamental beliefs we are taught about race?
- How did we develop these notions of race?
- How is race defined?

Interrogating the Construction of Race

At this point in the discussion, it is helpful to have the students view the documentary *Race: The Power of An Illusion, Volume 1* (Adelman, 2003). This documentary provides excellent definitions of race and how it is a social construction. Some questions to consider after the viewing are the following:

- Why is race a social construction?
- Why do students believe race is no longer an issue in our society?
- What were some common beliefs you had regarding race that were brought up in the video?
- How is race perpetuated socially?
- Why is race such a difficult topic to discuss?
- How can we critically analyze race?
- How does race impact students?
- Why is it important to recognize race even though it is a social construction and scientifically it does not exist?

Summative Question: What is the role of counselors in examining race, and why is it important not to use a color-blind perspective?

Follow-Up Integration

- After the processing questions, ask participants to return to their seats or classroom. Ask individual students to reflect in writing for 5 minutes on the following: Why does racism exist in our society; how does it get perpetuated; and why must we critically examine race and deconstruct it? After participants have written their responses, group them according to a triad and have them discuss and share their written reflections with one another. After 5 minutes, ask participants to share comments about their writing and the entire activity with the class.
- For homework, ask students to read Janet Schofield's (2006) article, "The Colorblind Perspective in School." Let students know that this is just the beginning of the critical examination of the social construction of race.

References

Adelman, L. (Executive Producer). (2003). *Race: The power of an illusion* (Vol. 1) [Television PBS Documentary]. Available from California Newsreel at http://newsreel.org

Kandaswamy, P. (2007). Beyond colorblindness and multiculturalism. *Radical Teacher, 80,* 6–11.

Schofield, J. W. (2006). The colorblind perspective in school: Causes and consequences. In J. A. Banks & C. A. McGee Banks (Eds.), *Multicultural education: Issues and perspectives* (6th ed., pp. 271–295). New York, NY: Wiley.

Additional Readings

D'Andrea, M. (1999, Winter). Evolution and transformation of a White racist. *Journal of Counseling & Development, 77,* 38–42.

Howard, G. (1999). *We can't teach what we don't know.* New York, NY: Teachers College Press.

McIntosh, P. (1989, July/August). White privilege: Unpacking the invisible knapsack. *Peace and Freedom,* 8–10.

Scheurich, J. J., & Young, M. D. (1997). Coloring epistemologies: Are our research epistemologies racially biased? *Educational Researcher, 26*(4), 4–16.

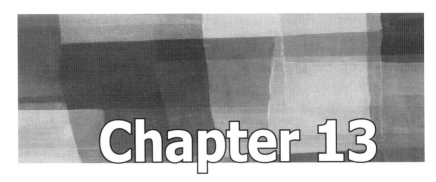

Chapter 13

Who Am I?

Arpana G. Inman

Topics: Introduction to Multicultural Counseling
Definitions of Cultural Diversity
Cultural Identity Development
Human Growth and Development

Purposes: This activity aims to provide participants with opportunities to explore the effects of social identities on one's sense of self. In particular, this activity will enhance one's understanding of marginalized and dominant identities.

Learning Objectives: As a result of this activity, students will (a) have a better understanding of the various groups that one may identify with, (b) gain knowledge about oneself in context, and (c) appreciate the potential for ignoring or being unaware of relevant identities in others.

Target Population: Beginning or advanced undergraduates, master's- or doctoral-level students

Group size: Any number

Time Required: 30 minutes (10 minutes to conduct the activity and 20 minutes for processing)

Setting: A regular class setting or a workshop

Materials: Handout 13.1

Instructions for Conducting Activity

Give each student a handout, then read the instructions: "Listed in the handout are various social groups that we all belong to. Go through the list and check the extent to which you think about each of your social identities while engaged in interactions with others." Instruct students not to spend too much time reflecting on the list; instead, they should respond to it as quickly as possible.

Process questions include the following: (a) Which identity seemed to stand out as salient every time or often, and which identity was never in the forefront? (b) How can this awareness or lack of awareness affect one's interactions with others? (c) Why engage in this activity?

Handout: Handout 13.1: Who Am I?

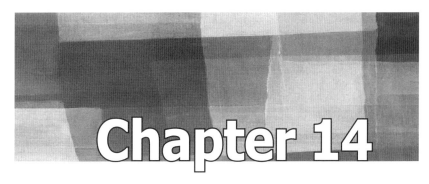

Chapter 14
Diversity Quiz

Mark D. Mason and Minsun Lee

Topics: Definitions of Cultural Diversity
Four Forces in Counseling
Oppression and Discrimination
Dimensions of Worldviews
Advocacy and Social Justice
Poverty, Social Class, and Socioeconomic Status (SES)

Purposes: Students often demonstrate varying types and levels of resistance to change in multicultural courses (Brown, 2004). One type of resistance may be manifested in students' worldviews and an underlying belief in a just world (e.g., Ibrahim, Roysicar-Sodosky, & Ohnishi, 2001). The belief in a just world theory posits that people have a tendency to want to believe so strongly that the world is just and fair that when they observe an otherwise inexplicable injustice, they will rationalize it by looking for things that the victim might have done to deserve it (Hafer & Begue, 2005; Lerner, 1978, 1980, 1997). Individuals who share a worldview that supports belief in a just world tend to rationalize inequities and injustices (Ibrahim et al., 2001). As such, many individuals, in their desire to sustain their beliefs in a just world, may struggle to integrate conflicting information about the disparities in health, income, SES, education, and mental health according to race, gender, sexual orientation, and ability.

 The purpose of the diversity quiz activity is to (a) introduce knowledge about cultural diversity facts into psychology coursework and cultural diversity experiences, (b) explore the practical implications of dominant and subordinate identity groups in the United States, and (c) initiate discussion about students' experiences of cultural diversity and privilege. Overall, the diversity quiz has become a popular tool to introduce cultural diversity into a variety of curricula. Also, the diversity quiz is a thought-provoking and engaging activity to begin discussions, to heighten awareness about difference, and to further explore oppression and discrimination.

Learning Objectives: As a result of participation in this activity, students will (a) be better able to identify disparities in income, education, SES, and health according to race, gender, sexual orientation, and ability; (b) appreciate the effects of membership according to dominant and subordinate group status; and (c) begin to understand the complexities of multiculturalism and the effects of difference according to power and privilege of dominant and subordinate identities.

Target Population: This activity has been designed to introduce graduate counseling students to the practicalities and real-life experiences of oppressed groups within society, often within the context of psychology courses or structured diversity experiences or programs. However, instructors are encouraged to tailor the activity according to their needs.

Group Size: This activity is best conducted with a group of 50 participants or less. However, larger groups may be accommodated within a larger lecture setting.

Time Required: Depending on the role of the activity in the lesson and the learning objectives, the diversity activity may be used within a limited duration (e.g., 20 minutes) or as part of a more extended discussion and processing time (1 hour 15 minutes).

Setting: The classroom setting should support small-group discussion. Therefore, classroom settings with moveable chairs and tables are recommended in order to facilitate participation and communication in the activity.

Materials: Materials needed for this activity are Diversity Quiz handouts and answers. The Diversity Quiz may be administered through presentation (e.g., PowerPoint) or through traditional paper-and-pencil format.

Instructions for Conducting Activity

First, students are instructed to complete individually the Diversity Quiz. The instructor should caution participants that diversity facts are rarely taught in a formalized way in the educational system; hence, the quiz is difficult. Second, because this activity is often used as an icebreaker, students are grouped into teams of four to share and compare answers. Teams of four students dialogue and formulate answers to the Diversity Quiz as a group and may also compete against other teams. Third, instructors provide the answers to the Diversity Quiz in order to grade and assess the individual and team responses. Finally, instructors lead the group in discussion about the activity, inviting participants to share experiences and feelings that surfaced during the activity. Some suggested facilitation questions include (a) Which facts are most surprising? (b) How are these disparities maintained? and (c) Given these significant differences according to culture and identity, how do they impact the counseling relationship?

Handout: Handout 14.1: Diversity Quiz

References

Brown, E. L. (2004). What precipitates change in cultural diversity awareness during a multicultural course? *Journal of Teacher Education, 55,* 325–340.

Hafer, C. L., & Begue, L. (2005). Experimental research on just-world theory: Problems, developments, and future challenges. *Psychological Bulletin, 131,* 128–167.

Ibrahim, F. A., Roysicar-Sodosky, G., & Ohnishi, H. (2001). Worldview: Recent developments and needed directions. In J. G. Ponterotto, J. M. Casas, & C. M. Alexander (Eds.), *Handbook of multicultural counseling* (pp. 425–456). New York, NY: Sage.

Lerner, M. J. (1978). "Belief in a just world" versus the "authoritarianism" syndrome . . . but nobody liked the Indians. *Ethnicity, 5*(3), 229–237.

Lerner, M. J. (1980). *The belief in a just world: A fundamental delusion.* New York, NY: Plenum Press.

Lerner, M. J. (1997). What does the belief in a just world protect us from: The dread of death or the fear of undeserved suffering? *Psychological Inquiry, 8,* 29–32.

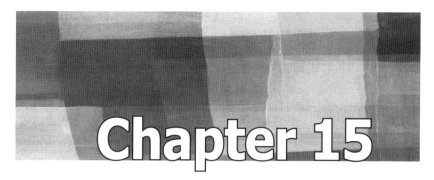

Chapter 15
Let's Talk About It

Krista M. Malott

Topics: Introduction to Multicultural Counseling
Definitions of Cultural Diversity
Cultural Identity Development
Professional Identity and Ethical Practice

Purposes: Purposes of this activity are to (a) define *diverse*, as it applies to subgroups; (b) engage students in an initial discussion of the topic of diversity; (c) recognize potential difficulties of discussing the topic, and identify the source of this discomfort; and (d) provide rules to encourage future discussion. In addition, this activity creates ready-made, diverse groups that can continue to be used for future discussions and assignments.

Learning Objectives: As a result of this activity, students will (a) be able to define diversity in relation to subgroups, (b) recognize a broader definition of which groups could be considered multicultural, (c) understand their own and others' reluctance to discuss the topic and the origins of that discomfort (e.g., cultural pressure to avoid taboo or controversial topics), and (d) create a set of rules to increase personal comfort with class discussions centered on multicultural topics.

Target Population: Counseling students, master's or doctoral level, in a multicultural counseling course

Group Size: 15 and up

Time Required: 25 minutes

Setting: Small- to average-sized classroom or larger

Materials: Whiteboard or chalkboard, chalk or marker

Instructions for Conducting Activity

1. Inform students you want to create groups to be used throughout the semester. To provide a mix of persons with a variety of experiences and opinions, these groups must be as diverse as possible. Ask them to list all the different elements of a multicultural group. Write these on the board—suggest groups if ideas are minimal (e.g., such as different socioeconomic groups, different gender orientations, cultural/generational differences, and so forth).

2. Ask students to stand and wander with the goal of forming the most diverse small groups possible (depending on preference, groups can have three to five students). Observe interactions (e.g., silences, nervous laughter, reluctance to speak, and so forth).

3. After they have seated themselves with their groups, discuss the experience. Possible questions/comments are as follows:

   a. Tell me about your groups' diverse elements (address each group if the number of groups is small).

   b. What was the experience like?

   c. Which questions were you comfortable asking one another? Why?

   d. Were there any questions that you refrained from asking? (What makes these questions taboo?)

   e. Who taught you they were taboo?

   f. What do we fear when it comes to broaching these topics?

   g. As the instructor, share your observations, using humor and terminology to increase student comfort level with topics. For example, "I noticed a lot of nervous laughs and silence." Or, "I didn't hear anyone shouting out, 'Who's poor in here?' 'Who's gay?' Why not?"

4. Ask them to create rules for the class to make talking about those topics easier and safer. Examples include confirming confidentiality, using "I" statements (speak from own experience), and practicing tolerance and respect toward classmates' opinions.

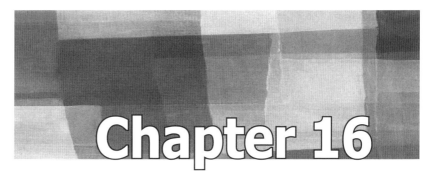

Chapter 16

Enhancing Cultural Competency With Diversity Definitions

Allison C. Paolini

Topics: Introduction to Multicultural Counseling
Definitions of Cultural Diversity
Cultural Identity Development
Culturally Skilled Counselor

Purposes: The purpose of this activity is to enhance counselors' awareness about the meaning of phrases and terms pertaining to cultural diversity. Knowledge of this terminology is imperative so that counselors will have a more comprehensive understanding about issues regarding diversity and will become more competent and knowledgeable multicultural counselors.

Learning Objectives: As a result of this activity, students will become familiar with and learn terms and vocabulary that play an integral role in multicultural counseling.

Target Population: This activity is specifically designed for undergraduate students taking sociology, education, or psychology courses. This activity can also be used for graduate students who are obtaining a degree in school counseling, mental health counseling, or psychology.

Group Size: 15–30 students

Time Required: 25–30 min

Setting: This activity can be conducted in a classroom setting. Students will be required to sit in a circle to encourage classroom discussion after the activity is completed.

Materials: Pens, pencils, and handout

Instructions for Conducting Activity

Using the vocabulary words provided in the word bank, the facilitator will ask students to define each of the terms listed. The facilitator will then lead a discussion regarding the accuracy of the definitions to develop a common language among the group members. Once students acquire the necessary knowledge, they can then complete the handout.

   Handout: Handout 16.1: Diversity Definitions

Additional Readings

Anti-Defamation League. (2009). *101 ways to combat prejudice: Developing a common language.* Retrieved July 29, 2009, from http://www.adl.org/prejudice/prejudice_terms.asp

Callahan, P., Corey, M. S., & Corey, G. (2007). *Issues and ethics in the helping professions.* Pacific Grove, CA: Thomson Brooks/Cole.

Pedersen, P. (2000). *A handbook for developing multicultural awareness* (3rd ed.). Alexandria, VA: American Counseling Association.

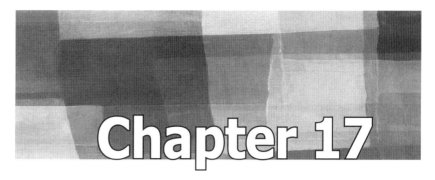

Chapter 17

My Culture/Drawing

Adelaida Santana Pellicier

Topics: Definitions of Cultural Diversity
Cultural Identity Development
Human Growth and Development
Creative Arts

Purposes: The purposes of this activity are to define *culture* and to engage students in reflecting on their respective cultures.

Learning Objectives: Students' understanding will increase about how all individuals have a culture and can define themselves in terms of culture.

Targeted Population: Students at any level, kindergarten through doctorate level, studying issues related to multiculturalism, diversity, and social justice; or participants in workshops on racism, diversity, social justice, and/or culture. Procedures and discussions will need to be adapted to the age level.

Group Size: Any size

Time: 1 hour

Setting: Any classroom or conference room, depending on class/group size. It is best to have desks and/or tables.

Materials: Drawing paper or any blank paper for each participant; markers and/or crayons to share

Instructions for Conducting Activity

1. Distribute drawing paper or any unlined paper to each participant.
2. Distribute markers/crayons to share with one another.
3. Explain to students that you will not define the term *culture* but they are being asked to define it for themselves through drawing pictures and symbols that define their culture. Encourage them to make their drawings colorful.
4. Remind students that artistic ability is not required, nor is it necessary. Cutting pictures and symbols from magazines is an alternative technique but requires additional materials, such as magazines, glue, and scissors. It is important to be frugal with materials to minimize complexity of what is a potentially emotional activity.

Processing

1. Processing is dependent on participant's responses; therefore, flexibility in processing is required.
2. Divide class into groups of three to five, depending on the total number of participants.
3. Ask participants to share their drawings and talk about them in their groups—their reasons for selecting each representation of their culture and their meanings. Ask that they talk about how they defined culture as well as what they were feeling as they drew.
4. Ask each group to discuss whether or not they each have a culture.
5. Ask each group to draw some inferences on the definition of *culture* as well.
6. Reconvene the class to process their group work as well as to share comments related to the activity.
7. For adult classes, the instructor may provide a myriad of definitions from the resources below to generate a more in-depth discussion related to the complexity in defining this term. One may further engage in some discourse in terms of such questions as the following: Are there elements in some of the definitions that are similar? Can we arrive at a working definition? Further discussions may generate reasons for the following questions: Why do some individuals define themselves culturally whereas others do not? What are the reasons for the differences in how each individual defines himself or herself? Why does society often use the term *culture* synonymously with *ethnicity*? Why is there a need for a precise definition to distinguish the differences between the terms *ethnicity* and *culture*?
8. Provide the group with an acceptable working definition of *culture* (Mio, Trimble, Arredondo, Cheatham, & Sue, 1999) as well as *ethnicity* and other terms that will be used frequently in their readings and/or in class.
9. The previous two items (i.e., Items 7 and 8) must be adapted according to the group level and/or the goal of the exercise as defined by the instructor or facilitator.

Handouts: None are necessary, though a list of definitions may be shared with students as a handout, depending on age of students.

References

Mio, J. S., Trimble, J. E., Arredondo, P., Cheatham, H. E., & Sue, D. (Eds.). (1999). *Key words in multicultural interventions: A dictionary.* Westport, CT: Greenwood Press.

Additional Readings

Santiago-Rivera, A., Arredondo, P., & Gallardo-Cooper, M. (2004). *Counseling Latinos and la familia: A practical guide.* Thousand Oaks, CA: Sage.

Sue, D. W., & Sue, D. (2008). *Counseling the culturally diverse: Theory and practice* (5th ed.). New York, NY: Wiley.

Chapter 18

Cards of Life

Torey L. Portrie-Bethke

Topics: Introduction to Multicultural Counseling
Definitions of Cultural Diversity
Cultural Identity Development
Counseling Lesbian, Gay, Bisexual, Transgender (LGBT), and Other Sexual Minority Clients
Counseling People With Disabilities
Human Growth and Development
Helping Relationships
Poverty, Social Class, and Socioeconomic Status (SES)

Purposes: The purpose of this activity is to enhance students' integration of cultural beliefs, biases, and values. The activity is provided to challenge students' beliefs about ethnicity, race, SES, age, sexual orientation, and disabilities to further develop counseling skills and awareness for working with diverse populations.

Learning Objectives: As a result of this activity, students will (a) have a greater understanding of their personal biases and beliefs related to race, ethnicity, social status, sexual orientation, age, and disabilities; (b) identify how their personal worldviews affect their conceptualizations of the client's needs in the counseling relationship; and (c) develop counseling approaches for meeting the needs of diverse individuals. The activity may be used to initiate the discussion and practice of working in the moment with clients' personal needs and worldviews.

Target Population: Master's-level counseling students enrolled in counseling skills courses or students who are learning to integrate theory with diverse client needs and experiences

Group Size: 5–40 participants/students

Time Required: 1 hour

Setting: Classroom—the activity is designed to begin with individual personal exploration followed by a transition into small-group discussions and then a large-group discussion. To begin the first phase of the activity, the students are instructed to work independently on developing their client's identity. In the second phase of the activity, the students will need to be placed in groups of three to six students. After the second phase of the activity is completed, the students will move into a large group circle for a group discussion.

Materials: Chairs and tables for the students to be seated; one or several decks of playing cards (one deck may be used for 16 students); the script for the playing cards (refer to Handout 18.1); and the "Counseling Theory Objectives" handout (refer to Handout 18.2).

Instructions for Conducting the Activity

The instructor begins by providing the students with instructions to begin the activity.

1. Each student will be given one card, either the ace or a face card, and five of the numbered playing cards and the script (Handout 18.1). The script will identify the created client in which the student will provide a case conceptualization of the client's life experiences and worldview in relation to a specific counseling theory.
2. Once the students have created their client based on the cards allotted and the script, the student will begin the conceptualization of the client and the counseling needs in relation to the student's chosen counseling theory.
3. After the students have completed conceptualizing the clients in relation to their counseling theories, the students will move into groups of four to address their created clients and the counseling theory objectives (refer to Handout 18.2).
4. Concluding experience: In a large group the students will explore their perceptions of this experience and the importance of awareness of self and others in the counseling relationship.

Handouts: Handout 18.1: Cards of Life Script
Handout 18.2: Counseling Theory Objectives

Definitions of Cultural Diversity

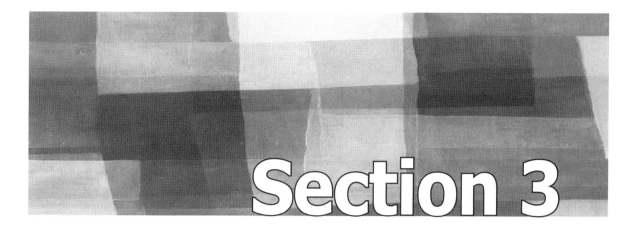

Barriers to Effective Cross-Cultural Counseling

These experiential activities provide an opportunity for students to reflect and explore concepts of stereotypes, prejudice, discrimination, and cultural identity. These activities also encourage students to consider the ways in which a counselor's life experiences and personal biases can help or hinder effective cross-cultural encounters. These activities can be used in a variety of core counseling classes throughout a student's counseling training and can be particularly useful in clinical courses at both the master's and doctoral levels.

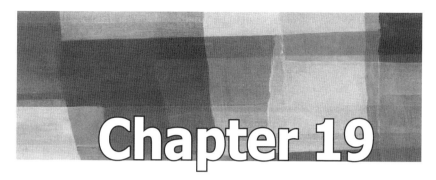

Chapter 19

Having a Voice and Being Heard: Exploring the Impact of Multiple Social Identities on the Self

Hector Y. Adames and Milton A. Fuentes

Topics: Barriers to Cross-Cultural Counseling
Oppression and Discrimination
Group Work
Multiple Identities/Biracial, Multiracial

Purposes: Stereotypes remain prevalent in today's society, despite great efforts to eliminate them. In many ways, stereotypes can be harmful in nature as they perpetuate often incorrect notions and ignore individual differences (e.g., Smith & Hopkins, 2004; Spencer, Steele, & Quinn, 1999; Steele, 1997). Even more damaging are the potential negative psychological effects on members of stereotyped groups. This activity has four purposes: (a) to provide a process that will welcome participants to experience the powerful ways in which stereotypes may impact behavior, affect, and cognition; (b) to highlight the ideology that all people possess multiple social identities; (c) to help participants understand and appreciate the visible and invisible aspects of diversity within the group; and (d) to help participants identify ways in which stereotypes and bias, both implicit and explicit, can serve as barriers to the psychotherapeutic relationship.

Learning Objectives: As a result of this activity, participants will (a) increase their awareness and knowledge that both prejudice and discrimination come in a variety of forms; (b) have concrete and in-vivo examples of how people's behavior, affect, and cognition are impacted in powerful ways by stereotypes; (c) appreciate and understand that all people benefit from cultural diversity training; and (d) identify personal biases that serve as barriers to interpersonal cross-cultural encounters

Target Population: Undergraduate and graduate students as well as professionals

Group Size: Works best with a group size of 10 or more participants

Time Required: 60–90 minutes

Setting: No specific room design is required

Materials: Paper and writing utensils

Instructions for Conducting Activity

- Welcome members to the group activity.
- Have participants fill out "Exploring Our Multiple Identities" handout.

- Facilitator will then collect each sheet of paper.
- Facilitator should tally up and organize the various categories according to identities (e.g., African American, lesbian, middle-class, ability status). Having participants fill in this information will ensure that the facilitator will call out the social categories represented in the group, thus giving all participants an opportunity to stand before the group and make their statements.
- Now you are ready to begin.
- Instruct participants to all stand and move to one side of the room.
- Group members should all be facing the facilitator while the facilitator faces the group members.
- Facilitator will then read the following instructions:

> This experiential exercise will provide an opportunity for you to voice your thoughts about statements you no longer want to hear regarding your identities. You will be provided with a sentence stem to complete. For this exercise the sentence stem is, "I don't want to hear any more that . . ." So, for instance, I will welcome all members who identify as a woman to stand where I am standing and address the group. You are welcome to come up and say something that you no longer want to hear that is often said about women. You are welcome to make more than one statement. Also, since we have more than one identity—for instance, someone can identify as biracial, gay, immigrant, and male—it is very likely that this individual will have four chances to address the group.

- Allow participants to ask questions regarding the instructions.
- Facilitator will call each social category one at a time and allow participants to begin completing the sentence stem.
- After all social categories represented in the room (as self-identified in the filled-out "Exploring Our Multiple Identities" handout) have been called, group process begins. Ask the group to discuss what they have learned from the exercise. As you process the exercise with the larger group, consider the following questions:

  1. What was this like for you?
  2. What struck you the most about the exercise?
  3. What were you most pleased by?
  4. What were you most surprised by?
  5. What was the greatest lesson for you?
  6. What was your greatest disappointment?
  7. Complete this sentence: "Because of this exercise, I will now . . ."
  8. How might this play out with our clients?
  9. How might our clients do this with us?

Points to Remember

- We have found that many participants report that this activity provided a new experience for them to voice how social stigmas and stereotypes have affected them. They have discussed the power of being "heard" by members of the dominant group while standing in solidarity with members of their own group. Thus, it is not uncommon for participants to become emotional during the exercise.
- Because some individuals may be hesitant to complete the sentence stems, even in small groups, it can be effective for facilitators to be active participants in the exercise. If the facilitator makes himself or herself vulnerable, others will be more comfortable doing the same.
- We often do this exercise during the middle of the semester or after group cohesion has been established.

Handout: Handout 19.1: Exploring Our Multiple Identities

References

Smith, C. E., & Hopkins, R. (2004). Mitigating the impact of stereotypes on academic performance: The effects of cultural identity and attributions for success among African American college students. *Western Journal of Black Studies, 28,* 312–321.

Spencer, S. J., Steele, C. M., & Quinn, D. M. (1999). Stereotype threat and women's math performance. *Journal of Experimental Social Psychology, 35,* 4–28.

Steele, C. M. (1997). A threat in the air: How stereotypes shape intellectual identity and performance. *American Psychologist, 52,* 613–629.

Additional Readings

Dworkin, S. H. (2002). Biracial, bicultural, bisexual: Bisexuality and multiple identities. *Journal of Bisexuality, 2,* 93–107.

Hays, P. A. (2001). *Addressing cultural complexities in practice: A framework for clinicians and counselors.* Washington, DC: American Psychological Association.

Chapter 20

Increasing Self-Awareness: Identifying Counselors' Potential Strengths and Barriers to Effective Multicultural Counseling

Michael D'Andrea and Judy Daniels

Topics: Introduction to Multicultural Counseling
Barriers to Effective Cross-Cultural Counseling
Culturally Skilled Counselor
Human Growth and Development
Multiple Identities/Biracial, Multiracial

Purposes: This activity is intended to serve a threefold purpose. First, it is aimed at increasing counseling students' self-awareness of how their own development has been affected by multiple factors that comprise the RESPECTFUL counseling model (D'Andrea & Daniels, 2001). Second, this activity is aimed at increasing counseling students' knowledge of the cultural multidimensionality of their clients' development. Third, it is designed to assist counselors in thinking about the strengths and potential barriers they bring to counseling situations with persons from diverse groups and backgrounds; these strengths and potential barriers are a result of their own cultural conditioning and life experiences.

Learning Objectives: As a result of completing this activity, students will (a) develop a better understanding of their own cultural multidimensionality and identity; (b) become more knowledgeable of the personal, cultural, and developmental strengths they bring to counseling settings; (c) expand their thinking about their clients' cultural multidimensionality; and (d) increase their awareness of the potential limitations and biases that are linked to their own personal, cultural, and professional development as it affects the work they do.

Target Population: This activity is designed for counseling students in graduate training programs. It is especially useful to implement during the early stage of graduate students' training program, perhaps during their first semester.

Group Size: "The RESPECTFUL Counseling Self-Assessment Activity Form" (Handout 20.2) can be used in groups of counseling students as small as 3 to as many as 20 individuals.

Time Required: 1.5 hours

Material: "Description of the RESPECTFUL Counseling Model" (Handout 20.1); "The RESPECTFUL Counseling Self-Assessment Activity Form" (Handout 20.2)

Setting: This activity can be done in a classroom setting where the students' and instructor's desks/chairs are arranged in a semicircle.

Instructions for Conducting Activity

In the week preceding the use of the activity form, the course instructor should state the following instructions and distribute the accompanying handout materials.

> In order to be an effective counselor and a culturally competent counselor, it is important to be aware of the ways that your own life experiences and cultural conditioning have affected your development. As you become aware of these issues, you will also be better positioned to understand many of the personal and professional biases you have acquired and bring to the work you will do as a professional counselor.
>
> It is very important to become as aware of these forces as well as your biases so you can consciously work to resist imposing such biases in your counseling endeavors. Given the importance of developing this awareness, I would like you to read the information that describes the RESPECTFUL counseling model I am distributing to you at this time.
>
> After you have read this information and become aquainted with this theoretical model, I would like you to complete "The RESPECTFUL Counseling Self-Assessment Activity Form" that I am also providing to you. In doing so, you will become more aware of your own multidimensional nature. As you work through this exercise, you also will be encouraged to think about some of the generalized assumptions and biases you may have developed about persons from other groups and backgrounds as a result of your own sociocultural conditioning. We will discuss your reactions to completing this form at our next class meeting.

The next week, the instructor should have the students arrange their seats/desks in a semicircle at the beginning of class and provide the following instructions:

> Now that you have had time to read about the RESPECTFUL counseling model and complete the self-assessment activity form that was distributed last week, I would like to do a few things in this class meeting. First, I would like to hear your general reactions to this model. Second, I would like to take time to learn about your thoughts and feelings as a result of completing the activity form. Third, I would like to hear what you think are some of the implications of the reactions you had to completing this form in terms of the different clients you will work with in the future.

It is important for the instructor to manage the discussion of the above-stated issues in such a manner that all three areas are covered in the class meeting. In many classes where we have used this activity, we have found benefits from having students spend about 20 minutes discussing their general reactions to the RESPECTFUL counseling model, 30 minutes discussing their reactions to completing "The RESPECTFUL Counseling Self-Assessment Activity Form" handout, and 30 minutes discussing the implications of their reactions to RESPECTFUL counseling theory for the different clients they will work with in the future. Instructors are encouraged to use about 10 minutes for a short break at an appropriate time.

Handouts: Handout 20.1: Description of the RESPECTFUL Counseling Model
Handout 20.2: The RESPECTFUL Counseling Self-Assessment Activity Form

Instructors need to make copies of these handouts and distribute them to the students a week before the class meeting when the exercise will be used, as noted above.

References

Cartwright, B., & D'Andrea, M. (2004). Counseling for diversity. In T. F. Riggar & D. R. Maki (Eds.), *Handbook of rehabilitation counseling* (pp.111–122). New York, NY: Springer.

D'Andrea, M., & Daniels, J. (2001). RESPECTFUL counseling: An integrative model for counselors. In D. Pope-Davis & H. Coleman (Eds.), *The interface of class, culture and gender in counseling* (pp. 417–466). Thousand Oaks, CA: Sage.

Duran, E., & Duran, B. (1995). *Native American postcolonial psychology.* Albany, NY: State University of New York.

Kelly, E. W. (1995). *Spirituality and religion in counseling and psychotherapy: Diversity in theory and practice.* Alexandria, VA: American Counseling Association.

Lewis, J. A., Lewis, M. D., Daniels, J. A., & D'Andrea, M. J. (2003). *Community counseling: Empowerment strategies for a diverse society* (3rd ed.). Pacific Grove, CA: Brooks/Cole.

Liu, W. M. (2001). Expanding our understanding of multiculturalism: Developing a social class worldview model. In D. B. Pope-Davis & H. L. K. Coleman (Eds.), *The intersection of race, class and gender in multicultural counseling* (pp. 188–197). Thousand Oaks, CA: Sage.

Sprinthall, N. A., Peace, S. D., & Kennington, P. A. D. (2001). Cognitive–developmental stage theories for counseling. In D. C. Locke, J. E. Myers, & E. L. Herr (Eds.), *The handbook of counseling* (pp. 109–130). Thousand Oaks, CA: Sage.

Worrell, J., & Remer, P. (2003). *Feminist perspectives in therapy: Empowering diverse women* (2nd ed.). Hoboken, NJ: Wiley.

Additional Readings

Ivey, A. E., D'Andrea, M., Ivey, M. B., & Simek-Morgan, L. (2007). *Counseling and psychotherapy: A multicultural perspective* (6th ed.). Boston: Allyn & Bacon.

Sue, D. W., & Sue, D. (2003). *Counseling the culturally diverse: Theory and practice* (4th ed.). New York: Wiley.

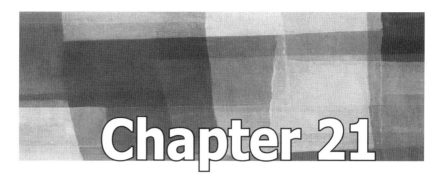

Chapter 21

Cross-Cultural Interviews: Understanding Attitudes Toward Counseling and Mental Health Services

Michael Goh, Julie Koch, and Michael Starkey

Topics: Barriers to Effective Cross-Cultural Counseling
Culturally Skilled Counselor
Helping Relationships
Use of New Technology
Creative Arts

Purposes: The purposes of this exercise are to encourage students to (a) challenge themselves to interact with and learn about persons culturally different from themselves, (b) learn about help-seeking attitudes and preferred sources of help held by members of a culturally distinct group, (c) dialogue with other class members about help-seeking attitudes and preferred sources of help held by members of a culturally distinct group, (d) create a visual collage of responses from the interviews, and (e) consider and discuss creative methods of overcoming barriers to help-seeking.

Learning Objectives: As a result of this activity, students will (a) experience interviewing and conversations with someone culturally and possibly ethnically different than themselves, (b) understand help-seeking attitudes held by some members of cultural and ethnically diverse groups, (c) understand preferred sources of help for some members of cultural and ethnically diverse groups, and (d) learn about nontraditional methods of working with these groups.

Target Population: Students currently enrolled in an introductory or advanced multicultural counseling course or general introduction to counseling course

Group Size: It is recommended that this activity be conducted with at least 10 participants but no more than 30 participants.

Time Required: This activity will require time in at least two class meetings as well as time spent outside of class. The bulk of the activity will take place in one class meeting and will take an hour to an hour and a half.

Setting: No special setting is needed for this activity. A classroom or group room is appropriate.

Materials: Colored paper (8 ½″ × 11″)—four reams in four different colors, markers, masking tape

Instructions for Conducting Activity

The instructor should determine a point allotment for this assignment/activity and include it on the course syllabus. An example may read like this:

> Conduct a structured interview based on questions agreed on in class with **two** members of **one** culturally distinct group (including international students, new immigrants, persons with disabilities, and so forth) to understand their perception of counseling/helping services and preferred sources of help. Complete a summary of what you have learned from persons of this culture group about their help-seeking behavior and perceptions. Include a one-page candid self-analysis about your feelings (not thoughts) of comfort or discomfort with your interview experience (six to seven pages).

During one class session early in the semester, introduce the activity, provide students with instructions, and allow them four to six weeks to make contacts and conduct interviews. When introducing the assignment to students in class, the instructor may want to use a PowerPoint slide to offer an example of an interview question for each aspect of this assignment:

- "Source(s) of help" sample question:

  "If you needed help on a personal issue or problem, who would you go to for help? Why?" (Repeat the question for an "academic issue," "career issue," and so forth.)

- "Attitudes toward seeking professional psychological help" sample question:

  "What is your opinion, if any, about going to see a psychologist or mental health counselor for help?"

Outside of class students are to interview two members of one culturally distinct group, such as international students and new immigrants, those with disabilities, the elderly, or sexual-orientation minorities, to understand their perception of counseling/helping services and preferred sources of help. Students complete a summary of what they have learned from persons of the culture-group they chose about their help-seeking behaviors and perceptions. Students include a one-page candid self-analysis about their feelings (not thoughts) of comfort/discomfort with the interview experience (6–7 pages)

Later Class Session

Students bring their summaries to class. At the front of class, students are shown four piles of 8 ½″ × 11″ paper in four different colors. Two of the colors are used to represent attitudes toward seeking professional psychological help. One color will be for one positive attitude (e.g., "trustworthy" or "trained"). Students will use one sheet of paper for one description. In a similar manner, students will use another colored paper to list all the negative attitudes described by their interviewees (e.g., "stranger" or "shameful"). The other two stacks of paper will reflect whom interviewees listed as their preferred sources of help. One color is used to list professional helpers mentioned (e.g., social worker, licensed professional counselor) and the other color for other sources of help (e.g., clergy, family member).

The next stage of this class session requires one wall in the classroom to be designated the wall for the positive attitudes about counseling and for professional sources of help. The other wall is designated for the negative comments about counseling and for informal sources of help. It is helpful to put up a sample colored paper on the designated walls to aid students. Whenever students are ready, they will take their stack of colored papers and use masking tape to stick their results on the corresponding walls. In the 10 years that Michael Goh has conducted this exercise, it is striking how the "negative" wall is regularly overflowing and the "positive" wall is sparsely filled. Students are invited to walk around the room to review what is written on the walls and to contemplate the meaning of it all.

The instructor then leads a discussion focused on questions such as the following:

1. What does this mean about our profession? How do you feel about this career choice you made?
2. Why do the negative impressions about our field exist?

3. What barriers of access exist for cultural and ethnic minority groups to receive help?
4. How should we understand the pervasive informal network of helpers that people prefer?
5. Are there ways in which we can work with these informal helping networks?
6. What can we do to remove stigmas and to educate the public about our profession?
7. Why do you think so many people find it hard to trust counselors?

Obviously, questions can be added or removed depending on the flow of the discussion.

Additional Readings

U.S. Department of Health and Human Services. (2001). *Mental health: Culture, race, and ethnicity—A supplement to mental health: A report of the surgeon general*. Rockville, MD: Author.

Chapter 22

Creating Diversity-Based Policies in Schools or Agencies

Marty Jencius

Topics: Barriers to Effective Cross-Cultural Counseling
Oppression and Discrimination
Professional Identity and Ethical Practice
Group Work
Research and Program Evaluation
Advocacy and Social Justice

Purposes: This activity aims to provide participants with the opportunity to simulate the development of a diversity policy for their current or future workplace. Participants develop a policy that addresses the equity needs of marginalized clients or students, the diversity development needs of staff and/or practitioners, or the organizational policy needs of a school or agency. This activity also creates dynamic small-group discussion about the challenges involved in establishing workplace policies related to diversity. Discussion leads to discovering macrosystem barriers that marginalized groups face in acquiring services from schools and community agencies.

Learning Objectives: As a result of this experience, participants will (a) have a better understanding of how agencies and schools address and develop a diversity policy, (b) experience "mock" resistance that policy advocates face when presenting diversity policy, and (c) explore some of the public arguments for and against equity issues in schools and community agencies.

Target Population: The target population is counselor trainees preparing for school or mental health practice. This activity can easily be adapted and used in a school or agency in-service training.

Group Size: Optimal size is approximately 20, and minimum size is 8 participants. Groups larger than 40 participants are difficult to coordinate with the time allotted.

Time Required: 12 hours, depending on the group size

Setting: This activity is best designed for a room with moveable seating so the participants can aggregate in smaller work groups.

Materials: Because the teams will be creating a policy for presentation, it is best to have supplies available for team members to create a policy that can be displayed and viewed by the whole participant group. For this purpose, the activity leader can provide the following: flipcharts, markers, blank overhead transparencies, or in the case of a technology-rich setting, a document projector or digital projector for PowerPoint developed by the groups. Because the groups will be working simultaneously and independently, there should be enough supplies for each team to work on their own. The activity leader may also want to have a reward for the team with the best policy (e.g., a bag of chocolate candy!).

Instructions for Conducting Activity

1. The activity leader introduces the activity to the larger group of participants, explaining the steps found in the instructions.
2. The larger group of participants is divided into working teams of four or five members each. Depending on the context of the training and the nature of the participants, teams can be formed on the basis of their future or current work setting (e.g., K–12 school, mental health, college counseling) so that team members have a common setting where their policy will apply.
3. The teams are given directions to create a policy for their designated setting. The policy they create should have a defined target (a school district, teachers in a same school, counselors in a same agency).
4. Teams are directed to create a policy statement that has the following elements: (a) a clear policy statement to be enacted by their setting, (b) a target of the policy, (c) an action plan and description of how the policy will be enacted, and (d) a method of evaluating the success of the policy on the setting.
5. Teams engage in independent small-group work discussing and creating documents to present to the larger group of participants.
6. The activity leader visits teams as they work, answers questions, and keeps the work of the teams moving.
7. After the teams have finished their work, the activity leader asks for all materials to be brought to one location. (This interrupts teams from continuing to work during others' presentations.)
8. Teams are chosen (in a random-order selection) to present their policy to the other teams as a larger audience. They have limited time to present. Time is monitored by the activity leader (usually 5–10 minutes).
9. Viewing teams are given a few minutes to consult with their team members and develop **only one** question they can ask of the presenting team. Each viewing team can ask their one question, and then the presenting team members are given a chance to defend their proposal. The activity leader picks the order of team questions and monitors (and interrupts, if necessary) the process of the questioning.
10. Once every team has presented and responded to questions from opposing teams, the activity leader engages the larger group of participants in a reflective process regarding the experience of working in the team, developing the policy, and defending the policy.

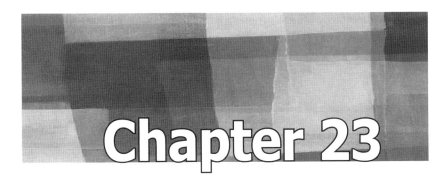

Chapter 23

Earliest Memory Related to Race: Feelings and Messages

Minsun Lee and Mark D. Mason

Topics: Barriers to Effective Cross-Cultural Counseling
Oppression and Discrimination
Dimensions of Worldviews
Counseling African Americans
Counseling Native Americans
Counseling Asian Americans
Counseling Hispanic/Latino Americans
Counseling European Americans
Gender Issues in Counseling
Helping Relationships

Purposes: This activity is based on an activity described by Tatum (2003, pp. 31–32), in which she asked participants to name the feelings associated with their earliest race-related memory. The purpose of this activity is to help participants understand the prevalence of race-related messages and how they affect their views of race and race relations. Although people's experiences, and consequently their worldviews, are shaped by their race (Frankenberg, 1993), individuals are taught to deny how their experiences are situated in a racially hierarchical structure. By explicitly asking about racial experiences, this activity seeks to make visible how individuals become socialized about race through covert and overt race-related messages. Awareness of society's pervasive messages about race makes it less likely for individuals to maintain a color-blind attitude. Color-blind attitude has been linked to various factors, such as racial identity development (Chen, LePhuoc, Guzman, Rude, & Dodd, 2006; Gushue & Constantine, 2007), multicultural competence (Spanierman, Poteat, Wang, & Oh, 2008), and empathy for clients (Burkard & Knox, 2004).

Learning Objectives: As a result of this activity, participants will be better able to (a) identify and clarify the messages they have received about race; (b) understand how these messages have shaped their unexamined views on race, including assumptions and stereotypes about racial groups; (c) process their feelings about these messages; and (d) examine how these feelings relate to the counseling relationship.

Target Population: This activity is appropriate for both undergraduate and graduate students in multicultural courses.

Group Size: Although a group of 10 to 20 participants is ideal, this activity can be accommodated for various group sizes.

Time Required: 45 to 75 minutes, depending on the number of participants

Setting: It is best if the seating arrangement in the room is flexible so that chairs can be moved for small- and large-group discussions. The room should also have a black- or whiteboard.

Materials: Black- or whiteboard with chalk or markers. Each participant needs a blank sheet of paper and pen.

Instructions for Conducting Activity

Although this activity may be used to segue into a discussion on the socialization around race, it may be helpful for the participants to have had a preliminary discussion of race and racism prior to the activity.

1. Ask each participant to write about the following anonymously:
   a. What is your earliest memory related to race?
   b. What were the feelings associated with the incident?
   c. What was the message you received about race from that incident?
2. Collect the anonymous writings.
3. Have the participants get into dyads and redistribute the anonymous writings, making sure that no one receives her or his own writing. Ask them to make sure the writing is not their own. If anyone receives his or her own, redistribute the writing.
4. Ask the dyads to discuss what is written, including their answers to the following questions:
   a. How do you feel about what is written?
   b. Are there common themes in the two writings?
   c. Are they similar to what you wrote about?
   d. Were the messages and/or feelings associated with the incidents positive or negative?
   e. How would you feel if the incident in the writing was something that happened to you? How might it have influenced your views about race?
5. Ask the participants to come back to the larger group.
6. Divide the black- or whiteboard in half by drawing a vertical line down the middle, and entitle one column "Messages" and the other "Feelings."
7. Have one person from each dyad come up and write on the board the messages and feelings associated with the incident in the writings.
8. After all the dyads have had a chance to write on the board, ask the participants what they notice about what is written on the board. For example, what is a common message or feeling listed on the board? How do these messages and feelings affect how we view ourselves and others?
9. Ask the participants to discuss what they talked about in their dyads.
10. Ask if they would like to share what they wrote about in their original writing; invite feedback from others after each person shares.
11. If the activity is conducted within the context of a counseling course, discuss how these incidents, messages, and feelings may affect the counseling relationship.

References

Burkard, A. W., & Knox, S. (2004). Effect of therapist color-blindness on empathy and attributions in cross-cultural counseling. *Journal of Counseling Psychology, 51*, 387–397.

Chen, G. A., Le Phuoc, P., Guzman, M. R., Rude, S. S., & Dodd, B. G. (2006). Exploring Asian American racial identity. *Cultural Diversity and Ethnic Minority Psychology, 12*, 461–476.

Frankenberg, R. (1993). *White women, race matters: The social construction of whiteness.* Minneapolis: University of Minnesota Press.

Gushue, G. V., & Constantine, M. G. (2007). Color-blind racial attitudes and White racial identity attitudes in psychology trainees. *Professional Psychology: Research and Practice, 38*, 321–328.

Spanierman, L. B., Poteat, V. P., Wang, Y.-F., & Oh, E. (2008). Psychosocial costs of racism to White counselors: Predicting various dimensions of multicultural counseling competence. *Journal of Counseling Psychology, 55*, 75–88.

Tatum, B. D. (2003). *"Why are all the Black kids sitting together in the cafeteria?" and other conversations about race*. New York, NY: Basic Books.

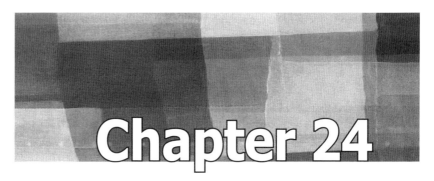

Chapter 24
Who's Got the Money?

Krista M. Malott

Topics: Barriers to Effective Cross-Cultural Counseling
Oppression and Discrimination
Helping Relationships

Purposes: The purpose of this activity is to provide participants with the opportunity to explore the effect of privilege on their own and others' professional and personal lives.

Learning Objectives: As a result of this activity, students will (a) be able to define and recognize privilege, (b) recognize how privilege affects them and their clientele in personal and professional settings, and (c) develop a level of comfort in discussing issues of power and privilege.

Target Population: Master's- or doctoral-level counseling students in any counseling course

Group Size: 10–30 participants

Time Required: 45 minutes

Setting: Small- to average-sized classroom or larger

Materials: Quotes, each typed on separate piece of paper; play money; tape

Instructions for Conducting Activity

1. Tape privilege statements throughout the room. For examples of statements, refer to McIntosh (1998) or Johnson (2006). A broader definition of *privilege* (e.g., race, gender, sexual orientation, socioeconomic status, and disability) will ensure that every student leaves the room feeling he or she has at least one privilege.
2. Place a stack of play money, equal to the number of students present, beneath each privilege statement around room.
3. Write and review the definition of *privilege*: "Privilege: a special right, advantage, immunity, benefit or exemption not enjoyed by all; exempts persons from certain obligations or liabilities" (Allee, 1987).
4. Ask students to pair up with the person that most differs from them (e.g., men with women, African American students with White students). Explain that they must wander as a pair, read each statement, and collect a bill according to the ones that apply to their partner. Give an example: "If the statement 'I can be fairly sure that when I apply for a job, those in power will be the same gender as I am,' is true for your partner, collect a bill from the stack of bills.

5. Once finished, have them count their partner's money and share the amount. To provide a powerful visual, ask students to shout out the amount of money they amassed and draw a vertical line on a board, putting the largest amount amassed on top, lowest on bottom, and a few in-between numbers. Refer back to this as you process the experience.

6. Process the experience as a group. Suggested questions are as follows:
   a. What was the experience like?
   b. What was it like to collect the money (or not collect the money) for your partner?
   c. How were you different from your partner in the amount you amassed?
   d. Were there any of the statements that surprised you? How so?
   e. How do you think this (in this moment, you can refer back to the scale on the board) relates to privilege?
   f. The bills were placed randomly. However, if you were going to assign the largest bills to what you perceived as the most valuable privileges, which would those be?

7. Next step, optional: Ask if there were any privileges that they did not have but wished that they did. When a student notes a privilege, ask him or her to take that bill from another student who has it. Continue with several other students in this manner.

8. Discussion suggestions are as follows:
   a. What was it like getting your "privilege" taken from you? What feelings did you experience?
   b. In reality, do you have anything to lose if you give up some of those privileges?
   c. What was it like to take the money? What feelings did you have?
   d. How is privilege like money in the bank?
   e. How is privilege connected to power?

9. Final activity: Talk 3 minutes with a partner about how your life is influenced by privilege and how this matters as a professional when working with clients that differ from you.

10. Ask students to share their reactions to the activity with the entire class. If the class is reluctant to divulge, have them journal their thoughts.

References

Allee, J. G. (1987). *Webster's dictionary*. Baltimore, MD: Ottenheimer Publishers.

Johnson, A. G. (2006). *Privilege, power, and difference* (2nd ed.). New York, NY: McGraw Hill.

McIntosh, P. (1998). White privilege: Unpacking the invisible knapsack. In M. McGoldrick (Ed.), *Re-visioning therapy: Race, culture, and gender in clinical practice* (pp. 147–152). New York, NY: Guilford Press.

Barriers to Effective Cross-Cultural Counseling

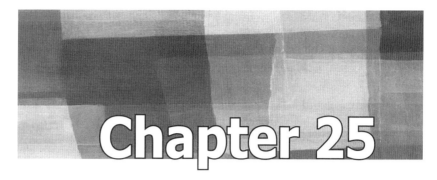

Chapter 25
Depression and the *Bruja*

Krista M. Malott

Topics: Barriers to Effective Cross-Cultural Counseling
Oppression and Discrimination
Poverty, Social Class, and Socioeconomic Status (SES)
Immigrant Experience

Purposes: The purpose of this activity is to increase intellectual and affective understanding of the barriers faced by clientele of other cultures or socioeconomic levels or who do not speak English. This activity will also expose students to alternative healing practices, encouraging discussion of alternative healing as a viable form of helping.

Learning Objectives: As a result of this activity, students will (a) increase knowledge of barriers faced by persons of different cultures when attempting to access mental health services, (b) increase knowledge regarding ways to provide more culturally competent services for clientele of different culture backgrounds or for those who are English language learners, (c) increase awareness of alternative healing practices.

Target Population: Master's- or doctoral-level counseling students in any counseling course

Group Size: Any number

Time Required: 30–40 minutes

Setting: Any conducive to class discussion

Materials: Questionnaire (Handout 25.2); copies of the actual situation for students who are visual learners (Handout 25.1)

Instructions for Conducting Activity

1. Inform students that you want them to imagine they are in a situation that you will present to them. They can close their eyes if it helps them better imagine themselves in the setting. Ask those who are visual learners if they would like a copy of the written scenario.
2. Read the situation (Handout 25.1) to the group (note: you can change the situation and setting to better fit the subgroup most represented in your area or to accomodate your level of comfort with Spanish in this situation).
3. Afterward, hand out the questionnaire and asks students to fill it out.

4. Discuss questionnaire responses as a class.
5. Final questions (in small groups or as a class):
   a. Call out all of the barriers that you faced as a client in this scenario.
   b. As a future professional, what are ways to reduce client barriers to locating, approaching, and accessing services?
   c. How could you make sure the services you offer are culturally congruent or, at the least, comprehensible (or meaningful) for the clientele?
   d. How would you collaborate with alternative healers, and what type of alternative healers would you work together with?

Handouts: Handout 25.1: Depression and the *Bruja*
                Handout 25.2: Questionnaire

Additional Readings

Fong, R. (Ed.). (2004). *Culturally competent practice with immigrant and refugee children and families.* New York, NY: Guilford Press.

Chapter 26
I Imagine You Imagine I Am and I Observe, I Imagine

Brian J. Mistler

Topics: Introduction to Multicultural Counseling
Barriers to Effective Cross-Cultural Counseling
Four Forces in Counseling
Culturally Skilled Counselor
Group Work

Purposes: The purpose of this activity is to provide participants with an opportunity to explore and share their projections about each other, to discover how this may limit their effectiveness in cross-cultural counseling, and to modify some of their prejudices through experiences that contrast with their preconceptions and stereotypes.

Learning Objectives: As a result of this activity students will have a better understanding of (a) their prejudices and projections onto people and cultures different from their own, (b) how they are perceived by others, (c) how others' perceptions of them and their projections onto others may lead to biases in the counselor and/or client and may be an obstacle to cross-cultural communication, (d) practical techniques for confronting projections with real-world data, and (e) further steps to take for improving cultural competency and investigating projection.

Target Population: Multicultural groups, therapists in training (may be replicated with clients as well)

Group Size: 3–100 (as a class or in smaller groups, as preferred)

Time Required: 20 minutes to 3 hours, as preferred

Setting: Any room

Materials: None required. Pencil and paper are optional.

Instructions for Conducting Activity

1. The instructor or class leader begins by introducing the activity and, if appropriate, providing one or two examples to demonstrate the technique and set an open, accepting tone.
2. Each individual (in round-robin sequence or speaking up as ready) makes a statement in the form "I imagine you imagine I am . . ." directed at another member of the group. It is important that individuals direct these statements to a specific member, even if she or he feels that multiple

people have the same feeling. Examples include, "I imagine you imagine I am a bad therapist," "I imagine you imagine I am a spoiled rich kid," "I imagine you imagine I'm smarter than I really am," or "I imagine you imagine I spend all my time outside of class with other people of my race." At this step, the person being spoken to should not reply but, rather, should simply listen to the projection. Notice the format of the statement is not about the person it is directed to; instead, it is a statement about what the speaker imagines.

3. Next, introduce participants to the distinction between observation and imagination. Data perceived by the senses and more-or-less accepted as objective is directly observable. Inferences made from such observations are labeled *imagination*. For example, "I observe you furrow your brow when I speak to you, and I imagine you don't understand what I'm saying," "I observe you clenching your fists when you talk to me, and I imagine you're angry at me," or "I observe you reading during class, and I imagine you're not interested in what we're talking about."

4. Next, individuals are instructed to again go around and this time are asked to make statements in a similar form: "I observe . . . and I imagine. . . ." You can ask people to pay special attention to their habit of making statements not in this form, and the instructor or group leader can help guide participants if they're struggling. For example, someone who says, "I observe you're not excited to see me," might be reminded to look for the data points that she or he sees that leads her or him to **imagine** that "you're not excited to see me." And someone who says, "I observe that many Muslims are angry at American politics, and I observe you're Muslim, and I imagine you're angry at me" could be guided into reflecting about the degree to which the observation is about the person in the room and not about a stereotype.

5. The same activity can be repeated to preface the "I imagine you imagine I am . . ." statement. For example, one could say things like, "I observe you give me a *C* on most assignments, and I imagine you imagine I am stupid," or "I observe that you make jokes about people of my race, and I imagine that you imagine I and my whole family are criminals." At this point, many students may find it difficult to identify specific observations with the individuals in the room that lead to their imaginings. If time allows, this may be an appropriate time to talk about what individuals have observed **outside** of the room (e.g., from the media, from past family situations, and so forth) that have led them to imagine certain things about people in the room. The central question of this step is, "**How** did I come to imagine this?"

6. In this step, participants can "check out" their perceptions by soliciting feedback from fellow participants. This process is done by asking straightforward questions that will either support or provide evidence against their imaginings. For example, one participant may turn to the person who she or he imagined thought him/her stupid and ask, "Do you think I'm stupid?" Or, someone might ask, "When you clench your fists, are you angry at me?" The participants at whom the questions are directed are encouraged to reply if they wish. Some students will find their imaginations are on target (e.g., "When I read during class it is because I'm not interested"), and others may find their imaginations disconfirmed (e.g., "No, I'm not angry. I clench my fists because I'm so energized about what we're talking about," or "I don't think your family members are criminals; I just tell those jokes because I think they're funny").

7. Finally, students are asked to think about how to change their imaginations, beliefs, and actions based on this feedback. Students can do this step in private, or they may share if they wish, and they may even record their decisions to change in writing. A student who learns that people yawning while she or he is speaking doesn't mean they're not interested may decide "When I observe someone yawning, I know they're just tired sometimes, and I won't immediately imagine they're bored with me." Equally, students may decide to change their actions based on feedback, "I understand that when I tell racist jokes other people imagine I'm making judgments about them, so I don't want to do that anymore." The emphasis of this step is both on changing the pattern of irrational thoughts and feelings that occur as the result of an observation into more rational ones and on changing actions based on feedback about the way they're perceived.

8. Discuss the results and implications for therapy. Encourage others to speak about their own experience, and avoid criticizing or judging other group members.
   a. How much of what you imagined turned out to be true?
   b. What surprised you about what others imagined about you?
   c. How does imagination not based on observation get in the way of your work with clients? How could you use the ability to consciously separate observation from imagination to improve your cross-cultural communication and counseling skills?
   d. Do you feel more comfortable "checking out" your perception and projections with others? How could you do this with clients?
   e. What sorts of things do you need to learn about certain cultures to be a better cross-cultural counselor? What areas do you still have a lot of unfounded imaginings in?
   f. What sorts of things might your clients imagine about you from things you do? Which things do you want to keep, and which do you want to change?
   g. How might this activity be useful in group therapy settings? How could you use "I observe" and "I imagine" with clients in individual therapy?
   h. What about in supervision? Consider being both supervisor and supervisee—how might it feel different to give or receive clinical feedback or semester evaluations using this form?
   i. What can you learn about what clients imagine about you or others in the therapy room? How can you help them "check it out?"

Additional Readings

Abdullah, S. M. (1999). *Creating a world that works for all*. London, England: Berrett-Koehler.

Mistler, B. J. (2009). Gestalt therapy. In American Counseling Association (Ed.), *The ACA encyclopedia of counseling* (pp. 211–212). Alexandria, VA: American Counseling Association.

Perls, F. S., Hefferline, R., & Goodman, P. (1994). *Gestalt therapy: Excitement and growth in the human personality*. Gouldsboro, ME: Gestalt Journal Press.

Van De Riet, V., Korb, M. P., & Gorrell, J. J. (1980). *Gestalt therapy, an introduction*. New York, NY: Pergamon Press.

Chapter 27
Physical Space Appraisal

*Jacqueline Peila-Shuster, Edward J. Brantmeier, Nathalie Kees,
Sharon K. Anderson, and Antonette Aragon*

Topics: Barriers to Effective Cross-Cultural Counseling
Culturally Skilled Counselor
Career Development

Purposes: Rationale—Hormuth (1990) indicated that physical artifacts, which are the created objects of a culture, provide important and often powerful messages (as cited in Banning, 1997). These artifacts can be expressions of cultural beliefs and assumptions that are often just below the surface of conscious thought (Kuh & Whitt, 1988). Visual ethnography has been used to observe artifacts and appraise the cultural climate of educational institutions (Banning, 1997; Banning & Bartels, 1997). It can also provide a framework to assess one's physical work environment to see what messages are being given regarding the cultural sensitivity of the organization and the counselor.

The purpose of this activity is to increase awareness of the messages one's counseling environment sends to clientele. It provides a way to look at one's physical space through a broader lens and critique the messages it may send to others, especially those who are marginalized in today's society. This activity allows counselors to make changes to improve the inclusivity of their physical space, and it provides them with the opportunity to reflect on their own worldviews (exhibited in choices about their physical space) and how that may affect their counseling.

Learning Objectives: As a result of this activity, participants will be able to (a) gain greater awareness of their physical space and the nonverbal messages it transmits, (b) identify ways that they can provide a more inclusive environment, (c) contemplate on their own level of privilege and how that affects their counseling.

Target Population: Counseling (school, community, career) students and professionals

Group Size: Varies. This can be done individually or in small groups.

Time Required: External assignment with in-class presentation and process time. Allow for 20 minutes per presentation in class and 15–30 minutes for follow-up processing with entire class upon completion of all presentations.

Setting: Student's own office, counseling, or internship space; classroom for presentation and processing

Materials: Visual depiction of one's space can allow for greater opportunities for others to provide feedback; thus, the use of personal cameras or disposable cameras is recommended.

Instructions for Conducting Activity

- Go into your work space and take a look around with a new lens. Think in terms of the client, an outsider to your office. What do you see? What messages are being delivered by the physical space? Take pictures of what you discover.

    Be sure to look at the layout of the furniture, the books on your shelves, the posters and pictures on the walls. What displays of self and culture are there? Are they appropriate, safe, and welcoming for your clients? How have you exhibited a welcoming environment for diversity? Think in terms of a wide variety of diversity, including, but not limited to, gender, race, ethnicity, sexual orientation, and other ability. Don't overlook the little things. In addition to the visual, be sure to use your other senses as well. For example, what do you hear? What do you smell? How does it feel?

- Write all of your observations down, and see if you notice any themes or patterns. What are these?
- What can be done? Are there ways that you can make your physical space a safer and more welcoming environment for your clientele? What observations may be beneficial to discuss with your work colleagues?
- Present your findings to the class in a 15- to 20-minute presentation that includes your pictures, themes that emerged, and ideas that you have for making adjustments.
- Be sure to solicit feedback from your peers regarding their observations and suggestions.

Process Questions

- How did it feel to critique your own space? What were the benefits and the limitations?
- Was there a certain group that you more closely identified with as you completed your appraisal? Were there certain groups that seemed to be less included?
- What public messages are being given about you, the place you work for, and the profession that you represent?
- What can you do to help improve your appraisal of your environment? What supports can you enlist to help you?

Follow-Up Integration

Follow up in the next few weeks with a brief (one-page) written report on adjustments you are making to your physical environment to improve inclusivity.

References

Banning, J. H. (1997). Assessing the campus' ethical climate: A multidimensional approach. In J. Fried (Ed.), *Ethics for today's campus: New perspectives on education, student development, and institutional management* (pp. 95–105). San Francisco, CA: Jossey-Bass.

Banning, J. H., & Bartels, S. (1997). A taxonomy: Campus physical artifacts as communicators of campus multiculturalism. *NASPA Journal, 35*(1), 29–37.

Hormuth, S. (1990). *The ecology of the self.* Cambridge, England: Cambridge University Press.

Kuh, G. D., & Whitt, E. J. (1988). *The invisible tapestry: Cultures in American colleges and universities* (ASHE-ERIC Higher Education Report No. 1). Washington DC: Association for the Study of Higher Education.

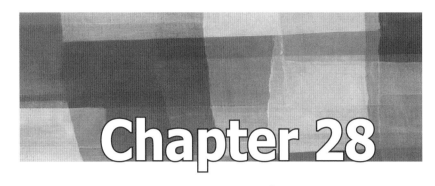

Chapter 28

Who Am I?

Adelaida Santana Pellicier

Topics: Introduction to Multicultural Counseling
Definitions of Cultural Diversity
Barriers to Effective Cross-Cultural Counseling

Purposes: The purpose of this activity is multifaceted: (a) to introduce the professor within the myriad of concepts and microtopics encompassed in a multicultural counseling class and (b) to enlighten the audience to their own unconscious and subconscious assumptions about individuals.

Learning Objectives: Students will have a better understanding of their preconceived ideas about individuals and will also gain a better understanding of their underlying thoughts and feelings that may affect their behavior with clients.

Target Population: Graduate students in the fields of counseling, psychology, social work, and the helping professions in general

Group Size: Any size

Time Required: 1 hour

Setting: Any classroom or conference room, depending on class/group size

Instructions for Conducting Activity

1. This activity starts the class, that is, it begins on the very first day of class. The professor may write her or his name and the class title on the board. The professor says nothing else other than giving instructions for the activity.
2. Distribute note cards to the group, one per student.
3. Request that they do not write their names on the cards; it is an anonymous exercise.
4. Ask students to write on the note card their response to every item given by the facilitator/professor. Each item will be mentioned once and quickly. They must then write their response quickly.
5. Ask them to write their responses to the following: "Tell me who you think I am with respect to . . ."
   a. My ethnicity, culture, sex, gender, sexual orientation, socioeconomic status (SES)/class, country of origin, home language/native language, marital status, highest degree, with/out children, number and sex of children, visible disabilities, and age?
   b. I often add the following for levity: favorite color, favorite food, leisure activities, make of car, and housing type.

6. Introduce self to the class, ensuring coverage of all above categories.
7. Discuss with the class that these are at least some of the assumptions that we glean about people, some without evidence. These, then, are concepts within the area of multicultural counseling that will be covered within the class and will be defined and studied throughout the course of the class. Students may sometimes want to brag about their success in accurately identifying who the professor is. Facilitator may ask for a show of hands on the number of correct items, followed by, "What may accuracy and/or lack of it suggest about a person's knowledge and/or beliefs?"

Additional Readings

Keung Ho, M. (1992). *Minority children and adolescents in therapy*. Newberry Park, CA: Sage.

Santiago-Rivera, A., Arredondo, P., & Gallardo-Cooper, M. (2004). *Counseling Latinos and la familia: A practical guide.* Thousand Oaks, CA: Sage.

Sue, D. W., & Sue, D. (2008). *Counseling the culturally diverse: Theory and practice* (5th ed.). New York: Wiley.

Tatum, B. D. (1997). *"Why are all the Black kids sitting together in the cafeteria?" and other conversations about race*. New York, NY: Basic Books.

Witko, T. M. (Ed.). (2006). *Mental health care for urban Indians: Clinical insights from Native practitioners*. Washington, DC: American Psychological Association.

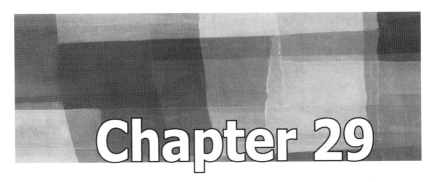

Chapter 29
Addie Appleseed

Adelaida Santana Pellicier

Topics: Introduction to Multicultural Counseling
Definitions of Cultural Diversity
Barriers to Effective Cross-Cultural Counseling
Professional Identity and Ethical Practice
Human Growth and Development

Purpose: This activity is designed to provide participants with an opportunity to explore the uniqueness of individuals.

Learning Objective: As a result of this activity, participants will develop a clearer appreciation of the physical uniqueness of individuals.

Target Population: Graduate students in the fields of counseling, psychology, social work, and the helping professions in general.

Group Size: 10–20 participants (cost per pound of apples makes this exercise prohibitive for large groups)

Time Required: 1–1.5 hours

Setting: Classroom or conference room

Materials
- Select Delicious apples (red or yellow, or does it matter? Be specific), Macintosh apples, and/or green apples that resemble each other as closely possible. Remove any stems and make sure none has identifiable markings. The number of apples varies according to the number of people in a group and/or class.
- One wide and shallow basket/container to hold all apples and one paper bag.
- Butcher paper/flipchart or dry-erase board with a dark ink marker.

Instructions for Conducting Activity
1. Ask the participants to each select an apple from the basket/container.
2. Ask the participants to study the apple for approximately 2 minutes (in order to be able to pick it out of a basket of apples). Instruct them not to make any markings on their apple but to notice its unique features.

3. After 2 minutes, ask the participants to place their apples back in the basket or container.
4. Facilitator should mix/displace the apples so that they are not in the same position as where the owner placed them. You might place them in a bag and shake them carefully to mix them, then replace them onto the basket to make them visible to the class.
5. Ask each individual to pick his or her respective apple out of the basket.

Processing

1. Ask the participants to discuss how they were able to identify their respective apple.
2. Engage the class or group in a discussion around what this activity meant for them.
3. Ask the class or group to draw some generalizations/inferences they may take away from this activity as they relate to the overall barriers to effective cross-cultural counseling and the notion of prejudice.
4. Record these on a flipchart and distribute to the class or group at the following meeting date (you may ask for a volunteer to do this).

Additional Readings

Bergen, T. J., Jr. (2001). The development of prejudice in children. *Education*, *122*, 154–162.

Chapter 30

Hero, Messenger, or Mystic: Cross-Cultural Symbol Understanding

Jordan S. Potash and Cheryl Doby-Copeland

Topics: Barriers to Effective Cross-Cultural Counseling
Cultural Communication Styles
Dimensions of Worldviews
Professional Identity and Ethical Practice
Creative Arts

Purposes: The purpose of this activity is to encourage helping service professionals to carefully ascertain the meaning their clients ascribe to various words and symbols. Careful attention should be paid to this area to avoid misunderstanding and possible misdiagnosis. This activity uses art to facilitate participants' understanding of how a narrow worldview affects their interactions with others. The goal of the activity is based on the fact that different cultures attribute different meanings to the same symbols and colors.

Learning Objectives: As a result of this activity, participants will (a) be able to see the impact of culture on understanding symbols and art, (b) understand the importance of learning about a client's cultural background, and (c) understand the need to carefully assess their own biases and worldviews before applying them to another.

Target Population: The target population is students and professionals in the helping service professions. It may be especially pertinent for those who use art or images in their interventions.

Group Size: This activity can be adapted to various size groups. The ideal number of participants is 10–30.

Time Required: 15–30 minutes

Setting: Classroom or large space

Materials: This activity requires very few materials: art printed out or projected on a screen, instruction sheet handouts, and paper and pens/pencils

Instructions for Conducting Activity

Art is often thought of as a universal language that transcends language and cultural boundaries. Although it is true that every culture has an art tradition, people of different cultures do not ascribe the same meaning to similar symbols (e.g., Cirlot, 1971; Eberhard, 1983). In fact, visual perception and production of symbols is a learned trait that relates to specific historical and cultural contexts (Mangan, 1978). Gude (2001) wrote that the "unexamined and unchallenged assumptions about the normalcy of color associations becomes a vehicle for re-inscribing racially charged symbolism into current consciousness" (p. 41). In one example, she discussed artistic language that calls dark values "low" and light values "high." She was careful to point out that they may not have been designed with race relations in mind, but these terms and what they represent take on different contexts in today's pluralistic world.

In the helping service professions, art is often thought of as a tool for communication or diagnosis. Even though practitioners are becoming increasingly aware of the cultural limitations of projective tests, there are therapists who try to make interpretations of art without cultural, developmental, or historical context. Chebaro (1998) described the limitations in assumptions on symbolic expression in projective tests. She gave the example of "Draw a Person in the Rain," which assumes that rain is symbolic of stress. Although this interpretation may be appropriate for some, there are parts of the world where rain is viewed as a blessing and necessity for life. Wegman and Lusebrink (2000) conducted research to compare kinetic family drawings completed by children from different cultures. The study showed that some drawings met the Western criteria for pathology, when in fact they were drawn in culturally appropriate ways for clients from a particular culture.

This activity, designed by art therapists, is intended to challenge these assumptions, while at the same time promoting awareness of the challenges of assumed symbolic expression. The danger in ignoring these concerns was made clear by Lofgren (1981), who described her work in art therapy with a Native American client. By researching her client's art traditions and cultural values, she was able to understand that her client's diagnosis was inappropriate. For those who use art in their profession and those who do not, this activity reinforces how unchecked biases can impact our worldview and affect our ability to attend to clients across cultural boundaries.

Preparation

Prior to the activity, make copies of the instruction sheet handouts, masking out the titles at the top of the page that identify the country or culture. What the facilitator knows but the participants do not is that there are three different sets of instructions. Each set should be copied to look identical so that the participants do not realize that each set contains a different set of directions. When it is time to hand the instructions out, the facilitator should be careful to conceal that there are different sets.

Experiential

Divide participants into groups of three to five students, making sure there are at least three groups. Make sure each group is far enough away from the others so that they cannot overhear each other. The facilitator should then read the directions at the top of the handout:

> In the initial session with a new client, you invite your client to create a symbolic family drawing. The client takes a lot of time to work on the art. At the end of the session, there is not enough time for the client to discuss the drawing, but the client promises to talk to you about it further the next time you meet. You are the first staff member to meet with this client and you are about to walk into a staffing meeting. You have to give a brief presentation on the client based on your initial impressions. Because you didn't have much time to talk, you have to base your opinion on the art itself.
>
> In order to help you understand the drawing, you take an article off your desk titled "Investigation of Symbol Meaning and Implications for Art Therapy Research." The article reports on the usage of various symbols, their meanings, and correlation to certain personality traits. The study seems to be credible based on the large sample size of the population and the longitudinal nature of the research project.
>
> Using the following excerpts from the article, prepare a brief presentation that you could offer in a staff meeting. You will have 5 minutes, after which you will be asked to report your findings.

Facilitator shows projected image of art or hands out a color copy to each group (see Handout 30.5). The facilitator also hands out the instruction sheets to the participants (see Handouts 30.2, 30.3, and 30.4). All participants in the same group should receive the same set of instructions.

After 5 minutes, each group should select a speaker who will present their findings. The facilitator should allow each group to present their interpretations. It is important that the facilitator encourage the groups to share their analysis without going into the details of how they arrive at their interpretations. (This is important as otherwise the groups will find out too early in the process that they are all using different meaning guides. We often have been able to prevent detailed analysis of interpretation by role-playing a demanding clinical team leader who is in a rush.). By the time the third group presents, there is usually some grumbling in the room. The participants can be led in large-group discussion to uncover why there are conflicting reports. This discussion can continue as long as the facilitator deems necessary or until someone in the group makes a comment related to whether everyone had the same set of instructions.

Debriefing

The facilitator tells the group that each subgroup was given a different set of instructions. The "large sample size of the population and the longitudinal nature of the research project" relates to three different cultures that have each long held onto their own beliefs as to the meaning of certain animals and colors (see Handout 30.1). Explain that one set of instructions relates to Chinese (Eberhard, 1983; see Handout 30.2), one to Western mythology (Cirlot, 1971; see Handout 30.3), and the third to Zuni, a Native American nation (Young, 1988; see Handout 30.4).

The facilitator should explain that it is important when working with clients to learn about their worldviews either through research or by asking them so as to avoid misinterpreting their use of terms or symbols. The facilitator may give some examples of how misunderstanding can lead to misdiagnosis or inappropriate treatment goals and interventions. The facilitator should also pay careful attention to how participants describe the relationships among the animals. In addition to the symbol meaning, any assumptions indicate a reference to one's own worldview, rather than that of another.

Please note, even within a specific culture symbols may have multiple meanings. The ones offered here represent a selection from the given culture as indicated in specific references. When researching this activity, we found several websites that gave listings of Zuni animal fetishes and their meanings. In further research of more scholarly sources, we found that the fetishes were originally created to represent six sacred animals. The other animals that are now being created are a more recent phenomenon, possibly influenced by contact with non-Native American people. Even when using culturally correct information, it may be best to share one's ideas with the client in order to determine the appropriate analysis for that person.

Handouts: Handout 30.1: Chart of Symbol Meanings
Handout 30.2: Chinese
Handout 30.3: Western Mythology
Handout 30.4: Zuni
Handout 30.5: Art

References

Chebaro, M. (1998). Cross cultural inquiry in art and therapy. In A. R. Hiscox & C.A. Calisch (Eds.), *Tapestry of cultural issues in art therapy* (pp. 229–240). Philadelphia, PA: Jessica Kingsley.

Cirlot, J. E. (1971). *A dictionary of symbols* (2nd ed.; J. Sage, Trans.). London, England: Routledge.

Eberhard, W. (1983). *A dictionary of Chinese symbols* (G. L. Campbell, Trans.). London, England: Routledge and Kegan Paul.

Gude, O. (2001, Spring). Color lines. *Teaching Tolerance, 19,* 38–43.

Lofgren, D. E. (1981, October). Art therapy and cultural difference. *American Journal of Art Therapy, 21,* 25–30.

Mangan, J. (1978). Cultural conventions of pictorial representation: Iconic literacy and education. *Education Communication and Technology, 26,* 245–267.

Wegman, P., & Lusebrink, V. B. (2000). Kinetic family drawing scoring method for cross-cultural studies. *The Arts in Psychotherapy, 27,* 179–190.

Young, M. J. (1988). *Signs from the ancestors: Zuni cultural symbolism and perceptions of rock art.* Albuquerque, NM: University of New Mexico.

Chapter 31

A Creative Project: Helping Children of Color Learn About Self-Concept and Career Options Through Life Span Career Development Theories

Varunee Faii Sangganjanavanich

Topics: Barriers to Effective Cross-Cultural Counseling
Cultural Identity Development
Oppression and Discrimination
Culturally Skilled Counselor
Professional Identity and Ethical Practice
Human Growth and Development
Career Development

Purposes: This activity aims to provide participants with opportunities to explore the impact of racial identity on the career development of children from different cultural backgrounds. This activity also enhances students' understanding of the obstacles and prejudice that children of color may encounter in constructing their self-concepts and searching for career information.

Learning Objectives: As a result of this activity, students will (a) have a better understanding of the impact of racial identity on ethnic and cultural minority children in terms of self-concept and career development and (b) be able to integrate multicultural counseling competencies in career development of children from different cultural backgrounds.

Target Population: Students in career theories, career development, and career counseling courses

Group Size: 15–20 students

Time Required: 40 minutes

Setting: Regular classroom size, round tables are preferred

Materials: Flipcharts and markers

Instructions for Conducting Activity

First, the instructor divides students into three groups, representing elementary, middle, and high school. Then, the instructor explains to students that they are school counselors or counselors working in school settings. They are assigned the task of developing a creative project intended to help a group of children of color learn about their career options. This group is made up of children of diverse backgrounds.

Students will address the following questions from the perspective of life span career development theories:

1. What are your roles as a counselor?
2. According to life span career development theories, what can you do to appropriately support the development of self-concept in children from that age group?
3. How does racial development influence the growth of self-concept and access to career information among children of color?
4. What are potential obstacles and prejudices you think these children of color might encounter?
5. How does your project assist in the development of their self-concept and career options?

The instructor informs students in each group that they have 15 minutes to complete the project and 5 minutes to present their project to the class. The project involves discussion among group members, understanding of life span career development theories and racial identity development, and integration of multicultural counseling competencies. The instructor also communicates to students that the project can be as creative as they would like. Students write their creative project on flipcharts, which they then present to the class. After finishing the group presentations, the instructor encourages students to discuss and reflect on both the creative projects and their general experience of this activity.

Additional Readings

Akos, P., & Ellis, C. M. (2008). Racial identity development in middle school: A case for school counselor individual and systematic intervention. *Journal of Counseling & Development, 86,* 26–33.

Helms, J. E. (2003a). Racial identity and racial socialization as aspects of adolescents' identity development. In R. Lerner, F. Jacobs, & D. Wertlief (Eds.), *Handbook of applied developmental science: Promoting positive child, adolescent, and family development through research, policies, and programs: Vol. 1. Applying developmental science for youth and families.* Thousand Oaks, CA: Sage.

Helms, J. E. (2003b). Racial identity in the social environment. In P. B. Pedersen & J. C. Carey (Eds.), *Multicultural counseling in schools: A practical handbook* (pp. 44–58). Boston, MA: Allyn & Bacon.

Sharf, R. S. (2010). *Applying career development theory to counseling* (5th ed). Belmont, CA: Wadsworth.

Trimble, J. E., Helms, J. E., & Root, M. P. P. (2003). Social and psychological perspectives in ethnic and racial identity. In G. Bernal, J. Trimble, & F. Leong (Eds.), *Handbook of racial and ethnic minority psychology: Part III. Social and developmental process* (pp. 239–275). Thousand Oaks, CA: Sage.

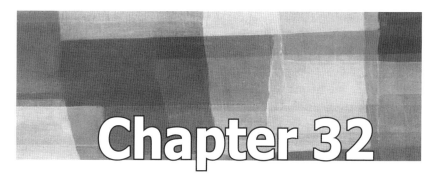

Chapter 32
Stereotypes and Generalizations

Hemla D. Singaravelu

Topics: Barriers to Effective Cross-Cultural Counseling
Cultural Communication Styles
Oppression and Discrimination
Dimensions of Worldviews
Helping Relationships

Purposes: Unintentional hidden biases may influence perceptions and actions even if we see and treat others as equals. Biases can be acquired through stereotypes and generalizations and tend to be barriers to effective communication, thus affecting effective cross-cultural counseling. This activity aims to provide an opportunity for participants to express and hear the different stereotypes associated with diverse populations in an anonymous fashion. Participants will discuss how generalizations and stereotypes can affect communication and the counseling process when working with diverse populations.

Learning Objectives: Upon completion of this activity, participants will (a) be aware of the different stereotypes affecting different groups of people, (b) understand how and where these stereotypes are derived, and (c) be aware of how stereotypes can impact cross-cultural communication.

Target Population: Participants in cross-cultural training programs and counseling students

Group Size: 5–25 participants

Time Required: 40–60 minutes

Setting: Classrooms or discussion rooms with chairs arranged in a semicircle or with participants facing each other

Materials: Index cards or a sheet of paper

Instructions for Conducting Activity

1. The instructor should instruct the participants, "I am going to list out some groups of people, one at a time. Please tell me what images or messages come to your mind when I say these groups. Using a sheet of paper provided, please write down these messages and/or describe these images."
2. Do not identify participants' names on the index cards. First, the instructor/trainer will say the name of each group, for example, "African Americans." "What images or messages come to your mind when I say African American?" The instructor will allow participants a few minutes

to respond to the question on the sheet of paper. Then the instructor will say the name of the next group (e.g., Latin Americans/Hispanics) and will then allow participants time to respond. Other groups that can be named include the following: gay, lesbian, bisexual, and transgender individuals; Asians; people with disabilities, and so forth.

3. When participants finish responding to the first questions, the second question is asked: "On the back of your paper, please state from where or how you received these images/messages."

4. The instructor will collect the sheets of papers from the participants, shuffle the papers, and redistributes them to the participants. If participants happen to receive their own paper, they are instructed not to reveal it. Then each participant will read the stereotypes listed on the paper for each group; that is, the first participant will read the response for the stereotypes for the first group mentioned (African Americans). The second participant will read the response for African Americans, and so on. Then, the first participant will start again and read the stereotypes listed on the paper for the second group: Latin Americans/Hispanics. This process continues until all the stereotypes of all groups are read by each participant in the room.

5. Then participants are asked, "How or from where have your received these images/messages?"

6. When all the responses have been read, including the response to where these stereotypes have been derived, the instructor will process the activity. Examples of processing questions include:
   a. "What did it feel like to hear these stereotypes about different groups?"
   b. "How have these stereotypes affected how you think and communicate with members of these groups?
   c. "As counseling professionals, how can these stereotypes pose a barrier to effective cross-cultural communication?"

Additional Readings

Ponteroto, J., Utsey, S., & Pedersen, P. (2006). *Preventing prejudice: A guide for counselors, educators, and parents*. Thousand Oaks, CA: Sage.

Ridley, C. R. (2005). *Overcoming unintentional racism in counseling and therapy: A practitioner's guide to intentional intervention*. Thousand Oaks, CA: Sage.

Rosenblum, K., & Travis, T. (2006). *The meaning of difference: American construction of race, sex, gender, social class, and sexual orientation*. Boston, MA: McGraw Hill.

Sue, D. W., & Sue, D. (2005). *Counseling the culturally diverse: Theory and practice*. New York, NY: Wiley.

Barriers to Effective Cross-Cultural Counseling

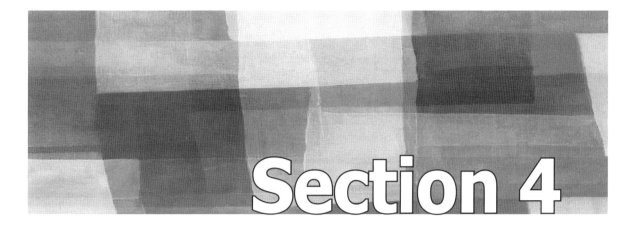

Section 4

Cultural Communication Styles

This section offers activities designed to assist students in uncovering the ways in which communication styles differ along cultural lines and can affect the nature of a counseling environment. These experiential activities can be used throughout the semester in all clinical and/or introductory multicultural courses. They can also be used in doctoral-level supervision courses to assist students in understanding cultural differences in communication styles that can strengthen or impede the counseling and/or learning process.

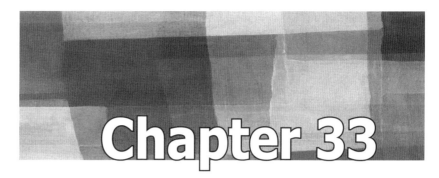

Chapter 33

Multicultural Career Dialogue

Stephanie A. Crockett

Topics: Barriers to Effective Cross-Cultural Counseling
Cultural Communication Styles
Dimensions of Worldviews
Career Development
Helping Relationships

Purposes: Multicultural career dialogue stems from Stone and Winkelman's (1985) voice dialogue technique. The technique maintains that a person's attitudes and beliefs are shaped by culture. As cultural voices become internalized, alternative perspectives are disregarded, one's thinking becomes rigid, and one's methods of social interaction become narrower. In order to provide effective multicultural counseling, counselors must be aware of their dominant beliefs and attitudes, understand how they affect the career counseling process, and increase flexibility in ways of interacting by seeking out and considering alternative, disregarded views of career development and counseling.

The purposes of this activity are to provide participants with the opportunity to examine and challenge their unquestioned, automatic cultural beliefs and attitudes as they relate to career counseling as well as to generate/identify alternate perspectives to those beliefs and attitudes. To be more specific, this activity helps participants to (a) identify personal cognitions, attitudes, and origins of internal messages associated with providing counseling to a hypothetical client presenting with career-related issues; (b) apply personal learning and reflection to future clients with career counseling concerns; and (c) reflect on personal cultural perspectives and their influence on career counseling. This activity also exposes participants to culturally diverse viewpoints concerning career development.

Learning Objectives: As a result of this activity, students will

- recognize how culture has shaped their beliefs and attitudes related to career development and counseling;
- attain a greater awareness of personal unquestioned, automatic cultural beliefs and attitudes and how they affect the career counseling process;
- generate alternate viewpoints concerning career counseling and vocational development;
- be better equipped to make a self-authorized choice concerning their cultural beliefs; and
- have a greater awareness of how to provide effective multicultural career counseling.

Target Population: This activity is designed for master's-level counseling students enrolled in a basic career development course. However, the activity can be used during supervision with master's-level practicum and internship counseling students.

Group Size: Flexible

Time Required: 30–45 minutes

Setting: A room with a large open space and at least six empty chairs.

Materials: Six chairs (you can substitute pillows if chairs are not available)

Instructions for Conducting Activity

1. Hand out copies of the provided case study to each student. Ask students to read through the case study independently. Then, have them designate one student to be the counselor. After the students have read the case study, ask the counselor to sit in a chair that has been placed in the middle of an open space.

2. Begin by asking the counselor to reflect on the case study and to become aware of his or her internal voices regarding the client and situation presented. You may wish to explain that internal voices are the inner thought dialogues that push us toward or stop us from executing certain behaviors and ideas. Some voices emit explicit messages, whereas others produce covert, implicit messages. Explain that some internal voices may be loud and easy to detect, whereas some are muted and difficult to identify. Encourage the counselor to become aware of both the loud and muted internal voices.

3. When the counselor is ready, ask him or her to begin to identify and separate the internal voices. Some examples of identification include the following: the voice that doesn't understand why the client won't change his major or the voice that does not feel equipped to work with a culturally diverse client. Again, it is imperative to encourage the counselor to share a variety of voices, even those that are alarming or uncomfortable. In the interest of time, the counselor may pick up to five voices to work with for the remainder of the exercise. Keep in mind that the exercise will be most beneficial if there is diversity in the five voices chosen.

4. As the internal voices are identified, the counselor must ascertain the strength and influence of each voice. To facilitate this awareness, instruct the counselor to designate a chair for each voice. Then ask the counselor to place the chair, based on the strength of the voice, in relation to his or her original chair. In other words, the chair of a domineering voice is close to the counselor's chair, whereas the chair of a muted, disowned voice is further away.

5. Next, ask the counselor to become each one of the voices by sitting in each chair. As the counselor sits in each chair, process the beliefs, attitudes, and origins of each voice through the following probes:
   a. What does this voice believe about the client?
   b. What does this voice believe about the client's situation?
   c. What does this voice believe about careers? Career development?
   d. Why do you think you hear this particular voice? What is the origin of this particular voice?

6. As the counselor becomes aware of the beliefs and attitudes associated with each voice, again make note of the proximity of each voice. Close voices represent dominant beliefs and attitudes, whereas distant voices symbolize disowned or alternate beliefs and attitudes.

7. After all voices have been processed, ask the counselor to return to his or her original chair. While sitting in the original chair, the counselor should consider how each internal voice affects him or her and his or her career counseling style. Questions to facilitate this exploration include:
   a. How does each of these internal voices help you work with the case study client? What rewards did they earn, or what dangers did they avoid?
   b. How might these internal voices hinder your ability to work with the case study client?

c. How might these voices help your future counseling work with clients who present with career issues? How might these voices hinder your future counseling work with clients who present with career issues?

d. How would you rearrange the strength of the internal voices to facilitate your work with the case study client?

8. When the counselor is done processing the influence of internal voices, invite the remaining class members to share additional observations and reactions regarding the counselor, case study client, and activity.

9. Through class discussion, generate and process ideas on how to work with the case study client. You may wish to specifically discuss career counseling as it relates to the cultural themes presented in the case study. Example questions include the following:

a. How would you work with a client whose family values/interests come before personal choice?

b. How do you provide career counseling to a client whose career choices are independent of his or her interests?

c. How do you work with a client who values saving face in his or her community?

d. How are these cultural themes different from the Western viewpoint of career development?

10. Finally, provide the class with an opportunity to examine and share their internal voices related to the case study client. Example discussion questions include the following:

a. What internal voices do you hear regarding the case study? What do they believe about the client and career development?

b. What might be the origin of these particular voices?

c. How does each of these internal voices help or hinder your work with the case study client?

Handout: Handout 33.1: Case of Manish

References

Stone, H., & Winkelman, S. (1985). *Embracing ourselves.* Marina del Rey, CA: Devross.

Additional Readings

Stone, H., & Stone, S. (n.d.). *Voice dialogue international.* Retrieved May 14, 2008, from http://www.delos-inc.com/

Chapter 34

Low-Context and High-Context Styles of Communication: Simulations for Counseling Students and Professionals

Cheryl Crippen

Topics: Definitions of Cultural Diversity
Cultural Communication Styles
Culturally Skilled Counselor
Helping Relationships

Purposes: The purpose of this activity is for participants to learn about different cultural styles of communication, such as low- and high-context. Participants will explore ways in which diverse styles of communication can affect the counseling or learning environment and ways to facilitate effective intercultural communication.

Learning Objectives: After completing this didactic lesson and simulation, counseling students and professionals will have (a) an enhanced understanding of how cultural norms and values affect styles of communication, (b) knowledge about the differences between low- and high-context communication styles, (c) the ability to recognize ways in which divergent styles of communication can impact their effectiveness as counselors and teachers, and (d) improved skills to facilitate effective intercultural communication.

Target Population: Counseling students or professionals

Group Size: Minimum six; no maximum

Time Required: Didactic portion takes 15–20 minutes, Simulation #1 (general concept) takes 10 minutes, and Simulation #2 (counseling application) takes 20 minutes.

Setting: Classroom or conference room; any seating arrangement (chairs only or desks) can accommodate this activity; space needs to be available at front of room for the simulations.

Materials: Dry-erase board or flipchart for didactic and discussion portions

Instructions for Conducting Activity

Didactic Portion

Introduction. Culture is a "frame of reference that consists of patterns of traditions, beliefs, values, norms, symbols, and meanings that are shared to varying degrees by interacting members of a community" (Ting-Toomey, 1999, p. 10). This frame of reference, or worldview, defines boundaries, expectations, rules for interactions, and communication patterns, such as low- and high-context styles of communication. Communication is "the primary vehicle by which we create community, perform ritual, convey identity, and discern meaning" (Leeds-Hurwitz, 2002, p. 29). Thus, it is likely that patterns of communication are culturally bound and vary among cultural groups. Hall (1976) found that different styles of communication are associated with different cultural value orientations identified by scholars such as Kluckhohn and Strodtbeck (1961) and Hofstede (1980, 2001).

In the counseling literature, Perel (2000) discussed how divergent styles of communication between individuals from different cultural backgrounds can lead to misinterpretation between the sender and receiver because of inherent differences in subtext and underlying meanings. In addition, the persistent use of different styles of communication that remain unrecognized can lead to an ongoing pattern of false attribution and misunderstanding in interpersonal relationships (Baucom, Epstein, & Rankin, 1995). Thus, it is important for counseling students and professionals to be aware of these differences, the most general of which are categorized into low- and high-context styles of communication.

Low- and high-context communication styles. In his seminal work on culture and communication, Hall (1976) delineated cultures along a dimension of low-context to high-context communication styles. A low-context communication style emphasizes direct verbal messages, explicit meanings, and a linear orientation. In contrast, a high-context communication style uses indirect nonverbal nuances and messages, implicit meanings, and a reliance on the social roles, position, and context of the exchange. Hall (1998) elaborated that "high-context communication . . . is one in which most of the information is already in the person, while very little is in the coded, explicit, transmitted part of the message. A low-context communication is just the opposite . . . the mass of the information is vested in the explicit code" (p. 61). Handout 34.1 titled "Low-Context and High-Context Styles of Communication" reviews various characteristics and examples of each communication style. Students and participants frequently have many other personal and professional examples to illustrate the different styles.

Simulation #1: General Concepts

This activity (see Handout 34.2) relies on two pairs of volunteers to simulate monocultural and cross-cultural interactions based on different communication styles. During a short break for participants, the volunteers (referred to as A1, A2, B1, and B2) are instructed to use the scripted dialogue to illustrate monocultural (Scenarios 1 and 2) and cross-cultural (Scenario 3) exchanges between friends. The narrative in italics denotes what is thought, rather than articulated, and volunteers are told to speak in a different manner to convey a nonspoken thought (e.g., off to the side with a gesture as if telling a secret, or speaking to the audience in a softer voice rather than speaking directly to the other volunteer).

After each scenario, discuss the characteristics of each exchange that indicate a low- or high-context communication style. After Scenario #3, discuss the assumptions of each speaker and receiver and the ways in which misunderstandings occur when messages are interpreted from the perspective of one's own communication style rather than being understood from the perspective of the other. As a conclusion, the group can discuss ways in which communication could be improved.

Simulation #2: Counseling Application

The second experiential activity (Handout 34.3) is designed to apply the general concepts of low- and high-context communication styles to a counseling scenario. This simulation works best with two volunteers who have had basic clinical training. The volunteers use the basic details of the attached case study to create an interaction between a counseling intern and a new client. After the volunteers conduct their cross-cultural counseling exchange, the facilitator can lead a group discussion using the questions provided. The discussion should focus on ways for the counselor to promote more effective communication with the client.

Handouts: Handout 34.1: Low-Context and High-Context Styles of Communication
Handout 34.2: Simulation #1—Experiential Practice: General Concepts
Handout 34.3: Simulation #2—Experiential Practice: Counseling Application

References

Baucom, D. H., Epstein, N., & Rankin, L. A. (1995). Cognitive aspects of cognitive-behavioral marital therapy. In N. S. Jacobson & A. S. Gurman (Eds.), *Clinical handbook of couple therapy* (pp. 231–246). New York, NY: Guilford Press.

Hall, E. T. (1976). *Beyond culture.* New York, NY: Anchor.

Hall, E. T. (1998). The power of hidden differences. In M. J. Bennett (Ed.), *Basic concepts of intercultural communication* (pp. 53-67). Yarmouth, ME: Intercultural Press.

Hofstede, G. (1980). *Culture's consequences: International differences in work-related values.* Los Angeles, CA: Sage.

Hofstede, G. (2001). *Culture's consequences: Comparing values, behaviors, institutions, and organizations across nations* (2nd ed.). Newbury Park, CA: Sage.

Kluckhohn, F. R., & Strodtbeck, F. L. (1961). *Variations in value orientations.* Evanston, IL: Row and Peterson.

Leeds-Hurwitz, W. (2002). *Wedding as text: Communicating cultural identities through ritual.* Mahwah, NJ: Lawrence Erlbaum.

Perel, E. (2000). A tourist's view of marriage: Cross-cultural couples—Challenges, choices, and implications for therapy. In P. Papp (Ed.), *Couples on the fault line: New directions for therapists* (pp. 178–204). New York: Guilford Press.

Ting-Toomey, S. (1999). *Communicating across cultures.* New York, NY: Guilford Press.

Additional Readings

Althen, G. (Ed.). (1994). *Learning across cultures.* Washington, DC: NAFSA.

Bennett, M. J. (Ed.). (1998). *Basic concepts of intercultural communication: Selected readings.* Yarmouth, ME: Intercultural Press.

Brislin, R. W. (2000). *Understanding culture's influence on behavior* (2nd ed.). Fort Worth, TX: Harcourt College.

Calloway, T. C., Cooper, P. J., & Blake, C. (1999). *Intercultural communication: Roots & routes.* Boston, MA: Allyn & Bacon.

Cushner, K., & Brislin, R. W. (1996). *Intercultural interactions: A practical guide* (2nd ed.). Thousand Oaks, CA: Sage.

DeVita, P. R., & Armstrong, J.D. (2002). *Distant mirrors: America as a foreign culture* (3rd ed.). Belmont, CA: Wadsworth.

Gudykunst, W. B. (1998). *Bridging differences: Effective intergroup communication* (3rd ed.). Thousand Oaks, CA: Sage.

Gudykunst, W. B., & Kim, Y. Y. (1997). *Communicating with strangers: An approach to intercultural communication* (3rd ed.). Boston, MA: McGraw-Hill.

Gudykunst, W. B., & Mody, B. (Eds.). (2002). *Handbook of international and intercultural communication* (2nd ed.). Thousand Oaks, CA: Sage.

Guirdham, M. (1999). *Communicating across cultures.* London, England: Macmillan.

Hall, E. T. (1976). *Beyond culture.* New York, NY: Anchor.

Harris, P. R., & Moran, R.T. (2000). *Managing cultural differences* (5th ed.). Houston, TX: Gulf.

Hofstede, G. (2001). *Culture's consequences: Comparing values, behaviors, institutions, and organizations across nations* (2nd ed.). Newbury Park, CA: Sage.

Hofstede, G. J., & Pedersen, P. B. (2002). *Exploring culture: Exercises, stories, and synthetic cultures.* Yarmouth, ME: Intercultural Press.

Kim, Y. Y. (2001). *Becoming intercultural: An integrative theory of communication and cross-cultural adaptation.* Thousand Oaks, CA: Sage.

Klopf, D. W. (2001). *Intercultural encounters: The fundamentals of intercultural communication* (5th ed.). Englewood, CO: Morton.

Kohls, L. R., & Knight, J. M. (1994). *Developing intercultural awareness: A cross-cultural training handbook* (2nd ed.). Yarmouth, ME: Intercultural Press.

Landis, D., Bennett, J. M., & Bennett, M. J. (Eds.). (2004). *Handbook of intercultural training* (3rd ed.). Thousand Oaks, CA: Sage.

Lewis, R. D. (1999). *Cross-cultural communications: A visual approach*. Yarmouth, ME: Intercultural Press.

Lustig, M., & Koester, J. (1999). *Intercultural competence: Interpersonal communication across cultures* (3rd ed.). New York, NY: Longman.

Martin, J. N., & Nakayama, T. K. (2000). *Intercultural communication in contexts* (2nd ed.). Mountain View, CA: Mayfield.

Martin, J. N., & Nakayama, T. K. (2001). *Experiencing intercultural communication*. Mountain View, CA: Mayfield.

Nolan, R. W. (1999). *Communicating and adapting across culture: Living and working in the global village*. Westport, CT: Bergin and Garvey.

Samovar, L., & Porter, R. (2001). *Communication between cultures* (4th ed.). Belmont, CA: Wadsworth.

Stewart, E. C., & Bennett, M. J. (1991). *American cultural patterns: A cross-cultural perspective*. Yarmouth, ME: Intercultural Press.

Storti, C. (2001). *The art of crossing cultures* (2nd ed.). Yarmouth, ME: Intercultural Press.

Ting-Toomey, S. (1999). *Communicating across cultures*. New York, NY: Guilford Press.

Ting-Toomey, S., & Gudykunst, W. B. (1996). *Communication in personal relationships across cultures*. Thousand Oaks, CA: Sage.

Ting-Toomey, S., & Oetzel, J. G. (2001). *Managing intercultural conflict effectively*. Thousand Oaks, CA: Sage.

Triandis, H. C. (1994). *Culture and social behavior*. New York, NY: McGraw-Hill.

Trompenaars, F., & Hampden-Turner, C. (2000). *Building cross-cultural competence: How to create wealth from conflicting values*. New Haven, CT: Yale University Press.

Chapter 35

Lamps of Speech: Proverbs as a Tool to Understand Differences in Cultural Communication

Mark D. Mason and Sally M. Hage

Topics: Introduction to Multicultural Counseling
Cultural Communication Styles
Culturally Skilled Counselor

Purposes: Proverbs are popular, short, repeated sayings representing a cultural group's accumulated wisdom and experiences. They are considered the "lamp of speech" and the "children of experience" (Baer, 2001). Proverbs reflect a people's primary values and beliefs, such as virtue, generosity, thrift, and patience, within a particular cultural and historical context. For example, a popular often-repeated proverb during times of economic hardship is, "A penny saved is a penny earned." Hence, proverbs provide a window to glimpse existing cultural differences and similarities within a particular historical setting, while also leading, at times, to the fallible use of national character stereotypes. For this reason, proverbs can be used to demonstrate psychological principles such as context and group values as well as highlight how we may stereotype groups of people based on their national origin or identity as a member of a cultural group.

As proverbs are often attributed to national identities, this activity serves to explore the emic versus etic nature of personality. Although research on the Five Factor Model of Personality (McCrae, 2001; McCrae & Allik, 2002) has established small differences in personality according to culture (McCrae, 2002; McCrae, Terracciano, & 79 Members of the Personality Profiles of Cultures Project, 2005), these differences have not corresponded to mean national character traits within or across cultures (Terracciano et al., 2005). Some scholars posit that there are no differences in personality across groups (e.g., Pinker, 2002), which reflects an etic or universal understanding of personality across cultures. In attempting to clarify this debate, Terracciano et al. found that perceptions of national character did not match actual, aggregate personality traits. Thus, national character differences may be nothing more than "groundless stereotypes" that serve to maintain a sense of national identity (McCrae, Terracciano, Realo, & Allik, 2007, p. 954). Yet culture likely influences the assessment, expression, and identification of personality traits (see Matsumoto & Juang, 2008).

This proverbs activity has a variety of purposes. This activity may be used to teach and reinforce the importance of differences in cultural communication concepts of context (high vs. low), especially within the context of cross-cultural communication. Students will understand how implicit meanings that are present in language and cultural expressions affect communication. A second purpose is to assist counseling students to explore individualist and collectivist values across perceived national identities. A third purpose is to invite counseling students to explore the social construction of stereotypes and the misconceptions and errors of cognitive schemas and heuristics about so-called national character. Finally, this activity may be used as a research tool to assist students in exploring cross-cultural group differences in personality, according to the Five Factor Model of Personality.

Learning Objectives: As a result of participation in this activity, students will (a) be able to identify proverbs as a representation of cultural communication, (b) be able to discuss proverbs within their cultural literacy and socialization experiences, (c) gain an understanding of existing scholarly debate about the etic versus emic nature of personality across national boundaries and cultures, (d) understand the social construction of stereotypes and national character, and (e) apply the principles of high and low context and individualist and collectivist values to proverbs.

Target Population: This activity has been designed for use with graduate students, often within the context of multicultural counseling courses or structured diversity experiences or programs; however, it may be tailored according to the presenter's needs.

Group Size: This activity is best conducted with a group of 35 participants or less, with students divided into groups according to proverb category. Larger groups can also be accommodated with more proverbs and categories.

Time Required: The time required for this activity varies from 30 to 90 minutes, depending on the specific purpose of the activity in the multicultural course. For example, the activity could be used early in the course to increase students' self-awareness or at other points in the course to also illustrate concepts such as high and low context in communication, microaggressions, or cultural stereotyping.

Setting: The classroom setting must support small-group discussion. Classroom settings with moveable chairs and tables are, therefore, recommended in order to facilitate small-group participation and communication in the activity.

Materials: Materials needed for this activity include the following: scissors, proverbs paper handouts (see Handout 35.1), and a flipchart or blackboard. Instructors must also bring additional proverbs handouts with corresponding populations to distribute to the students.

Instructions for Conducting Activity

First, introduce proverbs as a representation of cultural literacy or expression. Mieder's (2004) *Proverbs: A Handbook* further explains and illustrates the role of proverbs as a means of communication. Brainstorm with participants proverbs commonly used or heard as well as possible meanings, and list examples on the blackboard or flipchart. At the same time, encourage students to identify the historical context and cultural group associated with each proverb. In many cases, proverbs may reflect different meanings and values. Second, the instructor should introduce or review the concepts of high- and low-context communication styles and individualist and collectivist values, especially as they relate to counseling and communication. Third, assign students to small groups and distribute the proverbs handouts. Each group will be assigned a category of proverbs (e.g., age, happiness, wisdom, and so forth; see handout) and given an envelope of separated pieces of paper containing proverbs and cultural groups (e.g., "Youth is wasted on the young" and "French proverb"). Within their groups, students will pair the proverbs with the cultural groups and/or nationalities and discuss possible interpretations. Often, participants ascribe different and competing meanings and values to the proverbs and may struggle to identify the corresponding cultural group. In a large-group format, process students' experiences of pairing the proverbs. For example, presenters may ask, "What contributes to the difficulty of this activity?" or "How do proverbs and other idioms facilitate and/or hinder cross-cultural communication?" Fourth, ask groups of students to identify proverbs that *best* reflect high- and low-context styles of communication and individualist and collectivist values from each category. Review examples of context and cultural values with the participants in order to illustrate examples of high and low context and collectivist and individualistic values. Finally, distribute either McCrae's (2001) article about trait psychology or Terracciano et al.'s (2005) article about national character and lead a large-group discussion about the emic versus etic nature of personality. Students could explore the following questions: What is universal in human behavior that is also relevant to counseling? What is the relationship between cultural norms, values, and attitudes, on the one hand, and the manifestation of behavioral or personality disorders and their treatments on the other hand (Sue & Sue, 2003)?

Handout: Handout 35.1: Proverbs

See the Proverbs handout. Each proverb and corresponding group must be physically separated before distribution to the participants in envelopes. Proverbs or categories may be substituted according to the instructor's needs.

References

Baer, F. C. (2001). *Creative proverbs from around the world: Proverbial wisdom from around the world.* Retrieved December 23, 2008, from http://creativeproverbs.com

Matsumoto, D., & Juang, L. (2008). *Culture and psychology.* Belmont, CA: Wadsworth/Centage Learning.

McCrae, R. R. (2001). Trait psychology and culture: Exploring intercultural comparisons. *Journal of Personality, 69,* 819–846.

McCrae, R. R. (2002). NEO-PI-R data from 36 cultures: Further intercultural comparisons. In R. R. McCrae & J. Allik (Eds.), *The Five-Factor Model of Personality across cultures* (pp. 105–125). New York, NY: Kluwer Academic/Plenum Publishers.

McCrae, R. R., & Allik, J. (Eds.). (2002). *The Five-Factor Model of Personality across cultures.* New York, NY: Kluwer Academic/Plenum Publishers.

McCrae, R. R., Terracciano, A., Realo, A., & Allik, J. (2007). Climatic warmth and national wealth: Some culture-level determinants of national character stereotypes. *European Journal of Personality, 21,* 953–976.

McCrae, R. R., & Terracciano, A., & 79 Members of the Personality Profiles of Cultures Project. (2005). Personality profiles of cultures: Aggregate personality traits. *Journal of Personality and Social Psychology, 89,* 407–425.

Mieder, W. (2004). *Proverbs: A handbook.* Westport, CT: Greenwood Press.

Pinker, S. (2002). *The blank slate: The modern denial of human nature.* New York, NY: Penguin Books.

Sue, D.W., & Sue, S. (2003). *Counseling the culturally diverse: Theory and practice.* Hoboken, NJ: Wiley.

Terracciano, A., Abdel-Khalek, A. M., Ádám, N., Adamovová, L., Ahn, C.-k., Ahn, H.-n., . . . McCrae, R. R. (2005). National character does not reflect mean personality trait levels in 49 cultures. *Science, 310,* 96–100.

Chapter 36
Cultural Evidence

Anne M. Warren

Topics: Definitions of Cultural Diversity
Cultural Communication Styles
Cultural Identity Development
Use of New Technology
Creative Arts

Purposes: The purpose of this activity is to provide participants with an opportunity to explore how culture is transmitted through the media.

Learning Objectives: As a result of this activity, students will have a better understanding of the effect of cultural imagery on our cultural self-perception and our personal perception of other cultures.

Target Population: Graduate and undergraduate psychology, counseling, social work, and art therapy core cultural studies classes

Group Size: This exercise is suitable for group sizes from 8 to 25 participants.

Time Required: 1½ hours for artistic process plus 1 hour for discussion at the end of artistic process.

Setting: Tables and chairs to accommodate a chair for each participant and generous tabletop space for each participant should be provided. Tables should be large enough to accommodate a working area of a square yard on the table surface for each participant, though smaller areas may be accommodated as necessary and students may be encouraged to work on the floor. The door to the room should be closed to define the therapeutic space. The room size should match the need; for instance, a gymnasium may seem intimidating in size and scale for working with small groups.

Materials:
- One 12-inch round piece of cardboard for each participant. These may be bought in bulk through various art supply businesses
- A supply of magazines, newspapers, greeting cards, and various forms of advertising, including brochures
- Glue sticks, liquid white school-type glue, markers in assorted colors, colored pencils, oil pastels, crayons, and scissors to share
- Computer Internet access and television and radio access if possible

Instructions for Conducting Activity
- Facilitator hands out one cardboard round to each student.
- Provide students access to all other suggested materials and media.

- Students should be instructed to compose a collage of at least six found references to a chosen culture in the 1½-hour time allotted. Phrases heard or overheard from electronic media that reflect student's chosen culture or reflect intercultural assumptions or conceptions may be added in the form of script handwritten by the student/artist. Students should be encouraged to create an aesthetically pleasing art piece.
- Music, preferably instrumental, may be played during the art-making time of this activity.

Students may be encouraged to place cultural references on both sides of the cardboard. Students may be encouraged to use cultural references from media expressed by their chosen culture on one side of the cardboard and references to their chosen culture by those outside the culture on the other side.

This exercise may be given as an activity to be completed outside of class as homework.

At least 1 hour should be scheduled for sharing the images and discussing conclusions within the classroom.

Request that students think about the following when choosing material for their project and when coming to conclusions:

1. What is your personal culture, and how is your culture depicted in media? Does how your culture is depicted in media reflect your personal view of your own cultural identity?
2. What cultural attitudes and cultural worldviews are being expressed through media?
3. How do cultural depictions in media inform your knowledge of human systems and concepts of cultural identity formation and self-reference?

Additional Readings

Andersen, M. L. (2006). *Race, class & gender: An anthology*. Belmont, CA: Wadsworth.

Banks, J. A. (1997). *Teaching strategies for ethnic studies*. Boston, MA: Allyn & Bacon.

Sue, D. W., & Sue, D. (2007). *Counseling the culturally diverse: Theory and practice*. New York, NY: Wiley.

Takaki, R. (2008). *A different mirror: A history of multicultural America*. San Francisco, CA: Back Bay Books.

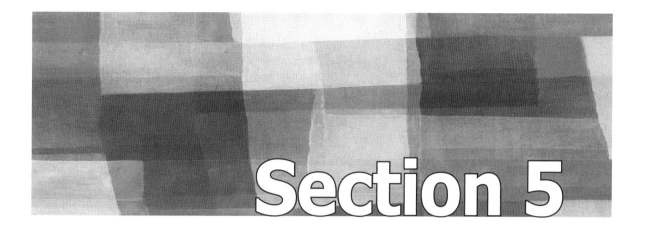

Section 5

Cultural Identity Development

This section highlights activities designed to assist students in examining issues of cultural identity development. Some of these activities address racial identity development using Helms's conceptual model. Some activities help students explore sexual identity development, whereas others explore concepts of multiple social identities. Other activities encourage the exploration of how family, community, and society can affect one's construction of cultural identity.

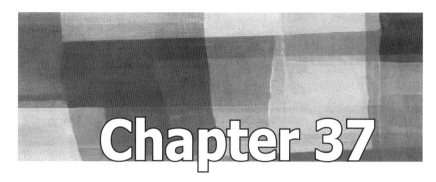

Chapter 37

Identities in Interaction: A Role-Play

Edward A. Delgado-Romero and Erin M. Schwartz

Topics: Introduction to Multicultural Counseling
Definitions of Cultural Diversity
Cultural Identity Development
Oppression and Discrimination
Culturally Skilled Counselor

Purposes: The purpose of this activity is to understand the dynamic interactions of the identities of the counselor and client in counseling. Usually identity models are used to understand counselors and clients in isolation, but this role-play exercise allows students to understand the interplay of identities and to speculate on possible outcomes. This exercise is based on Helms's (1984, 1995) Black and White racial identity interaction model.

Learning Objectives: As a result of this activity, students will

- understand the interplay of different identity statuses and be able to predict possible effects on the counseling process,
- be able to identify both effective and ineffective interactions in counseling,
- recognize the necessity for counselor multicultural competence, and
- understand the ethical implications of the interaction of identities in counseling.

Target Population: This activity is designed for students in a multicultural counseling course at any level. It is likely to be more effective if students have had some counseling experience with people who are different than they are in some way.

Group Size: Groups of four create the role-play and then act it out for the class.

Time Required: 30 minutes to discuss and create the role-play, then in a group setting 5 minutes to act out the role-play and 10 minutes to lead a discussion of the role-play.

Setting: This activity works best if students can find space to work on the role-plays apart from each other. For the class presentation, it would be helpful to present in a fishbowl set up.

Materials: A handout summarizing the four types of possible interactions (see Handout 37.1; Helms, 1984, 1995).

Instructions for Conducting Activity

The class session prior to this activity the instructor lectures on identity models and the interaction of the identities of the counselor and client. Although this activity is based on the Black and White racial interaction model (Helms, 1984, 1995), the topic does not have to be limited to race. The instructor should present various identity models and note the similarities in the development of relevant identities. Examples of other pertinent models to be considered in this activity include the feminist identity model, the womanist identity development model, and the gay and lesbian identity development model (Hoffman, 2006). Each of these models will allow the students to process other aspects of identity that extend past race and will, in turn, increase their awareness of multiculturalism. The instructor should also note the relevant multicultural counseling competencies related to the personal awareness and identity development of counselors.

The next session the instructor divides the class into groups of three or four students. The students are given a handout that summarizes Helms's four interaction types: parallel, crossed, regressive, and progressive. Each group is assigned a different type of interaction to create a role-play. Groups are not aware of what other groups have been assigned. They are then instructed that they have 30 minutes to create the role-play and that when they return to the larger group, they will perform the role-play and the rest of the class will discuss and try to guess (a) the type of interaction and (b) the identity statuses of the counselor and client. Students usually see this as a challenge and work harder to create more nuanced role-plays.

A few caveats: First, students are advised to try to make the interaction true to life and subtle versus overt. Second, students are reminded to avoid stereotyping. Finally, students will specify the relevant identity dimension (e.g., race, gender, sexual orientation) of the counselor and client rather than assuming that the counselor and client are playing people from their own identity group. For example, White students might be reminded that they do not have to represent their race in a paradoxical manner and be reminded not to pigeonhole minority students.

When the group comes together, it is the job of the instructor to keep the class focused on the task, facilitate the discussion, and keep the groups on time. It is usually helpful to remind the class that these are role-plays and that no student should be identified with the role he or she is playing. It is helpful for the instructor to facilitate the discussion by asking the following questions:

- What type of interaction is this?
- What is the identity status of the counselor? How can you tell?
- What is the identity status of the client? How can you tell?
- What is the likely outcome of this type of relationship?

This role-play can be a fun and interesting experience for a class if they are properly prepared (e.g., understand identity models, understand how prejudice and discrimination works in counseling). In particular, if groups can move beyond always assuming the counselor has to be from a dominant group (e.g., White, male, straight) and role-play interactions between members of oppressed groups, then a more complex discussion and understanding can be attained.

Handout: Handout 37.1: Helms's (1984, 1995) Interactional Model

References

Helms, J. E. (1984). Toward a theoretical explanation of the effects of race on counseling: A Black and White model. *The Counseling Psychologist, 12*, 153–165.

Helms, J. E. (1995). An update of Helms's White and people of color racial identity models. In J. G. Ponterotto, J. M. Casas, L. A. Suzuki, & C. M. Alexander (Eds.), *Handbook of multicultural counseling* (pp. 181–191). Thousand Oaks, CA: Sage.

Hoffman, R. M. (2006). Gender self-definition and gender self-acceptance in women: Intersections with feminist, womanist, and ethnic identities. *Journal of Counseling & Development, 84*, 358–372.

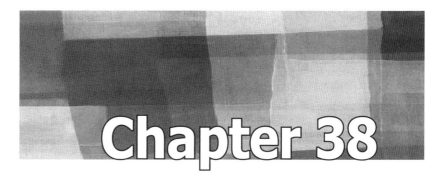

Chapter 38

"Pieces of Me": Cultural Identity Development Exploration

Kylie P. Dotson-Blake and Angela Rowe Holman

Topics: Definitions of Cultural Diversity
Cultural Identity Development
Dimensions of Worldviews
Gender Issues in Counseling
Counseling Lesbian, Gay, Bisexual, Transgender (LGBT), and Other Sexual Minority Clients
Creative Arts

Purposes: The purpose of this activity is to provide participants with opportunities to explore cultural identity development, including the familial and psychosocial factors that influence development.

Learning Objectives: As a result of this activity, participants will

- develop an enhanced awareness of how they conceptualize their process of cultural identity development,
- be able to identify social and familial impacts on their cultural identity development,
- have an increased awareness of how their cultural identities affect the counseling process, and
- become familiar with one effective tool for actively engaging clients in explorations of client cultural identity development.

Target Population: First- or second-year master's-level counseling students

Group Size: 20 or fewer students is ideal; if more than 20 students are participating, processing will be improved through the use of small groups.

Time Required: 90 minutes

Setting: Classroom

Materials: Paper, glue sticks, writing utensils (markers, colored pencils, or crayons), scissors

Instructions for Conducting Activity

1. Project development—personal reflection
   a. Provide students with several sheets of paper and markers, crayons, or colored pencils. Instruct them to draw a large shape that they feel best symbolizes their cultural identity on one of the pieces of paper.

b. Instruct the students to cut the other pieces of paper into small (no larger than ½″) differently shaped pieces. On the other pieces of paper, have students write single words characterizing or related to their cultural identity. Each word should be written on one of the small cut-up pieces of paper.

c. As they write each word, they are to change the size and shade intensity of each word to reflect their personal reactions to the word. For example, a student who identifies strongly with her religion but is less connected to her family may write "youngest daughter" in a faint, small font, while "Muslim" could be written in bold, large letters.

d. The students should then be instructed to paste each piece of cut-up paper (with words written on them) inside the shape on the first piece of paper. This collage of words is a composite of words relevant to ideas about their cultural identities.

e. Allow 15 minutes for development of the collage.

2. Processing—group reflection

a. When students have completed their collages, they are instructed to reflect on the different words in their pictures. Students should be encouraged to share with the group as they feel comfortable. Ask students to consider how they came to learn and understand these words and their meanings. Encourage students to reflect on which words serve to link them with their families of origin and which establish their identities separate from their families. Ask them to reflect on which words seem to expand their positive conceptualizations of their identities and which words contract or in some way limit their positive conceptualizations of their identities. How are their responses to the previous question linked to the fonts they chose to represent terms? Explore how students remember their families of origin using these terms, if at all. Reflect on how their family members and society view these words similarly or differently. Ask if the majority of fonts chosen are most related to how society views and uses the terms or how their families of origin used the terms. How are these similar or different? Reflect on how their associations with these words have or have not changed over their life span. Reflect on which components of their cultural identities are private and which are public. Encourage students to consider how the "pieces" of their cultural identities reflect their processes of cultural identity development. Ask students who are comfortable to share how their chosen shape (within which all of the pieces have been glued) represents their cultural identity and to explain how their "pieces" fit.

b. Ask students to consider the impact of cultural identity and the process of cultural identity development on counseling. How do their conceptualizations of their cultural identities affect their engagement with clients? How might the client's process of cultural identity development affect client engagement in counseling and the outcomes of counseling? Discuss how this tool, the "Pieces of Me" activity, might be used in a counseling session. Encourage students to brainstorm reflecting/processing questions to use with clients.

Processing should occur in a way that allows for flexible response to the developmental needs of students. Throughout the processing, it is imperative that the instructor fosters a safe, supportive learning environment.

Advanced Modification of Tool

This tool can be modified to focus on gender and sexual identity development and may be used with students who are at an advanced developmental level. In order to modify this activity in this manner, it is imperative that the instructor fosters a safe, supportive learning environment and that students not be pressured to share in the processing. To do this, change the focus of words written on the scraps of paper to be words related to gender and sexual identity development. During processing, the instructor and students should work together to determine appropriately challenging, but nonintrusive, questions to use from the ones suggested above. It is appropriate to allow students some opportunity for individual reflection, not to be shared with the group. Other useful questions in addition to the ones described above include the following:

1. Which words would students feel comfortable using in sessions with clients?
2. Which words do they feel would be important to know about their clients' identities and why?
3. Which words have multiple meanings in different contexts?
4. Which words promote the persistence of a heterosexist ideology? How?
5. How does language reflect internalized prejudices and perpetuate barriers?
6. How does language influence our case conceptualization and professional behavior?

By collaboratively developing the structure for processing the activity, the instructor honors the students' advanced developmental level and is able to most effectively create a safe, supportive environment. In addition to the learning objectives listed for the base activity, students who engage in the advanced version of this activity will

- have an increased awareness of how their personal sexual orientation and gender identities affect the counseling process;
- be able to identify internalized prejudices that may affect their perceptions of and interactions with sexual minority clients;
- be prepared to actively identify heterosexist assumptions; and
- develop increased comfort with sexuality-related dialogue, words, and vocabulary.

Additional Readings

Vinson, T. S., & Neimeyer, G. J. (2003). The relationship between racial identity development and multicultural counseling competency: A second look. *Journal of Multicultural Counseling and Development, 31*, 262–277.

Chapter 39
Creating a Sexual Orientation and Identity Dialogue

Angela Rowe Holman and Kylie P. Dotson-Blake

Topics: Cultural Identity Development
Counseling Lesbian, Gay, Bisexual, Transgender (LGBT), and Other Sexual Minority Clients
Professional Identity and Ethical Practice
Human Growth and Development

Purposes: The purpose of this activity is to create a dialogue among students about sexual orientation and identity by providing participants with opportunities to explore sexual orientation and identity development through language. This activity also promotes competencies for sexual minority clients by identifying heterosexist assumptions and promoting recognition of how personal biases may influence counselors' professional behavior.

Learning Objectives: As a result of this activity, participants will

- have an increased awareness of how their personal sexual orientation and gender identities affect the counseling process;
- be able to identify internalized prejudices that may affect their perceptions of and interactions with sexual minority clients;
- be prepared to actively identify heterosexist assumptions; and
- develop increased comfort with sexuality-related dialogue, words, and vocabulary.

    These learning objectives have been developed in accordance with the Association for Lesbian, Gay, Bisexual, and Transgender Issues in Counseling's (ALGBTIC's) competencies for counseling practice.

Target Population: First- or second-year master's and doctoral degree-seeking counseling students

Group Size: 20 or fewer students is ideal; if more than 20 students are participating, then the processing will be improved by breaking the large group into smaller groups.

Time Required: Approximately 90 minutes; could be adapted for longer periods of time with extended role-plays and group discussion

Setting: Classroom

Materials: Copies of student handouts and pens/pencils

Instructions for Conducting Activity

1. Provide students with Handout 39.1. Instruct students to review the words listed and identify, by circling on the handout, 10 words that have been significant to their own sexual orientation identity development, positively or negatively. Inform students that their handouts with circled words will not be shared with other students. Encourage them to quietly reflect about how they conceptualize their experiences of themselves with regard to their sexual identity and orientation. Reflect on which words expand their conceptualizations of their identities and which words contract, or in some way limit, their positive conceptualizations of their identities. Reflect on how they remember their family members' uses of these terms, if at all. Reflect on how their family members and society view these words similarly or differently. Reflect on how their associations with these words have or have not changed over their life span. Reflect on which components of their sexual and gender identities are private and public. Allow 10 minutes for this portion of the activity.

2. After guided individual reflection, students are then instructed to turn their attention to group processing. At this point, give each participant a copy of Handout 39.2. The professor will then read through the list of words and the accompanying definitions on Handout 39.2. Allow 5–10 minutes to review definitions as a group.

3. Students are then broken into groups of three. As time permits, each member of the triad is to have an opportunity to role-play being a counselor, client, and observer. Students in the role of the client are instructed to role-play a client with an identity relevant to the vocabulary on Handout 39.2 and use a different word from Handout 39.1 to create a counseling role-play scenario. The "counselor," without knowing which word from Handout 39.2 the "client" has selected, will use active listening skills to help the "client" process the issue related to the word selected from Handout 39.1. The observer is to take notes about the interaction. Allow 5 minutes of active role-play and 20 minutes total for each member of the triad to assume each role. Allow an initial 5 minutes to set-up the triadic role-plays. Total time for this portion of the activity is 25 minutes.

4. After each student has played a client, counselor, and observer, the students can then process the entire experience as a group. The following questions can be used to encourage classroom dialogue:

   a. How did the role-plays progress without knowing the sexual orientation identity of the client from Handout 39.2?
   b. What beliefs may have influenced the counselors' and clients' dialogue?
   c. Which words would students feel comfortable or uncomfortable using in session with clients?
   d. Which words do students believe would be important to know about their clients' identities and why?
   e. Which words from Handout 39.1 have multiple meanings in different contexts?
   f. Which words promote the persistence of a heterosexist ideology?
   g. How does language reflect internalized prejudices and perpetuate barriers?
   h. How does language influence our case conceptualizations and professional behaviors?

Handouts: Handout 39.1: Sample Word List Related to Sexual Orientation Identity Development
Handout 39.2: Gay, Lesbian, Bisexual, Transgender Vocabulary

References

Gay & Lesbian Alliance Against Defamation. (2007). *GLAAD media reference guide* (7th ed.). Los Angeles, CA: Author.

Chapter 40

Multicultural Literature for
Culturally Responsive Counseling

Paula S. McMillen and Dale-Elizabeth Pehrsson

Topics: Definitions of Cultural Diversity
Barriers to Effective Cross-Cultural Counseling
Cultural Identity Development
Dimensions of Worldviews
Human Growth and Development

Purposes: Information presented will either introduce or enhance participants' knowledge regarding the use of books in classroom and counseling settings, commonly referred to as *bibliotherapy*. This activity will increase understanding of specific criteria that should be considered when selecting books for therapeutic and developmental use with culturally diverse clients. Students will receive an overview of therapeutic mechanisms, implementation approaches, and the special benefits of using appropriate and high-quality multicultural literature with culturally diverse clients. These benefits include promoting positive cultural identity development and increasing empathic cross-cultural understanding. Children's picture books provide an engaging medium to introduce these ideas while requiring a minimal amount of time.

Learning Objectives: This activity is designed to help participants

- enhance their understanding of potential benefits—such as promoting positive cultural identity development—afforded to culturally diverse clients by using quality multicultural children's literature;
- discover and learn the basic concepts, benefits, therapeutic mechanisms, and implementation strategies of bibliotherapy;
- identify critical book evaluation criteria to consider when conducting culturally responsive counseling;
- improve bibliotherapeutic evaluation skills through interactive activities examining children's multicultural picture books; and
- understand the limitations, ethics, and cautions surrounding bibliotherapy techniques and interventions.

Target Population: This activity is designed for counselors in educational preparation programs. This module is usually incorporated as part of a creative, expressive, or child therapy "techniques" class but could be appropriately incorporated in a variety of classes in the counseling curriculum, such as social justice, human development, multicultural counseling, group counseling, practicum, internship, and advanced field experience classes.

Group Size: The activity is appropriate for groups up to 50 participants. Larger groups will be broken down into small groups for more individualized learning activity.

Time Required: 45–60 minutes

Setting: Any appropriate classroom setting will work, though flexible seating is helpful so that students can form themselves into small groups. Ideally the class should meet within a library or curriculum media center so students can explore the collection for additional multicultural literature.

Materials:

- Children's picture books that are representative of cultural diversity (preselected by instructor)
- Projection equipment for PowerPoint presentation (such as SmartBoard or a computerized projection system) or overhead projector
- PowerPoint file or overhead transparencies
- Evaluation worksheets

Instructions for Conducting Activity

- Present a brief overview of bibliotherapy (preferably using PowerPoint or via overhead slides). Include definitions, conceptual categories, benefits, therapeutic mechanisms, implementation models, and research support.
- Conduct an interactive activity where students work in small groups to examine books for cultural indicators using broad evaluation questions (see PowerPoint slide 40.2).
- Facilitate a group discussion with entire class to discuss discoveries in the books examined.
- Present (via overheads or PowerPoint) the specific criteria relevant for evaluation of multicultural materials. The instructor chooses a book and models the process first.
- Form the class once again into their previous small groups. Students reevaluate the original book(s) using the specific criteria presented that address cultural sensitivity and inclusion.
- Facilitate discussion with the entire class about the lessons learned between the first and second evaluation.

Handouts: Handout 40.1: Evaluation Criteria for Selecting Multicultural Literature
Handout 40.2: Multicultural Literature for Culturally Responsive Counseling PowerPoint

References

Baber, C. (1992). Ethnic identity development and literacy education. *Reading Psychology, 13*(1), 91–98.

Constantino, G., Malgady, R., & Rogler, L. (1986). Cuento therapy: A culturally sensitive modality for Puerto Rican children. *Journal of Consulting and Clinical Psychology, 54*, 639–645.

Council on Interracial Books for Children. *10 quick ways to analyze children's books.* Retrieved May 27, 2008, from http://www.birchlane.davis.ca.us/library/10quick.htm

Erikson, E. H. (1966). The concept of identity in race relations: Notes and queries. *Daedalus, 95*(1), 145–171.

Ford, D. Y., Tyson, C. A., Howard, T. C., & Harris, J. J. (2000). Multicultural literature and gifted Black students: Promoting self-understanding, awareness, and pride. *Roeper Review, 22*(4), 235–240.

Greenbaum, L., & Holmes, I. A. (1983). The use of folktales in social work practice. *Social Casework, 64*(7), 414–418.

Harris, T. L., & Hodges, R. E. (1995). *The literacy dictionary: The vocabulary of reading and writing.* Newark, DE: International Reading Association.

Holman, W. D. (1996). The power of poetry: Validating ethnic identity through a bibliotherapeutic intervention with a Puerto Rican adolescent. *Child and Adolescent Social Work Journal, 13*(5), 371–381.

Kaplan, J. S. (1994). Using novels about contemporary Judaism to help adolescents understand issues in cultural diversity. *School Counselor, 41*(4), 287–295.

Malgady, R., Rogler, L., & Constantino, G. (1990). Hero/heroine modeling for Puerto Rican adolescents: A preventive mental health intervention. *Journal of Consulting and Clinical Psychology, 58,* 469–474.

Mazza, N. (2003). *Poetry therapy: Theory and practice.* New York: Brunner-Routledge.

Pardeck, J. T., & Pardeck, J. A. (1998). An exploration of the uses of children's books as an approach for enhancing cultural diversity. *Early Child Development and Care, 147,* 25–31.

Shrodes, C. (1950). *Bibliotherapy: A theoretical and clinical-experimental study* (Unpublished doctoral dissertation). University of California at Berkeley.

Chapter 41
Create Yourself as a Cultural Being

Tina R. Paone

Topics: Introduction to Multicultural Counseling
Definitions of Cultural Diversity
Cultural Identity Development
Group Work
Creative Arts

Purposes: The purpose of this activity is to allow group members to creatively express who they are as a cultural person. The activity provides participants an opportunity to explore what is inside, how they feel about themselves, and their cultural competence. The discussion surrounding the activity aims to assist group members in understanding not only what they feel represents them culturally, but how those around them view culture.

Learning Objectives: As a result of this activity, participants will

- express their own cultural representations,
- learn about other group members' cultural representations, and
- explore and learn about how they, themselves, and others view culture.

Target Population: Preadolescents to adults; anyone wanting to learn more about himself or herself, culturally

Group Size: Two or more

Time Required: 30–40 minutes

Setting: Classroom setting is appropriate for this activity, although anywhere would work.

Materials: White Crayola Model Magic modeling clay, markers, shells, buttons, feathers, glue, jewels, glitter, ribbon, and a variety of other craft materials.

Instructions for Conducting Activity

The group facilitator will break up the Model Magic so that each of the group members has a piece about the size of a plum. Then the facilitator will instruct group members to "create yourself as a cultural being." No other specific directions are given. If group members question, the facilitator will respond, "You get to decide," allowing total freedom of expression to the members. Group members may choose to use markers, to glue feathers, to glue jewels, or to use other craft materials to create their being.

Once all participants have had time to create their being, the facilitator will process with group members. The following prompts may be used to stimulate discussion: What kind of being are you? What does your "cultural being" represent? What does your "cultural being" do? Describe your "cultural being's" strengths and weaknesses. Who does your "cultural being" interact with? How does being a "cultural being" impact others? How does it impact you? How does it impact the world? Is your "cultural being" influenced by others? How does the "cultural being" represent who you are? Tell the group more about your culture.

This activity can bring up very sensitive issues for group members. It is important to remember to follow through with each topic that is brought to light. It is also important to remember that the processing questions presented here are only a guideline. All groups are different; therefore, it is important to be flexible during processing, allowing group members to touch on issues that they feel are important.

Additional Readings

Paone, T. R. (2006). The comparative effectiveness of group activity therapy on the moral reasoning of at-risk high school students. *Dissertation Abstracts International, 67,* 848.

Chapter 42

My Cultural Awareness Lifeline

Carol A. Parker

Topics: Introduction to Multicultural Counseling
Barriers to Effective Cross-Cultural Counseling
Cultural Identity Development
Dimensions of Worldviews
Culturally Skilled Counselor

Purposes: This activity, modified from the diversity lifeline activity by Lindsey, Robins, and Terrell (2003), is designed to help students identify the significant events in their lives that made them aware of cultural differences and the impact of those experiences on their current behaviors and beliefs about cultures, races, and so forth. Participating in this activity helps students understand significant events and provides them with opportunities to explore how those experiences affect current beliefs and behaviors of others in the larger community.

Learning Objectives: First, participants will be able to discuss the impact of past experiences on their current attitudes about other cultures, races, ethnic groups, and so forth. Second, participants will be able to compare their experiences with the experiences of others in the group and design ways to enhance cross-cultural experiences.

Target Population: Graduate students in the first half of graduate studies for professional counselors, mental health professionals, and/or school leaders

Group Size: This activity is ideal for classes or groups of 8–24 participants. If the size of the group ranges from 8–12, processing may be done in one group; however, if the group has more than 12, use smaller groups of 3–8 participants. The purpose of the smaller group is to allow each participant ample time to explain his or her lifeline and respond to questions to clarify entries on the timeline that are not clear to anyone.

Time Required: 90 minutes (small group) to 2 hours (up to 24 participants)

Setting: Typical classroom suitable for 20 to 24 graduate students or the area needed to accommodate three large tables of six to eight participants. Space should be sufficient for each participant to draw a timeline on newsprint for the group to see.

Materials: Markers for each participant, newsprint or chart paper for each participant, masking tape, and enough wall space for each participant to hang his or her lifeline and discuss it in a small groups

Instructions for Conducting Activity

The facilitator gives a sheet of newsprint or chart paper and markers to each participant. The participants are organized into small diverse groups of two to three. The groups are kept small so that each person has sufficient time to adequately explain his or her timeline. The participants are allowed 20 minutes to make their timeline and 15 minutes to present the timeline to their small group. After all participants have shared with their small group, one large group comes back together to review all timelines, which are taped to the wall.

During the debriefing, participants are asked the following questions:

1. What did you feel as you began to fill in the times that you became aware of cultural or racial differences?
2. During the process of making the timeline, what did you learn or discover about yourself?
3. Did you learn something new about yourself during this process? If so, what did you learn about yourself?
4. What did you learn about your group members?
5. What did you learn about diversity?
6. How can you use what you learned with others?

References

Lindsey, R. B., Robins, K. N., & Terrell, R. D. (2003). *Cultural proficiency: A manual for school leaders* (2nd ed.). Thousand Oaks, CA: Sage.

Additional Readings

Moodley, R., & Palmer, S. (2006). *Race, culture and psychotherapy: Critical perspectives in multicultural practice*. New York, NY: Routledge.

Cultural Identity Development

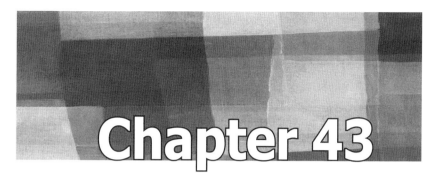

Multicultural Career Counseling Case Study

Jacqueline Peila-Shuster, Sharon K. Anderson, Antonette Aragon,
Edward J. Brantmeier, and Nathalie Kees

Topics: Cultural Identity Development
         Professional Identity and Ethical Practice
         Career Development

Purposes: Rationale—Case studies are an established approach that can help students to bridge the gap from theory to application (Niles, Goodman, & Pope, 2002). By practicing with case studies, students can learn from each other as well as the instructor, which can help move theoretical discussion toward practical application.

    The purpose of this activity is to provide a means for students to apply their knowledge about career counseling and career development and counseling theories within a framework of contextual and multicultural issues. It also provides an avenue in which students can think creatively about how they might provide culturally sensitive career counseling.

Learning Objectives: As a result of this activity, participants will be able to (a) identify and develop a variety of strategies or options that may be useful with diverse clientele, (b) gain greater awareness of internal and external barriers that may exist for diverse clientele, and (c) contemplate their own unearned privilege and worldview and how that can affect their interactions with clients.

Target Population: Career, school, and community counseling students and professionals

Group Size: 3–25 participants, broken into groups of 3–5 members

Time Required: 60 minutes

Setting: Classroom with room for students to get into discussion groups

Materials: Case studies (included in handouts), stimulus questions (see Instructions for Conducting Activity)

Instructions for Conducting Activity

1. Assign one case study to each group. Each group needs to discuss the case, with the following questions providing stimulus and focus:
    a. What are the cultural and contextual issues that need to be considered?
    b. What additional information is needed, especially in regard to these issues?
    c. How do these issues affect your choice of and/or application of theory as well as your intervention?
    d. What would you propose as your next steps or plans for career counseling with this client?

2. After completing the cases in individual groups, provide time to process and share with the larger group.

Process Questions

1. How might your worldview have affected your thoughts about the case?
   a. How do you know when you are projecting your worldview, values, or cultural assumptions onto a client rather than seeing and feeling the world from her or his viewpoint?
2. What emotions were brought up as you read and discussed the case?
3. How familiar or unfamiliar were you with the cultural and contextual issues that affected the individual in the case you studied?
   a. What was it like to try to take into consideration issues with which you were unfamiliar?
   b. What steps can you take to become more familiar with these areas?
4. How did theory inform and/or limit you?
5. What ideas can you share on becoming a more effective culturally competent counselor?

Follow-Up Integration

Have students write a 5-minute journal about what they will do to carry this forward for real-world application and/or how they will gain further skills to be become a culturally competent career counselor.

Handout: Handout 43.1: Multicultural Career Counseling Case Study Activity

References

Niles, S. G., Goodman, J., & Pope, M. (2002). *The career counseling casebook: A resource for practitioners, students, and counselor educators.* Tulsa, OK: NCDA.

Chapter 44
Cultural Knowledge Gaps

Brooke Rawson and Brian J. Mistler

Topics: Cultural Communication Styles
Cultural Identity Development
Oppression and Discrimination
Group Work
Poverty, Social Class, and Socioeconomic Status (SES)

Purposes: The purpose of this activity is to provide participants with an opportunity to discover the limits of their knowledge of other cultures and how these limits may place restrictions on their counseling.

Learning Objectives: As a result of this activity, students will have (a) a better understanding of their limited knowledge of various unfamiliar cultures, (b) a better understanding of how these limits may lead to biases in both counselor and/or client, (c) greater insight into practical possibilities for addressing cultural issues, and (d) insight into further steps to take for improving cultural competency.

Target Population: Students in undergraduate or graduate counseling theories or practice courses

Group Size: 6–30 participants

Time Required: 1 hour or one class period

Setting: A classroom with moving desks and chairs is preferable.

Materials: Paper, pens, dry-erase board, dry-erase markers

Instructions for Conducting Activity

1. Divide the class into three groups. Attempt to make the groups equal in number.
2. Assign Group 1 with White American Culture.
3. Choose two more cultures to assign to the other two groups. For example, assign Group 2 with African Americans and Group 3 with Asians.
4. Instruct the class to write down all the knowledge they have of the culture assigned to them. This could range anywhere from foods to religions.
5. After approximately 30 minutes (longer if need be), bring the entire class back together and discuss the list.

6. It may be helpful to make three columns on the dry-erase board and list what items each group put for their cultures to show the vast differences in the amount of knowledge of each culture especially when compared with the White Americans column.

7. Discuss the results with discussion questions.

   a. Do you feel that your knowledge of your assigned culture is based on stereotypes?

   b. Do you feel qualified to properly counsel your assigned culture or any other cultures discussed?

   c. If someone from another culture comes to you for counseling, would you counsel them without proper knowledge, or would you send them to someone with more education on their culture? Would this be ethical?

   d. Describe any similarities and differences you may see between the groups. How would you apply the similarities and differences you see to your counseling?

   e. Can you identify any other group divisions in the list? For example, economic differences.

Additional Readings

Abdullah, S. M. (1999). *Creating a world that works for all*. London, England: Berrett-Koehler.

McIntosh, P. (2007). White privilege and male privilege. In E. O'Brien & J. Healey (Eds.), *Race, ethnicity, and gender: Selected readings* (pp. 377–384). New York, NY: Sage.

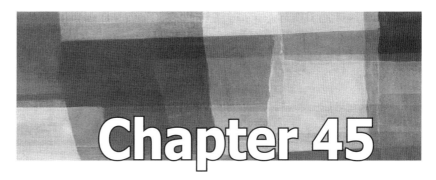

Chapter 45

The View From Where I Stand: Cultural Identities, Power, and Privilege

Carmen F. Salazar

Topics: Cultural Identity Development
Oppression and Discrimination
Helping Relationships
Group Work

Purposes: This activity provides participants the opportunity to increase understanding of the sociopolitical context of their cultural identities. It will allow them to consider the ways in which race, ethnicity, gender, sexual orientation, physical ability, and other identities interact within each individual and affect how we perceive ourselves and are responded to by others. It further provides participants a visual representation of how cultural identities position them in systems of power and privilege.

Learning Objectives: As a result of this activity, students will (a) identify which of their cultural identities are more salient to their sense of selfhood, (b) gain a better understanding of how their cultural identities position them in relation to characteristics that are ascribed power in U.S. society (e.g., White, middle-class, male, able-bodied), and (c) learn from others who are similar and different about the "view" from relative positions of power and privilege.

Target Population: Students in an advanced multicultural counseling course or a course on race, class, and gender. To prepare for the activity, students will have read at least two assigned articles listed in the Additional Readings section. The activity will be most effective if the class members have already developed rapport and a sense of safety with each other.

Group Size: Can be done with the entire class, providing there is enough space to move around

Time Required: Allow 1 hour; time may vary depending on the size of the class.

Setting: For Part 1 and Part 3 of the activity, seat students in a circle so they can see each other. Part 2 requires enough open floor space for the class to stand in a large circle and move around.

Materials: Handout 45.1, "The View From Where I Stand"; pens or pencils; masking tape

Instructions for Conducting Activity

The week before you intend to use this activity, assign two or more of the Additional Readings. It is recommended that you require McIntosh's *White Privilege and Male Privilege* paper. Choose at least one additional article from among the readings.

Begin the activity by discussing the readings, asking the class to brainstorm a list of cultural identity categories (e.g., race, ethnicity, gender, physical ability, sexual orientation, age). Write these identity categories on the board. Then draw a large circle on the board. Ask the students to identify what cultural identity characteristics are associated with power and privilege in U.S. society (e.g., White, male, middle-class, young, heterosexual, able-bodied). Write these characteristics in the circle. Tell them the circle represents the center of power and privilege in U.S. society.

Part 1

Give students the handout "The View From Where I Stand." They may wish to write in the "power and privilege" circle any additional characteristics the group identified. Draw their attention to the identity categories listed at the bottom of the handout. Tell them to **silently** consider the following about their own cultural identities before completing the handout:

- Which of your identities are most salient to your sense of selfhood?
- What other identities, if any, would you like to add that are not on the handout?
- In addition to visible identities, which of your less visible identities are you willing to reveal during the exercise? Do you feel safe to reveal them?
- How do your cultural identities position you with respect to the characteristics that appear in the power and privilege circle?

Instruct the students to draw an *X* or a symbol on the handout for each of their cultural identities in relation to the power and privilege circle. They may find it helpful to label the *X* or symbol if it is positioned outside the circle (e.g., female, visible physical disability). When each student has completed the handout, proceed to Part 2.

Part 2

For the next step, you'll need room for the students to walk around. Before starting the next step, use masking tape to mark a circle on the floor (approximately 3 feet in diameter) at the center of the activity space. Tell the students they will be creating a visual representation of their cultural identities and their position with respect to the power and privilege circle. Depending on the available space, instruct them to stand in a large circle (or around the perimeter of the room) with the power and privilege circle at the center. Then say:

> When I name a cultural identity (e.g., race or gender), I want you to position yourself closer, further away from, or in the circle, depending on how you see yourself positioned in relation to the center of power and privilege. When I name a cultural identity that is not visible, keep in mind how much you are willing to reveal to the group at this time and position yourself accordingly. For example, if you wish to keep this private, choose a nondescript position between the center and the periphery of the group.

For each cultural identity category, ask the group the following questions before moving on to the next category. (Note that as facilitator, you'll need to help the students keep the focus on their own thoughts and feelings; help them be descriptive versus evaluative when commenting.) Tell participants they need not respond to each question, especially if their point was made previously.

- What do you notice as you look around the room and see where your classmates are positioned and where you are positioned?
- When you positioned yourself, were you influenced by the position of other people in class?
- How easy or difficult was it to decide where to stand? If it was difficult, what made it so?
- What do you want others in the class to know about the view from your position?
- What do you want to ask others in the class about how they positioned themselves? Remember that your questions are intended to increase *your* understanding, not to ask others to defend their position. Your question could begin, "I wonder what it means . . ."

Cultural Identity Development

Part 3

After the group has completed this activity for each identity, tell students to return to their seats. Then ask the group the following questions:

- Which of your identities were you most aware of? Least aware of? What influenced your awareness?
- How might your position for a particular identity vary depending on setting (e.g., in school vs. your workplace or your community)?
- You were asked to position yourself one identity at a time. Were there any times when it was difficult to separate your identities in this way?
- Which identities were hard for you to separate? How do these intersecting identities influence how you see yourself positioned in relation to the center of power and privilege?
- Did anyone say something about themselves that angered you or hurt your feelings? Was that intentional?
- In a sentence or two, what did you learn about cultural identities, power, and privilege that you didn't know before you did this exercise?

Handout: Handout 45.1: The View From Where I Stand: Cultural Identities, Power, and Privilege

Additional Readings

Hays, P. A. (1996). Addressing the complexities of culture and gender in counseling. *Journal of Counseling & Development, 74,* 332–338.

McIntosh, P. (1988). *White privilege and male privilege: Coming to see correspondences through work in women's studies* (Working Paper No.189).Wellesley, MA: Wellesley College Center for Research on Women. (ERIC Document Reproduction Service No. ED335262).

Reynolds, A. L., & Pope, R. L. (1991). The complexities of diversity: Exploring multiple oppressions. *Journal of Counseling & Development, 70,* 174–180.

Robinson, T. L. (1999). The intersections of dominant discourses across race, gender, and other identities. *Journal of Counseling & Development, 77,* 73–79.

Salazar, C. F. (2006). Conceptualizing multiple identities and multiple oppressions in clients' lives. *Counseling and Human Development, 39*(1), 1–18.

Salazar, C. F., & Abrams, L. P. (2005). Conceptualizing identity development in members of marginalized groups. *Journal of Professional Counseling: Theory, Practice, and Research, 33,* 47–59.

Chapter 46

Weaving a Tapestry of Life Identities and Relationships

Rebecca Toporek

Topics: Cultural Identity Development
Dimensions of Worldviews
Cross-Cultural Family Counseling
Human Growth and Development
Career Development
Helping Relationships
Multiple Identities/Biracial, Multiracial
Creative Arts

Purposes: The purpose of this activity is to facilitate participants in identifying significant aspects of their cultural and life identities and in understanding the role that those identities play in their relationships and decisions. When used with counselors and counselor trainees, the exercise may be oriented toward developing an understanding of how their identities influence their interactions, assumptions, and values related to working with clients. When used with clients in career counseling, this exercise can be oriented toward developing an understanding of how their identities may influence their choices in careers, jobs, or time allocation. It can be used to help them consider rebalancing their distribution of efforts depending on their significant identities. In addition, it can be used to help them understand how these identities interact with the identities of those around them and how this interaction may influence family and work relationships. It is preferable to use the exercise in situations where participants can be in dyads because the interaction between two people optimizes the outcome.

Learning Objectives: By the end of this exercise, participants will be able to

- identify eight significant aspects of their identity and be able to talk about each;
- understand how another individual's identity structure may differ from their own;
- describe how their identity may influence the way they interact with others' identities and how their significant identities may fluctuate as a result of their interactions with others; and
- recognize how their significant identities may influence their choices, such as career, job, and relationships, and discover how their time and energy allocations may need to shift to realign with their significant identities.

Target Population: This exercise can be used successfully with graduate counselor trainees in multi-cultural counseling classes or career counseling classes; practicing career counselors, psychologists, and therapists in a workshop format; or undergraduate students in career life-planning or freshman-year-experience classes or other self-reflective classes.

Group Size: The exercise can be used with 1–50 people. It is optimal to have enough people to break into dyads.

Time Required: 60–90 minutes, depending on depth of processing and knowledge of group members regarding concept of identity

Setting: Room with chairs and tables where dyads can work together

Materials: Handout 46.1, A Tapestry of Identities; Handout 46.2, Identifying Your Most Salient Identities; one sheet of construction paper for each participant (each person in the dyad should have a different color); paper should be cut into eight strips lengthwise, with each strip 8″ long and no more than 1″ wide.

Instructions for Conducting Activity

The instructions that follow include setting the context; providing step-by-step instructions, including guiding the dyad discussions; and processing or debriefing the exercise in a large group. These instructions assume 90 minutes. If less time is available, facilitators may reduce the amount of dyad and large-group processing.

Setting the Context

Setting the context may vary depending on the group and the purpose of using this activity with the specific group.

1. Create a shared understanding of *identities*. Explain how we have many different aspects of ourselves, some that reflect our roles, some that reflect our community, some that reflect our family, some that reflect our biology.
2. I share a list of my identities: White, French-Canadian-Polish, U.S. and Canadian citizen, mother, sister, educator, counselor-advocate, writer, woman, partner, colleague, temporarily able-bodied, heterosexually identified, economically secure, midlife mom, recycler.
3. Distribute "Tapestry" handout (Handout 46.1) and discuss different aspects of identity and how the significance of each fluctuates depending on our developmental status, life circumstances, and context. I use my own example: At times, I am not conscious of the significance of my Canadian identity; however, whenever U.S. politics arise in conversation, in the news, or in my consciousness, my Canadian identity becomes prominent in my mind. My identity as a White person is significant much of the time because I have chosen professionally and personally to focus a lot of time and energy on understanding issues of privilege around race and ethnicity, which requires me to keep that present in my mind. There are definitely situations where that is more prominent than others. For example, when I am the only White person in an unfamiliar group or when I am in a group of all White people, this identity becomes more prominent. My identity as a midlife mom (vs. simply "mother") is rarely prominent, except when a stranger misidentifies me as "grandma" when I am with my young children.

Step-by-Step Instructions for the Exercise

1. Using the "Identifying Salient Identities" handout (Handout 46.2), ask participants to list all the identities that reflect who they are then choose the top eight (the ones that are most significant most of the time). For counselor trainees and in workshops with counselors, I ask them to choose at least three that reflect ethnicity, race, gender, ability status, socioeconomic status, religion, nationality, and sexual orientation.
2. Distribute eight strips of construction paper to each participant (each participant should haves strips of the same color). Ask participants to write each of their eight most significant identities

on a strip of paper. Once they have eight strips, ask them to weave the strips, four horizontally and four vertically. The result should look somewhat like this:

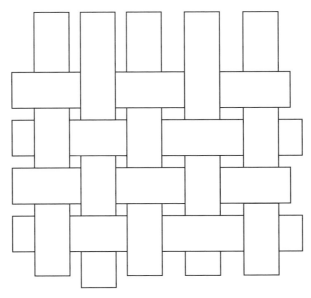

The identity labels will be showing in some areas and covered in other areas by other identities.

3. Ask participants to notice how their identities are showing in some areas and covered in others. Ask them to think about areas in their lives where one identity may overshadow another and how that may shift over time or circumstance. Depending on the purpose of this exercise, the facilitator may guide the participants in thinking about the shifting identities at work, family, school, community, and so forth.

4. Now ask participants to unweave their strips and meet with their partner. It is best if their partner's construction paper is a different color (e.g., Participant A has eight blue strips, Participant B has eight red strips).

5. In the dyads, participants should alternate briefly describing each identity to their partner, what that identity means to them, and why they chose this as one of their top eight. As they do this, they will need to collaboratively weave their identities together. The result will be a multicolored tapestry.

6. Ask the dyads to discuss where their identities may be similar or different. Ask them to discuss how these similarities and differences may help them understand each other or have difficulty with each other. Partners can help each other uncover how these identities influence different parts of their lives.

7. If the focus is on work relationships, facilitate further discussion regarding workplace values and communication and how these might be influenced by their identities.

Large-Group Processing

1. The extent and focus of group processing depends on the intent and purpose of the assignment. The intent of this level of processing is to help frame dyad experiences and summarize. I have grouped sample stimulus discussion questions below.

2. General discussion questions: How did it feel to talk about your identities and their meanings with your partner? What were some similarities and differences that were significant? What insights did you have? How did you and your partner negotiate the weaving process?

3. Work- and career-related discussion questions: What insights came out of the partner discussions regarding how different identities influence work life? Are there any goals participants identified based on the identities and work (e.g., better balance between a particular identity and work; the need to address issues of discrimination around a particular identity)?

Cultural Identity Development

4. Multicultural relationships: What insights were gained regarding similarities and differences that were unexpected? How might your assumptions of particular identities be changed? What insights were gained regarding the importance of your partner's identity that you may not have considered? How did the identities influence the way you interacted with your partner?

Handouts: Handout 46.1: A Tapestry of Identities
Handout 46.2: Identifying Your Most Salient Identities

References

Arredondo, P., Toporek, R., Brown, S., Jones, J., Locke, D. Sanchez, J., & Stadler, H. (1996). Operationalization of multicultural counseling competencies. *Journal of Multicultural Counseling and Development, 24*(1), 42–78.

Additional Readings

Abes, E. S., Jones, S. R., & McEwen, M. K. (2007). Reconceptualizing the model of multiple dimensions of identity: The role of meaning-making capacity in the construction of multiple identities. *Journal of College Student Development, 48*(1), 1–22.

Hays, P. A. (2001). *Addressing cultural complexities in practice: A framework for clinicians and counselors*. Washington, DC: American Psychological Association.

Jones, S. R. (1997). Voices of identity and difference: A qualitative exploration of the multiple dimensions of identity development in women college students. *Journal of College Student Development, 38*(4), 376–386.

Super, D. E. *(1990).* A life-span, life-space approach to career development. In D. Brown & L. Brooks (Eds.), *Career choice and development: Applying contemporary theories to practice* (2nd ed., pp. 197–261). San Francisco, CA: Jossey-Bass.

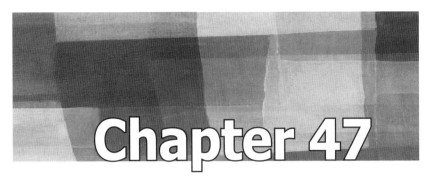

Chapter 47
Racial-Cultural Dyadic Role-Play

Gina C. Torino and Peter C. Donnelly

Topics: Introduction to Multicultural Counseling
Definitions of Cultural Diversity
Cultural Identity Development
Helping Relationships

Purposes: This activity aims to provide participants with an understanding of how racial-cultural identity attitudes manifest within the counseling relationship and to provide students with an opportunity to practice culturally appropriate microcounseling skills.

Learning Objectives: As a result of this activity, participants will gain a better understanding of (a) their own racial-cultural identity attitudes (e.g., race, gender, social class, ability, sexual orientation, religion, and so forth), (b) how racial-cultural identity attitudes affect the lives of clients, and (c) one's ability to use culturally appropriate counseling interventions.

Target Population: Advanced master's-level mental health and/or doctoral-level counseling, clinical, or social work students. Students must have taken or be taking a didactic course on race and/or multicultural psychology.

Group Size: Approximately four to six students per group

Time Required: 30 minutes per dyad. This activity can be conducted over several sessions or throughout an entire semester. The number of hours needed to complete this exercise will be based on the number of students in the course.

Setting: Classroom(s). The dyads will be seated in two chairs (preferably not desks) that are arranged approximately 2–3 feet across from one another. Observers will sit in a semicircle around the dyad. For the large-group discussion, the entire classroom will sit in a large circle.

Materials: Notebook and pen or pencil with which observers and participants can take notes

Instructions for Conducting Activity

Depending on classroom size, divide participants into groups of four to six. Ideally, two or three advanced-level teaching assistants would be used to facilitate each individual group; however, this activity can also be used with one instructor teaching a small multicultural course. If possible, each small group would work in a separate classroom; however, if it is a small group (10–12), then the two groups can work on opposite sides of the same room.

Prior to selecting the dyads (e.g., on the first day of class), the instructor or teaching assistants will ask all students to submit a sheet of paper with their self-identified race, gender, social class, ability, sexual orientation, and religion. Based on the students' self-identification, the instructor or teaching assistants will select the dyads. Dyad selection should be based on a heterogeneous grouping (e.g., one African American and one Asian American student). When dyadic groupings are finalized, assign one person to be the counselor and the other to be the client.

Dyads should be instructed to engage in a 10-minute role-play on a current concern (e.g., difficulties with school work, family members, and so forth). Direct the client to integrate a racial-cultural concern into the mock session, either at the content level (substance of the interaction) or process level (communication between the counselor and the client). For example, the client might discuss his or her financial hardships as a single parent paying for an education. Alternatively, the client might bring up the difficulties in working as a counselor from a particular racial group. Instruct the counselor to engage in the dyad as if it were an authentic counseling session. As in a real-life session, the counselor should be responsible for keeping track of time. Prior to commencing with the dyad, instruct other group members or observers to take notes on the counseling process. Please see Handout 47.1 for observer guidelines.

After the role-play, the counselor/client should take about 5 minutes to write reactions to the session. Ask them to pay particular attention to racial-cultural concerns. For the remaining 15 minutes, open up the discussion to the group. Use the observer guidelines to focus the discussion.

Next, select another dyad to participate in this exercise. Continue to repeat this exercise until each participant has had at least one opportunity to be the counselor and to be the client. When all students have had an opportunity to participate in this exercise (both as counselor and client), use one class session to engage students in a large-group discussion. Please see Handout 47.2 for discussion guidelines.

Handouts: Handout 47.1: Observational Guidelines: Racial–Cultural Dyadic Role-Play
Handout 47.2: Discussion Guidelines: Racial–Cultural Dyadic Role-Play

Additional Readings

Carter, R. T. (2005). Teaching racial-cultural counseling competence: A racially inclusive model. In R. T. Carter (Ed.), *Handbook of racial-cultural psychology and counseling: Training and practice* (Vol. 2, pp. 36–56). Hoboken, NJ: Wiley.

Mio, J. S., & Barker-Hackett, L. (2003). Reaction papers and journal writing as techniques for assessing resistance in multicultural courses. *Journal of Multicultural Counseling and Development, 31,* 12–19.

Rozas, L. W., & Miller, J. (2009). Discourses for social justice education: The web of racism and the web of resistance. *Journal of Ethnic & Cultural Diversity in Social Work, 18,* 24–39.

Spanierman, L. B., Poteat, V. P., Wang, Y. F., & Oh, E. (2008). Psychosocial costs of racism to White counselors: Predicting various dimensions of multicultural counseling competence. *Journal of Counseling Psychology, 55*(1), 75–88.

Sue, D.W., & Sue, D. (2008). *Counseling the culturally diverse* (5th ed.). Thousand Oaks, CA: Sage.

Sue, D. W., & Torino, G. C. (2005). Racial-cultural competence: Awareness, knowledge, and skills. In R. T. Carter (Ed.), *Handbook of racial-cultural psychology and counseling: Training and practice* (Vol. 2, pp. 3–18). Hoboken, NJ: Wiley.

Utsey, S. O., & Gernat, C. A. (2002). White racial identity attitudes and the ego: Defense mechanisms used by White counselor trainees in racially provocative counseling situations. *Journal of Counseling & Development, 80,* 475–483.

Chapter 48
Cultural Heritage Quilt Presentations[1]

Cheryl B. Warner and Rosemary E. Phelps

Topics: Introduction to Multicultural Counseling
Definitions of Cultural Diversity
Oppression and Discrimination
Culturally Skilled Counselor
Creative Arts

Purposes: This activity aims to engage each student in her or his own personal cultural exploration, ultimately answering the question, "Who am I?" Through the creation of individual presentations, this activity allows students to explore their histories and tell personal stories that introduce their cultural identities and identity development to their peers. This activity facilitates multicultural awareness and understanding as outlined by the Association of Multicultural Counseling and Development's (AMCD's; n.d.) Multicultural Counseling Competencies Standard 1—Counselor Awareness of Own Cultural Values and Biases, specifically relating to the following AMCD criteria:

- *A.2.* Culturally skilled counselors are aware of how their own cultural background and experiences have influenced attitudes, values, and biases about psychological processes.
- *B.1.* Culturally skilled counselors have specific knowledge about their own racial and cultural heritage and how it personally and professionally affects their definitions and biases of normality/abnormality and the process of counseling.
- *C.2.* Culturally skilled counselors are constantly seeking to understand themselves as racial and cultural beings and are actively seeking a nonracist identity.

Learning Objectives: As a result of this activity, students will (a) gain understanding of their cultural development by identifying critical incidents or factors significant to their personal growth and development; (b) connect their cultural heritage and socialization to their attitudes, values, and beliefs; (c) recognize the complexity of intersecting cultural variables (e.g., gender and race, sexual identity and religion) on personal development; and (d) gain awareness of how their cultural development is reflected in their professional development.

Target Population: Graduate students enrolled in cross-cultural awareness or multicultural counseling courses

Group Size: A maximum class size of 25

---

[1]Although the authors did not originally develop the idea of a cultural heritage quilt presentation, they have significantly modified it over the years.

Time Required: 15 to 20 minutes per participant

Setting: A regular classroom equipped with audio/visual equipment

Materials: Assignment description (see Handout 48.1) to be included in course syllabus.

Instructions for Conducting Activity

1. Include the activity description (Handout 48.1) in the course syllabus. Note: We recommend strategically scheduling the presentations after the fourth or fifth week of a 15-week semester. This allows sufficient time for (a) reviewing the definitions of cultural diversity, AMCD Multicultural Counseling Competencies, and professional and ethical guidelines and standards; and (b) allowing participants sufficient time to research their family histories, interview family members, and collect their artifacts. (Depending on the class size, several class sessions should be devoted to these presentations.)

2. Review the assignment, including its objectives and expectations on the first day of class. (Note: The ambiguity and personal nature of this assignment may cause concern and apprehension for some students.) Emphasize the importance for students to define and present their cultural heritage as they view themselves rather than how they perceive the instructor will evaluate the completed assignment.

3. Randomly assign students to the scheduled presentation dates. On the day of the presentation, the order of individual presentations can be determined by allowing students scheduled on that date to volunteer or by the instructor randomly assigning the presentation order.

4. Allow sufficient time at the end of each presentation for classmates to ask questions or make observations.

5. When all students have presented, process the activity with the entire class, using the following suggested discussion questions:
   a. With a show of hands, how many of you:
      (1) Were concerned about what and how much information you should reveal in your presentation? Were concerned about how others would perceive you if you shared certain information?
      (2) Learned new information about your family or yourself by doing this assignment?
      (3) Included stories and information about family members who are no longer living or who you have never personally met but were critical to your cultural history?
      (4) Could easily tell your cultural story without reference to the past?
      (5) Realized you had similar experiences with classmates who you thought were very different from you?
      (6) Realized that you had very different experiences from classmates that you perceived to be similar to you?
   b. What were the most difficult aspects of creating and presenting your cultural heritage? What were the easiest or most fun aspects of creating and presenting your cultural heritage?
   c. What emotions did you experience as you were preparing and presenting your cultural heritage?
   d. What insights have you gained by listening to each other's cultural stories?
   e. By examining your own cultural heritage, what insights have you gained about cultural identity development? Why is it important? What critical information would you have missed about your classmates if you did not know about their cultural heritage?
   f. How does our cultural identity development affect our professional development? How does learning about ourselves as "cultural beings" assist us in becoming multiculturally competent professionals?
   g. How can you use this experience in empathizing with or helping individuals who are culturally different from you? Culturally similar to you?

Handout: Handout 48.1: Course Assignment—Cultural Heritage Quilt Presentations

References

Association of Multicultural Counseling and Development. (n.d.). *Multicultural counseling competencies and standards.* Retrieved from http://www.counseling.org/Counselors/

Additional Readings

Arredondo, P., Toporek, M. S., Brown, S., Jones, J., Locke, D. C., Sanchez, J., & Stadler, H. (1996). *Operationalization of the multicultural counseling competencies*. Alexandria, VA: AMCD.

Smith, T. B. (Ed.). (2005). *Practicing multiculturalism: Affirming diversity in counseling and psychology*. Boston, MA: Pearson Education.

Sue, D. W., & Sue, D. (2008). *Counseling the culturally diverse: Theory and practice* (5th ed.). Hoboken, NJ: Wiley.

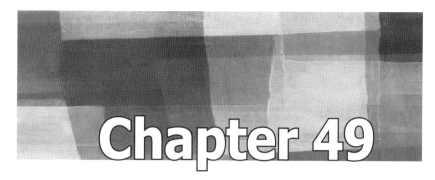

Chapter 49

Living in a Changing World: Personal Cultural Identification

Mary E. Walker and Linda L. Autry

Topics: Cultural Identity Development
Dimensions of Worldviews
Cross-Cultural Family Counseling
Counseling Asian Americans
Use of New Technology

Purposes: This activity is designed to enable students to

- identify their own unique culture,
- explore ways to move freely among diverse cultures, and
- choose aspects of their own culture that they will incorporate into their own personal identity and pass to future generations.

Target Population: Students in a multicultural or family course

Group Size: Small groups of four to six students

Time Required: Classroom activities that include a full-length movie and discussion will take 3 to 4 hours. Allow approximately 1 hour for discussion of movies watched by students outside of class. Instructors can adjust time allotments depending on length of class periods. If the entire activity is assigned as an independent assignment outside of class, allow students at least half a semester for completion.

Setting: The discussion part of this activity can be done in a regular classroom environment where chairs can be arranged in small groups. In addition, this activity is conducive to online coursework in the form of online discussions. Online work could include submission of written assignments, use of chat rooms, and use of videocams.

Materials: None needed for the classroom. Students will need to rent movies for some sections of the activity. All videos are available through movie rental companies, such as Netflix and Blockbuster.

Instructions for Conducting Activity

The instructor can begin the activity by relating the following story to students:

> Ed, a young engineer in a large U.S. company, shared his cultural heritage with a fellow worker. Ed had moved to the United States with his family at a very young age. His father, while seeking the advantages of living in the United States, worked to raise his children in a strict Korean culture. Ed attended a major university and excelled, securing a premium job on graduation. Holding to the traditions of his Korean heritage, Ed faced some difficulties both on the job and off with his customs such as dietary practices. In spite of these small problems, Ed remained loyal to his upbringing.
>
> At an appropriate age, Ed's father arranged for him to make a trip back to Korea to seek a wife. When he reached Korea, his family had some 30 girls for him to meet and consider for marriage. After a few meetings, Ed found a woman who he felt would make an appropriate wife and began the process of bringing her to the United States.
>
> What Ed's father and Ed had failed to consider was that the Korean culture over the past 25 years had been in the process of change. The older customs that Ed's family had faithfully observed as well as the attitudes toward family, lifestyles, and gender roles had changed drastically. The wife and family Ed was seeking were virtually nonexistent in a more modern Korea. The result of the assumptions made by Ed and his family about culture resulted in confusion and frustration. The expectations of the young man and his bride were very different and resulted in a difficult start for their marriage.

The authors believe that cultures in the 21st century must be personally identified and defined. The process of doing so requires people to reflect on those traditions, traits, and qualities that have been passed to them by previous generations and that they hope to pass on to the succeeding generations of their families. As counseling students experience a personal process of identifying their culture, they will better understand the culture of future clients in all of their variations. Through this process, the student should be able to use general knowledge of the dominant culture of a future client to allow the specific culture of that individual and her family of origin to facilitate a clearer picture of the real life of the person whom they are counseling.

The following activities are designed first to lead counseling students through a personal discovery of the culture that defines them and second teaches them to carry that process forward toward a greater understanding of the unique cultures of others. Rather than pigeonholing the client into a stereotypical view of a specific presenting culture, the counseling student will have a frame of reference for allowing future clients to define their personal culture and how that culture has shaped her or his sense of self and ultimately his or her current life.

Often a person's culture is reduced to specific foods. These exercises capitalize on the idea of the family recipe; however, the ingredients are the strands of cultural heritages that make up the modern version of living cultures shaping the lives of families and individuals. Looking at the ingredients of a person's cultural heritage allows a fresh perspective on the current emerging culture of the future counselor and subsequently of the counselor's clients in the 21st-century world.

The following activities are designed to explore three generations of the counseling student's heritage. Students with a limited knowledge of more than two generations can work within those parameters and still reach a satisfactory result. Students who are parents or who have a generation of nieces and nephews from whom they can draw information may choose to include that generation as a fourth level. In the event that adopted children are among the counseling students and may have a limited knowledge of past generations, the instructor can encourage the use of a deductive approach. Adopted students may want to explore traits that are not congruent with their adoptive family and could have roots in an unknown cultural heritage. From that, these students may choose to parallel their adoptive heritage with their unknown heritage. Those traits that cannot be explained within the framework of the adoptive family's culture could lead the student to explore possible birth family cultural origins that might support those traits and characteristics. For example, having a strong ability for oration could lead a student to search out cultures with an oral tradition.

After the students have learned to identify their own culture, this information will serve as a launching pad for students to begin to move freely within others' cultural background. The stigma of assimilation can be laid to rest as this approach allows for growth and change without demanding the acquiescence of one culture to another. Seeing cultures as a living and free-flowing approach to how a person structures his or her life will help future counselors become more accepting and relaxed about the multicultural experiences that are increasingly part of their profession. Approaching the processes of delineating a person's personal culture creatively and with an open mind will add to the future counselor's effectiveness over time as the world shifts from pockets of isolation to a heterogeneous global village.

Defining Your Cultural Identity

Looking down a city block in a large U.S. metropolitan area will generally reflect the multiplicity of the culture where most counselors work. Shops, doctor's offices, and restaurants can present a strongly visible cultural diversity existing and exchanging goods and services side by side. Yet, as these cultures move into mainstream areas, the ability to define one's own culture becomes increasingly hazy. This section draws from the individual's cultural heritage that has been influenced by marriages, partnerships, location, finances, and belief systems.

Students will carry out the groundwork of these assignments individually or in groups outside of class and then process the results in the classroom.

1. Create a cultural genogram that reflects at least three generations.
    a. Identify cultural characteristics and traditions, creating symbols for
        (1) Ethnicity or country of origin
        (2) Specific traditions demonstrated
        (3) Personal characteristics
        (4) Skills and talents
    b. Identify three significant characters
        (1) How does each influence or manifest the culture of the family?
        (2) What stories about the family or family member are told in the family?
    c. Discuss three of the following traits, traditions, or lifestyles that have been shaped by your culture:
        (1) How you view love and marriage
        (2) How you express grief
        (3) Your choice of professions
        (4) Education
        (5) Political views and affiliations
        (6) Your view of nature and the environment
        (7) Parenting styles
        (8) Gender roles
        (9) Your attitude toward class systems
        (10) Your attitude toward authority
        (11) Pets
        (12) Civic responsibility and/or charitable work/contributions
        (13) Religious beliefs
        (14) Celebration of holidays
        (15) Diet
        (16) Your taste in art, music, and drama/movies
        (17) Home and land ownership
        (18) Superstitions
        (19) Attitudes toward authority
        (20) Exploration of the unfamiliar
        (21) Your attitude toward other cultures/ethnicities
    d. Write a reflection paper about this experience addressing these questions:
        (1) How has your cultural heritage been shaped by family relationships?
        (2) How has money shaped your cultural heritage?
        (3) How has religion shaped your cultural heritage?

        (4) How has art shaped your cultural heritage?

2. Hollywood hits that reflect cultural struggles

   a. Watch the movie *Crash* (2005). You may have seen this movie but have not really observed the underlying assumptions about the cultures represented, especially your own.

     (1) What culture in this movie is most like your own?

     (2) How does your cultural identity vary from the stereotypes presented?

     (3) What do you think shaped those differences?

   b. Selecting on your own

     (1) Select a movie you believe closely reflects your own culture

     (2) Select a movie that you believe others would say reflects your culture but does not.

   c. Comparing and contrasting the two

     (1) What cultural struggles are depicted in the two movies you selected?

     (2) What cultural struggles have you dealt with?

     (3) If your heritage is a mixed culture, what unique struggles have you faced?

3. Depicting your cultural identity

   a. Watch a generational film, such as *Little Miss Sunshine* (Turtletaub, Saraf, Berger, Yerxa, & Friendly [Producers] and Dayton & Faris [Director], 2006).

   b. If Hollywood made a film covering three generations of your family, which actors and actresses would play major roles?

     (1) Why those choices?

     (2) Who plays you?

   c. In class, present a dramatic presentation of a major character in your family.

   d. Reflection: What have I learned about my cultural heritage as a result?

Moving Freely Among Diverse Cultures

In this section, students are challenged to explore cultures with which they are uncomfortable and typically attempt to avoid. Knowledge of self is not sufficient to counter fears and prejudices that have been learned. Students must use the knowledge of their self-identified culture to explore their ideas about the culture of others.

1. What three cultures are you least comfortable or familiar with that you might encounter as a professional counselor?

   a. Watch movies that are sensitive or sympathetic to these identified cultures or that members of these cultures might watch.

   b. Reflect on aspects of the cultures that made you uncomfortable before watching the movie.

   c. What, if any, impact did the movie have on your opinions of these cultures?

   d. Reflecting back on your cultural genogram, what traits, attitudes, or traditions from your culture are present in the ones that you are unfamiliar or uncomfortable with?

2. Facing fears and prejudices

   a. Watch the movie *Grand Canyon* (Gillo, Kasdan, & Okun [Producers] and Kasdan [Director], 1991) to determine what fears and misconceptions manifest in the movie.

     (1) How did cultural barriers manifest in the main characters?

     (2) What steps were taken by the main characters to bridge those barriers?

     (3) What benefits does each main character derive from the relationship?

3. Celebrating and appreciating other cultures

   a. Listen to music and observe art from diverse cultures.

   b. Consider how each made you feel and reflect on aspects of the art/music that you appreciate.

   c. Present to the class a musical piece or art/craft piece that you like from a diverse culture.

     (1) Describe to the class the positive thoughts and emotions the item evokes.

     (2) Discuss how this might become part of your culture.

Cultural Identity Development

Treating Multiculturalism as a Living Entity

These exercises are designed to broaden a student's perspective not only horizontally across cultural lines, but also in terms of the progression that is made over time. This perspective broadening can take the idea of multiculturalism out of the proverbial box and place it on the continuum of evolving world communication. Observing how cultures have progressed, not losing their definition but enhancing their uniqueness, gives greater hope of a world filled with diversity that is appreciated and understood.

1. Watch the movies *Guess Who's Coming to Dinner* (Glass & Kramer [Producers] and Kramer [Director], 1967) and *Guess Who* (Caracciolo [Producer] and Sullivan [Director], 2005).
   a. What transitions have occurred in attitudes toward the mixing of cultures between these two movies?
   b. Looking back at your own cultural genogram, what cultural transitions have occurred in the last three generations?
   c. What transitions should have occurred but have not?
2. Watch the movies *I Passed for White* (Wilcox [Producer and Director], 1960) and *Real Women Have Curves* (LaVoo & Brown [Producers] and Cardoso [Director], 2002).
   a. What differences have occurred between these two movies in the attitudes about leaving your culture?
   b. What disadvantages were there in leaving a culture in the 2002 film?
   c. What were the advantages?
   d. What personal breeches have you made in your cultural heritage?
   e. What did it cost you, and what did you gain?
   f. What part of your own culture do you want to leave behind, and what parts do you hope to pass on to the next generation?

Reflections

1. Reflecting back on the course exercises, what has the process been like for you?
2. In the process, what have you learned about yourself?
3. As a future counselor, what can you take from this exercise that will make you a better counselor?

Informal Student Evaluation

1. How could this activity be improved?
2. What parts were especially meaningful?
3. What should be left out?
4. What could be added?

In addition, the instructor may choose to have students write formally their reflections regarding the activity or have them process their reflections as part of a whole-group classroom discussion. Instructors are encouraged to use all or parts of the activity and to use their creativity to further enhance the activity based on the particular needs of their students.

Handout: Handout 49.1: Websites of Culturally Diverse Movies

References

Caracciolo, J. (Producer), & Sullivan, K. (Director). (2005). *Guess who* [Motion Picture]. United States: Sony Pictures.

Gillo, M., Kasdan, L., & Okun, C. (Producers), & Kasdan, L. (Director). (1991). *Grand Canyon* [Motion Picture]. United States: 20th Century Fox.

Glass, G., & Kramer, S. (Producers), & Kramer, S. (Director). (1967). *Guess who's coming to dinner* [Motion Picture]. United States: Columbia Pictures.

Haggis, P., Cheadle, D., & Moresco, B. (Producers), & Haggis, P. (Director). (2004). *Crash* [Motion picture]. United States: Lionsgate.

LaVoo, G., & Brown, E. (Producers), & Cardoso, P. (Director). (2002). *Real women have curves* [Motion Picture]. United States: HBO Films.

Turtletaub, M., Saraf, P., Berger, A., Yerxa, R., & Friendly, D. (Producers), & Dayton, J., & Faris, V. (Directors). (2006). *Little Miss Sunshine* [Motion picture]. United States: Fox Searchlight Pictures.

Wilcox, F. (Producer), & Wilcox, F. (Director). (1960). *I passed for White* [Motion picture]. United States: Allied Artist Pictures.

Additional Readings

At the discretion of the instructor

Chapter 50
Process Group Themes Project

Carlotta J. Willis and Debra Bergeron

Topics: Cultural Identity Development
Oppression and Discrimination
Group Work
Research and Program Evaluation
Use of New Technology

Purposes: The purpose of the activity is two-fold. The process groups, an on-going in-class and online activity, provide an opportunity for students to work in small groups to discuss readings and process personal reactions, integrate learning, and develop understanding while developing skills in group facilitation. The theme identification project at the end of the semester provides students with the opportunity to experience a modified consensual qualitative research (CQR; Hill, Thompson, & Williams, 1997) process for analysis of their process entries and helps them to develop skills in theme identification, especially racial identity development themes. The learning objectives below are based on the theme identification project. The process groups have additional learning objectives, as described in Rowell and Benshoff (2008).

Learning Objectives: For the theme identification project students will be able to

- describe their social background, ethnic identity, and socially and culturally shaped beliefs;
- identify themes of racial identity development within their own process entries; and
- have a basic understanding of a qualitative research method for analysis of process note data.

Target Population: Graduate students enrolled in a course in multicultural counseling

Group Size: Six and eight members are best for the process groups; class size could vary.

Time Required: Typically the groups meet for 30-40 minutes within each class session. Between class meetings, student post process entries in the course folder online. Students read the other students' postings and comment if they wish. The instructor will read all comments and observe the process groups but in most cases will not comment in the in-class process groups or online folders.

Setting: Classroom with space for groups of six to eight students to meet sitting in a circle. Also, online private discussion group folders with access only for group members and instructor.

Materials: Process entries are posted between class sessions in discussion folders (private to each group) through Sakai, Blackboard, or other electronic learning management system. Students may wish to use large paper or whiteboards for consensus discussions. Colored pencils or markers may be useful for organization of themes.

Instructions for Conducting Activity

1. Explain that this semester-long activity will consist of three different components: multicultural counseling process groups, reflective processing posting, and the theme identification project.
2. Describe multicultural counseling process groups: The class will be divided into small process groups that will work together throughout the semester to discuss readings and process personal reactions, integrate learning, and develop understanding while developing skills in group facilitation. Active participation in the group is required. Keep in mind that examining issues related to diversity and privilege is a lifelong process, and the material presented in this class represents part of a continuing process to which there is no final end point. Each student will begin at her or his own starting place, and learning will continue well beyond the end of the course. One group member will serve as facilitator and one as scribe each week for the in-class sessions. The scribe will identify the themes from the in-class session and will post these in the process group folder.
3. Divide group into small process groups of six to eight. If possible, mix according to gender, race, ethnicity, age, sexual orientation, experience in groups, and so forth. Provide weekly class time (30-40 minutes if possible) for process group discussion.
4. Distribute reflection postings instructions handout (see Handout 50.1).
5. Students participate in the semester-long course, posting their reflections in addition to meeting in small face-to-face groups weekly. The instructor reads and occasionally comments on the entries and observes the process groups, commenting only if necessary.
6. Three weeks before the end of the semester, distribute the theme identification project instructions handout (see Handout 50.2). The instructor should present briefly on qualitative research and Hill et al.'s (1997) CQR process. The modified process and application to this project should also be reviewed in class.
7. Students prepare at home by identifying the themes in their own process entries.
8. The next-to-last class of the semester, the students complete the theme identification project in their small process groups. This should take the entire class time, up to 3 hours.
9. Presentation of themes: Each process group will present the themes on which they reached consensus to the whole class at the final class session. Examples and discussion of key learning are encouraged.
10. The presentations are often followed by a sharing of traditional foods in order bring the semester to a celebratory conclusion and to honor the learning that has taken place.

Handouts: Handout 50.1: Instructions for Reflective Process Postings
Handout 50.2: Instructions for Theme Identification Project

References

Hill, C. E., Thompson, B. J., & Williams, E. N. (1997). A guide to conducting consensual qualitative research. *The Counseling Psychologist, 25*(4), 517–572.

Rowell, P. C., & Benshoff, J. M. (2008). Using personal growth groups in multicultural counseling courses to foster students' ethnic identity development. *Counselor Education and Supervision, 48,* 2–15.

Additional Readings

The course for which this activity was developed used the following core texts:

Andersen, M. L., & Collins, P. H. (2007). *Race, class, and gender: An anthology* (6th ed.). Stamford, CT: Wadsworth.

Johnson, A. G. (2006). *Privilege, power, and difference* (2nd ed.). Boston, MA: McGraw-Hill.

Sue, D. W., & Sue, D. (2008). *Counseling the culturally diverse: Theory and practice* (5th ed.). New York, NY: Wiley.

Young, R. J. C. (2003). *Postcolonialism: A very short introduction.* New York, NY: Oxford University Press.

Cultural Identity Development

Chapter 51
Exploring Racial Identity Development

Jill Miller, Sukie Magraw, Kayoko Yokoyama, and Liza Hecht

Topics: Introduction to Multicultural Counseling
      Definitions of Cultural Diversity
      Cultural Communication Styles
      Dimensions of Worldviews
      Culturally Skilled Counselor

Purposes: The purpose of this activity is for class members to reflect on particular (abbreviated) models of racial identity development for people of color and White people and then to reflect on their own racial identity development process, specifically, what they notice about membership in their cultural group and about the cultural groups of others. This exercise is used to enhance the readings and discussion related to racial identity models used in the field of psychology and counseling.

Learning Objectives: As a result of this activity, students will have enriched understanding of the racial identity development models proposed and/or discussed by psychologists W. Cross, J. Helms, J. S. Phinney, D. W. Sue, or B. D. Tatum; in addition, they will examine more deeply where they are in their own racial identity development and how they arrived at the current phase, stage, or status.

Target Population: Advanced undergraduate or graduate students who are learning about racial identity development and the impact it has on overall human development

Group Size: Optimal group size would be a diverse group of eight to ten students.

Time Required: About 75 minutes—allow 15 minutes to explain the assignment and for students to review the synopsis handouts on racial identity development, 10–15 minutes for students to identify their own phase in development, 20–30 minutes for students to reflect on stimulus questions and write about where they are in their journey of racial identity development, and 15 minutes for students to share with a partner, small group, or large group any of their responses to the stimulus questions.

Setting: Classroom

Materials: Handout of synopses of racial identity development models and stimulus questions (Handout 51.1, adapted from colleague Veronique Thompson, PhD, Wright Institute, 2001).

Instructions for Conducting Activity

1. Introduce activity by telling participants:

   As students become culturally competent therapists, it is important to have an understanding of the processes related to racial identity development. For people of color the task in racial identity development is to develop an empowered sense of self in the face of racist societal messages; these tasks may look different for different peoples of color, and their varied histories of immigration into the United States must also be considered (Tatum, 2003). For White people the task of racial identity development is to develop a positive White identity based in reality, not on assumed superiority (Sue, 2003). It is also important for students to understand that this identity development process begins in childhood and is dynamic and can continue over the course of one's lifetime.

The following exercise is designed to complement discussion on racial identity development models and processes. This exercise encourages within-culture and cross-cultural contemplation and dialogue.

2. Hand out "Racial Identity Development" (see Handout 51.1) and "Racial Identity Exercise" (see Handout 51.2) to all students.
3. Have students review the handouts and surmise where they are in their racial identity development.
4. Tell students that they will now have 20-30 minutes to review the stimulus questions and write on as many of them as they wish. Inform them that they will share their responses with a partner, within a small group, or with the entire class (depending on the class size and structure). Note: Small groups may or may not be broken up by cultural caucuses.
5. When everyone has finished, 15 minutes is allotted for sharing. The instructor can debrief and explore further with students for the remainder of the class.

Handouts: Handout 51.1: Racial Identity Development
Handout 51.2: Racial Identity Exercise

References

Sue, D. W. (2003). *Overcoming our racism: The journey to liberation.* San Francisco, CA: Jossey-Bass.

Tatum, B. D. (2003). *"Why are all the Black kids sitting together in the cafeteria?": A psychologist explains the development of racial identity.* New York, NY: Basic Books.

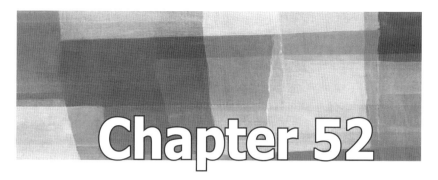

Chapter 52
Community Genogram and Parallel Process Links

Adam Zagelbaum

Topics: Definitions of Cultural Diversity
Cultural Identity Development
Cross-Cultural Family Counseling
Human Growth and Development
Group Work
Assessment

Purposes: This activity aims (a) to provide participants with opportunities to explore how their communities of origin and related community-based experiences help to form a sense of cultural identity and (b) to locate parallel processes and characteristics that other participants may have as well.

Learning Objectives: As a result of this activity, students will

- learn how to construct a community genogram,
- be able to recognize how the community and setting within which one lives help to form a sense of cultural identity,
- notice how similar characteristics can be found between participants with diverse cultural backgrounds and identities,
- help to form appropriate questions and interpersonal dialogue to engage participants in the discussion of similarities and differences between their communities of origin, and
- gain a better understanding of how one's setting can affect group dynamics and cultural variables that exist within groups composed of diverse individuals.

Target Population: Specifically designed for counselors in training of all ages but can also be conducted on client populations ages 13 and beyond

Group Size: Ideally, 8 to 10 members (has been conducted on as few as 5 members and as many as 30 in a single classroom)

Time Required: 50 minutes or less

Setting: Classroom or group room where tables can allow for individuals to draw; the seating arrangement generally works best when there are seats that are able to make a half-circle whereby one individual can be given undivided attention by group members but eye contact can be shared among all group members.

Materials: Dry-erase board and markers (if possible) for the group leader/model; 8.5″ × 11″ sheets of paper (or larger), with markers for each participant

Instructions for Conducting Activity

For individuals who are not familiar with the concepts of genograms, a brief lecture about how to construct a more traditional type of genogram is recommended. The basic symbols used to represent men (squares) and women (circles) within this traditional type of genogram can provide an important background on which the specific and different concepts of the community genogram can be better understood. Participants, however, are to be specifically informed about the fact that the community genogram does not follow the more traditional structures and symbols associated with the exercise designed to map one's family of origin and related family members. The reason as to why these differences exist is because family genograms are more about the people associated with one's family of origin and timeline, whereas the community genogram is more about the places and locations associated with one's growth and development.

Introducing the PowerPoint slides (Handout 52.1) at this time helps to illustrate the aforementioned points. The concepts of the person as community and the contact hypothesis help illustrate the importance of understanding that people are not the only variables that help individuals develop a sense of identity, but, rather, the settings in which people exist also help construct meanings and beliefs about themselves and their culture. Although people are certainly important when it comes to developing a cultural understanding of who we are as social beings, so are the physical locations where people exist. The instructor or group leader at this time approaches the class or group members with a brief lecture about the fact that cultural beings are shaped not only by the people with whom they are exposed to in their sociocultural surroundings, but also by the physical settings and locations in which they are contained. This specifically refers to the concept of the person as community (Ogbonnya, 1994).

The instructor or group leader may wish to assert at this point that many memories individuals have of their distant and recent past do not simply involve particular people, but also involve particular places in one's neighborhood or community. Presenting examples at this point is usually encouraged. For example, the instructor may wish to ask participants if they have a particular location that comes to mind when people in their respective communities wish to have meetings or gatherings of some kind. Also, the instructor may ask if there are places within one's community that people are constantly being told to stay away from. This type of Socratic questioning helps to engage the audience in the concept of noticing that specific areas of one's community are salient cues that indicate the values behind which many community members socialize or avoid contact with other community members.

At this point, the instructor is encouraged to display an example of a community genogram, using either the format of a map design or a star design, both of which are described on the enclosed PowerPoint slides (Ivey, Pedersen, & Ivey, 2001). The map design is explained as a schematic representation of physical locations within one's community of origin drawn in the form of a road map. The star design is explained as a more abstract version of the map, because it does not have any particular structures or schematics associated with it but, rather, is a series of statements and/or memories that an individual draws around a central point on a sheet of paper that reflect the places and occurrences that have happened within his or her lifetime of living within a particular community. Examples of these community genogram formats are available in many texts (Ivey et al., 2001) and can be independently generated by individuals who wish to place their own creative concepts onto this structure. Younger clients, especially children, tend to draw the star diagram because of its more basic design (Ivey et al., 2001).

Regardless of the type of community genogram to be used for the exercise, the instructor is encouraged to draw an example of one in front of the other participants so that the in vivo exposure to the exercise can be modeled effectively. Usually, drawing one's own community of origin is easiest, and the instructor is strongly encouraged to make certain that participants are not viewing the example as the only way a community genogram is supposed to look. The instructor should use a dry-erase board or large display tablet on which he or she can construct the genogram in front of other participants and speak out loud

Cultural Identity Development

while doing so. For example, stating to the participants, "The main street in my community of origin was Maple Avenue" while drawing a long line across the center of the board and labeling it "Maple Avenue" helps visually and verbally engage the audience while instructing them on how to construct the design. The instructor provides about 5 to 10 minutes of dialogue and drawing to show members what kinds of details are able to be included in the community genogram. Houses, buildings, gathering venues, transportation areas, open spaces, and neighboring communities are just some of the many components that a community genogram can contain. After completing the example, the instructor allows for the participants to ask questions about what has been drawn and uses these questions as opportunities to illustrate to participants how clients would normally respond to similar questions if this exercise were to be done in a counseling session of some kind. The PowerPoint slide about drawing out the story (slide #4) can also be displayed at this time to assist with the learning experience. The instructor, just like a client, reserves the right to answer or not answer particular questions depending on the level of comfort that the group appears willing to contribute. Some participants may wish to know about particular roadways that have been drawn on the board. Others may wish to enquire about why particular areas of the genogram appear to have gaps or larger spaces associated with them. Other participants may ask about particular events or memories that the instructor has about particular details that have been drawn in his or her genogram. All of these questions are opportunities for the group to process why they are focusing on particular details and what messages these focal points are saying about their community values. The instructor is encouraged to make observations and use Socratic questions at this point to engage the participants in an interpersonal dialogue regarding how they are viewing and valuing the community genogram exercise.

Then, the instructor uses the remainder of the session to have the participants draw their own community genograms on sheets of paper displayed in front of their desks. They are encouraged to draw community genograms that represent their community of origin and should be advised that they may be asked to share their creations with other participants and may be asked questions about what they have drawn. A designated time period of about 15 minutes should be sufficient for participants to draw their genograms. The remaining time during the session should be used to have willing participants display their community genograms to one another by having one person at a time, in a format similar to a show-and-tell exercise, hold up his or her constructed genogram and verbally explain to the other group members what details and content pieces of the genogram are important to him or her. Other participants are to act as observers but are free to ask questions of the presenter. The presenter is allowed to answer the posed questions that he or she feels are appropriate. The instructor serves as a facilitator who makes links between one person's genogram and another's. The results are often fascinating because of the links that people can find between different genograms.

For example, a person who displays a genogram that focuses on an urban community where people congregate in a particular part of the town on Friday nights for the purposes of socializing may have a link with a person who displays a genogram that focuses on a rural community where people congregate in a particular part of the area to socialize on a Saturday afternoon. Though the details and definitions of socializing may be different among the communities, the parallel processes that can be drawn are usually captivating points that allow the group members and instructor to showcase the power of the exercise as well as to learn how cultural values compare and contrast to one another based on the communities in which people were raised. The exercise can terminate at this point, but participants are certainly encouraged to follow up about their reflections and learning experiences as needed.

Handout: Handout 52.1: The Community Genogram for School Counseling Purposes PowerPoint

References

Ivey, A., Pedersen, P., & Ivey, M. (2001). *Intentional group counseling: A microskills approach.* Belmont, CA: Wadsworth.

Ogbonnya, O. (1994). Person as community: An African understanding of the person as an intrapsychic community. *Journal of Black Psychology, 20,* 75–87.

Additional Readings

Lynch, J., Modgil, C., & Modgil, S. (1992). *Cultural diversity and the schools* (Vol. 1). Washington, DC: Falmer.

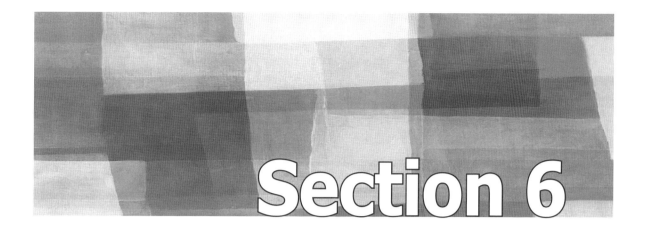

Section 6

Oppression and Discrimination

This section contains experiential activities that encourage students to explore concepts of oppression and discrimination. It contains several activities that assist students in beginning conversations about power and privilege and how these issues can affect an individual's interaction with others in and out of therapeutic settings. These activities are designed to address students' awareness and knowledge regarding racial, religious, gender, and ethnic oppression as well as to introduce the concept of micro-aggressions and its importance in daily life. Some activities incorporate a variety of learning approaches, including case studies and media use. These activities can be used in all core courses, including introductory and advanced multicultural courses.

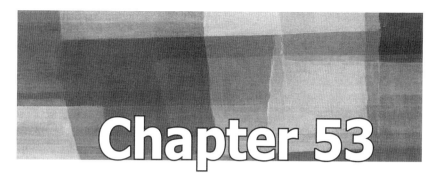

Chapter 53

Examining the Inner Circle: Unpacking White Privilege

Edward J. Brantmeier, Antonette Aragon, Nathalie Kees,
Jacqueline Peila-Shuster, and Sharon K. Anderson

Topics: Barriers to Effective Cross-Cultural Counseling
  Oppression and Discrimination
  Counseling European Americans

Purposes: Rationale—Peggy McIntosh's (1989) article on White privilege is nearly a classic for study-ing White privilege, an invisible system that grants unearned privileges to Whites and creates oppressive conditions for non-Whites based on skin color in the United States. Deep inner work needs to be done on the part of Whites in order to unravel the White dominance paradigm and move from honesty, to empathy, to advocacy, to social action toward change (Howard, 2006).

  The purpose of the activity is to provide an opportunity for students to understand how White privilege marginalizes non-White groups; this goal is accomplished via a physical experience of the distancing effects and power differentials inherent in a system of privilege. The activity also provides an opportunity for students to reflect on racism as an invisible system that confers advantage and dominance to some at the exclusion of others. It urges students to view how the structural aspects of racism promote inequity.

Learning Objectives: As a result of this activity, participants will be able to (a) deconstruct the emotions experienced by Whites and non-Whites that are associated with White privilege; (b) position-take and empathize with non-White and White groups; and (c) reflect on power, privilege, and dominance in a broader U.S. society.

Group Size: 10–40 participants

Time Required: 45–60 minutes

Setting: This activity works best when it is conducted outside in a large, open space. If weather does not allow, a large room is necessary.

Materials: Markers, paper, pens/pencils, copy of McIntosh's 1989 article "White Privilege: Unpacking the Invisible Knapsack" (Handout 53.1); McIntosh's "Some Notes for Facilitators on Presenting White Privilege and the Invisible Knapsack" (Handout 53.2).

Note. The original idea for this activity stemmed from a conversation with Nelson Soto, Indiana University—Purdue University at Indianapolis, and Rachelle Winkle, University of Nebraska—Lincoln, about a conference presentation that they had conducted as graduate students. Since then, the process and processing questions have morphed significantly based on trial and error in Ed Brantmeier's undergraduate and graduate diversity courses.

Instructions for Conducting Activity

- Ask students to prepare for class by reading Peggy McIntosh's article, "White Privilege: Unpacking the Invisible Knapsack" (see Handout 53.1).
- If done in a White-dominant context, ask certain participants to position-take with a person who is Native American, African American, Latino/a, or Asian American. Ask them to hold a sign with that label and to respond from that position: "I am a person who is Native American," "I am a person who is African American," and so forth. Give everyone in the group the option to not represent her or his own race or group. All other participants will represent White people.
- In a large, open space, gather participants into a tight, shoulder-to-shoulder formation of concentric circles. The concentric circles need not be perfect or even.
- Explain that it is very necessary that participants tighten the circle.
- Ask participants to remain silent during the activity and discussion.
- Read all 20 or so statements about White privilege from Peggy McIntosh's article. If a participant can answer "yes," he or she stays in the inner circle. If the answer is "no," he or she should take one large step backward.
- For example, read, "When I am told about our national heritage or about 'civilization,' I am shown that people of my color made it what it is." Based on who they are representing, a participant will remain still or take a step backward.

Process Questions

After all statements are read, reflect on the process and the formation.

- How does it feel to be on the outer circle? What thoughts did you have?
- How does it feel to be on the inner circle? What thoughts did you have?
- With whom do you feel closest? With whom do you feel most distant?
- If you did so, how did it feel to position-take with a person from another race? What were some of your thoughts during that process? How did it feel to operate on stereotypes?
- Did anyone have trouble hearing? Please explain yourself.

Interrogating Structural Racism

- What does the formation represent in larger society?
- Whose voice is heard? Whose voice is lost?
- Who has power at the decision-making table? Who decides what for whom?
- If this formation mirrors larger U.S. society, how can this formation be changed so that it is more inclusive and equitable? What specific changes would this take in the larger social, political, economic, and environmental spheres?
- How can we move toward more authentic racial equality and equity?
- Howard (2006) maintained that Whites go through a four-stage process in a healing response to unraveling the White dominance paradigm: honesty, empathy, advocacy, and social action toward change. If you identify as White, where would you place yourself in these stages and why?
- What is the role of counselors in contributing to that change process?
- Summative question: How would the inner circle change or remain the same if the focus of this activity was on ability privilege, sexual orientation privilege, gender privilege, religious privilege, class privilege, linguistic privilege, or other forms of privilege?

Follow-Up Integration

- After the processing questions, ask participants to return to their seats or classroom. Ask students to reflect in writing for 5 minutes on the following statement from McIntosh's article: "I was taught to see racism only in individual acts of meanness, not in invisible systems conferring dominance on my group."
- In dyads, ask students to share their written reflections with each other. After 5 minutes, ask participants to share comments about their writing and the entire activity with the class.

Handouts: Handout 53.1: "White Privilege: Unpacking the Invisible Knapsack" by Peggy McIntosh
Handout 53.2: "Some Notes for Facilitators on Presenting White Privilege and the
Invisible Knapsack" by Peggy McIntosh

References

Howard, G. (2006). *We can't teach what we don't know: White teachers, multiracial school.* New York, NY: Teachers College Press.

McIntosh, P. (1989, July/August). White privilege: Unpacking the invisible knapsack. *Peace and Freedom,* 8–10.

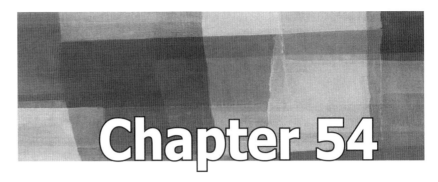

Chapter 54

Developing Knowledge of Others: Case Studies to Develop Studies of Other Diverse Cultures

Kate Davis Rogers

Topics: Definitions of Cultural Diversity
Barriers to Effective Cross-Cultural Counseling
Oppression and Discrimination
Dimensions of Worldviews
Culturally Skilled Counselor
Human Growth and Development
Creative Arts

Purposes: The activity/assignment is a challenge to students to look at images and see what reactions they might have toward clients.

Learning Objectives: To explore biases based on first impressions and to integrate knowledge, awareness, and skills from the readings, class discussions, and research

Target Population: Graduate students, who will identify clients they may work with in the future

Group Size: 8–20 participants would be ideal.

Time Required: This is an assignment to be done over time. I give it out in the first class and allow the students to develop it.

Setting: No specific setting required

Materials: I give eight images to each student. I look for images in news magazines, and my assistant looks for images on the Internet; we make packets that can be reused for each class. We look for images of people from a variety of racial and ethnic backgrounds, people of different ages, disabled people (a catalogue for physical and occupational supplies was very helpful), and other population groups that will be covered in the class.

Instructions for Conducting Activity

During the first class, I talk about this assignment. I tell the students that they are new employees of my agency and they have been randomly assigned a group of clients. I talk about how some agencies will use a variety of methods in assigning clients, such as giving clients a chance to request a particular type of counselor (e.g., whether they would prefer a male or female counselor). The students are told that clients can be assigned to a particular therapist based on that counselor's skills or specialties. I give them the option of referring out a client, but they have to discuss how and why they will refer out the client.

After handing out the eight images, I ask the students to write down their initial response to the client. I talk about the book *Blink* (Gladwell, 2005) and the human experience of making judgments on very little information. Then I allow time to help work with those snap judgments.

I then form small groups of three to four people to discuss their first impressions with each other. At the end of the class, I ask the students to post these images over the next weeks of the course and to write down additional thoughts on each client.

The following questions for each client need to be answered in the paper or collage that the students turn in at the end of the term:

- What was your original response to this image?
- What are the cultural factors that you see (gender, race, disability, and so forth)? What might be hidden (sexual orientation, cultural heritage, adoption, raised by a family member, disability, and so forth)?
- What might be some social concerns that this client faces? Any political structures that may affect this client?

The students may turn in a journal at the end of the term that reflects their process of thinking about each client. I have the students write about three pages per client. I ask the student to submit references from their reading, discussions, or speakers in classes that helped further their knowledge about each client.

For instance, an image of an African American client who looks about 14 years old with a cane is given to the student. One student reacts, "I realized that I have had very little interactions with teenagers. I have no idea what this child would like or what it would want in its life. I would have to ask several questions to help me understand him/her. I wonder about the cane. Does this mean the child is having problems with walking, or does it help out with a family member who needs the cane? I would like to know more before I make a decision."

Some of the areas that can be addressed in a paper include the following:

- Apply appropriate awareness and knowledge to a situation.
- Develop appropriate skills (i.e., listening, critical thinking, sensitivity).
- Develop the ability to analyze institutional inequality.
- Develop appropriate skills to be an ally.
- Explore what might be a multiculturally appropriate intervention.
- Learn ways to discuss the politics of an environment.
- Analyze your ability to go from being in an area of the continuum to facing a fractured society.
- Explore how to become culturally competent on the next level.
- Explore your unfamiliarity with this cultural group after your experience.

References

Gladwell, M. (2005). *Blink: The power of thinking without thinking.* New York, NY: Little, Brown, and Company.

Additional Readings

Sue, D. W., & Sue, D. (2007) *Counseling the culturally diverse: Theory and practice* (5th ed.). New York, NY: Wiley.

Chapter 55

The People in My Life:
A Personal Reflection on Power and Privilege

Kylie P. Dotson-Blake

Topics: Cultural Communication Styles
Oppression and Discrimination
Culturally Skilled Counselor
Human Growth and Development
Helping Relationships
Creative Arts

Purposes: The purpose of this activity is to encourage students who have a foundational understanding of the concepts of power and privilege to begin to critically assess the presence and impact of power and privilege in their daily lives. Hays and Chang (2003) asserted that privilege serves to separate social groups. As students become aware of the intersections of privilege, power, and oppression, they are more likely to advocate for social change (Ancis & Szymanski, 2001). Unfortunately, in counselor education, the concepts of power, privilege, and oppression are often discussed in the abstract, with the focus remaining primarily on the appreciation of diversity (Hays & Chang, 2003). Subsequently, students often miss the opportunity to reflect on the presence of power and privilege disparities within their own lives and the larger society. Thus, the purpose of this activity is to extend the learning of students who have previously explored the concepts of power and privilege at a foundational level by raising awareness of power relationships present in their lives and communities.

Learning Objectives: As a result of this activity, students will

- critically assess power relationships in their community,
- extend their understanding of the concepts of power and privilege,
- develop an enhanced awareness of the impact of social distance between cultural groups, and
- develop a better understanding of the impact of social distance on their personal conceptualizations of power and privilege.

Target Population: Master's-level counseling students who have been exposed to the concepts of power and privilege on a foundational level

Group Size: Any number of students can participate in this activity. For groups larger than 20, small groups should be used to process the activity.

Time Required: 90 minutes

Setting: Classroom setting. Participating students will need to have desks or flat surfaces on which to work.

Materials: Handouts for all students; power grids (printed on transparency sheets) for all students; colored candies or beads; dry-erase markers; and board on which to write the races/ethnicities and genders of the colored pieces (chalkboard, white-board/flipchart, or projector)

Instructions for Conducting Activity

1. Distribute a mix of colored candies or beads to each table.
2. Students should work as a group to write down the race and gender of the colored candies or beads. Make a list noting each candy's race and gender on the board. Most likely the list will not be totally inclusive because of limited numbers of different colors of candies. An example is as follows:
   a. Blue gummy bears = Asian women
   b. Red gummy bears = European American Women
3. Distribute one "The People in My Life" handout (Handout 55.1) to each student.
4. Have the students place the candy that represents the majority of people indicated by each grid square prompt into the square. For example, if as a European American (EA) woman, a student was raised in a single-parent EA female-headed household and she is currently living alone, she may place one red gummy bear in the box stating "The primary income producer in my family is and/or was . . ." Students should feel free to place more than one candy in each square if they need greater representation.
5. Distribute the "Power Grid" transparency handout (Handout 55.2).
6. Have the students lay the power grids over "The People in My Life" handout without removing the candies.
7. Have the students discuss which grid squares represent positions holding power and privilege. Facilitate a discussion of why these positions hold power and what privilege means for the positions. After the group reaches consensus on the positions/grid squares holding power and/or privilege, they should use dry erase markers to mark those squares on the power grid transparency with a *P*.
8. Process the activity by discussing the following:
   a. How is critical analysis important for one to become fully aware of power and privilege?
   b. Which races and gender are most often representative of positions holding power and/or privilege on student grid sheets?
   c. How are the students' individual "People in My Life" sheets representative of our larger society?
   d. What can we do to bridge the social distance between cultural groups in our lives?
   e. If students are in practicum or internship placements, it is useful to explore where the majority of their clients would fall on the chart and how this affects counselor-client interactions.
   f. It is necessary to structure processing in a manner congruent with the developmental needs of the students. If students need more concrete structure during processing, it would be appropriate to develop more specific processing questions aligned with student needs.
9. This activity can be adapted and modified for online course delivery by using a Word document version of "The People in My Life" handout, multicolored *X*s typed into grid squares to represent people, highlighting of grid squares to denote power grid squares, and discussion posts or blogs for processing.

Handouts: Handout 55.1: The People in My Life
Handout 55.2: The People in My Life: Power Grid

References

Ancis, J. R., & Szymanski, D. M. (2001). Awareness of White privilege among White counseling trainees. *The Counseling Psychologist, 29*, 548–569.

Hays, D. G., & Chang, C. Y. (2003). White privilege, oppression, and racial identity development: Implications for supervision. *Counselor Education and Supervision, 43*, 134–145.

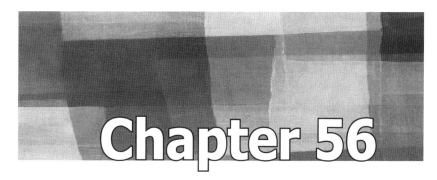

Chapter 56

The Socio-Cultural Profile (SCP)

Milton A. Fuentes and Hector Y. Adames

Topics: Definitions of Cultural Diversity
Four Forces in Counseling
Cultural Identity Development
Oppression and Discrimination
Dimensions of Worldviews
Gender Issues in Counseling
Counseling Lesbian, Gay, Bisexual, Transgender (LGBT), and Other Sexual Minority Clients
Multiple Identities/Biracial, Multiracial

Purposes: The purpose of this activity is to provide a comfortable and safe process for discussing the multidimensional and synergistic nature of identity as it relates to power, privilege, and oppression.

Learning Objectives: As a result of this activity, participants will

- appreciate the multidimensional, fluid, and synergistic nature of identity;
- understand the influence of context on identity;
- recognize the differences between ethnicity, race, and nationality;
- distinguish between biological sex and gender; and
- realize how power, privilege, and oppression are fluid and will fluctuate depending on identity dimensions and contexts.

Target Population: Undergraduate and graduate students as well as professionals

Group Size: The activity works with groups of all sizes. We have conducted this activity with groups as large as 100 and as small as 10.

Time Required: 30–45 minutes

Setting: No specific room design is required. For these types of activities, we usually prefer a circle, but it can be done comfortably with an auditorium design as well.

Materials: The "Socio-Cultural Profile" (SCP) handout and writing utensils

Instructions for Conducting Activity

This is a useful activity when the course lecture or training workshop involves concepts related to power, privilege, and oppression. Hence, it is recommended that facilitators first provide background information to participants on these concepts. Tatum's (2002) article provides a helpful discourse on systems of advantage. The terms used in this exercise are *dominant* (i.e., associated with power and privilege), *subordinate* (i.e., associated with oppression), and *mixed* (i.e., associated with power, privilege, and oppression based on the context, situation, and perspective—personal vs. systemic). Explain to participants that membership in a particular sociocultural group is dominant when the larger system is set up to promote the financial, social, or political interests of that group. Facilitators may want to provide examples (males, heterosexuals, and so forth). In the mixed status, participants often realize that there may be personal oppression (e.g., men are discouraged from expressing their feelings and are at greater risk of substance abuse), but systemic power and privilege exist (e.g., men in general make more money and have more legislative power).

Once the background information has been provided, ask participants to fill out the SCP by identifying their membership in the various categories. For each category, have participants identify whether their membership is dominant, subordinate, or mixed. Let participants know that they can skip any factors they wish, as they may be sharing their profile with a partner. The so-called pair and share is optional, but we have found that it helps participants get comfortable with sharing their thoughts in this area with a person or two first. If you opt to pair participants, we suggest you do it randomly, as it helps build group rapport and cohesion. Allow participants to share their overall experiences with their partner or small group, enumerating lessons learned, questions generated, or confusions produced. If done in dyads, provide 5 minutes; if done in small groups of four or five, provide 15–20 minutes.

Once the participants have had a chance to process the exercise with their partners or groups, consider the following questions with the larger group:

- What did you learn from this activity?
- Was it difficult to identify your membership in a particular factor?
- What role did context play?
- What did you do with sex and gender as identity categories? Did you have one response or two?
- Were their factors that were overtly visible (e.g., skin color)? Invisible (e.g., sexual orientation)? What are the implication of this in terms of power, privilege, and oppression?
- Did you identify memberships for other factors? Past participants have included age, level of education, nationality, language, physical appearance, and so forth.

Facilitators may want to close the activity by sharing key lessons that have been gained from the SCP. For example, Velasquez, Fuentes, Grady, and Gadalla (2004) found in their content analysis the following key lessons:

- Identity is multidimensional. It is made up of a number of sociocultural factors.
- Identity is dynamic and fluid. These factors may interact to enhance, compromise, or neutralize each other.
- Identity is defined by context.
- Aspects of identity are associated to power, privilege, or oppression.
- The SCP promotes comfortable and safe dialogue.

Handout: Handout 56.1: Socio-Cultural Profile

References

Tatum, B. (2002). *"Why are all the Black kids sitting together in the cafeteria?": A psychologist explains the development of racial identity*. New York, NY: Basic Books.

Velasquez, A. E., Fuentes, M. A., Grady S. K., & Gadalla, R. (2004, July). *Teaching multicultural diversity in psychology classes*. Poster session presented at the 112th annual convention of the American Psychological Association, Honolulu, HI.

Additional Readings

Bloom, L. R. (2002). Stories of one's own: Nonunitary subjectivity in narrative representation. In S. B. Merriam (Ed.), *Qualitative research in practice: Examples for discussion and analysis* (pp. 289–309). San Francisco, CA: Jossey-Bass.

Falicov, C. J. (1998). *Latino families in therapy.* New York, NY: Guilford Press.

Fuentes, M. A. (2001, Fall). All Hispanics are not alike. *The Community Psychologist, 34, 35*–36.

Fuentes, M. A. (2003, Fall). Deconstructing diversity: Lessons learned from six blind men and an elephant. *The Community Psychologist, 36,* 23.

Gainor, K. (2001). *Difficult discussions: Talking openly with our students and colleagues about race and privilege.* A keynote presentation at the 2000 January Advance, Agenda for Education in a Democracy, Center of Pedagogy, Montclair State University, Upper Montclair, NJ.

Jones, S. R., & McEwen, M. K. (2000). A conceptual model of multiple dimensions of identity. *Journal of college student development, 41,* 405–413.

Kaplan, J. B. (2003). Use of race and ethnicity in biomedical publication. *Journal of the American Medical Association, 289,* 2709–2716.

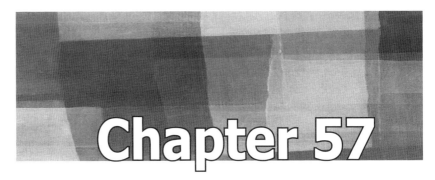

Chapter 57

A Microcosm of My Community

Stephanie F. Hall and Bianca M. Puglia

Topics: Introduction to Multicultural Counseling
Barriers to Effective Cross-Cultural Counseling
Oppression and Discrimination
Multiple Identities/Biracial, Multiracial

Purpose: This activity aims to provide participants with an opportunity to explore and discuss the demographics of the community in which they live, issues and barriers faced by underrepresented populations in their community (e.g., institutional and other types of racism; gender discrimination; and discrimination based on sexual orientation, socioeconomic status [SES], and so forth), and the effects of oppression and discrimination on employment, education, and mental-health-services-seeking behavior. In addition, participants are encouraged to begin exploring White privilege, personal biases, and ways of challenging socialization.

Learning Objectives: As a result of this activity, students will (a) have a better understanding of the ways in which racism, sexism, and other forms of oppression operate in the communities in which they live; (b) gain knowledge about the effect of culture on their behavior as a counselor; and (c) begin to understand cultural barriers to seeking mental health and other community services.

Target Population: Students enrolled in an introductory multicultural counseling course

Group Size: 25 students (or less)

Time Required: 60–90 minutes

Setting: Classroom (chairs can be moved out of the way so that there is a large space for students to interact with one another)

Materials: 3″ × 5″ index cards, demographic data for the community in which the university is seated, flipchart or blackboard

Instructions for Conducting Activity

This activity will require advance preparation by the instructor. Prior to conducting the activity, the instructor should research the community demographics based on race, gender, age, disability, religion, sexuality, and SES. The instructor should begin by engaging the students in a discussion about the demographics of the community in which the university is seated (e.g., Norfolk, VA, or Richmond, KY). Begin by asking the students to guess at demographics related to race, gender, disability, religion, sexual orientation, and SES. Likely, the students will not be aware of the actual numbers, so the instructor should then present them to the class. Next, the instructor will create a microcosm, or mini model, of the community within the classroom. For example: "Out of 25 students, we should have 12 Caucasian students, 9 African American students, 2 Asian students, and 2 Hispanic students. Out of those 25, 15 should be female and 10 should be male. There should be 4 people with a disability." These numbers would also be generated for categories such as religion, sexual orientation, and SES.

Likely, the classroom breakdown will not accurately reflect the community demographics, so then the instructor will generate a discussion of reasons why this might be the case. For example: "In this class, we see that the diversity of this community is not accurately reflected. Let's think of some reasons why that might not be the case." Students are then encouraged to discuss barriers to education based on the above factors. For example, if the class is mostly female, the instructor could ask, "Why do you think that the majority of counseling students are female? Could it be because women are socialized in a way that makes them more comfortable with discussing feelings, helping others, and so forth?" The instructor should discuss topics such as institutional racism and discrimination based on gender, age, disability, religion, sexual orientation, and SES.

Next, students will be asked to stand and will be divided into the appropriate categories. All 25 students will be given an index card on which they will write their profile. First, students will be categorized by race (irrelevant of which categories they actually belong to), then by gender, then age, then disability, then religion, then sexual orientation, then SES. After all categories have been assigned, my profile card might read: "I am an African American male. I have a disability. I am Catholic and heterosexual, and my family income is below poverty level." Another card might read: "I am a Caucasian female. I don't consider myself religious. I am a lesbian, and I fall into the category of high SES." Once all students have a profile card, they are given 5–10 minutes to brainstorm possible challenges that might exist (based on their profile) related to education, employment, and likelihood to seek mental health services.

After brainstorming, students will be divided into groups of two or three for discussion of those challenges and asked to take 20 minutes to share with one another. Then students return to the large group for discussion. As instructor, you will process the comments, reactions, and so forth, and discuss topics such as White privilege, institutional racism, overt and covert racism, sexism, and discrimination based on sexual orientation, religion, SES, age, and so forth. It might be helpful to use a blackboard or flipchart to make lists of the items discussed by members. Then the instructor should ask the class to brainstorm community resources that are available for members of different cultural groups. If students have trouble generating resources, how might they find those resources in the community? As a means of ending the activity, reactions to the discussion should be processed with questions such as the following:

- How did you feel during the activity?
- What did you learn about yourself and others?
- What was the most important learning point for you?
- How will this inform your work as a counselor with other cultural populations?

Additional Readings

Arthur, N., & Achenback, K. (2002). Developing multicultural counseling competencies through experiential learning. *Counselor Education and Supervision, 42,* 2–14.

Kim, B., & Lyons, H. Z. (2003). Experiential activities and multicultural counseling competence training. *Journal of Counseling & Development, 81,* 400–408.

Sue, D. W., Arredondo, P., & McDavis, R. J. (1992). Multicultural counseling competencies and standards: A call to the profession. *Journal of Counseling & Development, 70,* 477–486.

Watson, Z., Herlihy, B. R., & Pierce, L. A. (2006). Forging the link between multicultural competence and ethical counseling practice: A historical perspective. *Counseling and Values, 50,* 99–107.

Zerbe Enns, C., Sinacore, A., Ancis, J. R., & Phillips, J. (2004). Toward integrating feminist and multicultural pedagogies. *Journal of Multicultural Counseling and Development, 32,* 414–427.

Chapter 58
Ethnic and Religious Immersion

Arpana G. Inman

Topics: Introduction to Multicultural Counseling
Oppression and Discrimination
Culturally Skilled Counselor
Career Development
Spirituality

Purposes: This activity aims to provide participants with opportunities to explore the effects of oppression and privilege on members from different cultural backgrounds. In particular, this activity will enhance intergroup and within-group understanding of ethnic and religious communities.

Learning Objectives: As a result of this activity, students will (a) have a better understanding of the effect of racialization of ethnic communities, (b) gain knowledge of the within-group differences, (c) appreciate the similar principles underlying different religions, and (d) develop an empathic stance on the ethnic and religious community experience in the United States.

Target Population: Beginning- or intermediate-level undergraduate, master's, or doctoral students

Group Size: 15 students

Time Required: 5–6 hours (about one-half hour per group) or two class periods, with one class addressing ethnicity and the second addressing religion

Setting: A regular class setting

Materials: Students are encouraged to be creative in terms of their presentation and can be encouraged to bring in any materials they believe would best suit their representation of the community they are presenting. Use of PowerPoint presentations can be an added aspect of the presentation.

Instructions for Conducting Activity

In this didactic and experiential activity, student groups will be formed to address two major topics: ethnicity and religion. For the topic of ethnicity, the group should be further divided into five groups, such as the following: African American, Asian American, Native American, Hispanic American/Latina, and White Americans. For religion, students can be divided into five or six groups labeled, for example, Christianity, Judaism, Hinduism, Buddhist, Muslim, and Atheist. (Additional groups can be added or deleted based on number of students in class and need.) Each group will consist of two or three students (depending on the size of class), who will be responsible for assigned readings, additional research, class presentation, and a summary handout. Based on the readings and research pertinent to the group assigned (e.g., African American or Muslim), group members will learn what it is to be a member of their chosen group and try to articulate how the members of these ethnic and religious groups perceive themselves in context. Most important, for the half-hour presentation, these students will assume the role of the ethnic/religious group. They will present as if they are members of that particular group. Using this lens, three views will be presented: how members of your ethnic/religious group perceive themselves, how others perceive them, and how they would like to be perceived. These three perspectives will be the focus of the presentations and must be supported by statistics and demographics of the group, perceptions/stereotypes held by others, values, challenges, oppressions, and aspects of privilege particular to this ethnic/religious group. The student handout will be a one- or two-page summary that highlights salient issues and includes a reference list (in American Psychological Association's *Publication Manual* format).

Process questions after the activity can include the following: (a) How did it feel to assume (or not assume) the role or persona of a particular group? (b) What was an "aha" moment in learning about this group? (c) How might you apply this learning to your work or interactions with people?

▨ Additional Readings

Anderson, M. L. & Collins, P. H. (2006). *Race, class, and gender: An anthology.* (6th ed.). Belmont, CA: Wadsworth.

Ethnicity

African Americans
Cose, E. (1999, June). The good news about Black America. *Newsweek National Affairs,* 28–37.
Hacker, A. (2003). Dividing American Society. In A. Hacker's *Two nations: Black and White, separate, hostile, unequal* (pp. 3–16). New York, NY: Charles Scribner's Sons. Originally published in 1992.

Native Americans
Ashley, J. S., & Jarratt-Ziemski, K. (1999). Superficiality and bias: The (mis)treatment of Native Americans in U.S. government textbooks. *American Indian Quarterly, 23,* 49–61.
Bird, M. Y. (1999). What we want to be called: Indigenous peoples' perspectives on racial and ethnic identity labels. *American Indian Quarterly, 23,* 1–21.

Asian Americans
Wu, F. H. (2002). The model minority: Asian American "success" as a race relations failure. In F. H. Wu, *Yellow: Race in America beyond Black and White* (pp. 39-77). New York, NY: Basic Books.

Hispanic Americans/Latinas
Melville, M. B. (1988). Hispanics: Race, class, or ethnicity. *The Journal of Ethnic Studies, 16,* 67–83

Religion

White Americans
Adams, M. (2000). Anti-Semitism: Introduction. In M. Adams, W. J. Blumenfeld, R. Castaneda, H.W. Hackman, M. L. Peters, & X. Zuniga (Eds.), *Readings for diversity and social justice: An anthology on racism, anti-Semitism, sexism, heterosexism, ableism, and classism* (pp. 133–137). New York, NY: Routledge.
Eck, D. L. (2003). American Muslims: Cousins and strangers. In J. A. Banks & C. A. Banks (Eds.), *Multicultural education: Issues and perspectives* (5th ed., pp. A3–A31). New York, NY: Wiley.
Kaye/Kantrowitz, M. (2000). Jews in the U.S.: The rising cost of Whiteness. In M. Adams, W. J. Blumenfeld, R. Castaneda, H. W. Hackman, M. L. Peters, & X. Zuniga (Eds.), *Readings for diversity and social justice: An anthology on racism, anti-Semitism, sexism, heterosexism, ableism, and classism* (pp. 138–144). New York, NY: Routledge.
Kincheloe, J. L. (1999). The struggle to define and reinvent Whiteness: A pedagogical analysis. *College Literature, 24*(3)*,* 162–180.
Langman, P. F. (2000). Including Jews in multiculturalism. In M. Adams, W. J. Blumenfeld, R. Castaneda, H.W. Hackman, M. L. Peters, & X. Zuniga (Eds.), *Readings for diversity and social justice: An anthology on racism, anti-Semitism, sexism, heterosexism, ableism, and classism* (pp. 169–177). New York, NY: Routledge.

Lippy, C. H. (2007). Christian nation or pluralistic culture: Religion in American life. In J. A. Banks & C. A. Banks (Eds.), *Multicultural education: Issues and perspectives* (6th ed., pp.109–130). New York, NY: Wiley.

Mennis. B. (2000). Jewish and working class. In M. Adams, W. J. Blumenfeld, R. Castaneda, H. W. Hackman, M. L. Peters, X. Zuniga (Eds.), *Readings for diversity and social justice: An anthology on racism, anti-Semitism, sexism, heterosexism, ableism, and classism* (pp. 188–190). New York, NY: Routledge.

West, C. (2000). On Black–Jewish relations. In M. Adams, W. J. Blumenfeld, R. Castaneda, H. W. Hackman, M. L. Peters, X. Zuniga (Eds.), *Readings for diversity and social justice: An anthology on racism, anti-Semitism, sexism, heterosexism, ableism, and classism* (pp. 177–181). New York, NY: Routledge.

World Religions Index. (n.d.) *Table 2: Buddhism.* Retrieved January 18, 2008, from http://wri.leaderu.com/wri-table2/buddhism.html

World Religions Index. (n.d.) *Table 2: Hinduism.* Retrieved January 18 2008, from http://wri.leaderu.com/wri-table2/hinduism.html

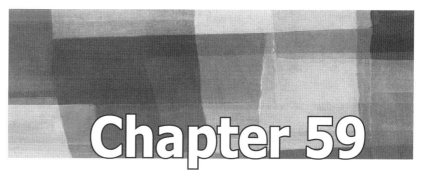

Chapter 59

Multicultural Career Case Conceptualization Role-Plays: Exploring Hidden Biases Through Reflections, Video-Recording, and Small-Group Processing

Margo A. Jackson

Topics: Oppression and Discrimination
Dimensions of Worldviews
Career Development
Helping Relationships
Use of New Technology

Purposes: The purpose of this activity is to develop multicultural self-awareness competencies in career counseling case conceptualization. This activity aims to help counselor-trainees (a) constructively explore and challenge their hidden biases in multicultural career counseling and (b) develop their empathic perspective-taking skills with clients vulnerable to discrimination.

Learning Objectives: As a result of this activity, students will

- increase their awareness of their own automatic negative and unhelpful reactions, attitudes, and worldviews toward issues that clients vulnerable to discrimination may present in career counseling;
- develop a better understanding of their own potential empathic strengths, as well as the client's personal resources or sources of support, that they might apply in multicultural career counseling; and
- practice incorporating their increased multicultural self-awareness of potentially hidden strengths and biases into a basis for refining their hypotheses and theoretical approaches to address career concerns presented by clients vulnerable to discrimination.

Target Population: Graduate student counselor-trainees in courses on career development and counseling

Group Size: Class size of 12–30; divided into role-play partners of two or three students each

Time Required: For activities conducted in class, approximate times required are as follows: (a) Counselor Demographics Exercise and explaining Case Selections homework assignment, 45 minutes; (b) reflecting on case selections, pairing role-play partners, and explaining the homework assignment of Pre-Role-Play Processing Questions, 45 minutes; (c) reflecting on first impressions and explaining the guidelines, 45 minutes; and (d) small-group consultations, 45 minutes for each group—depending on the number of students in the class, these small-group consultations may be scheduled over one to three class periods.

Approximate time required for five homework assignments (case selections, written responses to three sets of processing questions, and video-recording role-plays with partners) is 3–6 hours.

Setting: For in-class activities, a classroom is needed with equipment for viewing videos and chairs that can be moved into small groups. A similar setting (or any room with adequate space, light, and quiet) is needed for the homework assignment to video-record role-plays.

Materials: Materials needed include the textbook *Career Theory and Practice: Learning Through Case Studies* (Swanson & Fouad, 2010), handouts, and student access to equipment for video-recording and viewing.

Instructions for Conducting Activity

Overview

This learning activity spans much of the semester. It incorporates students video-recording role-plays in which they take turns in the counselor role in a multicultural career counseling case. It includes experiential and reflective processing exercises, facilitated in class and through homework assignments, and culminates in small-group consultations focused on students' own unintentional negative biases and hidden strengths in empathic perspective taking with clients whose multicultural issues they find most challenging. In conclusion, students examine how to integrate what they learned relevant to their developing multicultural self-awareness competencies in career counseling case conceptualization. (See Handout 59.1, "Guidelines.")

Swanson and Fouad's (2010) textbook is used as the source of the stimulus case vignettes (see Handout 59.3, "Multicultural Career Case Selections") and adapted core-processing questions (see Handout 59.4, "Pre- and Post-Role-Play Processing Questions for Challenging and Resonant Cases"). Following preparatory exercises in and out of class, core-processing questions are used in four stages of the activity: before and after role-plays, in small-group class consultations on viewing role-play videos, and culminating in reflections to integrate learning. In addition to facilitating in-class exercises, the instructor uses Handouts 59.1–59.5 to present, explain, and collect the products of each stage of the assignment (for which due dates are outlined in the syllabus).

Counselor Demographics Exercise

As a warm-up exercise in a class early in the semester, each student completes the "Multicultural Career Counselor-Trainee Demographic Self-Awareness" handout (Handout 59.2) and jots down his or her reactions; then the instructor facilitates a class discussion on students' reactions (positive or negative) and counseling implications. For example, students may explore their reactions to being asked to describe themselves in ways they might be categorized, stereotyped, or judged in a limited way. Then, they might discuss how their own reactions might be similar to or different from their clients' reactions to completing intake information, particularly information that is relevant to their group memberships or identities that are vulnerable to discrimination. The instructor facilitates a respectful, empathic, and constructively challenging discussion that includes considering the unique and substantial risks to health, safety, and career in disclosing homosexual orientation.

Thereafter, students are prompted at the beginning of each written homework assignment (Handouts 59.3–59.5) to indicate their own demographic information. This is intended as a reminder that they consciously reflect on the influence of their own demographic backgrounds, identities, and worldviews in generating and refining their hypotheses in case conceptualization.

Case Selections

The first homework assignment is to complete a handout (Handout 59.3, "Multicultural Career Case Selections"). Students are instructed to review 21 multicultural career case vignettes from Swanson and Fouad (2010), then to (a) select three cases about which they expect they would be most challenged in developing empathic understanding if they were the counselor, and (b) select three cases for which they could possibly play the role of the client most empathically (i.e., for which they have actual or vicarious experience in such a role and/or could identify with this client).

Pairing and Pre-Role-Play Processing Questions

Before collecting the first homework assignment, the instructor (a) facilitates a class discussion to explore students' reasons for the cases they selected as most challenging and resonant, and (b) prompts students to circulate in the classroom to find a partner to play the client role to his or her counselor role in a case he or she selected as most challenging. (For cases with a couple as clients, students may need more than one partner.) As a homework assignment, students are instructed to use that case (the challenging one in which they will role-play the counselor) to reflect on their first impressions and complete the "Pre-Role-Play Processing Questions" handout (Handout 59.4).

Guidelines for Role-Play Video-Recording Assignment

Before collecting the second homework assignment, the instructor facilitates a class discussion to explore students' responses to the pre-role-play processing questions. Then, the instructor reviews and explains the "Guidelines for the Multicultural Career Case Conceptualization Role-Play" handout (see Handout 59.1). Students are advised about options on how to arrange for an appropriate space and setting, how to gain access to video-recording equipment, and how to produce and store the video-recording on media that they test to ensure that it can reliably be played (clearly viewed and audible) in class for reflections and processing consultations. Also, the instructor gives a brief logistics demonstration in class of setting up and video-recording a test role-play of the first few moments of a mock career counseling session (e.g., with the instructor playing the role of the counselor and a student volunteer playing the role of client).

Small-Group Consultations and Integrating Multicultural Self-Awareness Competencies

On the due date for students to submit their video-recorded role-plays and written responses to the "Post-Role-Play Processing Questions" handout (Handout 59.4), students are required to be prepared in class to take turns in small groups (of four to six students, or two pairs of partners) to play back their video-recorded role-plays. In small-group consultations facilitated by the instructor, students take turns further exploring, from their experience in the counselor role, their own potential hidden biases and empathic strengths relevant to multicultural career counseling issues with the client(s) in the case they selected as most challenging and resonant.

The final homework assignment is to reflect in writing about how they might integrate what they learned overall from this activity relevant to their developing multicultural self-awareness competencies into career counseling case conceptualization (Handout 59.5).

Handouts: Handout 59.1: Guidelines—Multicultural Career Case Conceptualization Role-Play
Handout 59.2: Multicultural Career Counselor–Trainee Demographic Self-Awareness
Handout 59.3: Multicultural Career Case Selections: Most Challenging and Resonant
Handout 59.4: Pre- and Post-Role-Play Processing Questions for Challenging and Resonant Cases
Handout 59.5: Integrating Multicultural Self-Awareness Competencies Into Career Counseling Case Conceptualization

References

Swanson, J. L., & Fouad, N. A. (2010). *Career theory and practice: Learning through case studies* (2nd ed.) Thousand Oaks, CA: Sage.

Additional Readings

American Counseling Association. (1996). *AMCD multicultural counseling competencies.* Retrieved January 2, 2009, from http://www.counseling.org/Resources/

Byars-Winston, A. M., & Fouad, N. A. (2006). Metacognition and multicultural competence: Expanding the culturally appropriate career counseling model. *The Career Development Quarterly, 54,* 187–201.

Jackson, M. A., & Nutini, C. D. (2002). Hidden resources and barriers in career learning assessment with adolescents vulnerable to discrimination. *The Career Development Quarterly, 51,* 56–77.

Chapter 60

What Kinds of Privilege and Oppression Do I Experience?

Susan Kashubeck-West

Topics: Oppression and Discrimination

Purposes: The purpose of this activity is to heighten student awareness of the many cultural identities they possess and the oppression and/or privilege associated with each of these identities.

Learning Objectives: As a result of this activity, students should be able to

- identify their multiple cultural identities,
- discuss levels of oppression and privilege they experience with regard to each of their cultural identities, and
- understand their experiences of privilege and oppression in the context of societal power relations.

Target Population: Graduate students in the mental health professions

Group Size: Any size. If classes are large, break the students into smaller groups for discussion.

Time Required: 30 minutes

Setting: For the discussion portion of this exercise, movable chairs would be helpful if the class is larger than 10 people.

Materials: Enough copies of Handout 60.1, "Who Am I?" for each person in the class. The handout could be modified to add or delete identities that are deemed necessary or unnecessary.

Instructions for Conducting Activity

Have each student complete his or her own handout, "Who Am I?" (adapted from Worell & Remer, 2003). This process will take approximately 5–10 minutes. Following completion of the handout, form discussion groups of 5–10 people.

Sample discussion questions include the following: Were there new identities you had not thought about? Did you identify areas of privilege or oppression you had not been aware of? Which identities are sources of privilege? Which are sources of oppression? Any surprises? How do your identities converge? How does your own experience of privilege/oppression mirror or fail to mirror society's treatment of individuals in this cultural group? How does your own experience of oppression/privilege make you more or less aware of societal oppression/privilege that other individuals might face? Why might your experience of oppression/privilege be different from that of many others with similar identities?

Handout: Handout 60.1: Who Am I?

References

Worell, J., & Remer, P. (2003). *Feminist perspectives in therapy: Empowering diverse women* (2nd ed.). Hoboken, NJ: Wiley.

Additional Readings

Anderson, S. K., & Middleton, V. A. (2011). *Explorations in diversity: Examining privilege and oppression in a multicultural society* (2nd ed.). Belmont, CA: Thomson Brooks/Cole.

Johnson, A. (2005). *Power, privilege, and difference* (2nd ed.). Boston, MA: McGraw-Hill.

Kiselica, M. S. (Ed.). (1999). *Confronting prejudice and racism during multicultural training.* Alexandria, VA: American Counseling Association.

Oppression and Discrimination

Chapter 61

The Greeting Card Experience

Nancy Nishimura

Topics: Barriers to Effective Cross-Cultural Counseling
Cultural Communication Styles
Oppression and Discrimination

Purposes: The purposes of this activity are to have each student experience the impact of White privilege and cultural racism first-hand and to increase their awareness of how an individual's ethnic culture influences everyday activities.

Learning Objectives: As a result of this activity, students will have a better understanding of the effect of White privilege and cultural racism on themselves as well as on persons from other cultural backgrounds.

Target Population: Students in introductory multicultural courses

Group Size: Because this is an out-of-class assignment, group size can vary. It will, however, stimulate much class discussion, so it is recommended that the group be no larger than 20 students.

Time Required: Students should be allowed at least two weeks time to complete the assignment and write a short reaction paper. Class discussion on the day the reaction paper is due will take at least 1 hour. Expect an animated class discussion.

Setting: The room should be arranged in a manner that is conducive to group discussion, that is, chairs or desks arranged in a circle.

Materials: Instructors do not need specific materials. Per instructions below, students must seek out their own materials to complete the task.

Instructions for Conducting Activity

1. Identify a person in your life whom you hold in high esteem.
2. Purchase an "I appreciate you" type card from a store (e-cards are **not** acceptable) that (a) expresses your sentiment toward that person and (b) has a picture on it of a person(s) from a different racial background than the recipient.
3. Mail or deliver the card.

The reaction paper will focus on your (the student's) thoughts **and** feelings, expectations, reactions, and so forth surrounding the experience. This is **not** a "test" for the recipient in any way, although it may be of interest to include his or her reactions or nonreactions in your comments.

Note to the instructor: I have been using this activity for over 8 years and it never fails to create frustration, anxiety, and increased awareness in all the students, both majority and minority students alike. They struggle in locating a card that communicates the sentiment they want to convey **and** has a picture on it of someone who looks different. They often end up going to several stores as a result, making a simple errand a frustrating task.

Additional Readings

Atkinson, D.R. (2004). *Counseling American minorities* (6th ed.). Boston, MA: McGraw-Hill.

Baruth, L. G., & Manning, M. L. (2007). *Multicultural counseling and psychotherapy: A lifespan perspective* (4th ed.). Columbus, OH: Prentice-Hall.

Sue, D. W., & Sue, D. (2003). *Counseling the culturally diverse: Theory and practice* (4th ed.). New York, NY: Wiley.

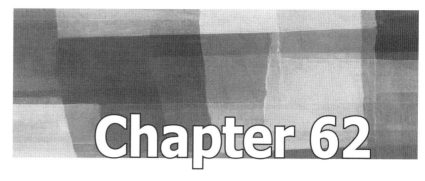

Chapter 62

The Token Activity

Shawn Patrick and Colleen M. Connolly

Topics: Introduction to Multicultural Counseling
Barriers to Effective Cross-Cultural Counseling
Cultural Identity Development
Oppression and Discrimination
Dimensions of Worldviews
Culturally Skilled Counselor
Group Work

Purposes: This activity simulates a group experience wherein participants can gain awareness of dynamics and social forces related to oppression and privilege. Using an experiential approach in a group format provides students with opportunities to examine their behaviors, responses, and judgments experienced (Katz, 1985). As an in-class group activity, this experiential process creates an atmosphere where students reflect on and discuss behaviors, feelings, and thoughts related to this difficult topic in a controlled classroom environment. It allows them to experience the meaning behind being a member of an oppressor group (Kim & Lyons, 2003). This experience also provides students who differ in their individual identity development opportunities to interact with and discuss the activity together (Fier & Ramsey, 2005; Ramsey, 1996). Debriefing and processing of this activity aids students in understanding their own experiences around oppression, places them in a cultural context, and helps develop empathy toward other students with different experiences. Although this particular activity has been used to increase racial awareness, it can also be easily adapted to other important areas, such as disabilities, sexual/affectional orientation, or gender (Collins & Pieterse, 2007).

Learning Objectives: As a result of this activity, students will

- create an experience and develop insight into the experience of holding a great or small amount of power,
- increase knowledge about the effects of oppression on individual actions and thoughts,
- enhance understanding about interactions between those experiencing more versus less power,
- experience the immediacy of a racial/cultural experience and integrate that with their awareness (Collins & Pieterse, 2007),
- integrate the varied and uncomfortable feelings experienced during the activity through the essential debriefing process (Arthur & Achenbach, 2002),
- apply this knowledge and skills acquisition to larger societal processes in order to gain a greater awareness of the systemic nature of oppression,

- expand the class experience from a fixed goal to an ongoing process of engagement in and commitment to future increased levels of awareness (Collins & Pieterse, 2007), and
- amplify cultural self-awareness and move toward eliminating racism and prejudice (Arredondo et al., 1996; Collins & Pieterse, 2007).

Target Population: Graduate-level students in professional counseling programs

Group Size: 15–25 participants

Time Required: Allowing 90 minutes for the entire process is ideal. A minimum of 20 minutes is required for the activity, and approximately 45–60 minutes is necessary for a sufficient debriefing/processing of the experience.

Setting: A classroom where desks or chairs can be arranged on opposite sides of the room and facing each other is recommended. A room allowing adequate space for students to move around is ideal.

Materials: Materials needed include:

- nonmonetary items, such as poker chips, to be used as tokens;
- a time-piece to measure the length of the activity;
- a quarter or other coin for a coin-toss;
- a sufficient number of copies of a culture-specific test that tests specifically within a designated non-White culture (Samuda, 1996, as cited in Gruber, 2000), for example, the Dove Counterbalance General Intelligence Test (Dove, 1968) or the Black Intelligence Test of Cultural Homogeneity (Samuda, 1996, as cited in Gruber, 2000); and
- paper and pencil for facilitator notes.

Instructions for Conducting Activity

1. Set-up of the activity
   a. Begin this token activity in a blind format so that students are initially unaware of the activity's true intent.
   b. The instructor tells students they will be taking a pop-quiz that can cover any material related to the class. Provide a sense of realism by indicating that the "Performance on the quiz is related to success in the course."
   c. To avoid intimating the true nature of the activity, do not answer any questions related to the quiz; instead, provide neutral and ambiguous responses when asked questions.
2. Group designations
   a. To arbitrarily create groups and break up typical groupings, tell students to number off in "ones and twos" and instruct them to separate into two different areas of the room.
   b. Determine the "winning" group through a heads-or-tails coin toss and provide only those members in the winning group with three tokens per person. Announce to the class that each person on the winning side has three tokens.
3. Experiential activity
   a. The instructor informs the class that the quiz will commence in 15 minutes. The instructor states, "Those students who hold two or more tokens will automatically receive a score of 100% on the quiz and will not need to take it. Those students holding less than two tokens or no tokens will receive the grade that is earned. The class gets to decide who will automatically pass and who will not." Do not provide any more instructions, and when asked questions, repeat the instructions. No more instructions are provided, and any questions are answered with a repeat of the instructions.
   b. During these 15 minutes, refrain from contact with the students, make observations about student interactions and dynamics, and discreetly take process notes. These steps will help to more effectively facilitate the debriefing and processing section of this activity.

Oppression and Discrimination

c. Continuing the activity for the full 15 minutes is essential so as to allow sufficient time for students to gain a more accurate sense of their emotions, thoughts, and reactions. Even when students come to a quick initial decision, the ensuing discussion remains very useful to the experience.

d. It should be noted that students may attempt to "bend the rules" by attempting to share tokens with each other or steal tokens from the instructor. The instructor can respond to these situations with simple statements such as, "That would be considered cheating on the test, and those who cheat would automatically fail." These behaviors and attempts, though, should be noted in the process notes and discussed during the debriefing.

e. The instructor alerts when 1 minute remains then calls time when the 15 minutes are up.

4. Quiz administration

a. The instructor asks students with one or no tokens to raise their hand and distributes the quiz to those students. Once all quizzes are distributed, students may begin. They are given 5 minutes to complete the quiz.

b. Students with two or more tokens are provided a copy of the quiz, reminded they are not required to take the quiz, but are encouraged to see how many questions they would have answered correctly.

c. After 5 minutes, the instructor calls time. It is essential at this point to inform the class that no grade is attached to the quiz or to anyone's behavior from the activity. Grading the quiz can be saved until later in the class to prevent the quiz experience from clouding the activity experience. If so, announce to the class that the quiz will be graded later, but first it is important to debrief and process the activity.

5. General and contextual debriefing

a. Begin by processing what the students thought were the intentions of the activity. After they generate their own ideas about the activity, then inform them that the intended purpose of the activity was to highlight power and the strong influence power has on behaviors, beliefs, and self-concept.

b. Convey to the students that the thoughts, actions, and feelings generated in the activity were related to being placed in an intolerable situation. It is important to highlight that this activity was not intended to judge anyone's character but, rather, to allow them to experience the processes that can spawn from an oppressive system.

c. Occasionally students attempt to criticize behaviors they deemed "unworthy." If students begin to direct such comments toward certain individuals, the instructor must immediately intervene and facilitate a discussion. These discussions can result in rich opportunities for addressing emotions and generating meaning around social interactions that are shaped by feelings of power or powerlessness. These discussions should not be glossed over, ignored, or dismissed.

d. This time is also critical for addressing students' feelings about the experience, and opportunities should be used to help generate meaning around and normalize potentially uncomfortable feelings.

6. Group processing

a. The instructor starts by asking for any general comments or observations students have about their experience.

b. The instructor then asks specific questions of each group, starting with the group who had tokens at the start and then shifting to the non-token group. Maintaining some structure around having one group speak at a time often aids the discussion as students are often eager to jump in with their immediate thoughts. However, slowing the discussion to focus on one group at a time allows others to listen and incorporate more information and experiences.

c. Questions that involve the decisions and methods of either giving or receiving tokens and the feelings of power or disempowerment are important to address. Some examples are as follows:
   (1) What were the students' feelings and thoughts when they realized that they had three tokens or no tokens?

(2) Which group acted first?

(3) Who did most of the talking?

(4) Who declined to speak?

(5) What methods were used to gain tokens or to persuade others to give up tokens?

(6) What thoughts and feelings motivated the responses?

d. The instructor then guides the questions back to the large group in order to link the activity back to the textbook (Sue & Sue, 2008), readings, class concepts, and real-world scenarios. Examples are as follows:

(1) What made the first group powerful?

(2) How was power displayed?

(3) How is power usually determined?

(4) How was it assigned here?

(5) How does this activity relate to real-life situations?

(6) What actions and attitudes did students see people engage in that are similar to those people or groups who are continually oppressed and to those who tend to hold more power?

e. Elicit specific examples of what occurred within the activity to allow students to situate those actions into a broader context and make more sense of the situations experienced.

7. Quiz processing:

a. After processing the activity, the quiz can be graded as a group. Group grading allows for discussion around the content of the questions. After grading, the ratio of students who "passed" to those who "failed" can be determined.

b. Regarding the quiz itself, because there are usually very few who pass, this experience can also lead to a discussion on the effects of biased testing and the impact of such decisions on society.

▨ References

Arredondo, P., Toporek, R. L., Brown, S. P., Jones, J., Locke, D. C., Sanchez, J., & Stadler, H. (1996). Operationalization of the multicultural counseling competencies. *Journal of Multicultural Counseling and Development, 24*, 42–78.

Arthur, N., & Achenbach, K. (2002). Developing multicultural counseling competencies through experiential learning. *Counselor Education and Supervision, 42*, 2–14.

Collins, N. M., & Pieterse, A. L. (2007). Critical incident analysis based training: An approach for developing active racial/cultural awareness. *Journal of Counseling & Development, 85*, 14–23.

Dove, A. (1968, July 15). Taking the chitling test. *Newsweek, 72*(3), 51–52.

Fier, E. B., & Ramsey, M. (2005). Ethical challenges in the teaching of multicultural course work. *Journal of Multicultural Counseling and Development, 33*, 94–107.

Gruber, G. A. (2000, March). *Standardized testing and employment equity career counseling: A literature review of six tests*. Retrieved from the Employment Equity Career Development Office, Public Service Commission of Canada, http://www.psc-cfp.gc.ca/ee/eecco/pdf/standardized_e.pdf

Katz, J. H. (1985). The sociopolitical nature of counseling. *Counseling Psychologist, 13*(4), 615–624.

Kim, B., & Lyons, H. (2003). Experiential activities and multicultural counseling competence training. *Journal of Counseling & Development, 81*, 400–408.

Ramsey, M. (1996). Diversity identity development training: Theory informs practice. *Journal of Multicultural Counseling and Development, 24*, 229–240.

Sue, D. W., & Sue, D. (2008). *Counseling the culturally diverse: Theory and practice* (5th ed.). Hoboken, NJ: Wiley.

▨ Additional Readings

DeRicco, J. N., & Sciarra, D. T. (2005). The immersion experience in multicultural counselor training: Confronting covert racism. *Journal of Multicultural Counseling and Development, 33*, 2–16.

Helms, J. E., Malone, L. T. S., Henze, K., Satiani, A., Perry, J., & Warren, A. (2003). First annual diversity challenge: How to survive teaching courses on race and culture. *Journal of Multicultural Counseling and Development, 31*, 3–11.

Patrick, S., & Connolly, C. M. (2008). *The token activity: Generating awareness of power in counseling relationships.* Manuscript submitted for publication.

Pedersen, P. (2000). *A handbook for developing multicultural awareness* (3rd ed.). Alexandria, VA: American Counseling Association.

Reynolds, A. (1995). Challenges and strategies for teaching multicultural counseling courses. In J. G. Ponterotto, J. M. Casas, L. A. Suzuki, & C. M. Alexander (Eds.), *Handbook of multicultural counseling* (pp. 312–330). Thousand Oaks, CA: Sage.

Sevig, T., & Etzkorn, J. (2001). Transformative training: A year-long multicultural counseling seminar for graduate students. *Journal of Multicultural Counseling and Development, 29*, 57–73.

Sue, D. W., Arredondo, P., & McDavis, R. (1992). Multicultural counseling competencies and standards: A call to the profession. *Journal of Counseling & Development, 70*, 477–486.

Sue, D. W., & Sue, D. (2008). *Counseling the culturally diverse: Theory and practice* (5th ed.). Hoboken, NJ: Wiley.

Website

The following website is given as a source for locating public-domain versions of tests that demonstrate cultural bias. Copies of the tests, along with scoring information, are provided at the following Internet address: http://www.wilderdom.com/personality/intelligenceCulturalBias.html

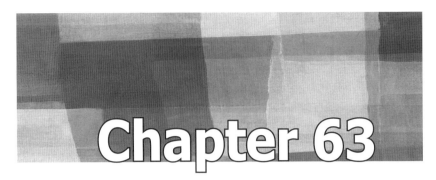

Chapter 63
Oppression Blues/Rap

Adelaida Santana Pellicier

Topics: Oppression and Discrimination
      Creative Arts

Purposes: The purpose of this activity is to review and verbalize the effects of oppression (and -isms, including racism; xenophobia; and so forth) on victims.

Learning Objective: Students will be able to verbalize a definition of and feelings about the impact of oppression on the victims.

Group Size: 10–30 participants

Time Required: 1–2 hours, depending on group size

Materials: Pens or pencils and paper; music to a rap or blues song in which the artist is singing about something quite painful

Instructions for Conducting Activity

1. This activity may be used as an introduction to the concept of oppression, racism, and so forth (inclusive of homo- and xeno- phobias); it also may be used immediately after viewing a film such as *Color of Fear* (Mun Wah, 1994), *Last Chance for Eden* (Mun Wah, 2003), or *Prayers for Bobby* (Mulcahy, 2009).
2. Form small groups of three or four individuals.
3. Explain to the class that they are to write two stanzas using the music to their favorite rap or blues song, or they may select the music from those provided by the facilitator.
4. Ask each group to select a group member to record the stanzas with the names of all group members.
5. Ask the class to recall how they felt after watching a video/DVD on oppression (racism, homophobia, and so forth) and to write out these feelings as a rap or blues song of how it feels to be oppressed (or how they felt as they watched the film). Remind groups to select their own rhythm or use one provided by the facilitator. Each group will be presenting their rap or "song" to the class collectively, or the group may select an individual to rap or sing it.
6. Allow at least 15 minutes for the groups to complete this part of the assignment. It may take 20 minutes; facilitator can watch groups to determine when more time is necessary.
7. After all groups are finished, ask each group to sing or rap their respective song.
8. After all groups have contributed their work, collect the songs and type into a word-process or for distribution at the next class. You may ask for a volunteer to do the latter.

Processing

1. Ask each group to report on the process they undertook to write their stanzas and to share their feelings on the process.
2. Ask the class to share any additional illuminating thoughts or reactions that they experienced during the exercise (or the film).

References

Mulcahy, R. (Director). (2009). *Prayers for Bobby* [Television Broadcast]. U.S.A.: Lifetime.

Mun Wah, L. (Director). (1994). *The color of fear* [DVD]. Berkeley, CA: StirFry Seminars and Consulting.

Mun Wah, L. (Director). (2003). *Last chance for Eden* [DVD]. Berkeley, CA: StirFry Seminars and Consulting.

Additional Readings

Sue, D. W., & Sue, D. (2008). (5th ed.). *Counseling the culturally diverse: Theory and practice*. New York, NY: Wiley.

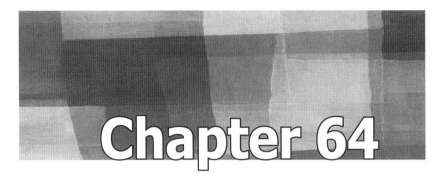

Chapter 64

Oppression Oppresses: Which "Dominant" or "Target" Cultures Do You Belong To?

Mark Pope

Topics: Introduction to Multicultural Counseling
Definitions of Cultural Diversity
Four Forces in Counseling
Oppression and Discrimination
Dimensions of Worldviews

Purposes: This activity is designed to enable students to understand that oppression oppresses; that is, those exposed to discrimination and prejudice are most likely to internalize negative feelings about their cultural groups. This goal is accomplished by having students explore the difference between a dominant culture and a target culture to see that culture is complex and dynamic and may vary from one country to another. It is a particularly effective activity to conduct early in the development of a classroom's culture, as it aids in the development of the common definitions and sensitizes the students to these important issues.

Learning Objectives: After the activity, participants will

- understand that oppression oppresses even the mentally healthy people in a society and that those exposed to discrimination and prejudice are most likely to internalize negative feelings about their cultural groups;
- have knowledge of the definitions of *dominant culture* and *target culture*;
- understand that culture is complex, dynamic, broad, and inclusive; and
- understand that the categorization of dominant and target cultures may vary from one country to another.

Target Population: Undergraduate or graduate students in counseling, education, psychology, or social work

Group Size: 15–30 participants

Time Required: 50–90 minutes

Setting: Classroom setting

Materials: White- or chalkboard or flipcharts, handouts of the "Diversity Profile" (Handout 64.1) and "Umbrella of Oppression" (Handout 64.2)

Instructions for Conducting Activity

1. The instructor will first read instructions for completing the diversity profile at the top of that handout (see Handout 64.1): "For each personal descriptive category below (i.e., ethnicity, gender, and so forth), place a check in the appropriate column indicating whether you **perceive** yourself as belonging to a dominant or target group. *Dominant* is defined as membership in the majority group that possesses the most power and influence in our society and tends to unintentionally or deliberately discriminate against, devalue, or oppress the target groups."

2. Then the instructor will allow the students time to complete the handout, instructing them not to talk to each other during this process and reminding them that it is important for their responses to describe their beliefs and attitudes.

3. In small groups (five or six persons), have the students identify and develop a consensus of the dominant culture of the United States in each category (ethnicity, gender, sexual orientation, and so forth) and also compare their completed handout with the dominant culture consensus, noting especially where they were in the target culture.

4. In the full class, have each group report their consensus for the United States' dominant culture categories selections and discuss the differences between each group's responses. Discuss how they arrived at their responses. Discuss how power and influence affected their responses. Identify who's in and who's out.

5. Introduce the "Umbrella of Oppression" handout as a way to continue the debriefing of the group. For example, here are some discussion starters:
   a. "All of this fits under the big, overarching ways that individuals can be oppressed, can be discriminated against in our society."
   b. "Oppression oppresses, and those exposed to discrimination and prejudice are most likely to internalize negative feelings about their cultural identity."
   c. "When someone keeps telling you how bad you are, it is difficult to feel good about yourself."
   d. "Positive identity is not easily attained in a society."
   e. "Sometimes a person from a target culture overidentifies with the dominant culture and feels that some aspect of his or her own culture is especially negative."
   f. "There must be something wrong with me because they say I'm . . ."
      (1) African American—maybe my hair **is** too curly.
      (2) Asian American—maybe I need to dye my hair blonde.
      (3) Native American—maybe I shouldn't smudge my new house before I move in.
      (4) Latin American—maybe I should **only** speak English.
      (5) Lesbian, gay, bisexual, or transgendered—maybe I **am** sick and perverse.

Handouts: Handout 64.1: Diversity Profile
                 Handout 64.2: The Umbrella of Oppression

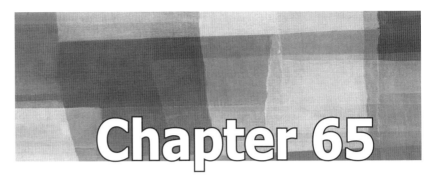

Chapter 65

Systemic/Organizational/Institutional (S/O/I) Transference Exercise

Ellen L. Short

Topics: Definitions of Cultural Diversity
Four Forces in Counseling
Oppression and Discrimination
Culturally Skilled Counselor
Career Development

Purposes: The purpose of this activity is to provide participants with opportunities to explore their conscious and unconscious transferential relationships to systems, organizations, and institutions (S/O/I) in which they work and/or are educated. The activity is psychodynamically oriented because of its emphasis on transference; it can also access/identify issues of institutional oppression and discrimination; and it emphasizes the importance of understanding systems and role for the culturally skilled counselor. The activity also provides participants with opportunities to (a) identify and explore the cultural profile of their chosen S/O/I; (b) identify and explore their own cultural identities/affiliations (outside of the S/O/I); (c) explore the relationship between their cultural identity/affiliation and the cultural profile of their S/O/I and the impact that the relationship may have on their professional behavior, identity, and work ethic; (d) identify and explore their role within the S/O/I as it exists; (e) explore the relationship between their family role and their S/O/I role; and (f) explore the possibility of change and transformation of their S/O/I role to facilitate increased satisfaction and attainment of goals.

Learning Objectives: As a result of participating in these exercises, students will (a) have a better understanding of the effect of culture and systems on their behavior as group leaders/facilitators, (b) have increased levels of cultural self-awareness that will help them be supportive of their clients' needs to identify and explore their own personal and systemic cultural identity/affiliation in group settings, (c) have increased levels of cultural self-awareness that will help them to more effectively manage their anxieties (e.g., as group leaders/facilitators) about openly exploring cultural and systemic issues with clients in groups, and (d) have a clearer focus on aspects of change and transformation concerning boundaries, authority, role, and task within S/O/Is—for themselves as group leaders/facilitators (and potential agents of change) and for their clients.

Target Population: Adults in all occupational, educational, and mental health settings

Group Size: 5–10 participants

Time Required: Each section of the exercise should be done in discrete sessions of 1 hour each: one introductory session + six sessions, for a total of seven sessions/hours.

Setting: Boundaried space—to assure confidentiality, the space should have privacy; chairs should be in a circle.

Materials: Large Post-it pages, markers of different colors

Instructions for Conducting Activity

An introduction to the exercise should be provided. The group leader/facilitator should explain the purpose of the exercise, emphasizing the need for respect among group members and confidentiality. Specific language and terms that will be used in the exercise should be outlined (see Handout 65.1). It is recommended that the group leader/facilitator provide a warm-up and/or introductory exercise before beginning the exercise for each session (e.g., playing music for relaxation, using meditation exercises, and so forth to stimulate creativity and the unconscious processes). For the drawings, Post-it pages can be placed on the walls, tables, floors, and so forth for participants to use. The participants should use the Post-it pages and markers for all of their drawings, and the drawings should be reflective of their individuality and creativity for each exercise. The drawings should be saved at the end of each session by the group leader/facilitator, stored in a safe and confidential space, and brought back to each session for participants to revisit, review, and connect to drawings done in subsequent sessions. At the end of all six sessions, the group members should be allowed to take their drawings with them. Exercises 1-5 will require the group members to create a specific drawing. For example, in Exercise 1 the group leader/facilitator will instruct the members to draw a picture of their S/O/I (see Exercise 1), and for Exercise 2, the group members will be asked to draw pictures of themselves (see Exercise 2). For Exercise 3 the group members will be asked to draw a picture of their S/O/I and themselves together on the same page. Exercise 4 will require them to draw themselves in their family and S/O/I roles, and Exercise 5 requires them to draw themselves in their transformed S/O/I roles (see Exercises 3, 4, and 5). During each session, it is recommended that the group leader/facilitator instruct all of the group members to draw at the same time and place a time boundary around the amount of time provided to complete the drawing task, which will then allow more time for interpretation and discussion. The drawings often reveal conscious and unconscious material; group leaders/facilitators should encourage group members to provide interpretations of their drawings during each session. If individuals are from the same S/O/I within the group, the group leader/facilitator should encourage them to comment on their peers' descriptions and drawings in order to provide multiple perspectives of what the member has expressed. To ensure confidentiality and freedom of expression, it is recommended that groups be composed of individuals who are peers and/or at the same levels of hierarchy (e.g., when from the same S/O/I). The final review and discussion session should focus on integrating material focused on in all of the sessions. Individual attention by the group leader/facilitator should be given to each group member, and members should be encouraged to provide concrete examples of their learning as well as ideas about application of it to their S/O/Is and other group affiliations. Group leaders/facilitators should caution the group members to be careful with applications of new learning within their S/O/I and other environments. Group leaders/facilitators should also encourage members to seek additional support from counseling and psychotherapy, should they need more guidance.

Participants will be asked to do the following activities:

1. Identify and explore the cultural profile of their chosen S/O/I.
   Describe your S/O/I's cultural profile:
   a. Does your S/O/I have a *universal* culture (Carter, 2000)?
   b. Does your S/O/I have a *ubiquitous* culture (Carter, 2000)?
   c. Does your S/O/I have a *traditional* culture (Carter, 2000)?
   d. Does your S/O/I have a *race-based* culture (Carter, 2000)?

   Describe your S/O/I's levels of *embeddedness* (Alderfer, 1997, 2000).

Systemic/Organizational/Institutional Transference Exercise

e. What country is it located in?

f. What city or region is it located in?

g. What entity is the S/O/I owned by? Are there more than one of your S/O/I?

h. What are some of the known rules and regulations of your S/O/I?

i. What are some of the secrets, myths, and unspoken rules and regulations of your S/O/I?

j. What type of resources does your S/O/I have?

k. What is the history of your S/O/I (as you know it)?

l. What does your S/O/I look like? Is it vertically shaped (e.g., with a distinct hierarchy of power from top to bottom) or horizontally shaped (e.g., with even levels of power)?

What metaphor would you use to describe your S/O/I?

Draw a picture of your S/O/I.

2. Identify and explore your own cultural identities/affiliations.

a. What is your race?

b. What is your ethnicity?

c. What is your gender?

d. What is your age?

e. What is your sexual orientation?

f. What is your religious or spiritual affiliation?

g. What is your level of physical ability/disability?

h. What language(s) do you speak?

Describe any other aspects of your identity that are important to you.

What metaphor would you use to describe yourself?

Draw a picture of yourself.

3. Explore the relationship between your cultural identity and your S/O/I's cultural profile.

a. Think about the metaphor that you've chosen to describe yourself.

b. Think about the metaphor that you've chosen to describe your S/O/I.

c. Explore how the two metaphors are related or not related.

d. Draw a picture of your S/O/I and yourself together (on the same page).

e. Explore how the two drawings are related or not related.

f. Explore what the two drawings look like together and your feelings about them.

4. Identify and explore your role in the S/O/I as it exists. Using your S/O/I's cultural profile:

a. Describe your S/O/I's boundaries (BART; Hayden & Molenkamp, 2004).

b. Describe your S/O/I's levels of authority (BART; Hayden & Molenkamp, 2004).

c. Describe your role in your S/O/I (BART; Hayden & Molenkamp, 2004).

d. Describe your task in your S/O/I (BART; Hayden & Molenkamp, 2004).

Identify and explore your family role as it exists.

e. Describe your family role.

f. Draw yourself in role in your family (Beck, 2008).

g. Describe your S/O/I role (use above description).

h. Draw yourself in role in your S/O/I (Beck, 2008).

Explore how the family + S/O/I roles are similar or dissimilar (Beck, 2008).

What metaphor would you use to describe your role in your family?

What metaphor would you use to describe your role in your S/O/I?

5. Explore the possibility of change and transformation of your role in your S/O/I.

a. Describe your S/O/I role as you would like it to be.

b. Draw yourself in your transformed S/O/I role.

Explore how the drawings of your family role, your current S/O/I role, and your transformed S/O/I role look.

What similarities and/or differences between the drawings do you notice?

Handout: Handout 65.1: Systemic/Organizational/Institutional (S/O/I) Transference Exercise

Oppression and Discrimination

References

Agnes, M., Goldman, J. L., & Soltis, K. (Eds.). (2002). *Webster's new compact desk dictionary and style guide*. Cleveland, OH: Wiley.

Alderfer, C. P. (1997). Embedded intergroup relations and racial identity development theory. In C. E. Thompson & R. T. Carter (Eds.), *Racial identity theory: Applications to individual, group, and organizational interventions* (pp. 237–263). Mahwah, NJ: Erlbaum.

Alderfer, C. P. (2000). National culture and the new language for race relations. In R. T. Carter (Ed.), *Addressing cultural issues in organizations. Beyond the corporate context* (pp. 19–31). Thousand Oaks, CA: Sage.

Beck, U. (2008, April/May). Psychodynamic coaching. *Leadership across the globe: Transforming organizations and relationships*. Symposium conducted at the A. K. Rice Institute 2008 Workshop, Chicago, IL.

Carter, R. T. (2000). Perspectives on addressing cultural issues in organizations. In R. T. Carter (Ed.), *Addressing cultural issues in organizations: Beyond the corporate context* (pp. 3–18). Thousand Oaks, CA: Sage.

Corey, G. (2009). *Theory and practice of counseling and psychotherapy* (8th ed.). Belmont, CA: Thomson/Brooks/Cole.

Hayden, C., & Molenkamp, R. J. (2004). Tavistock primer II. In S. Cytrynbaum & D. A. Noumair (Eds.), *Group dynamics, organizational irrationality, and social complexity: Group relations reader 3* (pp. 135–157). Jupiter, FL: A. K. Rice Institute for the Study of Social Systems.

Short, E. L. (2009, March). *Systemic/Organizational/Institutional (S/O/I) transference exercise*. Paper presented at the Families Symposium, sponsored by the New York Center for the Study of Groups, Organizations and Social Systems, New York, NY.

Chapter 66

Exploring Power and Privilege:
Making the Invisible Knapsack Visible

Allison L. Smith

Topics: Definitions of Cultural Diversity
Oppression and Discrimination
Dimensions of Worldviews
Culturally Skilled Counselor
Group Work
Creative Arts

Purposes: The purpose of this activity is to explore privilege and disadvantage using Peggy McIntosh's (1989) notion of the invisible knapsack (an invisible package of unearned resources and special supplies). The activity serves as a way to enhance the notion of White power and privilege along with other types of power and privilege (i.e., dominant group status with regard to sexual orientation, gender, race, religion, class, region, handedness, nationality, and so forth). By using the concept of the invisible knapsack, participants will be encouraged to unpack their own experiences of having been given unearned resources and special supplies. This process will bring to life their unique experiences with power and privilege.

Learning Objectives: As a result of the activity students will (a) increase their knowledge of White and/or majority status power and privilege, (b) explore ways that power and privilege impact their lives, and (c) "unpack" their knapsacks in order to gain a deeper understanding of their unique experience with power and privilege.

Target Population: This activity is designed for students in a counseling or counseling-related program enrolled in a multiculturalism course.

Group Size: The activity is designed for both large- and small-group formats, with no more than five members per small group.

Time Required: The activity will take approximately 1 hour and 45 minutes.

Materials: Materials include a copy of Peggy McIntosh's (1989) article (Handout 53.1); Peggy McIntosh's "Some Notes for Facilitators on Presenting White Privilege and the Invisible Knapsack" (Handout 53.2); and collage-making materials, such as magazines, scissors, markers, glue, pastels, colored pencils, and crayons.

Instructions for Conducting Activity

1. Instructor assigns McIntosh's article, "White Privilege: Unpacking the Invisible Knapsack" (Handout 53.1), for students to read prior to class. As a large group, instructor discusses the ideas of privilege and disadvantage.
2. Instructor asks students to form small groups (up to five students per group) and discuss the following questions:
   a. Discuss some elements of your own privilege and disadvantage. What kinds of privilege and power do you have, in particular? What kinds of unearned disadvantages? What types of privilege or disadvantage apply to you—for example, White privilege, male privilege, able-bodied privilege, sexual orientation privilege?
   b. Is the notion of power and privilege a new concept for you? Or were you aware of systemic advantage and disadvantage before this class?
   c. Out of Peggy McIntosh's autobiographical examples of daily effects of privileges, are there any that apply to your experience?
   d. What parts of your invisible knapsack do you feel are especially important for you to explore, understand, and unpack? (15 minutes)
3. Make your invisible knapsack of privileges visible. In the small groups, each group member creates his or her own invisible knapsack. Use words, pictures, colors, and so forth to create the knapsack in order to make it visible. Students create their knapsacks by using collage materials, such as magazines, scissors, markers, glue, pastels, colored pencils, and crayons (30 minutes).
4. After creating knapsacks, students share their collages in the small groups (15 minutes).
5. Pick one volunteer per group to share and describe her or his knapsack to the large group (15 minutes).
6. As a large group, process how the knapsacks were similar and unique.
   a. What kinds of individual power and privileges were unpacked?
   b. How can we continue to explore and unpack these privileges?
   c. Are there other privileges and power that were not mentioned?
   d. Why is it important to explore power and privilege as a counselor-in-training? (15 minutes)

Handouts: Handout 53.1: McIntosh's (1989) article, "White Privilege: Unpacking the Invisible Knapsack"
Handout 53.2: McIntosh's "Some Notes for Facilitators on Presenting White Privilege and the Invisible Knapsack"

References

McIntosh, P. (1989, July/August). White privilege: Unpacking the invisible knapsack. *Peace and Freedom*, 10–12.

Additional Readings

Ancis, J., & Szymanski, D. (2001, July). Awareness of White privilege among White counseling trainees. *Counseling Psychologist, 29*, 548–569. Retrieved December 10, 2008. doi: 10.1177/0011000001294005.

Bell, L., Love, B., & Roberts, R. (2007). Racism and White privilege curriculum design. In M. Adams, L. A. Bell, & P. Griffin (Eds.), *Teaching for diversity and social justice* (2nd ed., pp. 123–144). New York, NY: Routledge/Taylor & Francis Group. Retrieved December 11, 2008, from PsycINFO database.

Black, L., & Stone, D. (2005). Expanding the definition of privilege: The concept of social privilege. *Journal of Multicultural Counseling and Development, 33,* 243–255.

Liu, W. M., Pickett, T., & Ivey, A. (2007). White middle-class privilege: Social class bias and implications for training and practice. *Journal of Multicultural Counseling and Development, 35,* 194–206.

Manglitz, E. (2003, February). Challenging White privilege in adult education: A critical review of the literature. *Adult Education Quarterly, 53,* 119–134. Retrieved December 10, 2008. doi: 10.1177/0741713602238907.

Niehuis, S. (2005, December). Helping White students explore White privilege outside the classroom. *North American Journal of Psychology, 7*, 481–492. Retrieved December 10, 2008, from PsycINFO database.

Sue, D. (2006). The invisible Whiteness of being: Whiteness, White supremacy, White privilege, and racism. In M. G. Constantine & D. W. Sue (Eds.), *Addressing racism: Facilitating cultural competence in mental health and educational settings* (pp. 15–30). Hoboken, NJ: Wiley. Retrieved December 10, 2008, from PsycINFO database.

Chapter 67

Take a Walk in My Shoes

Sherri Snyder-Roche

Topics: Introduction to Multicultural Counseling
Cultural Identity Development
Culturally Skilled Counselor
Multiple Identities/Biracial, Multiracial

Purposes: The purpose of this experiential exercise is to expand students' awareness of discrimination; increase student's ability to be compassionate and empathic toward individuals with disabilities and "differences"; increase students' ability to observe and reflect on their own biases, prejudices, and stereotypic thoughts; increase students' ability to understand how societal discrimination and prejudice may affect an individual (and create barriers and limitations); and increase students' awareness of barriers (psychological, physical, societal) to individuals' obtaining support and culturally effective psychotherapy. The activity aims to provide participants with opportunities to explore the effect of prejudice, oppression, and stereotyping on their professional development. This activity also enhances participants' compassion for differences. Guided imagery is a powerful tool, and in this exercise it is used to help students increase empathy for others by "stepping into their shoes" momentarily.

I have used this experiential exercise with a variety of populations and settings, including college classrooms (both undergraduate and graduate level), corporate settings, small and large companies, counseling agencies, and municipalities. Unlike didactic or lecture-type workshops, which provide information, this workshop is experiential in nature. As cited in the *Handbook of College Teaching: Theory and Application*, experiential learning provides more active learning and self-exploration and increases participants' sense of ownership of learned material. With increased ownership comes greater likelihood of students' internalizing and actually using what they learn outside of class (Prichard & Sawyer, 1994, p. 114). We can never really know how another person feels or thinks. However, through this exercise, students are challenged to imagine how another person might experience life and, it is hoped, to draw inward and outward toward inquiry.

Learning Objectives: As a result of this exercise, students will (a) increase their awareness of their own prejudices, (b) increase their sensitivity to the impact of societal prejudice on potential clients, (c) increase their awareness of creating a culturally sensitive counseling environment (through use of language, written material, and so forth), and (d) use guided imagery to increase their empathy for others who are different from themselves.

Target Population: This activity is specifically designed for graduate students studying in the counseling and mental health field (including, but not limited to, the expressive therapies, psychology, counseling, human health services, and social work).

Group Size: The ideal group size is less than 30 to provide sufficient trust, intimacy, and time to process reactions to the exercise. Ideal group size is 15–25 participants.

Time Required: 1.5 to 2 hours, depending on the size of the group

Setting: Students will need tables or desks on which they may write or draw after the exercise. To promote classroom discussion, tables may be set up in a U shape.

Materials: The instructor will need to create identity index cards in advance. Each index card will have one identity written on it. A list of suggested identities is given below. Collect the cards after the completion of the exercise so they may be reused. Participants will need writing materials (pen and paper is sufficient). Drawing materials may also be used and made available (large paper 18″ × 24″, markers, oil pastels), providing participants a choice of response materials.

Instructions for Conducting Activity

A script is prepared for the instructor and may be read exactly as is to students. Make sure to leave ample pause-time between questions. No other introduction is necessary.

Script to Be Read to Participants

Today's exercise is to explore stereotype, discrimination, and oppression and the impact of these on our potential counseling clients. Rather than discuss these, we will go on a journey together through a guided imagery. Each of you will be given an identity on an index card. You will become this person temporarily for the purpose of this exercise. I will then lead a guided imagery, which will take about 20 minutes. For some people, you may feel uncomfortable, silly, or even anxious. Please pay attention to the feelings that are evoked. This is a learning exercise and is not meant to be traumatizing. However, for some people, it can bring up very uncomfortable emotions. If you need to leave the room, you may do so, but try to return to complete the exercise. After the guided imagery, you will be invited to process your experience through writing or drawing. You will have approximately 20 minutes for this part. Following that, we will have a group discussion about your reactions and responses. Any questions before we get started? (*Distribute index cards to all participants.*) If an identity is too similar to whom you really are, I suggest that you change cards. The exercise is meant to challenge you. As you take your index card, take a few minutes to take on your identity." (*Pause. If there is chatter, encourage quiet space for students to imagine their new identity.*)

Guided Imagery Script

(**Instructor:** *Make sure to pause between statements and questions to provide participants ample time to process image information*). You may either keep your eyes open or close them. Take a few deep breaths to get settled in your chair. Image yourself as the individual on the card. Imagine what you are wearing. What kinds of clothes, jewelry, hairstyle? Imagine your living environment, your home, apartment? House? And who lives with you? Who cooks? Who cleans? What does your home look like? What kind of furniture do you have? How is it decorated? Who decorated it? How do you feel in your home? (*Longer pause here.*) Now, imagine you are leaving your home on your way to work: as you proceed down the street, how do others look at you? As you proceed to work, how do you travel? Are you with anyone? Do you need assistance? When you arrive at work, what is the atmosphere? Do you have friends at work? How do you relate to your coworkers? Would you feel comfortable talking with them about personal issues? Are there any barriers to this? How do you think others perceive you? (*Longer pause.*) After work, you decide to go shopping. Where do you shop? How do others look at you? Are you shopping alone or with another person? Do you experience any limitations? How do you feel? Do you experience any limitations or barriers while shopping? (*Longer pause.*) Then you proceed to a building—a counseling office for the first time. You enter the building. Imagine its appearance and location. You approach the front desk and give your name. You are asked to take a seat and wait. Several minutes later, out comes this spry, Caucasian woman, dressed nicely and says that she is your new counselor and to follow her to the counseling office. You proceed down a long hallway. What are you thinking? Feeling? As you enter the office with her, she hands you some paperwork to complete then asks how you are? How do you think she perceives you? What is your perception of the counselor? Are there any potential barriers to your working together? What is your initial emotional reaction to this interaction?

Your journey ends here. At this point, I would like you to hold on to the images, emotions, thoughts, reactions. And slowly come back into the room. And using the provided materials, either write or draw your reactions to this guided imagery. Don't analyze, just let your reactions flow from you. (*Allow for approximately 20 minutes to process. When there are 5 minutes left, let the participants know.*) There are about 5 minutes left. (*Then,*) There is about 1 minute left, so start to wind down and wrap up where you are.

At this point, I want everyone to take a deep breath and exhale out any discomfort you may have experienced. Come back into the room. At this point, I invite you all to openly discuss your reactions and responses to this exercise. You may share as much or as little as you feel comfortable, including what you may have learned about yourself.

(**Instructor:** *Be prepared for a variety of emotional reactions, including crying, anger, self-disclosure of personal incidents of discrimination. Toward the last 5 minutes of discussion, try to refocus the group to discuss how a client may feel entering therapy, what we may have learned about ourselves, our blind spots that can affect our clinical work, what we learned about prejudice (our own prejudices) that may affect our clinical work.*).

(**In closing**): Before you leave, I want you to brush off your borrowed identity, leaving whatever discomfort you might have felt or experienced in this room. You may even brush it into the garbage as you leave the room today. If thoughts or feelings emerge later or during the week, I encourage you to write in a journal or notebook.

Modification of Exercise

This experiential activity may be modified and extended to have participants take on the identity of the index card for one week. During the week, the student is expected to imagine what it would be like to be this individual during the week. The student is expected to write and/or draw thoughts and reactions during the week and then share in the following class.

Handout: Handout 67.1: Identity Cards

References

Prichard, K. W., & Sawyer, R. M. (1994). *Handbook of college teaching: Theory and application.* Santa Barbara, CA: Greenwood Press.

Additional Readings (*At least one article should be listed as a required reading.*)

Goode, T. D. (2000). *Promoting cultural competence and cultural diversity in early intervention and early childhood settings,* and *Promoting cultural competence and cultural diversity for personnel providing services and supports to children with special health care needs and their families.* Available at http://nccc.georgetown.edu/documents/ChecklistBehavioralHealth.pdf

Magellan Health Services. (n.d.) *Magellan cultural competency resource kit.* Available at https://www.magellanprovider.com/MHS/MGL/education/culturalcompetency/resourcekit.pdf

Olson, L., Bhattacharya, J., & Sharf, A. (2006). *Cultural competency: What it is and why it matters.* Available at http://www.lpfch.org/programs/culturalcompetency.pdf

Saldana, D. (2001). *Cultural competency: A practical guide for mental health service providers.* Available from Hogg Foundation for Mental Health, University of Texas at Austin, at www.hogg.utexas.edu/PDF/Saldana.pdf

Sue, S. (1998). In search of cultural competence in psychotherapy and counseling. *American Psychologist, 53,* 440–448.

Sue, S. (2006). Cultural competency: From philosophy to research and practice. *Journal of Community Psychology, 34*(2), 237–245.

Sue, S., Zane, N., Nagayama Hall, G. C., & Berger, L. K. (2009). The case for cultural competency in psychotherapeutic interventions. *Annual Review of Psychology, 60*, 524–548.

Sutton, M. (2000). Improving patient care: Cultural competence. *Family Practice Management, 7*(9), 58–62. www.aafp.org/fpm/20001000/58cult.html

Bridging the Gap[1]

Rose M. Stark-Rose, Jayne M. Lokken, Martha S. Norton, and
Suzanne Zilber

Topics: Introduction to Multicultural Counseling
Definitions of Cultural Diversity
Cultural Identity Development
Oppression and Discrimination
Counseling Lesbian, Gay, Bisexual, Transgender (LGBT), and Other Sexual Minority Clients
Counseling Aging Clients
Counseling People With Disabilities

Purposes: The purposes of the discrimination simulation activity are to (a) raise awareness of group privilege and of differential treatment based on group identity or factors beyond an individual's control, (b) challenge the idea that rules and access to resources are systematically fair and apply to everyone, (c) activate participants' empathy for the experience of being systematically disadvantaged, (d) explore the difficulty of dialogue about race, and (e) promote racial and cultural awareness.

Learning Objectives: After participation in the simulation activity, students will (a) increase their awareness of when people are being systematically treated differently based on factors (cultural or subcultural) beyond their control; (b) notice their own verbal and nonverbal treatment of groups other than their own and alter their behavior to treat people equally; (c) increase their awareness of social privilege on dimensions such as culture, ability, age, size, and sexual orientation; and (d) increase their awareness of the emotional and practical/physical impact of differential treatment.

Target Population: Undergraduate and graduate students

Group Size: 15–25 students

Time Required: 1 hour

Setting: A medium to large room where desks, chairs, and/or tables may be easily rearranged or moved

Materials:

- Color sash for each participant. Red, yellow, and green sashes are made out of crepe paper;
- red, yellow, and green boards, 20″ × 33″, made out of construction paper;
- 64 different "feeling" words with a combination of negative and positive words (e.g., *sad, angry, anxious, happy*) typed onto paper;

---

[1]This activity is an adaptation of the original *Bridging the Gap* workshop by Martha Norton and Suzanne Zilber.

- an assortment of small toys and suckers for "Happyland";
- a sign made out of paper with "Happyland" written in boldface;
- toy bowling ball and toy bowling pins;
- toy hockey puck, toy hockey stick, toy hockey net;
- 3″ × 5″ index cards;
- two small tables;
- copy of Handout 68.1, "The Parables of the Ups and Downs," by Dr. Robert Terry; and
- transparent tape.

Instructions for Conducting Activity

This activity requires two facilitators. An option for instructors who wish to use this activity in their class would be to train an advanced undergraduate student or a graduate student on conducting the activity.

Prior to the start of the exercise, the room will need to be set up. In one corner of the room the facilitators will place the bowling game; in another corner the hockey game is placed; and in another corner the "Happyland" sign is taped to a wall, with the toys and candy placed nearby on a small table. At the front of the room, the three boards should be taped either to the blackboard or to a wall. The 64 feeling words are placed on a small table near the three boards.

As participants enter the classroom, they are randomly given a sash of red, yellow, or green. They are asked to wear the sash throughout the entire exercise. One facilitator says, "Welcome to the program Bridging the Gap. You are going to participate in two games today." A facilitator then explains to participants that they will be working toward a goal of ending up in "Happyland." This is a place where their dreams have come true, where they have met or achieved their goals. Ask participants to take a few moments to imagine a goal or wish that would be attained if they reached Happyland. They are told that they will have two opportunities to get to Happyland: by demonstrating skill at either a bowling activity or a hockey activity. Following each activity, they are asked to find a feeling word (from the 64 different feeling words) that represents their reaction to the experience and tape it to a board of the same color as their sash.

Half of the participants start with one game, half with the other. One facilitator runs one game, the other facilitator runs the other game. To start, ask for a volunteer to go first, or select someone wearing a green sash. Continue to ask for volunteers or randomly select people to play the game. Each player is treated differently based on the color of her or his sash. Green players are not given any obstacles to achieving their goals: They stand closest to the games, always succeed, and always get into Happyland. Yellow players are given tasks that make it harder, but not impossible, for them to get to Happyland. Yellows are questioned about their abilities and are challenged in the games, but they sometimes can make it to Happyland. Red players are not given much of a try. They are encouraged to find other goals. No matter what they do, they are not allowed into Happyland. If by chance they complete the game task, it is seen as a fluke and they have to do it again and are not allowed to succeed. As an alternative to getting into Happyland, the facilitator may offer the red player an opportunity to be "near" Happyland (red player may be offered to stand near Happyland). Remember, the facilitators interact with the different colors differently, giving encouragement and strong affirming messages to the green, expressing some encouragement and some doubt to the yellows, and discouraging the red.

After each person has a chance to play both games, the group is brought back together, each participant is given two index cards, and the group begins to process what they experienced and what they observed. At this point, participants begin identifying the different rules that were applied to each group. Ask participants when they first noticed that people were being treated differently. Often times you may find that green players are oblivious to the different treatment until later on in the game, but red players notice fairly soon the differences in treatment. Next, the facilitators read the feeling words that were placed on each of the three boards then asks the group, "What did you notice about the feeling words that participants posted on the boards?" Also, ask participants about any observations regarding the behaviors of the facilitators. Next, facilitators ask, "Where does this kind of thing happen in the

Oppression and Discrimination

real world?" Possible answers for green include: This color may represent but is not limited to people who are rich, elite, white males, movie stars, college seniors, university presidents, faculty, heterosexual individuals, prestigious professionals, or athletes. Possible answers for yellow include: This color may represent but is not limited to women in business, fair-skinned minorities, middle class, and some lower socioeconomic classes. Possible answers for red include: This color may represent but is not limited to gays, minorities, low socioeconomic classes, and first-year college students.

After this is processed, participants are asked to identify a time when they felt treated like one of the colors and to write about it briefly on an index card. They are told to mark their card with an *X* in the upper corner if they do not want their card read to the group. The facilitators gather the cards and read the examples aloud, asking people if they want to add comments. Next, one of the facilitators reads a poem called "The Parable of the Ups and Downs" (see Handout 68.1) by Terry (n.d.). A handout of the parable is included, which the facilitator can refer to. Finally, the facilitators thank individuals for participating in the activity.

Effort is also made at the conclusion of the exercise to clarify facilitator behavior. For example, during the activity, participants are asked to identify a personal goal. Depending on the color of sash they have, they are either encouraged or discouraged from that goal. At the end of the activity, facilitators should clearly state that they have a strong belief in each individual's ability to achieve his or her goals and that the discouraging comments were a part of the exercise rather than the facilitator's belief. Finally, participants are asked to write on another index card feedback for facilitators or something they have learned.

Handout: Handout 68.1: The Parable of the Ups and Downs (Terry, n.d.)

Additional Readings

Black, L. L., & Stone, D. (2005). Expanding the definition of privilege: The concept of social privilege. *Journal of Multicultural Counseling and Development, 33*, 243–255.

Bonilla-Silva, E., & Forman, T. A. (2000). "I'm not a racist but . . .": Mapping White college students' racial ideology in the USA. *Discourse & Society, 11*(1), 50–85.

Croteau, J. M., Talbot, D. M., Lance, T. S., & Evans, N. J. (2002). A qualitative study of the interplay between privilege and oppression. *Journal of Multicultural Counseling and Development, 30*, 239–258.

Dovidio, J. F., & Gaertner, S. L. (1986). How do attitudes guide behavior? In R. M. Sorrentino & E. T. Higgins (Eds.), *The handbook of motivation and cognition: Foundations of social behavior* (pp. 204–243). New York, NY: Guilford Press.

Johnson, A. G. (2006). *Privilege, power, and difference* (2nd ed.). Boston, MA: McGraw-Hill.

McGregor, J. (1993). Effectiveness of role playing and antiracist teaching in reducing student prejudice. *Journal of Educational Research, 8*, 215–226.

McIntosh, P. (1989, July/August). White privilege: Unpacking the invisible knapsack. *Peace and Freedom*, 10–12.

Ponterotto, J. G., Utsey, S. O., & Pedersen, P. (2006). *Preventing prejudice: A guide for counselors, educators, and parents*. Thousand Oaks, CA: Sage.

Stark-Rose, R. M., Lokken, J. M., & Zarghami, F. (in press). Increasing awareness of group privilege with college students. *College Student Journal*.

Terry, R. (n.d.). *Parable of the ups and downs*. Available at http://www.action-wheel.com/parableofupsanddowns.html

Whitley, B. E., Jr., & Kite, M. E. (2006). *The psychology of prejudice and discrimination*. Belmont, CA: Wadsworth.

Williams, A., & Giles, H. (1992). Prejudice-reduction simulations: Social cognition, intergroup theory, and ethics. *Simulation & Gaming, 23*(4), 472–484.

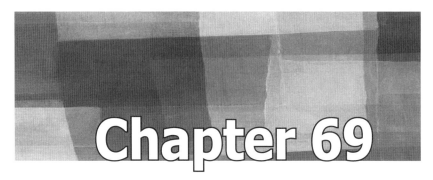

Chapter 69
Hierarchy of Social Power

Cheryl B. Warner

Topics: Introduction to Multicultural Counseling
Cultural Identity Development
Oppression and Discrimination
Advocacy and Social Justice

Purposes: This activity aims to engage participants in discussing the presence of social structures associated with power, privilege, and influences of cultural group membership in the United States. In addition, the outcome of this activity requires participants to rank-order cultural group membership ranging from the group that holds the most social power to the group that holds the least amount of social power. This task is accomplished by participants working in small groups, which requires group consensus.

Learning Objectives: As a result of this activity, participants will (a) identify the existing relationship between social power, privilege, and cultural group membership within United States' culture; (b) engage in small-group discussions that reveal individual thought and perceptions of social power and privilege; and (c) consider how group membership affects one's sense of personal power and social mobility.

Target Population: Undergraduate and graduate students enrolled in multicultural or cross-cultural awareness courses examining social and cultural dynamics. This activity is also appropriate for multicultural and diversity training in business and industry.

Group Size: Small groups of three to five participants

Time Required: 35 to 40 minutes (5 minutes to introduce the activity, 15–20 minutes to complete the activity, and 15 minutes to discuss the results and process the activity)

Setting: A room large enough to accommodate movement of participants and furniture to allow small working groups of three to five participants. One table per group is needed to allow participants to arrange the materials required by the activity.

Materials: Each group will receive an envelope in which there are slips of paper with descriptors of cultural groups (see Handout 69.1) written on them. Different color paper can be used for each group. Facilitators can modify the list provided by adding or deleting descriptors.

Instructions for Conducting Activity

1. Prior to facilitating the activity, determine the number of small groups (e.g., 20 participants can be organized into five small groups)

2. Copy the template of descriptors (see Handout 69.1) for the total number of small groups and cut individual slips of paper with descriptors along the dotted lines.
3. Place one set of descriptors into an envelope.
4. Prior to the activity, randomly assign participants to small groups (e.g., have participants count off from one to five and place all the ones in one small group, twos in another, and so forth.
5. Have each small group designate a spokesperson who will verbally report the group's results to the entire group of participants when reassembled
6. Distribute the envelope with set of descriptors to each group.
7. Read the following instructions to the entire group:

Each group has an envelope filled with descriptors representing the diversity of cultural group membership in race/ethnicity, sexual identity, sex, socioeconomic status, able-bodiness, religion/spirituality, and age. For this activity, there are three basic assumptions that should be considered: (a) the U.S. culture is rooted in a system of oppression that resulted in unequal social power and privilege associated with cultural group membership, (b) social power is defined as "access to institutional or structural resources (money, leadership positions, education) as opposed to resources based on personal qualities (intelligence, beauty, strength)" (Power & Reiser, 2005, p. 557), and (c) higher social power associated with cultural group membership provides social currency for in-group members that is unavailable to out-group members. Thus, the purpose of this activity is for each of your small groups, through group consensus, to determine the hierarchy of social power by ranking the descriptors from those who hold the most social power to those who hold the least amount of social power. You will have 15 to 20 minutes to complete this activity. At the end of the allotted time, each group will report its ranking to the entire group of participants.

8. At the end of the allotted time, have each group report their rankings. Expect variability among the groups on the ranking; however, there will be some similarities across the groups among the top six and bottom six. Reiterate to the participants that a "correct" answer to the activity will not be provided because the purpose of the activity is to acknowledge and discuss the presence and impact of social power on individuals.
9. Process the activity with the full group of participants, using the following suggested discussion questions:
   a. What were the descriptors that were the easiest for your group to agree on? Why were they easier for the group? What were the descriptors that were the most difficult for your group to agree on? Why were they harder for the group?
   b. What resources or modifications can an individual in the lower half of the ranking use to ensure upward mobility and increase his or her social power? What factors can lower the ranking of an individual with higher social power?
   c. Ask the group to compare and contrast the lifestyle and social currency of two individuals from different cultural groups and ranking levels. For example, compare and contrast the social currency of a White, heterosexual male who is college-educated and a Latino, gay male born outside the United States who has low English language skills.
   d. What insights were gained from the small-group discussions? How would the outcome of this activity differ if it was completed by individuals instead of small groups?
10. In closing the activity, acknowledge that completing this activity taps into the years of cultural socialization that occur in our society. Emphasize to the group that acknowledging social power and the inequality associated with it assists us in understanding the relationship and dynamics between individuals and cultural groups as well as the privilege and powerlessness present in our society.

Handout: Handout 69.1: Cultural Groups—Handout for Hierarchy of Social Power Activity

References

Power, R. S., & Reiser, C. (2005). Gender and self-perceptions of social power [Electronic version]. *Social Behavior and Personality, 33*, 553–568.

Additional Readings

Georgesen, J., & Harris, M. J. (2006). Holding onto power: Effects of powerholders' positional instability and expectancies on interactions with subordinates [Electronic version]. *European Journal of Social Psychology, 36*, 451–468.

Ramirez, A., & Soriano, F. I. (2001). Differential patterns of intra- and interethnic interaction in social power systems [Electronic version]. *The Journal of Social Psychology, 133*, 307–316.

Smith, T. B. (Ed.). (2005). *Practicing multiculturalism: Affirming diversity in counseling and psychology.* Boston, MA: Pearson Education.

Sue, D. W., & Sue, D. (2008). *Counseling the culturally diverse: Theory and practice* (5th ed.). Hoboken, NJ: Wiley.

Chapter 70
Concentric Circle Dialogues

Rebecca A. Willow

Topics: Introduction to Multicultural Counseling
Definitions of Cultural Diversity
Cultural Communication Styles
Cultural Identity Development
Oppression and Discrimination
Helping Relationships

Purposes: This exercise provides a forum for cross-cultural communication through one-on-one and group dialogues within a classroom setting. The activity is designed to increase participants' awareness of their personal experiences of privilege and oppression. In addition, the exercise promotes skill in dialogue about cultural differences.

Learning Objectives: As a result of this exercise, participants will (a) become more aware of personal experiences with privilege and oppression, (b) become more aware of barriers to cross-cultural counseling, (c) explore their own cultural identity development process, (d) develop counseling skills in broaching and discussing sensitive cultural issues, and (e) increase their awareness of potential countertransference issues.

Target Population: Most applicable for students in counseling or other related programs

Group Size: 6–16 students is ideal; adaptations may be made to accommodate more or fewer.

Time Required: Approximately 2 hours (depending on group size)

Setting: An open area without desks is needed for half of the group to sit in an outer circle. The other half of the participants sit in an inner circle of evenly matched chairs facing the outer circle. In other words, participants sit in concentric circles of chairs facing a partner.

Materials: Chairs, open space, list of prompt questions, stopwatch (helpful but not necessary)

Instructions for Conducting Activity

This exercise needs to be conducted within an environment where a sense of emotional safety has been established and where group norms for confidentiality have been discussed.

1. Have participants arrange themselves in two concentric circles: an outer circle facing inward and an inner circle facing outward. Each participant should be facing a partner. Adaptations can be made by arranging a group of three in the event of an uneven number. There will be six rounds

of questions. During the first half of a round, the outer-circle participants are the speakers and the inner-circle participants are the listeners. For the second half of a round, the roles reverse.

2. For each round, the facilitator will present a question. Outer-circle speakers will have 2 minutes to share their responses with their inner-circle partner. Inner-circle partners will demonstrate active listening skills. They are not to interrupt or shift the attention away from the speaker. The facilitator will signal when the 2-minute period is up by calling, "Time." She or he will then direct the same question to the inner-circle participants, who become the speakers and have 2 minutes to respond. Likewise, the outer-circle participants become the active listeners.

3. At the end of the round (when both outer- and inner-circle partners have responded to the same question), the facilitator will instruct the outer-circle participants to stand and move one seat to the right. (The inner-circle participants do not move.) In this way, new pairs are formed for each round.

Prompt questions:

a. Tell your partner what your cultural background is and something about that background of which you are proud.

b. When did you first realize that people were treated differently based on their race/ethnicity? Briefly describe your experience.

c. Share with your partner one stereotype that disturbs you about your racial, ethnic, or religious group.

d. What is a stereotype/image about a cultural group other than your own that you sometimes find yourself responding to even though you don't want to?

e. Describe a time when you were discouraged from doing something because of your race, ethnicity, gender, religion, or economic status.

f. Share with your partner a time when you did not interrupt prejudice.

4. Reconvene in the circle and debrief the exercise using the following prompts. Prompt questions may be altered to suit the needs of the group.

a. What was it like for you to share some personal information with your different partners?

b. Were there particular questions that were more difficult to answer? Easier?

c. Are there any parallels between what was difficult for you to discuss and cultural barriers to cross-cultural counseling?

d. Did you develop awareness or insights about the relationship between childhood messages and your current life experiences or worldview?

e. How did this process affect your awareness of your own experiences with privilege or oppression?

f. How will this experience inform you as a counselor? Are there any potential issues of countertransference of which you need to be aware?

Additional Readings

Johnson, A. G. (2001). *Privilege, power, and difference*. Mountain View, CA: Mayfield.

Katz, J. (2003). *White awareness: Handbook for anti-racism training*. (2nd ed.). Norman: University of Oklahoma Press.

YWCA of Greater Pittsburgh Center for Race Relations and Anti-Racism Training. (2001). *Study Circle program facilitator's guide*. Unpublished handbook.

Oppression and Discrimination

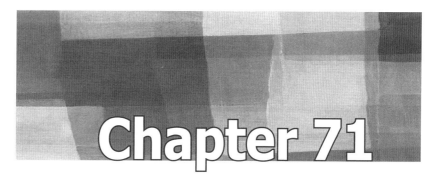

Chapter 71

Interrupting Oppression: Finding Ways to Speak Out Against Overt Oppression and Everyday Microaggressions

Kayoko Yokoyama, Sukie Magraw, Jill Miller, and Liza Hecht

Topics: Oppression and Discrimination
Helping Relationships
Advocacy and Social Justice

Purposes: The purpose of this activity is to help students formulate specific responses to interrupt oppression and everyday microaggressions. Through this activity, students will better understand the psychological impact of everyday microaggressions and oppression on themselves and others. In addition, this activity aims to provide participants with opportunities to explore their feelings, fears, and hopes related to interrupting oppression as well as to develop their skills in responding and interrupting oppression and microaggressions. This activity enhances multicultural self-awareness for counselors/psychologists-in-training and allows students to practice social justice and advocacy.

Learning Objectives: As a result of this activity, students will have a better understanding of the subtleties of microaggressions and oppression. Students will gain a greater awareness of their feelings, hopes, and fears and will acquire skills related to ways of interrupting or responding to oppression.

Target Population: Advanced undergraduate or graduate students in a multicultural awareness course

Group Size: Optimal group size would be a diverse group of 8–10 students.

Time Required: Total of 60 minutes (5 minutes for students to write down their recent experience, 15 minutes for each student to discuss their experience, and 40 minutes for reactions, reflections, and brainstorming)

Setting: Classroom

Materials: None

Instructions for Conducting Activity

1. At the beginning of the activity period, have students read "Interrupting Oppression Exercise: Finding Ways to Speak Out Against Both Overt Oppression and Everyday Microaggressions" (see Handout 71.1)

2. Make certain that students understand ground rules, including respect, safety, and privacy/confidentiality before conducting this activity.

3. Have students think of and write down a recent encounter with a microaggression or someone saying something oppressive, with the following questions as a guide:

   a. How did you feel? What did you do? What did you say? What did you wish you could have done or said?

   b. If you did have a discussion with the person who said or did something oppressive, how did the discussion go? How did the discussion leave you feeling?

   c. How has this discussion or interaction affected how you see others today?

   d. How does who you are affect your ability to interrupt oppression? What are the gifts and barriers that you bring to these discussions?

4. Brainstorm as a class about possible responses to these forms of microaggressions or oppressions.

   a. How would you have responded to another student's experience with microaggression or oppression?

   b. What might be some "back pocket responses," given that these types of microaggressions and oppressions occur regularly?

   c. What do you think would have been an educational or useful response to the person making the remark?

5. What was it like for you to discuss this experience with others in this class?

   a. What feelings or reactions did you have after hearing other students' feedback, reactions, and ideas?

6. In what other ways can others in this class provide support to you?

Handout: Handout 71.1: Interrupting Oppression Exercise

References

Sue, D. W., Capodilupo, C. M., Torino, G. C., Bucceri, J. M., Holder, A. M. B., Nadal, K. L., & Esquilin, M. (2007). Racial microaggressions in everyday life: Implications for clinical practice. *American Psychologist, 62,* 271–286.

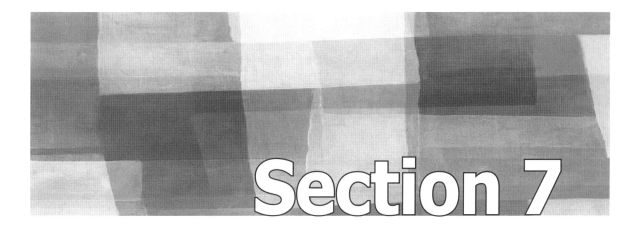

Section 7

Dimensions of Worldviews

This section offers activities intended to introduce students to concepts and terms related to the construction of differing cultural worldviews. Through these activities, students learn how cultural worldviews inform client and counselor values, assumptions, and biases. These activities also facilitate student awareness about how differing worldviews can affect the therapeutic match between counselor and client. Some of the activities offer theory (e.g., critical race) to explore how individuals construct and make sense of their environments and experiences based on sociopolitical realities. Many of these activities are intended for use in introductory multicultural counseling courses but can be infused in a variety of counseling courses.

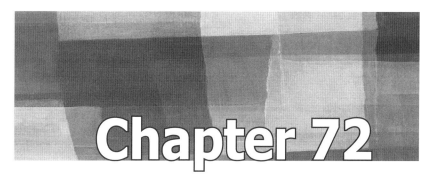

Chapter 72

Perspective Taking: Practicing to Really Hear the Other Person's Point of View

Sharon K. Anderson, Antonette Aragon, Edward J. Brantmeier, Nathalie Kees, and Jacqueline Peila-Shuster

Topics: Introduction to Multicultural Counseling
Dimensions of Worldviews
Culturally Skilled Counselor
Professional Identity and Ethical Practice

Purposes: Rationale—Perspective taking is a critical skill for all counselors to develop. Whether we are dealing with a client from another culture or a colleague with another worldview, we need to develop the skill of entering into dialogue to gain perspective taking.

The purpose of the activity is to provide an opportunity for students to understand the internal processes of perspective taking that can lead to true dialogue. Many times when we are confronted with a worldview or difference that pushes an emotional button inside, we move to a position of defense or right and wrong. This activity encourages students to stay engaged in a true dialogue or communication process where perspective taking or true understanding (not necessarily agreement) occurs.

Learning Objectives: As a result of this activity, students will be able to (a) better understand another person's value set, worldview, or point of view; (b) hear the other person's perspective as real and true for that person; and (c) suspend one's own internal push to evaluate and defend one's own position.

Target Population: Graduate students in the fields of counseling, psychology, social work, and the helping professions in general.

Group Size: Up to 30 participants

Time Required: 45–60 minutes

Setting: A large space or room is necessary.

Materials: Paper; pens/pencils; markers; whiteboard or news print; Flick's (1998) book, *From Debate to Dialogue: Using the Understanding Process to Transform Our Conversations*

Instructions for Conducting Activity

1. Ask students to prepare for activity by reading the first four chapters of Flick's (1998) book, *From Debate to Dialogue: Using the Understanding Process to Transform Our Conversations*.
2. Review the model discussed in the text—the difference between the "conventional discussion process" and the "understanding process."
3. In the large group, give students the opportunity to express their reactions to the model. Provide or initiate questions that promote healthy discussion about the model's utility in working with people who have a different worldview or who are from a different culture. This discussion is important. You want to address any misgivings, misunderstandings, or misperceptions about the model before students try to use it.
4. Begin to construct lists of cultural values or different worldviews. Depending on the class composition and dynamics that you are aware of thus far, you may wish to create a couple of different lists. One list might be a rather benign listing that prompts little to no emotional response (i.e., it doesn't really push anyone's real emotional buttons), and another list would be those values or worldviews that push people to debate—to win at all costs.
5. Carry out the following steps:
   a. Have the class or group break out into triads. Each person in the triad will have an opportunity to experience all three roles: (a) initiator of conversation, (b) responder to conversation, and (c) observer of conversation.
   b. Have initiator select one area or topic from the list. The initiator states his or her position on the area as clearly as possible. For example, "Multicultural issues should be discussed in every course" or "Abortion is not the answer. Personhood begins at conception."
   c. Have responder come from the conventional discussion process mode, with the goal being to "win the argument" and convince the initiator to see the issue from the responder's view. Allow the conversation to go about 5 minutes.
   d. Next have the initiator start the conversation again, but this time have the responder come from the understanding process mode—with the goal of understanding the other person's point of view.
   e. Process both conversations. Encourage all three students to share their experience and observations of the conversations.
   f. Have participants change roles two more times so that each person gets an experience with each role.
   g. See process questions below.

Process Questions

1. During the conventional discussion process conversation, use the following questions:
   a. What was your experience of the activity as
      (1) Initiator?
      (2) Responder?
      (3) Observer?
   b. What came naturally for you in your role as
      (1) Initiator?
      (2) Responder?
   c. What surprised you in your role as
      (1) Initiator?
      (2) Responder?
      (3) Observer?
2. During the understanding process conversation, use the following questions:
   a. What was your experience of the activity as
      (1) Initiator?
      (2) Responder?
      (3) Observer?

    b. What came naturally for you in your role as
       (1) Initiator?
       (2) Responder?
    c. What was a struggle for you in your role as
       (1) Initiator?
       (2) Responder?
    d. What surprised you in your role as
       (1) Initiator?
       (2) Responder?
       (3) Observer?

References

Flick, D. L. (1998). *From debate to dialogue: Using the understanding process to transform our conversations.* Boulder, CO: Orchid.

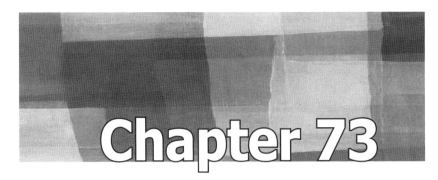

Chapter 73

The Squiggle Perspective

Laurie M. Craigen and Danica G. Hays

Topics: Cultural Identity Development
Dimensions of Worldviews
Helping Relationships

Purposes: The purpose of this activity is to provide participants with opportunities to consider the influences of an individual's worldview and its impact on the development of a positive counselor–client relationship. This activity also enhances the student's ability to perspective take, a vital skill for a professional counselor to develop.

Learning Objectives: As a result of this activity, students will

- be able to operationalize the concept of worldview,
- understand the importance of worldview and how differences in worldview affect the client–counselor relationship,
- gain experience in perspective taking, and
- learn the value of perspective taking as a professional counselor.

Target Population: Professional counselors or counselors-in-training (all levels)

Group Size: Size can vary. Activity can be completed with a range of group sizes, from small groups with as few as two people to very large groups such as classrooms or workshops.

Time Required: Approximately 30 minutes.

Setting: Many settings are conducive for this activity. Circular seating is the best fit for this activity.

Materials: Markers, squiggle handout (see Handout 73.1)

Instructions for Conducting Activity

1. Distribute squiggle handout.
2. Instruct students to do the following: "In front of you, you will notice a 'squiggle.' For the next 10 minutes, you are to add elements to the squiggle to represent whatever you see in this design." (Students may ask for more directions. However, you are to give no further instructions).
3. After 10 minutes, ask students (if they feel comfortable) to share their designs. With large groups, you may want to have students share their designs in dyads or triads.
4. Have students reflect on what they noticed about themselves and others in doing this activity. Immediately, students will note that each person interpreted his or her squiggle differently.

5. Introduce the concept of worldview. For example, "*Worldview* is defined as a person's relationship with the world. To be more specific, it is the core assumptions, values, and beliefs that individuals, families, and groups hold about the world based on their life experiences. Some influences of worldview might include the following:
   a. cultural identities (e.g., race, ethnicity, gender, religion);
   b. a judgment about how core or basic values are across individuals (i.e., holding an etic versus emic perspective);
   c. beliefs about human nature (good versus evil);
   d. the structure of social relationships (e.g., hierarchical, collaborative/collectivistic, individualistic);
   e. the interaction between humans and nature (e.g., mastery over nature, respect for nature);
   f. time orientation (i.e., past, present, future); and
   g. the idea of being versus doing."
6. Ask the students to explain how this activity relates to worldview and how differences in worldview affect the client–counselor relationship.
7. Ultimately, the goal is for students to understand that we all bring out unique frameworks for generating and applying knowledge to any relationship and particularly to the counseling relationship. Conversely, our clients will likely bring alternate worldviews. To generate discussion, you can ask the following questions:
   a. How can differences in worldview affect the counseling relationship?
   b. What obstacles are you likely to encounter?
   c. What strategies can you use to consider and understand these differences?

Handout: Handout 73.1: The Squiggle Perspective

Additional Readings

Ibrahim, F. A. (1991). Contribution of cultural worldview to generic counseling and development. *Journal of Counseling & Development, 70,* 13–19.

Sue, D. W. (1978). Worldview and counseling. *Personnel & Guidance Journal, 56,* 458–462.

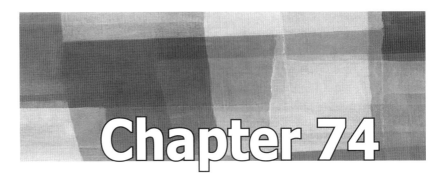

Chapter 74

Understanding Career Values

Danica G. Hays and Laurie M. Craigen

Topics: Dimensions of Worldviews
Professional Identity and Ethical Practice
Career Development
Assessment

Purposes: The purposes of this activity are to explore the importance of various internal and external career values in career decision making and to impart knowledge on how to assess the role of career values in clients' lives.

Learning Objectives: As a result of this activity, students will be able to

- understand prominent definitions of career or work values in the counseling literature,
- gain knowledge about the types of career or work values and its relationship to cultural and lifestyle values,
- gain self-awareness in what career values counselor trainees find most important in their lives, and
- learn how, as counselors, they may assist clients in understanding the role of career values in their personal, social, and occupational decisions.

Target Population: Master's- and doctoral-level counseling students in career development courses; students in internship and practicum courses

Group Size: This activity may be used in graduate classrooms or may be adapted to work with clients in individual and group settings dealing with career decision-making concerns.

Time Required: 30–45 minutes

Setting: Individual or group settings. If activity is conducted in a group setting, place chairs in a circle.

Materials: "Career Values Worksheet" (Handout 74.1), pens

Instructions for Conducting Activity

Instructor should do the following (please note that the instructor may adapt these instructions when using this activity with clients in an individual or group setting):

1. Distribute the "Career Values Worksheet" to counselor trainees (see Handout 74.1).
2. State the following: "Values are one aspect of the career decision-making process. In general values are individual beliefs and personal standards that guide behaviors and decision making.

Three main types of values are lifestyle values, cultural values, and career values. These three types of values often overlap in career decision making as oftentimes we select and prefer careers that best suit other aspects of our lives, such as family and social relationships, leisure activities, or cultural group memberships. Also, individuals prioritize career values based either on their own needs and preferences, others' needs and preferences, or a combination of both. Career or work values are either internal or external. Some examples of internal values are opportunities to be creative, personal satisfaction from helping others, and experiencing excitement from your job. Some examples of external work values are making money and having travel opportunities, social status, and work recognition. What I would like you to do is review the list of eight career values on the "Career Values Worksheet" and rate each value using a scale of 1 to 10, with 1 being that a particular value is of no importance to you and 10 being a particular value of greatest importance to you."

3. Allow the students time to complete the worksheet (typically 5–10 minutes).

4. After students have completed the worksheet, state the following, "Next, prioritize these values and circle your top four."

5. Have students present their top four values and their reasons for selecting them.

6. Have students reflect on the experience. Sample process questions include the following:
   a. How was this experience for you?
   b. What were some of your initial reactions to the career values?
   c. What did you notice about yourself as you prioritized the career values?
   d. What did you notice about others as they shared their career values?
   e. Are there values you believe have not been included on this worksheet? What priority would each value hold if you included those on the worksheet?
   f. How do your career values relate to values in other areas of your life?
   g. How do your career values relate to your cultural background?
   h. How do your career values differ from your cultural background?
   i. To what extent are your selected career values congruent with your aspirations to become a professional counselor?
   j. How do career values in general influence the career counseling process? How is value exploration beneficial for clients? How is it challenging for clients?
   k. How might you integrate information about clients' career values with other types of their values?

Handout: Handout 74.1: Career Values Worksheet

Additional Readings

Brown, D. (2002). The role of work and cultural values in occupational choice, satisfaction, and success: A theoretical statement. *Journal of Counseling & Development, 80,* 48–56.

Dawis, R. V., & Lofquist, L. H. (1984). *A psychological theory of work adjustment.* Minneapolis: University of Minnesota Press.

Rosenberg, M. (1957). *Occupations and values.* New York, NY: Free Press.

Wozny, D. (2009). Work values. In American Counseling Association (Ed.), *The ACA encyclopedia of counseling* (pp. 569–571). Alexandria, VA: Author.

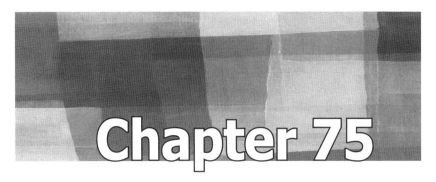

Chapter 75

Using Critical Race Theory and Narratives to Explore Cultural Differences

Matthew E. Lemberger and Cheryl Holcomb-McCoy

Topics: Barriers to Effective Cross-Cultural Counseling
Oppression and Discrimination
Dimensions of Worldviews
Counseling African Americans
Advocacy and Social Justice

Purposes: To increase student awareness of the dimensions of worldviews and the cultural implications of storytelling.

Learning Objectives: As a result of this activity, students will

- experience the intercentricity of race and racism with other forms of subordination (gender, class, immigration status, sexuality, disability);
- increase their commitment to social justice; and
- be better able to appreciate and understand the experiences of racial minorities, which will enhance their ability to counsel clients of racially diverse backgrounds.

Target Population: Racially diverse students in a graduate counselor education program. This activity works best when students are racially and/or ethnically diverse.

Group Size: 10–30 students (small groups of two or three for activity)

Time Required: 3–6 hours (enough time for students to write brief racialized narratives)

Setting: Classroom with movable chairs (preferred) but can be done with fixed-chair seating as well

Materials: Copies of the handout "Writing a Narrative on Race" (Handout 75.2) for each person in the class or group

Instructions for Conducting Activity

Begin the session with a lecture on critical race theory (see Handout 75.1). After the lecture, distribute Handout 75.2 and have students begin writing their narratives using the handout, including questions/ probes that act as a narrative writing guide. After students have completed their narratives (which can be a homework assignment), they are instructed to get into dyads or triads (the instructor should assign groups to ensure that there is one student of color in each dyad or triad, if possible) to share their narratives. In the small dyads or triads, students are instructed to determine at least three common themes in the narratives and three distinct differences in their narratives or experiences.

Discussion

The instructor leads a full-group discussion of this process and the students' insights to the specific themes (common and different themes) of each group. Questions to facilitate the discussion could include:

1. How does race and/or racism influence people's daily lives?
2. Which part of the narrative writing was most difficult or easiest for you?
3. Why do you think people avoid talking about race and racism?
4. As a White person, how does it feel hearing about others' "racialized" stories?
5. As a person of color, how does it feel hearing about White people's "racialized" stories?
6. How might the themes uncovered in the narratives influence the counseling process? Client–counselor relationship? Counseling outcomes?

Handouts: Handout 75.1: Lecture Narrative
Handout 75.2: Writing a Narrative on Race

References

Crenshaw, K., Gotanda, N., Peller, G., & Thomas, K. (Eds.). (1995). *Critical race theory: The key writings that formed the movement*. New York, NY: The New Press.

Delgado, R., & Stefancic, J. (2001). *Critical race theory: An introduction*. New York, NY: University Press.

Garcia, S. B., & Guerra, P. L. (2004). Deconstructing deficit thinking: Working with educators to create more equitable learning environments. *Education and Urban Society, 36,* 150–168.

Yosso, T. J. (2005). Whose culture has capital? A critical race theory discussion of community wealth. *Race, Ethnicity, and Education, 8,* 69–91.

Chapter 76
Transforming Our Worldview

Simone Alter-Muri

Topics: Barriers to Effective Cross-Cultural Counseling
Definitions of Cultural Diversity
Oppression and Discrimination
Dimensions of Worldviews
Advocacy and Social Justice
Creative Arts

Purposes:

1. This activity provides an opportunity for students to visualize and explore their current worldview and prejudices and to begin a process of transforming these beliefs in accordance to fundamental principles of social justice and multicultural and diversity awareness.
2. This activity enhances awareness of stereotypical views that are inherent in our Western culture and in the beginning practitioner's frame of reference.
3. This exercise augments class discussions of prejudice and oppression and issues in multicultural and diversity awareness.
4. This activity allows students to extend their knowledge and create a visual aid in their journey of becoming culturally competent and aware counselors/group workers.

Learning Objectives: As a result of the exercise, participants will

- examine their prejudices related to multicultural and diversity issues through an art exercise,
- synthesize their knowledge to create metaphorical and visual changes to their prejudices and/or worldviews through a visual representation,
- demonstrate their ability to understand and visualize their prejudices and/or worldviews, and to begin steps to alter or augment their prejudices, and
- comprehend how to transfer insights from a visual format to their practice as counselors and helping professionals.

Target Population: This exercise is appropriate for individuals of all ages and from different backgrounds. It can benefit the beginning student as well as students in upper-level classes.

Group Size: Group sizes may vary.

Time Required: This activity can be completed in either two class periods or in approximately 2 hours, depending on the size of the group.

Setting: A room with moveable tables

Materials: Drawing or watercolor paper 9″ ×12″ or larger. An assortment of marking instruments and/or painting materials should be available, which may include the following: Craypas (oil pastels), colored pencils, crayons, watercolor paints, brushes, containers for water, permanent markers (Sharpies), markers, scissors, and pencils.

Instructions for Conducting Activity

1. Students are led in a discussion/lecture about their underlying prejudices and worldviews. They are asked to think about their prejudices and or worldviews in relationship to issues of multicultural counseling and diversity.
2. Students are given a piece of paper and marking/painting instruments and asked to create colors, lines, and shapes that represent their prejudices and or worldviews.
3. Students are reassured that they do not need to view themselves as artists, that no one will be judged for his or her artistic abilities, and that the process of creating is important. Being nonjudgmental of oneself is an important component in counseling.
4. Students create lines, shapes, and colors or representational objects that visually represent their prejudices.
5. After the picture is completed (and has been left to dry if it was made with watercolors), students are encouraged to have a discussion about their work and thoughts.
6. Then students are asked to fold their paper in eight equal boxes. First the paper is folded in half, held in a landscape/horizontal format. Then each half is folded toward the middle, making eight squares on the paper.
7. The paper is creased strongly at the folds.
8. A cut is made in the middle of the paper horizontally on the middle fold that extends to the second fold on each side. The cut is not made to the end of either side of the paper.
9. The picture will then have a cut/slit in the center of the page that extends only two squares.
10. The paper is folded in half horizontally with the picture side facing the viewer.
11. The paper is pinched and folded.
12. This creates a folded book in a star shape. The pages with art on them can be glued to the neighboring page so the book now has four pages.
13. Students are asked to look at the pages and to see what has changed.
14. They are asked to accentuate the changes they see by adding words or images with permanent markers or other art materials. These changes should also relate to the students' transformation of their prejudices and/or their worldviews.

Additional Readings

Sue, D. W., & Sue, S. (2008). *Counseling the culturally diverse: Theory and practice* (5th ed.). Hoboken, NJ: Wiley.

White, L. M. (1988). *Printmaking as therapy: Frameworks for freedom*. London, England: Jessica Kingsley.

Wronka, J. (2008). *Human rights and social justice: Social action and service for the helping and health professions*. Thousand Oaks, CA: Sage.

Chapter 77

Out of Your Comfort Zone

Kate Davis Rogers

Topics: Definitions of Cultural Diversity
Oppression and Discrimination
Dimensions of Worldviews
Professional Identity and Ethical Practice

Purposes: For students to experience a cultural group in order to expand their knowledge and skills with cultural groups outside of their previous experience

Learning Objectives:

1. The students are to learn about a particular group or culture with which they have had limited or no experience before attending the class.
2. The students will learn how to become better counselors by staying open to how they learn about new cultures and client populations throughout their careers.

Target Population: Undergraduate and graduate students

Group Size: 8–20 would be ideal.

Time Required: At the discretion of the instructor

Setting: An assignment for outside of the classroom

Materials: An art response is included in my assignment but is not necessary. However, some students have taken pictures of their experience to share with the group. The art can be a collage of their experience. It can be a series of drawings of the way they felt before the experience, during the experience (if appropriate), and after the experience.

Instructions for the Conducting Activity

The students are told that they need to identify a group that they have very little experience in being around. Choosing the group is left open to the students' discretion. I make some suggestions, such as an age group that they may not be familiar with (e.g., an early intervention program that works with the newborns to 3-year-old children and their families); a religious or spiritual group, such as a Buddhist meditation or Catholic mass; and so forth. Some students have gone into a tattoo parlor, a casino, a Jewish wedding, and a Sufi dance. The possibilities are endless and open to whatever types of groups may be available in your area.

I asked that the students think about the feelings that they have before, during, and after the event. I remind them the clients will enter into their culture of therapy. I talk about how we expect clients to be emotional and yet still be able to relax when they come into the therapy room. I remind them that clients will often be anxious, just as they may be in meeting with a new population. This experience gives the student a chance to track what it is like to be in a new situation. In addition, it gives the student a chance to learn more about a potential client who may walk through the door.

After the student does this activity, you can have them either report verbally to the entire class or write a one-page report that can be shared with the class as information for the rest of the class.

Additional Readings

Gladwell, M. (2000). *Blink: The power of thinking without thinking.* New York, NY: Little, Brown & Company.

Sue, D. W., & Sue, D. (2007). *Counseling the culturally diverse: Theory and practice* (5th ed.). New York, NY: Wiley.

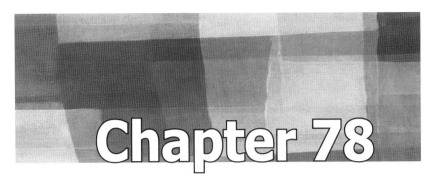

Chapter 78
Reflections on Culture:
Social Construction Plans

Tarrell Awe Agahe Portman and Anna M. Williams-Viviani

Topics: Barriers to Effective Cross-Cultural Counseling
Cultural Identity Development
Dimensions of Worldviews
Culturally Skilled Counselor
Professional Identity and Ethical Practice
Human Growth and Development
Helping Relationships
Group Work

Purposes: The purpose of this activity is to help counseling students understand their own cultural development from a social constructionist perspective. This understanding allows students to identify their cultural values and constructs and classify them as acceptable or unacceptable based on the *ACA Code of Ethics*. The normalization of "becoming" that which we have been exposed to and have learned from others helps students to deconstruct and then reconstruct perspectives of culture. The activity is shared with peers and helps develop a community where cultural competence is sought.

Learning Objectives: As a result of this activity, students will (a) develop a personal awareness of how their human social growth and development affects their cultural beliefs and values, (b) have the opportunity to develop skills necessary to change or retain appropriate cultural perspectives for ethical practice as a counselor, and (c) develop a dialogue about difficult cultural issues with clients and peers.

Target Population: This activity has been used with master's-level counseling graduate students.

Group Size: 14–18 participants

Time Required: The activity requires ongoing interaction and processing, intermingled with learning course content over the course of one semester.

Setting: Any standard classroom will work.

Materials: Students will need to provide their own transportation to events outside of class, depending on the plan they develop.

Instructions for Conducting Activity

1. Read the social construction plan introduction statement (see Handout 78.1).
2. Read the assignment descriptions (see Handout 78.1).
3. Complete the first assignment, "Past Social Construction Experiences—A Reflective Exercise."
4. Complete the second assignment, "Social Construction Plan Activity."

Handout: Handout 78.1: Assignment Descriptions

Additional Readings

Adams, M., Blumenfeld, W. J., Castañeda, R., Hackman, H.W., Peters, M. L., & Zúñiga, X. (Eds.). (2000). *Readings for diversity and social justice*: *An anthology on racism, anti-Semitism, sexism, heterosexism, ableism, and classism*. New York, NY: Routledge.

American Psychological Association. (2010). *Publication manual of the American Psychological Association* (6th ed.). Washington, DC: Author.

Pedersen, P. B., & Carey, J. C. (2003). *Multicultural counseling in schools: A practical handbook*. Boston, MA: Pearson Education.

Robinson, T. L., & Ginter, E. J. (Eds.). (1999). Racism: Healing its effects [Special issue] *Journal of Counseling & Development, 77*(1).

Robinson, T. L., & Howard-Hamilton, M. (2005). *The convergence of race, ethnicity, and gender: Multiple identities in counseling*. Columbus, OH: Merrill Prentice Hall.

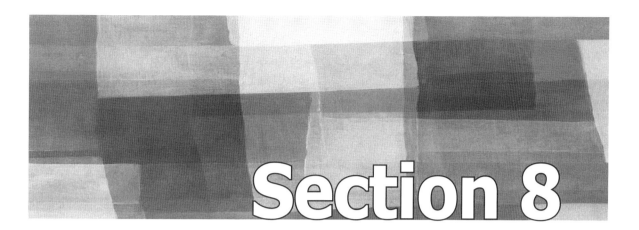

Section 8

The Culturally Skilled Counselor

This section highlights activities designed to assist students in developing multicultural competencies in the areas of awareness, knowledge, and skills. Through many of these activities students learn about the importance of culture awareness (both their own understanding and their client's). Some of the activities help students assess their developing strengths as culturally aware counselors-in-training. These activities use a variety of teaching formats, including case studies, popular movies, and life review strategies.

Chapter 79

The Cultural Encounter: An Exercise in Working Through One's Cultural Biases

Peter C. Donnelly and Gina C. Torino

Topics: Cultural Identity Development
Culturally Skilled Counselor
Counseling African Americans
Counseling Native Americans
Counseling Asian Americans
Counseling Hispanic/Latino Americans
Counseling European Americans
Gender Issues in Counseling
Counseling Lesbian, Gay, Bisexual, Transgender (LGBT), and Other Sexual Minority Clients
Counseling Aging Clients
Counseling People With Disabilities

Purposes: This activity aims to provide counselors-in-training with an opportunity to identify and work through their emotional and cognitive schemas by facing cultural issues that they deem challenging based on their personal biases.

Learning Objectives:

Counselor: For the "counselor," the objectives of this exercise are to (a) gain awareness of his or her cognitive/emotional reactions and biases toward cultural differences, (b) learn to exercise appropriate management of those reactions in the counseling session, and (c) practice culturally appropriate counseling skills.

Client: Through role-playing the "client," students will be able (a) to experience/observe the effectiveness (both strengths and limitations) of their "counselor's" interventions, which will intrinsically inform their own counseling style when faced with similar challenges, and (b) to increase their cultural knowledge and empathy by attempting to present the role-play through the client's perspective.

Observer: The observer(s) will have an opportunity to (a) provide constructive feedback, (b) observe process from the fly-on-the-wall position, and (c) gain familiarity with multicultural counseling interventions.

Target Population: Advanced master's-level mental health and/or doctoral-level counseling, clinical, or social work students. Students must have taken or be taking a course on race and/or multicultural psychology. This exercise should also be used after students have already done some work in acknowledging and identifying their cultural biases. The exercise is largely focused on enhancing cultural awareness.

Group Size: A minimum of three-person triad consisting of the counselor–client dyad and one or more observers

Time Required: The exercise will take approximately 2 hours. Five minutes should be allotted for the "client" to read the "counselor's" prepared responses to Handout 79.1 and think about how he or she will perform the role. Depending on the counselor's skill level, a 15-minute mock counseling session should be followed by a 20-minute feedback period. Less skilled counselors, however, may need to work in shorter periods and allow for more feedback. Ultimately, depending on the objectives and structure of the course, this exercise may be performed across several class sessions with a specific cultural group focus for each class (e.g., race-based challenges in one class and sexual-orientation-based challenges in another), or time frames can be increased as counselors become more skilled—dedicating a full class period to each student in the role of counselor and addressing multiple cultural domains.

Setting: A classroom is acceptable, but a clinical observation room is most desirable. The counselor and client will be seated in two chairs (preferably not desks) across from one another. Counselors are charged with setting up the seating arrangement and should be encouraged to provide a culturally relevant rationale for proximity (i.e., consider what might be appropriate from the client's perspective). The observer will sit outside of the dyad such that both the counselor's and client's faces can be observed.

Materials: Notebook and pen/pencil with which observers and participants can take notes

Instructions for Conducting Activity

Counselors must answer questions that identify cognitive/emotional schemas around those who are culturally different prior to the class (see Handout 79.1). Instructors should review responses and encourage greater insight where necessary. Counselors should be able to describe their anticipated challenges in working with culturally different clients. Prior to beginning the exercise, the student portraying the client must read the counselor's responses and plan to portray the characteristics or scenarios described by the counselor as culturally challenging. The goal of the client is to create the counselor's worst-case scenario.

Counselors should engage in the dyad as if it were an authentic counseling session. While remaining present in the counseling session, the counselor should attempt to be aware of his or her thought processes, emotional reactions, and rationales for interventions, as he or she will be required to discuss them during the feedback session.

Throughout the role-play, the observer is responsible for taking notes that describe the interaction between the client and counselor. He or she should attempt to observe and record the reactions of both counselor and client when addressing culturally loaded material. To accomplish this task, the observer should use Handout 79.2 in order to identify effective and ineffective interventions.

After the 15-minute role-play, each group member should take about 5 minutes to write about his or her reactions/observations of the session. For the remaining 10 minutes, the group should provide feedback to the counselor and discuss observations of his or her process. Please see Handout 79.3 for discussion guidelines. All notes should be submitted to the counselor. Participants should then rotate roles and repeat the exercise until each participant has had at least one opportunity to be the counselor and to be the client.

Handouts: Handout 79.1: Counselor Questionnaire
Handout 79.2: Observer Guidelines: The Cultural Encounter
Handout 79.3: Discussion Guidelines: Cultural Encounter Role-Play

Additional Readings

Fowers, B. J., & Davidov, B. J. (2006). The virtue of multiculturalism: Personal transformation, character, and openness to the other. *American Psychologist, 61*, 581–594.

Ivey, A. E., D'Andrea, M., Ivey, M. B., & Simek-Morgan, L. (2008). *Theories of counseling and psychotherapy: A multicultural perspective* (6th ed.). Thousand Oaks, CA: Sage.

Ivey, A. E., & Ivey, M. B. (2003). *Intentional interviewing and counseling* (5th ed.). Pacific Grove, CA: Brooks/Cole.

Pedersen, P., Draguns, J. G., Lonner, W. J., & Trimble, J. E. (2008). *Counseling across cultures*. Thousand Oaks, CA: Sage.

Sue, D. W., & Sue, D. (2008). *Counseling the culturally diverse: Theory and practice* (5th ed.). New York: Wiley.

Utsey, S. O., Gernat, C. A., & Hammar, L. (2005). Examining White counselor trainees' reactions to racial issues in counseling and supervision dyads. *The Counseling Psychologist, 33*, 449–478.

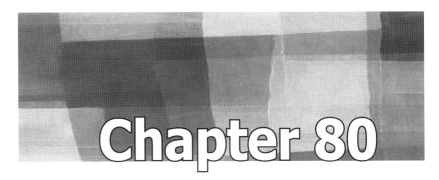

Photovoice:
Understanding Social Privilege

Bengü Ergüner-Tekinalp and Amney Harper

Topics: Introduction to Multicultural Counseling
Oppression and Discrimination
Culturally Skilled Counselor
Advocacy and Social Justice
Creative Arts

Purposes: Over the last three decades, multicultural counseling has become the fourth force in the counseling profession. Recently, scholars have begun to move toward including social justice as a part of multicultural counseling competency. Since the beginning of the 1980s, there has been a significant change in the focus of counselors and counselor educators to serve culturally diverse populations (Pedersen, 1991). Over the years, training multiculturally competent counselors has been emphasized (Locke & Kiselica, 1999); however, discussion on social justice and advocacy in counselor education programs has just begun to gain momentum. Today, the focus has shifted toward infusing social justice advocacy competencies in counselor education programs. An important dimension of social justice advocacy competencies is developing awareness of one's own culture and social status. The activity described here delves into the realm of social justice by helping the counseling student develop insight into his or her experiences as an individual in this society and how that experience might be different from others'. This activity was adapted from a research project that focused on participatory action research (PAR) and specifically on the concept of *photovoice* (Graziano, 2004). The aim of PAR is to enhance awareness of social justice issues in the participants' social world through their participation in research (Graziano, 2004). Specifically, in photovoice participants use photography to capture images that reflect the greater social structure in their specific environments and examine their images through discussion (Graziano, 2004). Here, the activity was adapted in order to enhance counseling students' understanding, perceptions, and conceptualization of social privilege in order to enhance their multicultural counseling competency and their identification with their role in creating social justice. They do this through taking an honest look at their status in the social system through the images they capture and completing writing and discussion exercises to further their understanding. This activity fosters creative expression and requires students to think and reflect on the concept of social privilege.

Learning Objectives: As a result of this activity, students will

- have a better understanding of social privilege,
- develop an awareness of their own social status,
- develop an awareness of how their social status and privileges may have an effect on their work as counselors, and
- develop an understanding of how they might be different from their clients in terms of the privileges they experience.

Target Population: This activity was designed for master's- or doctoral-level counseling students. The activity may also be used in in-service multicultural counseling workshops and trainings for counselors.

Group Size: No limitations

Time Required: (a) 1 hour to discuss the term *social privilege*; (b) at least a couple of days for students to brainstorm, take photographs, and complete writing reflections on their images; and (c) 12 hours on the discussion and classification of pictures

Setting: Classroom

Materials: Camera, board, transparent tape, and markers

Instructions for Conducting Activity

Step 1: Developing an Understanding of Social Privilege

Discuss the concept of social privilege. You can use the description provided in Handout 80.1. Provide the definition and ask students about the privilege, or lack thereof, they hold in society.

Step 2: Taking Photographs

Provide a copy of the handout to the students. Before the next meeting time, have students take a photograph of something that represents social privilege in their environment. Read students the instructions and definition listed in Handout 80.1.

Step 3: Reflections on Photographs

Collect the photos from students. Arrange and tape photos randomly on the board. Ask students to choose their photos and tell the story in their photos. Ask students to engage in a dialogue about their reflections of the photo. After each student reflects on his or her photo, ask the entire class to identify common themes and issues that have emerged from the photographs. Divide the board into sections based on the themes that have emerged. Write the themes on each section and place each photo that belongs to that theme in the designated area. Have students discuss the following:

1. How might these privileges be different for different cultural groups?
2. How might a lack of such privilege affect the well-being of their clients?
3. How might having differences in privileges affect the counseling relationship?
4. What are their roles as counselors to challenge the privileged system?
5. What are their roles as social justice agents?

Handout: Handout 80.1: Reflections of Social Privilege

References

Barndt, J. R. (2007). *Understanding and dismantling racism: The twenty-first century challenge to White America.* Minneapolis, MN: Fortress Press.

Graziano, K. J. (2004). Oppression and resiliency in a post-apartheid South Africa: Unheard voices of Black gay men and lesbians. *Cultural Diversity and Ethnic Minority Psychology, 10,* 302–316.

Locke, D., & Kiselica, M. S. (1999). Pedagogy of possibilities: Teaching about racism in multicultural counseling courses. *Journal of Counseling & Development, 77,* 80–87.

Pedersen, P. (1991). Multiculturalism as a generic approach to counseling. *Journal of Counseling & Development*, 70, 6–12.

Additional Readings

Ancis, J. R., & Szymanski, D. M. (2001). Awareness of White privilege among White counseling trainees. *The Counseling Psychologist*, 29, 548–569.

Freire, P. (1970). *Pedagogy of the oppressed.* New York, NY: Seabury.

Hays, D. G., Chang, C. Y., & Dean, J. K. (2004). White counselors' conceptualization of privilege and oppression: Implications for counselor training. *Counselor Education and Supervision*, *43,* 242–258.

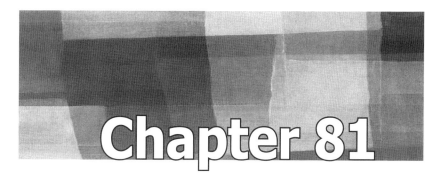

Cultural Formulation Exercise: Making Culturally Appropriate Formulations in the Treatment of Culturally Diverse Individuals

Michael Goh, Michael Starkey, and Julie Koch

Topics: Culturally Skilled Counselor
Counseling People With Disabilities
Helping Relationships
Assessment
Use of New Technology

Purposes: The aim of this exercise is to provide students with an opportunity to use an often ignored client conceptualization tool: the "Outline for Cultural Formulation" in the *Diagnostic and Statistical Manual of Mental Disorders* (4th ed., text rev.; *DSM-IV-TR*; American Psychiatric Association, 2000). The purpose of this tool is to help students consider culture's effects on a person's psychological functioning. Furthermore, this activity encourages students to reflect on how culture influences symptomatology, treatment planning, and case conceptualization.

Learning Objectives: As a result of this activity, students will (a) have a better understanding of how a client's culture influences treatment planning, diagnosis, and the therapeutic relationship; (b) consider culture as a major determinant in how a client understands his or her disorder; and (c) understand the inextricable nature of a client's culture and his or her psychological functioning.

Target Population: Students currently enrolled in an introductory or advanced multicultural counseling course or students in counseling practicum—basic or advanced. This exercise may also be conducted in a class about diagnosis and assessment of psychological disorders.

Group Size: Because discussion and consultation are critical aspects to this exercise, we recommend that classes have about four to seven students. In larger classes, this exercise can still be conducted with students broken up into groups of four to seven students.

Time Required: This activity will require time in at least two class meetings as well as time spent outside of class.

Setting: No special setting is needed for this activity. A classroom or group room is appropriate.

Materials: Stationery for taking notes. Copies of *DSM-IV-TR* (American Psychiatric Association, 2000).

Instructions for Conducting Activity

The instructor should determine a point allotment for this assignment/activity and include it on the course syllabus. A description of the activity in the course syllabus may read like this:

> Cultural formulation exercise is a small-group project working with two or three other students and involves three main phases. The first involves a class meeting, arranged by the course instructor, with a mental health provider(s) to interview about details of a case. The second phase involves writing an 8- to 10-page paper, consisting of (a) a traditional case presentation of a patient or client, and (b) a discussion of the case with special attention to cross-cultural, religious, or ethnic factors, according to the format of the *DSM-IV-TR*'s "Outline for Cultural Formulation" (see page xx of this syllabus). Students may also refer to the Committee on Cultural Psychiatry Group for the Advancement of Psychiatry text "Cultural Assessment in Clinical Psychiatry" for a detailed description on how to perform a cultural formulation. The third phase involves submitting the paper to a refereed journal. For example, the *Journal of Muslim Mental Health* features a "Cultural Formulation" section intended to demonstrate a cross-cultural approach to mental health assessment and treatment in a case-based format.

Early in the semester, the instructor should arrange a meeting with an area mental health agency, a college counseling center, or a counselor/therapist in private practice to present a client case.

Optional, but highly recommended, is to set aside another class meeting to view and discuss the video *The Culture of Emotions: A Cultural Competence Training Program* (Koskoff, 2002) in preparation for this exercise.

On the day of presentation the counselor/therapist may come to the class session at the university or the class may travel to the counselor/therapist's agency. The counselor/therapist then presents a client case to the class. All identifying information should already have been removed or masked. The information should include presenting problem, cultural background, family history, educational/vocational background, medical history, abuse history, outpatient treatment history, inpatient treatment history, substance abuse history, psychotropic medication history, and other relevant history. Along with this, the counselor/therapist should also provide information on the therapeutic relationship, any countertransference experienced, and length of treatment. Throughout this process, students are encouraged to ask questions and to interact with the presenter(s).

After the presentation, the students may either work in groups or individually to write a case study based on the *DSM-IV-TR*'s "Outline for Cultural Formulation" (American Psychiatric Association, 2000, pp. 897–898). The students' papers should include a summary of the client's history, multiaxial diagnosis, and cultural identity as well as cultural explanations of the client's disorder, cultural factors related to the client's functioning, and cultural elements that influence the relationship between the clinician and client.

Students are given one week to complete a draft of this paper. They return to class the subsequent week to meet again with the mental health providers. This meeting is an opportunity to seek new information as well as to clarify aspects of the case. A discussion about the entire cultural formulation exercise is recommended around the following questions:

1. What did you learn from this exercise?
2. How might our conceptualization of this case be different without the cultural formulation framework?
3. How can we develop the skills to make culturally appropriate treatments for all culturally diverse clients all of the time?

Students are strongly encouraged to submit their manuscript for publication. An example of one such manuscript that was published is Starkey et al. (2008).

References

American Psychiatric Association. (2000). *Diagnostic and statistical manual of mental disorders* (4th ed., text rev.). Washington, DC: Author.

Koskoff, H. (Producer). (2002). *The culture of emotions: A cultural competence training program* [Motion picture]. Boston, MA: Fanlight Productions.

Starkey, M., Lee, H. K., Tu, C. C., Netland, J., Goh, M., McGraw Schuchman, D., & Yusuf, A. (2008). Only Allah can heal: A cultural formulation of the psychological, religious, and cultural experiences of a Somali man. *Journal of Muslim Mental Health, 33,* 145–153.

Additional Readings

Committee on Cultural Psychiatry, Group for the Advancement of Psychiatry. (2002). *Cultural assessment in clinical psychiatry*. Washington, DC: American Psychiatric Publishing.

Chapter 82

Run for the Wall:
The Myth of the Level Playing Field

Nathalie Kees[1], Jacqueline Peila-Shuster, Sharon K. Anderson, Antonette Aragon, and Edward J. Brantmeier

Topics: Oppression and Discrimination
Culturally Skilled Counselor
Helping Relationships
Group Work

Purposes: It is often difficult for beginning counselors to empathize with clients who have different experiences and backgrounds from themselves. At the beginning stages of learning to empathize with others, counseling students may hold a strong belief in meritocracy, that each individual has equal opportunities for success if they work hard enough and pull themselves up by their bootstraps (Anderson & Middleton, 2005; Diller, 2007). The purpose of this activity is to help counseling students explore the myth of the level playing field, that is, the myth that they and their clients begin at the same place, with equal access to resources and experiences and, therefore, equal opportunities for success and attainment of goals.

Learning Objectives: As a result of this activity, participants will (a) become aware of the inequities experienced by their clients as a result of life experiences, institutionalized oppression and discrimination, and unearned privilege; (b) develop empathy and understanding for clients whose life experiences may be different from their own; and (c) reflect on the concept of meritocracy within the larger society and its effect on their role as counselors.

Target Population: Graduate students in the fields of counseling, psychology, social work, and the helping professions in general

Group Size: 10–30 participants

Time Required: 45–60 minutes

Setting: This activity is best conducted outside or in a large, spacious room with tables and chairs removed.

---

[1]Nathalie Kees was introduced to this activity by Barbara Catbagan of Naropa University in Boulder, CO, and has adapted it here for working specifically with counselors-in-training. The author would like to extend a special thank you to Barbara and her colleagues at Naropa.

Materials: Client role sheets, list of instruction statements found below, and participant journals

Instructions for Conducting Activity

1. In written form, provide each participant with a client role they are to play. Ask them not to share their role with other participants. Make the roles specific with information such as the client's age, race, gender, ethnicity, family history, sexual orientation, religion, educational background, disability, socioeconomic status, and work history. Make sure the roles are representative across all groups and include White and non-White clients, clients with privileges and those without, and so forth. Allow participants time to read and assume the client role they are to play.

2. Choose a large open space, indoors or out, where participants can form one line, shoulder to shoulder, all facing the same wall that is about 20 feet in front of them. Ask participants to hold hands with the persons next to them and to continue holding hands as long as they are able.

3. As the facilitator reads a statement from the following list, participants move either forward or backward in response to the directions provided.

4. As participants move further apart, it becomes more difficult to continue holding hands. Ask participants to be aware of any feelings this situation may bring up.

5. After all of the statements have been read, tell participants that, on the count of three, they must run for the wall and that the first one to touch the wall wins. Say, "One, two, three, GO!"

Sample Instruction Statements

You can change or add to these depending on the client roles you have given your participants.

1. If neither of your parents graduated from college, take one step backward.
2. If you have never experienced discrimination or violence based on the color of your skin, your gender, your age, or your sexual orientation, take one step forward.
3. If you are younger than 21 or older than 45, take one step backward.
4. If you are illiterate, take one step back.
5. If you can legally get married, take one step forward.
6. If you can comfortably walk in the town you live in while holding your partner's hand, take one step forward.
7. If you graduated from high school, take one step forward.
8. If you have an untreated substance abuse problem or mental illness, take one step backward.
9. If you have a disability, take one step backward.
10. If you have never had to worry about your weight, take one step forward.
11. If you are homeless, take one step backward.
12. If you were shown role models of people of your race or gender while you were in school, take one step forward.
13. If you have lost a job nonvoluntarily, take one step backward.
14. If you have never experienced discrimination based on your religion, take one step forward.
15. If you or your family's income is below the poverty level, take one step back.
16. If you struggle with English as your second language, take one step back.
17. If your parents paid for your college education, take one step forward.
18. If you or your family members are in this country as undocumented workers, take one step back.
19. If you have a valid driver's license and own a vehicle, take one step forward.

Processing Questions

Regroup in one large circle and discuss the following questions:

1. What did you notice about your client's experience?
2. What feelings did you have during your client's experience?
3. What did you notice about your client's position in relation to others in the line?

4. Who made it to the wall first, and who didn't? How did that feel?
5. How might your client's experience be similar or different from your own?
6. What did you learn that might help you empathize with your client or any of the others represented? Which clients will be easiest for you to empathize with? Which will be most difficult?
7. What did this exercise help you realize about meritocracy and the concept of the level playing field?
8. What struggles or questions did this exercise bring up for you?
9. What might you take from this experience into your work with clients?
10. What implications might this exercise have for your role as an advocate for your clients in the societal structures they are a part of? How might you advocate for societal change? Who might you speak up for who does not currently have a voice within the system? How might you help them gain a voice?

Follow-Up Integration
1. After processing the activity, ask participants to journal on their personal reflections from the exercise. Ask them to list any commitments or next steps they might take as counselors.
2. Provide participants with follow-up readings on privilege, institutionalized oppression, and meritocracy.

References

Anderson, S. K., & Middleton, V. A. (2005). *Explorations in privilege, oppression, and diversity.* Belmont, CA: Brooks/Cole.
Diller, J. V. (2007). *Cultural diversity: A primer for the human services.* Belmont, CA: Brooks/Cole.

Additional Readings

McIntosh, P. (1989, July/August). White privilege: Unpacking the invisible knapsack. *Peace and Freedom*, 8–10. (See Handout 53.1.)

Note. For a reverse example of a similar exercise, see *Tools for activists: Turning privilege disparities into just and sustainable action* by Adrienne Maree Brown, available at http://wiretapmag.org/movement/43496/

Chapter 83

Case Scenarios:
Issues in Multicultural Supervision

Julie Koch and Ling-Hsuan Tung

Topics: Barriers to Effective Cross-Cultural Counseling
Cultural Identity Development
Culturally Skilled Counselor
Human Growth and Development
Helping Relationships

Purposes: The purpose of this exercise is to encourage participants to consider covert and overt issues that may occur in multicultural counselor supervision. Participants will explore and problem-solve issues related to supervision, such as the supervisory relationship, supervisor roles, supervisor disclosure, and informed consent in the context of a cross-cultural supervisory dyad or triad.

Learning Objectives: As a result of this activity, students will (a) expand their knowledge and awareness of potential issues that may emerge in multicultural supervision, including visible and invisible cultural differences, differing levels of cultural identity development, differing communication styles, level of acculturation, and others; (b) learn of preventive measures supervisors may take to promote understanding and positive communication; and (c) develop solutions to problems in multicultural supervision.

Target Population: These scenarios may be used with students learning about counselor supervision, students learning about multicultural counseling, and students enrolled in a supervision practicum. They may also be useful for continuing education of practitioners, faculty members, and current supervisors wanting to expand their knowledge of multicultural counseling and supervision.

Group Size: These scenarios may be used with small or large groups of participants. When used with a large group, it is recommended that the larger group be broken up into dyads or small groups of three to four participants for role-plays or discussion.

Time Required: For each scenario, it is recommended that 5–10 minutes be allowed for small-group discussion and an additional 5–10 minutes be allowed for larger group discussion with the instructor. If role-plays are used, it is recommended that 5–10 minutes be spent for each role-play and an additional 5–10 minutes be used for processing the role-play. For the processing, first the counselor and supervisor can discuss their feelings and thoughts playing the role, and then the observer can provide both positive and constructive feedback.

Setting: No special setting is needed for this activity. A classroom or group room is appropriate. If using small groups, an auditorium-style or stadium-style seating arrangement might present problems.

Materials: No special materials are needed for this activity. If students are visual learners, it might be helpful to make copies of the scenarios and pass them out; scenarios may also be written on PowerPoint slides (one slide per scenario) for easy reference.

Instructions for Conducting Activity

There are many ways in which these scenarios (see Handout 83.1) may be used for discussion:

- *Individual work (works well in classes with large number of introverted students or where discussion is not desired):* The instructor reads a scenario aloud or provides students with handouts of scenarios. Students put their thoughts down on paper by writing answers to the questions in free-form. The instructor may ask for individual responses or may allow for large-group discussion after all students have written responses.
- *Large group:* The instructor reads a scenario aloud or provides students with handouts of scenarios. Students raise their hands, and the instructor facilitates a large-group discussion.
- *Small groups or dyads:* The instructor reads a scenario aloud or provides students with handouts of scenarios. The instructor may assign each small group a different scenario or may assign all groups the same scenario. Time is allowed for small-group discussion. The instructor then facilitates a large-group discussion related to the scenarios.

There are also many ways in which these scenarios may be used for role-plays:

- Role-plays can be used alone or after discussion of the questions.
- *Dyads:* The instructor divides students into dyads and provides two scenarios to each dyad. The students take turns to play the roles of the counselor and the supervisor. After the role-play, the counselor and the supervisor may discuss their feelings and thoughts.
- *Triads (preferred):* The instructor divides students into triads and provides three scenarios to each triad. The students take turns to be the counselor, supervisor, and observer. After the role-play, the counselor and supervisor may discuss their feelings and thoughts first, and then the observer can provide both positive and constructive feedback.

Handouts: No handouts are necessary for this activity, although some instructors may choose to provide participants with written scenarios (see Handout 83.1, Case Scenarios: Issues in Multicultural Supervision) in order to assist students who may be visual learners.

Additional Readings

Bernard, J. M. (1994). Special issue: Cross-cultural counseling supervision. (1994). *Counselor Education and Supervision, 34*, 114–171.

Bernard, J. M., & Goodyear, R. K. (2004). *Fundamentals of clinical supervision*. Boston, MA: Pearson Education.

Constantine, M. G. (Ed.). Special issue: Perspective on multicultural supervision. (2001). *Journal of Multicultural Counseling and Development, 29*, 98–158.

Norton, R. A., & Coleman, H. L. K. (2003). Multicultural supervision: The influence of race-related issues in supervision and outcome. In D. B. Pope-Davis, H. L. K. Coleman, W. M. Liu, & R. L. Toporek (Eds.), *Handbook of multicultural competencies in counseling & psychology* (pp. 114–134). Thousand Oaks, CA: Sage.

Toporek, R. L., Ortega-Villalobos, L., & Pope-Davis, D. B. (2004). Critical incidents in multicultural supervision: Exploring supervisees' and supervisors' experiences. *Journal of Multicultural Counseling and Development, 32*, 66–83.

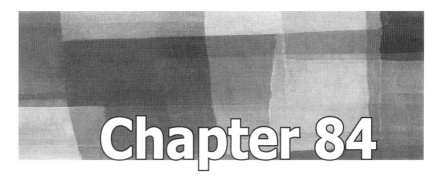

Chapter 84

Bridging the Gap of Multicultural Competencies

Imelda N. Lowe

Topics: Introduction to Multicultural Counseling
Dimensions of Worldviews
Culturally Skilled Counselor
Human Growth and Development
Helping Relationships

Purposes: The purpose of this activity is to provide students with an opportunity to reflect on their personal growth and development as counselors competent in multicultural issues. This activity also provides an opportunity for group discussion regarding individuals' personal experiences.

Learning Objectives: As a result of this activity, students will (a) be able to reflect on their personal growth relating to multicultural competence, (b) be able to represent their growth visually through the drawing activity, and (c) be able to discuss their personal process of gaining multicultural competence.

Target Population: This activity is designed for advanced students.

Group Size: Any size would be appropriate; this activity may be done with individuals or in a class-room setting.

Time Required: 1 to 1.5 hours

Setting: This activity may be conducted in a classroom setting. It is recommended that the students have a table for the drawing activity.

Materials: Markers, crayons, or colored pencils; one large piece of paper for each student

Instructions for Conducting Activity

Give each student a piece of paper, and provide markers, crayons, or colored pencils. Introduce the activity by inviting students to self-reflect on their prejudices and biases they believed as a child, adolescent, or young adult. Allow students a moment to visualize and reflect on their experiences. Next, have students consider their current beliefs and prejudices as well as their knowledge regarding multicultural counseling skills. Again, allow students a moment to visualize and self-reflect on their experiences. Inform the students that the activity they will be doing relates to the reflections that they just visualized.

Please note that some students may wish to verbally share their experiences during the introduction prompts. Encourage them to wait until the process time at the end if possible. This time is intended for students to self-reflect, and a time to process and share will be provided at the end.

Provide the following drawing instructions:

On the right side of the paper draw a representation of yourself before you entered the counseling program. This may be done in any way that you believe reflects your attitudes and beliefs you held at that time regarding multicultural issues (prejudices, assumptions, and so forth).

On the left side of the paper draw a representation of yourself currently. Again, visually represent your current attitudes and beliefs you have after learning about multicultural issues.

Between the two drawings, make a bridge that represents your personal journey from your previous belief system to your current belief system. Let the bridge be a symbol of the process you encountered while becoming more knowledgeable about multicultural issues.

Provide students with ample time to illustrate their drawing. Allow students to represent their drawings as they wish. The focus is on the process of the activity rather than the product of the drawing.

When the students are finished, allow them an opportunity to share their drawings either in small groups or as a class, depending on the size. Provide some of the following questions to assist in processing the experience:

- What resonated with you during the activity?
- What were the most notable differences between the drawing on the right side and the left side?
- What are your reactions to the differences?
- What feelings do you have when you see your picture?
- Where did you place yourself in relation to the bridge? Have you completed the journey across, or are you still on the bridge?
- Can you describe specific incidents that helped you cross your bridge?
- Is there anything that you would like to be different?
- What have you learned that you will take from today's activity?
- What was it like to hear other classmates share their stories?

Additional Readings

Coleman, M. N. (2006). Critical incidents in multicultural training: An examination of student experiences. *Journal of Multicultural Counseling and Development, 34*, 168–182.

Kim, B. K., & Lyons, H. (2003). Experiential activities and multicultural counseling competence training. *Journal of Counseling & Development, 81*, 400–408.

Chapter 85

Creating Multicultural Awareness and Understanding Through Establishing a Positive Learning Environment

Kelly Most

Topics: Culturally Skilled Counselor
Counseling Native Americans
Professional Identity and Ethical Practice
Helping Relationships
Group Work

Purposes: The purpose of this activity is to assist individuals in understanding and conceptualizing the general multicultural topics given in the course or training. This experiential activity is most effective when it is used early on in the course or training and then is revisited toward the end of the course.

Learning Objective: As a result of this experience, learners will gain awareness and general understanding into the broad multicultural topics given in their multicultural course or diversity training. Some of the areas of growth will include the following:

- understanding general information that will be presented in the course or training,
- learning the background knowledge of other participants in regard to the topic areas,
- achieving greater collaboration and openness between participants, and
- being a part of a reflective group work process.

Target Population: Individuals enrolled in a graduate multicultural counseling course or individuals attending a training on diversity

Group Size: A maximum of 50, but no fewer than 10

Time Required: 1–2 hours

Setting: Based on the amount of predetermined topics, seats would typically be arranged with four to six participants in each group. For example, if there are four topics and 20 participants, then there would be four groups with five participants in each group.

Materials: Because participants are required to record their ideas for the group to view, large Post-it paper (two for each topic) is required. Additional supplies for this activity include markers, note cards cut into fourths, and pens. A reward presented by the facilitator can also be given to the most creative group.

Instructions for Conducting Activity

1. Before the lecture begins, write the general topic areas for the multicultural course or training on the large Post-it paper, with one topic per paper (e.g., White privilege, acculturation models, multicultural competencies, biracial clients, Native American clients, diversity in public settings). Then place them evenly on the walls around the room, leaving space between them.

2. Group the tables and chairs together, creating the same number of groups as topic areas.

3. Place markers at each table.

4. Once all the participants are present, tell each group to go stand by one of the topics on the wall (all group members are required to physically go stand by the poster and participate in writing on the poster).

5. Explain the process: Students will first discuss as a small group what group members "know" about the topic area listed on the Post-it paper, then each group member will alternate writing on the Post-it paper words, concepts, and ideas that relate to the given topic.

6. Each group will be given approximately 5 minutes at each poster. The facilitator is responsible for telling the groups when to switch posters. The group as a whole will move from poster to poster in a clockwise fashion each time the facilitator calls "time." This process is called the carousal.

7. Once the groups have had the opportunity to write on each poster, they will end at the original poster where they started. Next, the group members will take their large Post-it paper off the wall and bring it to their seats.

8. The facilitator will give each group the note cards cut into fourths and pens to complete the next stage of the process.

9. Each group will record all the words and concepts written on the paper, one idea per note card. The groups will independently determine how to accomplish their task.

10. Next, each group will categorize all the concepts on their note cards by establishing headings and subcategories. Group members will collaborate on this process by putting all the note cards in front of the group members, who will move the cards around and establish category headings and subcategories. Many times the group members will have to establish these category headings, but other times they are given on the original Post-it paper.

11. Once the categories are organized, each group is given another large Post-it paper to record in a creative way the information constructed by the group.

12. Group members are also instructed to generate three questions that they wonder about in their topic area. They are not required to be able to answer the questions.

13. Once they have created a summary visual for the class and determined three questions about in their topic, they will present their information to the larger group. The presentations should focus on the topic information and reflect the overall group process. Each group member should present some information to the larger group.

14. The facilitator chooses the groups to present in random order and determines the amount of time available for each group to present (35 minutes).

15. Throughout this entire process the facilitator is moving between groups answering questions, helping generate ideas, and instructing the groups individually on the next step of the process.

16. Optional: Revisit this activity at the end of the course or training and see what the participants learned throughout their experience. Talk about what they came into the course knowing and wondering, then discuss what they learned based on the topic areas. Have them work by themselves initially and then in a small group; finally, ask people to share a summary of what was discussed in their smaller groups. The facilitator can also save the large Post-it pages created by the class and physically show the group what they learned.

Additional Readings

Ogle, D. (1986). K-W-L: A teaching model that develops active reading of expository text. *Reading Teacher, 38,* 564–570.

Chapter 86
Cultural Sensitivity Self-Assessment

Allison C. Paolini

Topics: Introduction to Multicultural Counseling
Cultural Identity Development
Culturally Skilled Counselor

Purposes: The purpose of this activity is to enable students to self-assess their comfort level and base of knowledge regarding multicultural counseling. This activity allows students to self-reflect about their feelings, beliefs, and possible existing biases pertaining to working with diverse populations.

Learning Objectives: As a result of this activity, students will become more aware of their own beliefs, feelings, and biases in terms of counseling diverse populations. This activity will also allow students to do introspective thinking and reflect on their attitudes and how their beliefs affect their ability to interact with individuals from a variety of cultural backgrounds. This activity will also give students the opportunity to use the knowledge that they have acquired about multicultural counseling by responding to the posed questions.

Target Population: This activity is specifically designed for undergraduate students taking sociology, education, or psychology courses. It can also be used with graduate students who are seeking to obtain a degree in school counseling, mental health counseling, or psychology.

Group Size: 15–30 students

Time Required: 25–30 minutes

Setting: This activity can be conducted in a classroom setting. After completing the activity, students can discuss their answers if they feel comfortable sharing their responses with their peers.

Materials: Pens, pencils, and handout

Instructions for Conducting Activity

Facilitator will preface this activity by stating that all individuals have certain prejudicial attitudes or beliefs. As students, it is important for individuals to be cognizant about their own biases and to understand the impact that their beliefs have on their interactions with culturally diverse populations. In this regard, the facilitator is creating a nonjudgmental environment for the students to respond in an open and honest manner. Students will read the statements posed (see Handout 86.1) and then circle "True" or "False" for each item based on their knowledge, beliefs, and attitudes regarding individuals from a variety of cultural backgrounds.

After the students have completed the activity, the facilitator will lead a discussion about the importance of recognizing one's own prejudices as well as the significance of being culturally sensitive when working with culturally diverse populations. In addition, the facilitator will need to address the consequences of being intolerant and narrow-minded when working with diverse cultural populations.

Handout: Handout 86.1: Multiculturalism Mania

Additional Readings

Callanan, P., Corey, M. S., & Corey, G. (2007). *Issues and ethics in the helping professions.* Pacific Grove, CA: Thomson Brooks/Cole.

MacCluskie, K. (2010). *Acquiring counseling skills: Integrating theory, multiculturalism, and self-awareness.* Upper Saddle River, NJ: Pearson/Merrill.

Sue, D. W., & Sue, D. (2003). *Counseling the culturally diverse: Theory and practice* (4th ed.). New York, NY: Wiley.

Chapter 87

Cultural Overtures

Mark Pope

Topics: Introduction to Multicultural Counseling
Cultural Communication Styles
Oppression and Discrimination
Dimensions of Worldviews
Culturally Skilled Counselor
Human Growth and Development

Purposes: This activity is designed to allow students to learn about other cultures while also learning about their fellow students. Hence, it is a particularly effective activity to conduct early in the development of a classroom's culture.

Learning Objectives: By participating in the activity, participants will (a) learn information about other cultures and (b) learn more about their fellow students.

Target Population: Undergraduate or graduate students in counseling, education, psychology, or social work

Group Size: 15–30 participants optimally, but really unlimited

Time Required: 30–50 minutes

Setting: Classroom setting

Materials: Copies of either "Cultural Overtures #1" (Handout 87.1) or "Cultural Overtures #2" (Handout 87.2); "Cultural Overtures Answers" (Handout 87.3)

Instructions for Conducting Activity

First, the instructor will decide which of the two handouts to use. Then, the instructor will pass out to each student a copy of that handout. Next, the instructor will read to the class the instructions at the top of the handout (see Handout 87.1 or 87.2):

1. "Read your Overtures Card below and note mentally which ones you, yourself, can answer.
2. You must sign your name and tell the other person what you know when you sign.
3. Each person may sign only one square on a card. Walk around and talk to others."
4. Students should walk around the room asking other students if they have knowledge of any of the items on that student's handout. The instructor may not sign the cards.
5. When almost all students have completed their cards, the instructor should tell the students to return to their seats.

6. Process the participants' feelings and reactions to the exercise. Here are some issues to guide your processing:
   a. What did it feel like to collect the signatures for each of the items? Did you approach it as a task to be completed or a learning process?
   b. How many students knew the answer to (a particular item on the card)?
   c. What do you think is the correct answer?
   d. What did you learn about your classmates?

Handouts: Handout 87.1: Cultural Overtures #1
            Handout 87.2: Cultural Overtures #2
            Handout 87.3: Cultural Overtures Answers

Chapter 88

Imagine a Cross-Cultural Experience

Janice Munro and Michael S. Rankins

Topics: Dimensions of Worldviews
Cultural Identity Development
Culturally Skilled Counselor
Group Work

Purposes: This cross-cultural activity is an interactive experience in guided imagery and invites participants to explore emotions associated with immersion in an unfamiliar cultural milieu while remaining in the group workshop setting. During this process, the facilitators will provide certain information intended to evoke strong imagery but will also require participants to draw on their own inner resources to complete the guided imagery experience. Through this experience, participants are led toward enhanced awareness of the means by which they interpret the world around them and the subjective nature of this interpretation. Ultimately, participants are encouraged to reflect on what they consider to be the most important dimensions of their own identity, how their identity may be more clearly examined as it is held up against a contrasting backdrop represented by the unfamiliar culture, and how the nature of so-called absolute truths may be challenged by developing a greater appreciation of the perspectives of persons from other cultures.

Learning Objectives: As a result of this activity, participants will have a greater awareness of how they interpret the world around them, how they engage in the construction of meaning, and how other persons may construct alternative meanings.

Target Population: Although perhaps of greatest interest to counselors and counselor educators, this activity is designed for all adults working or interacting with other adults in a diverse society.

Group Size: It is anticipated that this activity will work best with a group of 5–30 participants.

Time Required: This activity requires approximately 50–60 minutes.

Setting: It is essential that this activity take place in a quiet setting. Seating for all participants is important, as participants should be able to relax while engaging in the guided imagery exercise. Ideally, this activity requires a room large enough to allow all participants to be seated in a circle. If possible, facilitators should use a room in which the lighting can be dimmed.

Materials: The facilitator will need enough copies of Handout 88.1, "Imagine a Cross-Cultural Experience"; Handout 88.2, "Positive Feeling Words"; and Handout 88.3, "Negative Feeling Words" for all participants and facilitators.

Instructions for Conducting Activity

Prior to the workshop, the facilitator should modify the "Imagine a Cross-Cultural Experience" handout to reflect the cultural milieu into which participants will plunge during the guided imagery experience. If desired, the handout can remain generic and may be used as is. Rehearsal is advised: The facilitator will need to read the handout to participants during the guided imagery experience, as they will not be provided with copies of this handout until late in the workshop. Have copies of both the "Imagine a Cross-Cultural Experience" handout and the "Feeling Words" handout ready for participants, but only distribute these near the end of the workshop.

At the beginning of the activity, ask participants to form a circle if the room used for the workshop permits. If there is insufficient room or if other restrictions make forming a circle impossible, have participants assume an improvised arrangement so that all members of the group can regard one another. Invite participants to introduce themselves, and, if time permits, ask each person to share information about his or her culture of origin (e.g., heritage, birthplace, affiliations, and so forth). Following introductions, follow these steps:

1. Invite participants to join you in a guided imagery experience. Ask everyone to assume a comfortable and relaxed position and to remain seated for the duration of the experience. Ask everyone in the room to remain as quiet as possible during the next few moments.
2. Ask those wishing to participate to close their eyes and to keep their eyes closed during the entire guided imagery experience.
3. The facilitator should ask participants to allow themselves to focus on the sound of his or her voice as the remainder of the experience unfolds. The facilitator should inform participants that during the experience, he or she will ask them about what they are feeling at certain points. They should not speak when these questions are asked, but they should consider the feelings that they are experiencing at those points.
4. When the facilitator believes that participants are ready, he or she should begin reading the "Imagine a Cross-Cultural Experience" handout to the group. Read slowly, allowing participants to savor the richness of their own personal imagery as elicited by the words of the facilitator. Remember, participants should remain seated with their eyes closed and should not have copies of the handouts yet.
5. As the facilitator reads the handout, he or she should pause at certain predetermined points in order to allow participants to silently identify the feelings that they are experiencing at these moments during the experience.
6. As the facilitator concludes the reading of the handout, he or she should invite participants to emerge from the guided imagery experience and to open their eyes. After a brief moment, the facilitator should pose a number of postexperience questions to the group:
   a. Was Drew a man or a woman?
   b. Was Pat a man or a woman?
   c. What were the people wearing? What did they look like? What did they smell like? Sound like? What language was used during their chanting?
   d. What were **you** wearing? What car were you driving?
   e. What other assumptions did you make during the experience?
   f. What other sorts of details did you notice about the meeting?
   g. What other sorts of details did you notice about the people at the meeting?
   h. What other sorts of details did you notice during the experience?
   i. What if this was an Amway group meeting?
   j. What if this was a religious group meeting?
   k. What if this was a radical or reactionary political group meeting?
   l. What if this was another kind of meeting (invite participants to suggest various types of meetings).

7. At this point, the cofacilitator (or a volunteer) should begin distributing both sets of workshop handouts. The participants should continue sharing their feelings and the details they had noticed during the guided imagery experience.

8. After all participants have received copies of the two sets of handouts, the facilitator should invite participants to use the two "Feeling Words" handouts to help them articulate any additional feelings they wish to share with the group. Also invite participants to consider, as they glance through the "Imagine a Cross-Cultural Experience" handout, any discrepancies that exist between the words actually spoken by the facilitator and the images that were elicited for the participants.

9. The facilitator should pose to the participants the following critical questions for the group to discuss:

    a. Where did the information participants projected into the guided imagery experience come from?

    b. What thoughts were associated with the emotions participants experienced during the experience?

    c. What supported the assumptions that participants made during the experience?

    d. What process did participants go through in order to reach the conclusions drawn during the experience?

    e. Have participants had similar experiences in reality? If so, what similarities existed?

10. Conclude by inviting participants to propose ways in which their own background may have influenced their experience today, and how knowledge gleaned from today's guided imagery might help them achieve a more informed perspective when encountering different cultures and persons from those cultures.

Facilitator Notes

The success of this activity lies in the process of leading participants to realize how much of what they experienced during the guided imagery was drawn from their own frame of reference. Through the realization of how subjective their assumptions actually may have been (as evidenced by multiple, competing assumptions made by others), participants are encouraged to review both the cultural lens through which they view the world around them and the questionable accuracy of some conclusions drawn about that which is observed through such a lens. Remember that participants may not immediately demonstrate the benefits of such realizations. The facilitators should view the process of conducting this workshop as the planting of seeds.

Handouts: Handout 88.1: Imagine a Cross-Cultural Experience
Handout 88.2: Positive Feeling Words
Handout 88.3: Negative Feeling Words

Chapter 89

Reflections and Remembrances: Carrying Knowledge Into Practice

Anne M. Ober

Topics: Introduction to Multicultural Counseling
Cultural Identity Development
Dimensions of Worldviews
Culturally Skilled Counselor

Purposes: The purposes of this activity are to give participants an opportunity to reflect on their learning experiences in the introductory multicultural counseling course and to provide a method of transmitting this learning into their work with clients/students.

Learning Objectives: As a result of this activity, students will be able to (a) identify their strengths and growth edges related to multicultural counseling, (b) identify similarities and differences with a person from a different cultural background, and (c) reflect on personal insight and/or knowledge gained through the course.

Target Population: Students who have completed an introductory course in multicultural counseling and will soon begin their practicum and/or internship experience

Group Size: This activity can be used with any size group.

Time Required: Approximately 15–20 minutes for students to reflect and write

Setting: This activity can be used in almost any setting that provides a quiet and conducive space to write.

Materials: Worksheets (Handout 89.1), envelopes, and pens/pencils

Instructions for Conducting Activity

Introduce the activity by emphasizing the need for continual personal and professional growth and development with regard to multicultural counseling. This exercise is intended to help students reflect on what they have learned about counseling, others, and themselves over the time of the course and help them define areas of future growth. Hand out a worksheet (Handout 89.1) to each student and tell them that this piece of paper will be seen by them alone and will not be reviewed and/or graded by the instructor. Encourage them to take time to reflect and answer the questions honestly. After they are finished with the worksheet, have them fold it and place in envelope. Instruct them to place their name on the front of the envelope and sign over the seal at the back. Inform students that they will receive these envelopes in the future as they start working with clients/students to remind them of their learning experiences and to encourage continual development. It is the instructor's responsibility to provide these envelopes to students after they have begun their practicum or internship experiences.

Handout: Handout 89.1: Reflections and Remembrances

Additional Readings

Brockbank, A., & McGill, I. (2007). *Facilitating reflective learning in higher education* (2nd ed.). New York, NY: McGraw-Hill.

Hill, N. (2004). Promoting and celebrating multicultural competence in counselor trainees. *Counselor Education and Supervision, 43*, 39–51.

Rothenberg, P. S. (Ed.). 2007. *Race, class, and gender in the United States: An integrated study* (7th ed.). New York, NY: Worth.

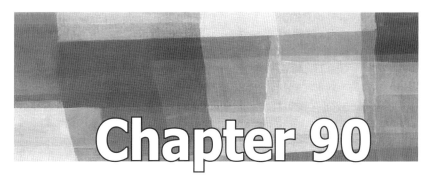

Chapter 90
Cross-Cultural Field Experience

Chippewa M. Thomas and Dorienna M. Alfred

Topics: Dimensions of Worldviews
Culturally Skilled Counselor
Helping Relationships

Purposes: The purposes of the cross-cultural field experience are (a) to encourage cultural immersion that challenges encapsulation and (b) to promote self-awareness and knowledge of specific ethnic/cultural groups to encourage multicultural counseling competence.

Learning Objectives: Consistent with the literature on experiential activities used to promote multicultural counseling competence (Arredondo & Arciniega, 2001; Arthur & Achenbach, 2002; Kim & Lyons, 2003), the objectives of this activity are to (a) provide students with opportunities to interact with individuals from cultures that are different than their own, (b) facilitate students' awareness of culture's impact on clinical practice, and (c) foster students' knowledge of specific groups' cultural practices that have implications for multicultural counseling competence.

Target Population: The target population for this activity is students in a beginning multicultural counseling and other core counseling courses.

Group Size: The designated group size for the activity includes the individual student and at least five or more people within a group at the cross-cultural experience.

Time Required: The duration of the activity includes the time needed for students to select the activity they will participate in, engage in the activity, and spend time reflecting on the experience. Finally, guided by the reflection questions, students will complete the reflection report. Students should be given approximately four weeks to prepare for and complete each cross-cultural experience.

Setting: Setting will be selected by the student, who will report it to the course instructor for approval.

Materials: Handout 90.1.

Instructions for Conducting the Activity

To become culturally competent, one must avoid being culturally encapsulated (Sue & Sue, 2003). Therefore, during the course of this semester, you will be asked to challenge the notion of encapsulation by participating in two cultural events/experiences with an ethnic/cultural group different from your own (e.g., gender, sexual orientation, religion, disability, race/ethnicity, socioeconomic status). You may be tempted to choose cultural events in which you may be a minority but that do not challenge you to reach a higher level of self-awareness or knowledge of a given culture. There is an expectation that you will engage in activities that provide opportunities for you to challenge any misperceptions you hold of the culture in which you choose to experience. You will have two opportunities to engage in a cultural field experience. Your second field experience should demonstrate your efforts to challenge your self-awareness toward and understanding of cultural/ethnic groups with whom you have struggled to effect multicultural competence. In addition to the field experience, you will be asked to write a three-page reflection in which you respond to questions or directives as they apply to your particular experience. Using the "Cross-Cultural Field Experience" worksheet, describe the field experience/setting, and answer the following questions: What was it like for you to be a participant in this event? What was your role in the activity/event? What feelings/thoughts did you have as you participated in the field experience? How did it feel to be an underrepresented person at the event? What cultural dynamics did you observe? What insights did you gain from this experience that will influence your awareness and knowledge as a culturally responsive professional? How could this information and/or experience inform your counseling practice? What cultural issues should be considered? Examine any legal or ethical concerns your experience could bring to bear in a counseling context. Prepare to discuss the content of the reflection in a class debriefing.

Handout: Handout 90.1: Cross-Cultural Field Experience

References

Arredondo, P., & Arciniega, G. (2001). Strategies and techniques for counselor training based on the multicultural counseling competencies. *Journal of Multicultural Counseling and Development, 29*, 263–273.

Arthur, N., & Achenbach, K. (2002). Developing multicultural counseling competencies through experiential learning. *Counselor Education and Supervision, 42*, 2–14.

Kim, B., & Lyons, H. (2003). Experiential activities and multicultural counseling competence training. *Journal of Counseling & Development, 81*, 400–408.

Sue, D. W., & Sue, D. (Eds.). (2003). *Counseling the culturally different: Theory and practice* (4th ed.). New York, NY: Wiley.

Additional Readings

Baruth, L. G., & Manning, M. L. (2007). *Multicultural counseling and psychotherapy: A lifespan perspective* (4th ed.). Upper Saddle River, NJ: Pearson/Merrill Prentice Hall.

Diaz-Lazaro, C. M., & Cohen, B. B. (2001). Cross-cultural contact in counseling training. *Journal of Multicultural Counseling and Development, 29*, 41–57.

Hansen, C. E., & Williams, M. R. (2001). Comparison of cross-cultural course changes: From traditional lecture course to contemporary course with biblio-learning, video-learning and experiential exercises. *Journal of Instructional Psychology, 30*, 197–206.

Langer de Ramirez, L. (2006). *Voices of diversity: Stories, activities, and resources for the multicultural classroom*. Upper Saddle River, NJ: Pearson/Merrill Prentice Hall.

Paniagua, F. A. (2005). *Assessing and treating culturally diverse clients: A practical guide* (3rd ed.). Thousand Oaks, CA: Sage.

Ponterotto, J. G., Casas, J. M., Suzuki, L. A., & Alexander, C. M. (1995). *Handbook of multicultural counseling*. Thousand Oaks, CA: Sage.

Rastogi, M., & Wieling, E. (Eds.). (2005). *Voices of color: First-person accounts of ethnic minority therapists*. Thousand Oaks, CA: Sage.

Welfel, E. R. (2006). *Ethics in counseling and psychotherapy: Standards, research and emerging issues* (3rd ed.). Belmont, CA: Thomson Brooks/Cole.

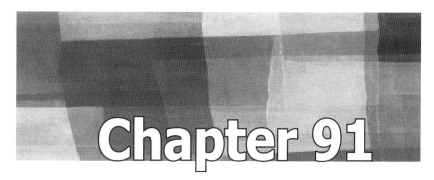

Chapter 91
Life Span Interview

Chippewa M. Thomas

Topics: Culturally Skilled Counselor
Counseling Lesbian, Gay, Bisexual, Transgender (LGBT) and Other Sexual Minority Clients
Counseling Aging Clients
Counseling People With Disabilities
Professional Identity and Ethical Practice
Career Development
Poverty, Social Class, and Socioeconomic Status (SES)

Purposes: The purpose of the life span interview activity is to involve participants in an activity in which they are exposed to cultures that are different from their own, thus fostering cross-cultural awareness (Dickson & Jepsen, 2007; Gardner & Kosmitzki, 2005).

Learning Objectives: As a result of this activity participants will (a) have experience in describing how individual differences in culture (e.g., heritage, environment, and lived experiences), race, social class, gender, sexual orientation, family structure, nationality, occupation, socioeconomic status, and religion/spirituality affect the course of development across the life span (Arredondo & Arciniega, 2001; Council for Accreditation of Counseling and Related Educational Programs, 2001); (b) use clinical interviewing skills to elicit personal histories (Gardner & Kosmitzki, 2005); and (c) use content from the interview to discuss the relationship of developmental and cultural considerations for counseling practice in a class group-processing context to enhance participant awareness (Arthur & Achenbach, 2002). Essentially, participants will gain awareness of psychosocial and emotional, social cultural and economic, and social political/historical factors that affect human growth and development across the life span.

Target Population: The target population for this activity is students (beginning) in a master's-level course of multicultural counseling applications to human growth and development/life span.

Group Size: The designated group size for the activity is the individual participant and the interviewee who volunteers to participate in the activity.

Time Required: The duration of the activity includes time needed for the participant to elicit the participation of a willing interviewee and plan the time and location the interview will take place; time to conduct the interview, which could span the course of 1 hour or more; and time to complete the paper detailing the interviewee's comments.

Setting: Setting will be selected and agreed on by the interviewee and participant.

Materials: Writing tablet, laptop and/or recording device to record the interviewee's responses, and comfortable setting in a location convenient for both the interviewee and the participant.

Instructions for Conducting the Activity

Participants select an interviewee representing a period of the life span and ask that person questions about the aspects of his or her life that have had and continue to have a profound developmental influence on him or her culturally and historically (Zingmark, Norberg, & Sandman, 1995). Participants complete a personal interview of any person 7 years of age or older. Participants are asked to reflect on the responses in regard to how they would approach counseling an individual with the concerns expressed in the interview. The interview will be conducted using the life span interview form provided (see Handout 91.1). The interview will be documented in a three- to five-page paper (descriptive paragraph in American Psychological Association style) and turned in to the instructor.

The interviewee's identifying information must **not** be recorded on the form or the final report, and the information gathered in the interview will not be used for any other purpose. The interviewee will be informed that the information gathered in interview will be used to fulfill a life span development class requirement and will not be used for any other purpose.

Participants will prepare to discuss the content from the interview in class group discussion and processing. Again, this content is anonymous, and the interviewee's identity is not revealed to the class. Using this content, participants are asked to reflect on developmental issues that would challenge them in providing multiculturally competent counseling and are asked to reveal concerns; thus, the course instructor or group facilitator may evaluate the participant's interview as well as his or her interpretive skills and judgment ability. Using the interview content in discussions that continue over the course of many classes, participants will be exposed to culturally appropriate responses and to practices of how to broach developmental issues with real-life clients (Arredondo & Arciniega, 2001; Day-Vines et al., 2007; Valario, 2001). The interview contextualizes various concerns that individuals experience at different periods of the life span and the various roles that culture plays in development across that time span.

Handout: Handout 91.1: Life Span Interview

References

Arredondo, P., & Arciniega, G. (2001). Strategies and techniques for counselor training based on the multicultural counseling competencies. *Journal of Multicultural Counseling and Development, 29,* 263–273.

Arthur, N., & Achenbach, K. (2002). Developing multicultural counseling competencies through experiential learning. *Counselor Education and Supervision, 42,* 2–14.

Council for Accreditation of Counseling and Related Educational Programs. (2001). *Standards.* Alexandria, VA: Author.

Day-Vines, N. L., Wood, S. M., Grothaus, T., Craigen, L., Holman, A., Dotson-Blake, K., & Douglass, M. J. (2007). Broaching the subjects of race, ethnicity, and culture during the counseling process. *Journal of Counseling & Development, 85,* 401–409.

Dickson, G. L., & Jepsen, D. A. (2007). Multicultural training experiences as predictors of multicultural competencies: Students' perspectives. *Counselor Education and Supervision, 47,* 76–95.

Gardner, H. W., & Kosmitzki, C. (2005). *Lives across cultures: Cross-cultural human development* (3rd ed.). Boston, MA: Pearson Education.

Valario, N. L. (2001). Creating safety to address controversial issues: Strategies for the classroom. *Multicultural Education, 8,* 24–28.

Zingmark K., Norberg A., & Sandman P. O. (1995). The experience of being at home throughout the life span: Investigation of persons aged from 2 to 102. *The International Journal of Aging and Human Development, 41,* 47–62.

Additional Readings

American Counseling Association. (2005). *ACA code of ethics.* Alexandria, VA: Author.

American Psychological Association. (2003). Guidelines on multicultural education, training, research, practice, and organizational change for psychologists. *American Psychologist, 58,* 377–402.

Baruth, L. G., & Manning, M. L. (2007). *Multicultural counseling and psychotherapy: A lifespan perspective* (4th ed.). Upper Saddle River, NJ: Pearson/Merrill Prentice Hall

Berk, L. E. (2007). *Development through the lifespan* (4th ed.). Boston, MA: Pearson Education.

Brinson, J. A., Brew, L., & Denby, R. (2008). Real scenarios and complementary lectures: A classroom training approach to increase counselor awareness, knowledge, and skill. *Journal of Counseling & Development, 86,* 11–17.

Broderick, P. C., & Blewitt, P. (2003). *The life span: Human development for helping professionals.* Upper Saddle River, NJ: Merrill Prentice Hall.

Collins, N. M., & Pieterse, A. L. (2007). Critical incident analysis based training: An approach for developing active racial/cultural awareness. *Journal of Counseling & Development, 85,* 14–23.

Crain, W. (2004). *Theories of development: Concepts and applications* (5th ed.). Upper Saddle River, NJ: Pearson Prentice Hall.

Gladding, S. T. (2006). *The counseling dictionary* (2nd ed.). Columbus, OH: Pearson.

Hansen, C. E., & Williams, M. R. (2001). Comparison of cross-cultural course changes: From traditional lecture course to contemporary course with biblio-learning, video-learning and experiential exercises. *Journal of Instructional Psychology, 30,* 197–206.

Hooks, B. (1994). *Teaching to transgress: Education as the practice of freedom.* New York, NY: Routledge.

Kim, B., & Lyons, H. (2003). Experiential activities and multicultural counseling competence training. *Journal of Counseling & Development, 81,* 400–408.

Ponterotto, J. G. (2001). *Handbook of multicultural counseling.* Thousand Oaks, CA: Sage.

Sue, D. W., & Sue, D. (Eds.). (2003). *Counseling the culturally different: Theory and practice* (4th ed.). New York, NY: Wiley.

Web Resources

ACA Association for Adult Development and Aging
http://www.aadaweb.org/

APA Division 20 Adult Development and Aging
http://apadiv20.phhp.ufl.edu/

Child and Adolescent Health Development
http://www.who.int/child-adolescent-health/

Kids Count
http://www.aecf.org/kidscount/

National Institute for Child Development & Human Development
http://www.nichd.nih.gov/

Society for Research in Adult Development
http://www.adultdevelopment.org/booklist.html

Society for Research in Child Development
http://www.srcd.org/

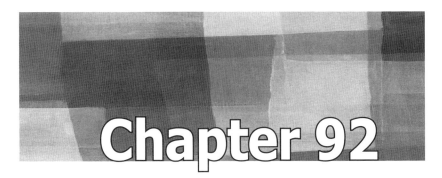

Chapter 92
Population Poster Conference

Carlotta J. Willis and Meg Connor

Topics: Introduction to Multicultural Counseling
Culturally Skilled Counselor
Professional Identity and Ethical Practice
Career Development
Research and Program Evaluation
Use of New Technology

Purposes: The purposes of this activity are to provide students with the opportunity (a) to thoroughly research a population of their choosing, applying theory and practice developed for a specific population, and (b) to develop some expertise in this area. Also, the activity is designed to encourage students to attend and present at conferences in the future by presenting their findings in a professional conference-like event within the classroom. Another purpose is to expose the students to a wide variety of potential career client groups by attending the presentations of their fellow students. Examples of populations to focus on include the following: lesbian, gay, bisexual, transgender (LGBT) adults; Hurricane Katrina survivors; laid-off workers; the deaf population; recent immigrants; returning veterans; sex-offenders or other forensic groups; farm workers; midlife career changers; English-as-a-second-language (ESL) speakers; Muslim Americans; and so forth.

Learning Objectives: As a result of this activity, students will be able to

- apply career theory appropriate to needs of diverse populations;
- integrate research findings for specific population career development needs;
- plan programs and interventions to meet the needs of a diverse client population;
- describe connections between career development and life roles, gender, culture, development, and life context for a specific population;
- be exposed to a wide variety of populations and specific effective career development approaches;
- present and exchange information in a professional forum; and
- experience the value of professional poster presentations.

Target Population: The activity was created for graduate mental health counseling students in a career lifestyle development course, although it can be used with students of other counseling specialties.

Group Size: The activity has been conducted with two sections of 24 each, combined into a 48-student mini-conference. It has also been successful with a single smaller section of 10 students. One of the advantages of the poster conference is that students who are afraid of public speaking can present to a smaller group of listeners multiple times, allowing for some desensitization around presentations.

Time Required: In-class time for the conference is 12 hours, depending on the size of the group. Students spend considerable time researching and preparing for the conference. This activity usually replaces the written research paper typically assigned in a graduate course.

Setting: A large room with tables or display boards, with space for participants and faculty members to circulate

Materials: Students will need access to PowerPoint, a printer, a poster board, and other materials as desired in order to create their poster. Students are encouraged to use their creativity to create an attractive poster representing their population group.

Instructions for Conducting Activity

Syllabus Description

Application to diverse populations research: Research a specific population around career development needs, using original source research and theoretical articles in the literature. You are encouraged to select a population whose mental health needs are primary, a cultural group, or an underserved population with which you may be working. Present a scholarly outline of your findings, including:

- description of the population,
- description of the specific career development needs of the group,
- recommendations for effective career development services for this population,
- appropriate theoretical approaches,
- culturally valid assessment,
- culturally valid intervention approaches, and
- abstract and references.

Using PowerPoint, create a poster presentation on this topic. Post the presentation in Sakai (Blackboard, etc.). Prepare a 5–10 minute presentation for the Population Poster Conference. Prepare a one-page handout of your poster. Use American Psychological Association style for poster, and see http://www.psichi.org/conventions/presentation_tips.aspx for tips on presentations and posters.

Instructions for the Poster Conference

On the day chosen for the conference, students present in rounds while other students and faculty members view and discuss the findings presented. Depending on the number of students, this could include two to four rounds of 30 minutes each, generally held during the class period. Each student, therefore, will present his or her topic multiple times to a small group of other students. Faculty members will rotate and view posters and listen to the presentations. Students also will have posted their PowerPoint presentations (used to make the poster) in the course folders so that the instructor will have more time to carefully review them for evaluation purposes. The campus community is invited to the poster conference, and typically other students, faculty, and library staff attend.

Handouts: Students will provide handouts of their presentations at the mini-conference.

Chapter 93

"I Am From" Poem

Sukie Magraw, Jill Miller, Kayoko Yokoyama, and Liza Hecht

Topics: Introduction to Multicultural Counseling
Definitions of Cultural Diversity
Cultural Identity Development
Culturally Skilled Counselor
Professional Identity and Ethical Practice

Purposes: The purpose of this activity is for class members to introduce themselves to each other. It enhances multicultural self-awareness for counselors/psychologists-in-training, and it encourages students to be curious about and appreciate differences.

Learning Objectives: As a result of this activity, students will have a better appreciation of their own histories and traditions and the histories and traditions of others.

Target Population: Linda Christensen (1998) does this exercise with high school students, but it can be adapted for use with advanced undergraduates and graduate students.

Group Size: Optimal group size would be a diverse group of 8–10 students.

Time Required: Total of 45 minutes (10 minutes to explain the assignment and for students to take turns reading some of the sample poems, 15 minutes for students and teacher to write their own poems, 10 minutes for everyone to read his or her poem, 10 minutes to discuss what people liked about others' poems).

Setting: Classroom

Materials: Handout of Linda Christensen's work (Available at http://youthvoices.net/node/2737).

Instructions for Conducting Activity

For Instructors

- Have students read activity introduction in Handout 93.1, "I Am From" Exercise.
- Distribute Linda Christensen's (1998) article, "Where I'm From: Inviting Student Lives Into the Classroom." Have a student read George Ella Lyon's (1999) poem, "Where I'm From." When finished, make note with the students of the devices that the author uses: items found around the home, yard, and neighborhood; names of relatives; sayings or words that were commonly repeated in childhood; names of foods from childhood; and where childhood memories are kept.
- Have students pick out other poems from Christensen's article to read aloud.

- Tell students that they will now write their own poem, which everyone will share with the class. Give them 10–15 minutes to write their poems. The instructor writes a poem along with the rest of the class.
- When everyone has finished, the instructor reads his or her poem first. Then the rest of the class takes turns reading their poems.
- The instructor then asks for comments on what students liked about each others' poems. The instructor can start off modeling this process by making a global comment about something she/he noticed in several or all of the poems and then making positive references to individual poems.

Handout: Handout 93.1: "I Am From" Exercise

References:

Christensen, L. (1998). Where I'm from: Inviting student lives into the classroom. *Rethinking Schools, 12*, 22–23.

Lyon, G. E. (1999). *Where I am from, where poems come from: A poetry workshop book for teachers and students.* Spring, TX: Absey & Co.

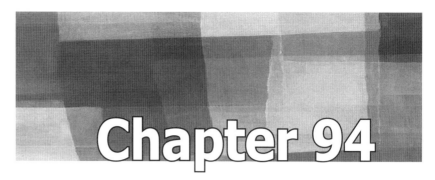

Chapter 94

Lights, Camera, Action!
Counselors, Treatment Planning,
and the Movies

Beth A. Durodoye

Topics: Culturally Skilled Counselor
Helping Relationships
Assessment
Use of New Technology

Purposes: This activity is designed to introduce students to the manner in which counselors conceptualize and assess clients.

Learning Objectives: As a result of this activity, students will (a) have the opportunity to acknowledge how their individual backgrounds may affect work with clients from culturally diverse groups, (b) have the opportunity to explore culturally relevant topics concerning specific ethnic and nonethnic minority populations, and (c) have the opportunity to review counseling theory and strategies as they relate to the cultural dynamics of various groups.

Target Population: This activity is specifically designed for beginning counseling students who have completed their foundational courses in counseling (i.e., introductory and theoretical courses).

Group Size: This is a small-group classroom activity. Group sizes range from three to seven individuals, depending on the number of students in class and the actual number of movies that are viewed.

Time Required: This activity is approximately 40 minutes in length.

Setting: The optimal room arrangement is one where there are movable chairs for the easy configuration of several small groups.

Materials: Students are assigned Cameron and turtle-song's (2002) article on case notes to read in advance. This article is used to help students complete the treatment plan form that is a requirement for the small-group activity (see Handout 94.1).

Instructions for Conducting Activity

Pre-Activity Preparation

It is important that instructors be familiar with the content of each movie placed on their class list. Given that movies are for entertainment purposes, instructors will find it necessary to ascertain which ones are more or less appropriate for use in the classroom (see Additional Readings section for a list of movies that I have found beneficial). It is strongly suggested that instructors familiarize themselves with the films of their choice before placing them on the movie viewing list.

In advance of the actual activity, students are directed to read Cameron and turtle-song's (2002) article in conjunction with watching one of several preselected movies. They will then choose a character from the movie and develop a counseling treatment plan for that character using the form provided. Students are asked to formulate their plans using the theory of their choice and pertinent cultural and other details about their client.

Group Activities

Students are assigned to small groups according to the movies that they watched. They are given 30 minutes to highlight each of their treatment plans. Group members are encouraged to query one another about what they thought and felt while working with their "clients," and to ask questions of one another related to each of their treatment plans. During the last 10 minutes following the small-group activity, the students come together as one large group to share any personal or small-group reactions.

Handout: Handout 94.1: Treatment Plan Form (to be completed following the movie viewing and in conjunction with the reading by Cameron and turtle-song, 2002).

References

Cameron, S., & turtle-song, i. (2002). Learning to write case notes using the SOAP format. *Journal of Counseling & Development, 80,* 286–292.

Additional Readings

Bass, R., Markey, P., & Tan, A. (Producers), & Tan, A., & Bass, R. (Writers), & Wang, W. (Director). (1993). *The joy luck club* [Motion picture]. United States: Hollywood Pictures.

Bressler, C., Estes, L., & Rosenfelt, S. (Producers), & Alexie, S. (Writer), & Eyre, C. (Director). (1998). *Smoke signals* [Motion picture]. Canada/United States: ShadowCatcher Entertainment.

Cantin, M., & Hurd, G. A. (Producers), & Jimenez, N. (Writer), & Jimenez, N., & Steinberg, M. (Directors). (1992). *The waterdance* [Motion picture]. United States: No Frills Film Production.

Cheadle, D., Haggis, P., Moresco, R., Schulman, C., & Yari, B. (Producers), & Haggis, P., & Moresco, R. (Writers), & Haggis, P. (Director). (2004). *Crash* [Motion picture]. United States/Germany: Bob Yari Productions.

Demme, J., & Saxon, E. (Producers), & Nyswaner, R. (Writer), & Demme, J. (Director). (1993). *Philadelphia* [Motion picture]. United States: TriStar Pictures.

Goetzman, G., Hanks, T., & Wilson, R. (Producers), & Vardalos, N. (Writer), & Zwick, J. (Director). (2002). *My big fat Greek wedding* [Motion picture]. United States: Warner Bros.

LaVoo, G., Brown, E. T., & Atlas, M. R. (Producers), & LaVoo, G., & Lopez, J. (Writers), & Cardosa, P. (Director). (2002). *Real women have curves* [Motion picture]. United States: HBO Independent Productions.

Nicolaides, S. (Producer), & Singleton, J. (Writer/Director). (1991). *Boyz n the hood* [Motion picture]. United States: Columbia Pictures Corporation.

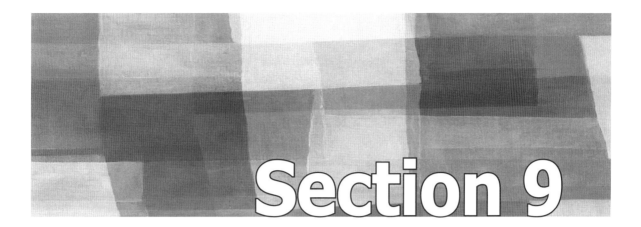

Section 9

Cross-Cultural Family Counseling

Activities in this section assist students in expanding their notions about what family means in a diverse society. Through these activities, students examine definitions of family from a lesbian, gay, bisexual, and transgender (LGBT) perspective as well as a Native American perspective and are given opportunities to explore the use of genograms when working with diverse populations. These activities may be used in courses on family counseling, human life span, and introductory and advanced multicultural studies; they may also be used in clinical/supervision courses.

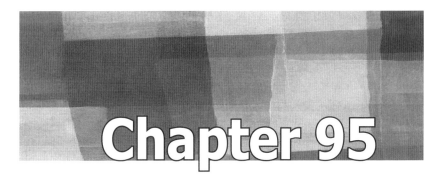

Chapter 95

And Tango Makes Three:
Promoting Understanding of LGBT Families

Kristin Meany-Walen and Casey A. Barrio Minton

Topics: Introduction to Multicultural Counseling
Definitions of Cultural Diversity
Cultural Identity Development
Culturally Skilled Counselor
Cross-Cultural Family Counseling
Counseling Lesbian, Gay, Bisexual, Transgender (LGBT), and Other Sexual Minority Clients

Purposes: The purpose of this activity is to engage students in discussion about same-sex parent families so that students can explore their beliefs and biases about gay and lesbian families.

Learning Objectives: As a result of this activity, students will (a) have an understanding of the similarities and differences between healthy families headed by heterosexual and same-sex parents; (b) have a better understanding of the effects of current laws and culture on same-sex parents, children of same-sex parent families, and children in foster and adoption systems; (c) recognize myths regarding same-sex households; and (d) have a resource to use with children and families in counseling.

Target Population: This exercise is developed for master's-level counseling students; however, it is also appropriate for adolescents and adults in general settings.

Group Size: Optimal groups would be small enough (e.g., no more than 20 participants) to allow for thorough discussion; however, the authors have conducted this exercise in a traditional classroom of over 30 students.

Time Required: The exercise may be completed in 30–60 minutes, depending on length and depth of discussion.

Setting: The exercise may be conducted in any classroom or meeting area that allows for group discussion.

Materials: *And Tango Makes Three* (Richardson & Parnell, 2005), dry-erase board or chalkboard, fact sheets/handouts.

Instructions for Conducting Activity

Begin the exercise by inviting students to do a brief guided imagery, which will be followed by discussion about their experiences as a child. Ask students to get comfortable, close their eyes, and picture a time in their childhood where they felt safest and happiest. Give students a minute or two to begin to form a picture in their minds. Ask students questions to help them more vividly build and explore those memories. Questions or prompts may include, but are not limited to, the following: Where are you? Who is around you? What do you see? What are you doing? What do you smell? How are you feeling? Allow students to sit with their images for a few minutes. Instruct students that the guided imagery is over and they can open their eyes and come back to the group when they are ready. After all students appear to be ready to move on, ask students to offer examples of their images and ideas of those times that they felt most secure. Record the essence of their memories and content on the board.

After students have shared their positive memories, ask students to draw from their collective experiences to develop a list of what they believe is important for children to experience in order for optimal development. On the dry-erase board, write down students' responses. Examples of answers may include things such as nurturance, love, safe relationships with parent(s), food, rest, play time, encouragement, and extended family involvement.

Next, let students know that you will be reading a book based on real events that developed at the Central Park Zoo. After reading *And Tango Makes Three* (Richardson & Parnell, 2005), ask students to share their immediate thoughts and reflections. After a number of students have shared their reactions to the book, guide the discussion so that students connect Tango's experience with the experiences they previously described as being necessary for optimal child development.

As students conclude discussion regarding Tango's experience, prompt students to consider things that might support or infringe on same-sex parent families' abilities to provide experiences that lead to children's optimal development. After brainstorming supports and challenges, distribute relevant fact sheets regarding laws affecting, myths regarding, and experiences of children of same-sex families. Encourage students to discuss the ways in which the information provided is similar to and different than their perceptions. Time permitting, you may choose to reveal to students that this book was the "most banned book" in 2006 and 2007 (Adamick, 2008) and to encourage students to discuss possible reasons for and consequences of banning such a book. Finally, note that this book may be an excellent resource when counseling children of same-sex parents. You may wish to entertain discussion regarding bibliotherapeutic uses of the book.

Handouts: Provide participants with at least two fact sheets regarding same-sex parent families. Fact sheets may be obtained from a number of reputable organizations, including the following:

- Parents and Friends of Lesbians and Gays: http://community.pflag.org/Page.aspx?pid=505
- Children of Lesbians & Gays Everywhere: http://www.colage.org/resources/research.htm
- American Academy of Child and Adolescent Psychology: http://www.aacap.org/
- American Psychological Association: http://www.apa.org/pi/parent.html
- Urban Institute: http://www.urban.org/publications/411437.html

References

Adamick, M. (2008, September 29). Banned books week: "And Tango makes three." *Babble.* Retrieved December 18, 2008, from http://www.babble.com/CS/blogs/strollerderby/archive/2008/09/29/banned-books-week-quot-and-tango-makes-three-quot.aspx

Richardson, J., & Parnell, P. (2005). *And Tango makes three.* New York, NY: Simon & Simon Books for Young Readers.

Additional Readings

American Academy of Child and Adolescent Psychotherapy. (2006, August). *Children with lesbian, gay, bisexual and transgendered parents* (Report No. 92). Retrieved January 3, 2009, from http://www.aacap.org

American Psychological Association. (2005). *Lesbian & gay parenting.* Washington, DC: Author. Retrieved January 3, 2009, from http://www.apa.org/pi/lgbc/publications

Crowl, A., Ahn, S., & Baker, J. (2008). A meta-analysis of developmental outcomes for children of same-sex and heterosexual parents. *Journal of GLBT Family Studies, 4,* 385–407.

Dunlap, D. W. (1996, January 7). Homosexual parents raising children: Support for pro and con. *New York Times.* Retrieved January 3, 2009, from http://query.nytimes.com/gst/fullpage.html?res=9D04E 3DE1339F934A35752C0A960958260

Gates, G., Badgett, L. M. V., Macomber, J. E., & Chambers, K. (2007, March). Adoption and foster care by lesbian and gay parents in the United States. *Urban Institute.* Retrieved December 21, 2008, from http://www.urban.org/publications/411437.html

Long, J. K., & Andrews, B. V. (2007). Fostering strength and resiliency in same-sex couples: An overview. *Journal of Couple & Relationship Therapy, 6,* 153–165.

Sears, B., & Hirsh, A. (2004, April 4). Straight-out truth on gay parents. *The Los Angeles Times.* Retrieved January 3, 2009, from http://www.rossde.com/editorials/childrenofgays.html

Sue, D. W., & Sue, D. (2008). *Counseling the culturally diverse: Theory and practice* (5th ed.). New York, NY: Wiley.

Chapter 96

Cultural Voices Across the Family Life Cycle

Torey L. Portrie-Bethke

Topics: Cross-Cultural Family Counseling
Counseling Lesbian, Gay, Bisexual, Transgender (LGBT), and Other Sexual Minority Clients
Human Growth and Development

Purposes: The purpose of this activity is to enhance students' integration of current life experiences with additional factors concerning diversity across the family life cycle. The activity is used to prepare students to meta-reflect on their life experiences and expand their personal knowledge and awareness of other cultures, diversity factors, and family dynamics.

Learning Objectives: As a result of this activity, students will (a) have a greater understanding of the family life cycle and how this is experienced by different cultures and abilities; (b) identify how the family life cycle is experienced by different groups based on ethnicity, race, sexual orientation, socioeconomic status, age, gender, and disabilities across the life span; and (c) develop counseling approaches specific to cultural needs across the family life cycle.

This activity is designed for counseling students in the family, marriage, and couples counseling course. The activity may be used to initiate the discussion of families as an introduction to the family life cycle.

Target Population: Master's of counseling students enrolled in a family course or students who are learning about the impact of the family life cycle on clients' experiences in order to integrate the family life cycle with conceptualization of client issues/factors

Group Size: 5–40 participants/students

Time Required: 1 hour

Setting: Classroom—the activity is designed to begin with small-group discussions, followed by a transition into a large-group discussion. To begin the first phase of the activity, the students will need to be placed in groups of three to six students. After the first phase of the activity is completed, the students will move into a large-group circle for a group discussion of the family life cycle.

Materials: Chairs and tables for the students to be seated, a variety of candy bars (Reese's peanut butter cups, Snickers, Milky Ways, Three Musketeers, Butterfingers, Kit Kat, Baby Ruth, and so forth), the identified family circumstances (see Handout 96.1), scissors, tape with which to attach the case scenarios located on Handout 96.1 to the candy bars, a large bag to hold the prepared candy that allows for easy access for the students to select their favorite piece, a PowerPoint of the presentation, and a board on which to write responses

Instructions for Conducting Activity

The instructor of the class begins by providing the students with the sequencing of the class events:

- define *family*,
- identify stages of the family life cycle,
- select candy for activity to begin,
- small-group discussions (first phase of activity),
- large-group discussion (second phase of the activity),
- PowerPoint integrated with large-group discussion, and
- redefine *family*.

The following information provides informative details of the class outline.

Define Family

The instructor asks the students to divide into groups of two or three. The groups are to define *family*. Have each group read their definition to the class. Write the definitions on the board for later discussion.

Identify Stages of the Family Life Cycle

After the students have defined family, ask the class as a whole to identify the stages of the family life cycle. Write the stages on the board and compare the students' stages with the actual stages identified by Carter and McGoldrick (1999) (see Handout 96.2, "Family Counseling").

Select Candy for Activity to Begin

Each candy bar is wrapped with a family life cycle scenario (see Handout 96.1 for family life cycle scenarios). After the students have selected the candy bar of their choice, have the students move into small groups of four. To be creative, have the students group with other students who have selected a different candy (each candy type needs to represent a different family life cycle scenario to ensure that duplication of scenarios does not occur within the groups).

Small-Group Discussions

The purpose of this experience is to provide each person a different scenario in the group. Each member reads his or her family life cycle scenario to the group, speaking from the perspective of the person in the scenario in relation to the family life cycle stage. The objective is for the group to conceptualize the person in the scenario experiences related to the life cycle.

Large-Group Discussion (PowerPoint)

After each member of the small group has discussed the scenarios with the family life cycle, the class will join as a large group for a discussion of the activity integrated with the family life cycle PowerPoint. At this time, students are encouraged both to speak from the voice of the person in the scenario across the family life cycle as well as to discuss their own personal journeys.

Redefine Family

Explore with the class their previously constructed definitions of family and whether these definitions are still representative of what they believe constitutes the definition of family following the activity. If the class determines that a more comprehensive definition is needed, then create the definition as a class.

Handouts: Handout 96.1: Family Life Cycle Scenarios
Handout 96.2: Family Counseling PowerPoint

References

Carter, B., & McGoldrick, M. (1999). *The expanded family life cycle: Individual, family, and social perspectives* (3rd ed.). Needham Heights, MA: Allyn & Bacon.

Chapter 97
Native American Ethics: Family

Anne M. Warren

Topics: Cultural Communication Styles
Cultural Identity Development
Cross-Cultural Family Counseling
Counseling Native Americans
Creative Arts

Purposes: The purposes of this activity are to explore Native American cultural mores and encourage students to reflect on Native American family beliefs and practices and how these beliefs may differ from students' beliefs about family.

Learning Objectives: As a result of this activity, students will

- have a better understanding of Native American family construct and beliefs about family,
- analyze stereotypes about and misconceptions of Native American beliefs about family groups,
- explore Native American cultural family values, and
- explore and compare Native American concepts of family with concepts of students' beliefs regarding family.

Target Population: Graduate and undergraduate psychology, counseling, social work, and art therapy core cultural studies classes

Group Size: In an educational context, this exercise may accommodate 4–12 participants.

Time Required: 3 hours

Setting: Tables and chairs to accommodate a chair for each participant and generous tabletop space for each participant should be provided. Tables should be large enough to accommodate a working area of a square yard on the table surface for each participant, though smaller areas may be accommodated as necessary and students may be encouraged to work on the floor. The door to the room should be closed to define the therapeutic space. The room size should match the need; for instance, a gymnasium may seem intimidating in size and scale for working with small groups.

Materials:

- Handout 97.1 ("Native American Family Proverbs")
- one cardboard circle for each student (12″, found in bulk through art supply stores);
- supplies to be shared: scissors; glue sticks and white school-type glue; glue gun and glue sticks; magazines and newspapers; drawing materials, such as markers, pastels, crayons, colored pencils, #2 pencils, and pens; various craft materials, such as ribbons, pieces of material, artificial

flowers, glitter, beads, and buttons; acrylic and watercolor paints; and natural materials, such as pinecones, buckskin, stones, sticks, leaves.

Instructions for Conducting Activity

This experiential activity begins with students reading a short informational written piece about Native American familial beliefs as expressed in Native American proverbs.

- Choosing one proverb from the handout, students are asked to work independently to create a collage in which they use available resources. The collage should reflect imagery that comes to mind when reading or hearing their chosen proverb and may incorporate elements from student's views of family that correspond or conflict with how they understand family values expressed in their chosen proverb.
- After the art-making process, students will meet in a circle, bringing chairs on which to sit in the circle. Within the circle they will lay their collages on the floor.
- Students will take a few minutes to walk around the circle of collages, looking at the images; next, those who wish to present their collage to the class and discuss it with the class may do so.
- Each student may be given a time limit for discussion and presentation of 5 to 10 minutes.
- No idea is wrong; exploration is key.

When students are working, Native American drum or flute music should play. Students may not chat while working so that they may focus on their process.

Request that students think about the following when coming to conclusions:

1. What are your personal beliefs about family constructs?
2. How do your personal beliefs about family constructs differ from Native American family constructs?
3. What are your attitudes about different kinds of families?
4. How do your attitudes about family influence how you view family constructs that are different from your own?
5. What is your knowledge of human systems and concepts of cultural identity formation?

Handout: Handout 97.1: Native American Family Proverbs

References

Neihardt, J. G. (1972). *Black Elk speaks*. Lincoln: University of Nebraska Press.

Additional Readings

Arden, H., & Wall, S. (1990). *Wisdomkeepers: Meetings with Native American spiritual elders*. Hillsboro, OR: Beyond Words Publishing.

Banks, J. A. (1997). *Teaching strategies for ethnic studies*. Boston, MA: Allyn & Bacon.

Barnes, B., Mitchell, M., & Thompson, J. (1984). *Traditional teachings*. Cornwall Island, Ontario, Canada: North American Indian Traveling College.

Beck, P. V., Walters, A. L., & Francisco, N. (1992). *The sacred: Ways of knowledge, sources of life*. Tsaile, AR: Navajo Community College Press.

Clifton, J. A. (1987). *The Potawatomi*. New York, NY: Chelsea House.

Duran, E. (2006) *Healing the soul wound*. New York, NY: Teachers College Press.

Fixico, D. L. (2003). *The American Indian mind in a linear world*. New York, NY: Routledge.

Graymount, B. (1988). *The Iroquois*. New York, NY: Chelsea House.

James, M. A. (1992). *The state of Native America: Genocide, colonization and resistance*. Boston, MA: South End Press.

Lombardi, F. G., & Lombardi, G. S. (1982). *Circle without end: A sourcebook of American Indian ethics*. Happy Camp, CA: Naturegraph.

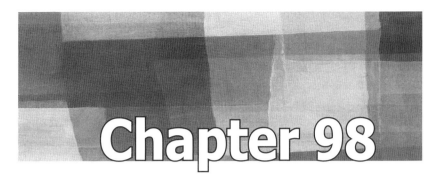

Chapter 98

Cultural Genograms

Kayoko Yokoyama, Sukie Magraw, Jill Miller, and Liza Hecht

Topics: Introduction to Multicultural Counseling
Definitions of Cultural Diversity
Oppression and Discrimination
Dimensions of Worldviews
Cross-Cultural Family Counseling

Purposes: The purpose of this activity is to help students reflect on the cultural worldview, biases, assumptions, and values that have been handed down through their families of origin. Through this activity, students will better understand the psychological impact of privilege and power, particularly as it relates to socialization within the family. This activity aims to provide participants with opportunities to explore the values of their family within the context of multicultural issues and reference group identities. This activity enhances multicultural self-awareness for counselors/psychologists-in-training and allows students to engage in culturally sensitive clinical practices.

Learning Objectives: As a result of this activity, students will have a better understanding of the intergenerational effects of privilege, oppression, and power as they relate to race, ethnicity, religion, gender, sexual orientation, ability, class, and so forth among other reference group identities. Students will gain a greater awareness of their own family's impact on their current worldviews, beliefs, assumptions, and values.

Target Population: Graduate students in an advanced multicultural awareness or family therapy course that includes a group process component

Group Size: Optimal group size would be a diverse group of 8–10 students.

Time Required: Total of 45 minutes is required for the presentation itself (20–30 minutes for each student's cultural genogram presentation plus 15 minutes for questions and reflection). In addition, background time of a few weeks is required for students to research and investigate their families and cultures of origin.

Setting: Classroom. Students often place their poster board on the ledge of a chalkboard/whiteboard.

Materials: Students may use poster board to graphically illustrate their cultural genogram.

Instructions for Conducting Activity

Give the following instructions to the participants:

1. All participants will present their cultural genograms in a 45-minute class presentation.

2. You will have 20–30 minutes to present your cultural genogram and 15 minutes for questions and further reflection.

3. The cultural genogram will not only describe your extended family structure (as in a traditional family genogram) but, more important, will explore, trace, and highlight the impact that oppression and privilege have had on you and your family.

4. Draw on as many sources of learning as you can to explore the themes of racism, ethnocentrism, gender oppression, religious oppression, ableism, classism, and homophobia/hetersexism/heterocentrism that have been passed down in your family.

5. In addition, consider the strengths, resilience, and gifts that have been transmitted through your family.

6. Each participant should attempt to go back at least three generations and provide a key for all of the symbols represented on the cultural genogram.

7. Please consult with McGoldrick, Gerson, and Petry's (2008) text on how to visually construct and organize your genogram.

8. Please consider the list of questions in Hardy and Laszloffy's (1995) article while constructing your genogram.

9. In addition, use the questions in the Cultural Genogram Exercise (see Handout 98.1) as a guide in constructing your genograms.

10. You have approximately one month to collect information about your family history and interview family members for information.

Handout: Handout 98.1: Cultural Genogram Exercise

References

Hardy, K. V., & Laszloffy, T. A. (1995). The cultural genogram: Key to training culturally competent family therapists. *Journal of Marital and Family Therapy, 21*(3), 227–237.

McGoldrick, M., Gerson, R., & Petry, S. (2008). *Genograms: Assessment and intervention* (3rd ed.). New York, NY: Norton.

Additional Readings

David, E. J. R., & Okazaki, S. (2006). Colonial mentality: A review and recommendation for Filipino American psychology. *Cultural Diversity and Ethnic Minority Psychology, 12*(1), 1–16.

McGoldrick, M. (1998). *Re-visioning family therapy: Race, culture, and gender in clinical practice.* New York, NY: Guilford Press.

McIntosh, P. (2003). White privilege: Unpacking the invisible knapsack. In S. Plous (Ed.), *Understanding prejudice and discrimination* (pp. 191–196). New York, NY: McGraw-Hill.

Schlosser, L. Z. (2003). Christian privilege: Breaking a sacred taboo. *Journal of Multicultural Counseling and Development, 31*, 44–51.

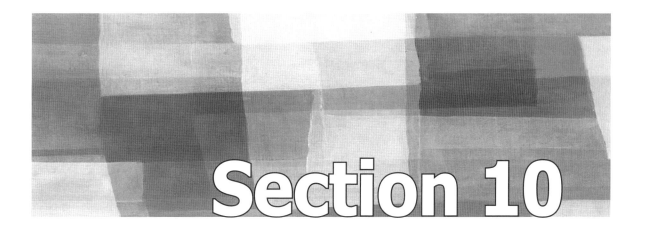

Section 10

Counseling Specific Cultural Groups

This section offers a variety of activities that assist students in understanding specific cultural groups (e.g., Native American clients; women; the elderly; and lesbian, gay, bisexual, and transgender populations). This section also includes an activity that addresses spiritual considerations. Through the use of these activities, students can increase their awareness and knowledge about specific considerations and challenges experienced by specific cultural groups. These activities can be used in introductory, advanced level, or cultural-specific counseling courses.

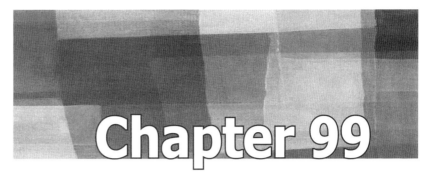

Chapter 99
Telling My Story

Rebekah J. Byrd

Topics: Introduction to Multicultural Counseling
Dimensions of Worldviews
Counseling Native Americans
Group Work
Creative Arts

Purposes: The purpose of this activity is to provide participants with an experiential activity incorporating Native American culture. It will introduce a Native American form of storytelling to aid in the opportunity to explore self and others. The importance of personal values will also be part of this activity as individuals seek to understand themselves and others.

Learning Objectives: As a result of this activity, students will (a) have a better understanding of the cultural custom of using different means (beads) to express, tell, or illustrate a story, event, or interest; (b) disclose personal values they possess through the process of storytelling; and (c) apply learning of values and group process to their work with diverse clients.

Target Population: This activity is designed to be used with counselor trainees in a multicultural course, group counseling course, or practicum/internship. However, it can also be used with children, adolescents, and adults.

Group Size: This activity can take place in a group, under classroom guidance, or on an individual basis. The description herein is for use in a graduate counseling classroom.

Time Required: 40–50 minutes

Setting: It can be used in different settings (graduate classroom, school, agencies, private practice) and in individual or group counseling.

Materials: Solid-colored beads (large or small depending on population); string, twine, or hemp (make sure the string you choose fits the beads, is sturdy, and is adjusted for specific age group); scissors (let adolescents and adults cut their own string, but pre-cut it for younger children so that they are all the same length); bowls to put beads in, one in the middle of each group of four or five individuals if using in a classroom guidance setting or with a large group

Instructions for Conducting Activity

Read the following statement to participants:

> Native Americans have a wonderful way of storytelling and remembering events through keeping records or artifacts and writing letters. They use beads and weave beautiful belts, necklaces, and other objects sometimes called *Wampum*. The designs made represent different ideas and hold different meanings according to the wampum language, and they have been used to pass stories down to future generations. Today you are each going to tell a story or represent something important to you by making an item of your choice with the materials provided. Be creative and think about an event, a person, a story, or a letter that you would like to depict using the beads and the string.

Provide the individual or group with approximately 15 minutes to create the object. Then, depending on time constraints, have each individual present and share his or her item to others. (You may elect to have them share in small groups or the large group, depending on group size.)

After each student has shared his or her object, the following process questions may be used:

- What was this activity like for you and why?
- What happened during the process?
- What did you learn about yourself during this activity?
- What did you learn about others during this activity?
- What were some common narratives among the group?
- How did this activity broaden your awareness of what is important to you?
- Why is it important to share stories, historical events, and so forth with others?
- How has this activity helped you with your work as a counselor-in-training?

Note: This activity was adapted from Byrd (2009) and can be adjusted to fit certain goals for the individual or group. For example, it could be used in a first group meeting, with group members making an item that tells something important about themselves so that the new group members get to know each other. In this same realm, the activity could be used as a termination activity, where all group members make an item about the most important thing they learned in the group and what they will take with them for the rest of their lives.

In an individual setting, this activity could provide an individual with a coping skill, assist in helping an individual tell his or her story (whatever it could be related to), or assist in helping someone cope with the death of a loved one.

References

Byrd, R. (2009). Beads of life. In C. F. Salazar (Ed.), *Group work experts share their favorite multicultural activities: A guide to diversity-competent choosing, planning, conducting, and processing*. Alexandria, VA: Association for Specialists in Group Work.

Additional Readings

Sidis, W. J. (n.d.). *The tribes and the states: 100,000-year history of North America*. Retrieved May 19, 2008, from http://www.sidis.net/TSContents.htm

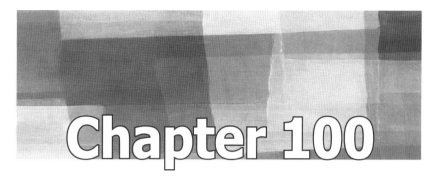

Chapter 100

Using Art and Discussion to Explore Myths and Realities About the First Thanksgiving

Laura Lake Catterton and Casey A. Barrio Minton

Topics: Oppression and Discrimination
Dimensions of Worldviews
Counseling Native Americans
Advocacy and Social Justice
Creative Arts

Purposes: This activity uses evidence-based teaching methods for American Indian populations (e.g., experiential, group activities, and storytelling; Reyhner, 2000) to help students uncover a more historically accurate and comprehensive story of the first Thanksgiving as opposed to dominant culture's adaptation of such. As a result of participating in this activity, students will be able to (a) describe accurate historical events and meanings surrounding Thanksgiving, (b) provide culturally based explanations of behavior and experiences from the perspectives of dominant and American Indian cultures, and (c) identify the pervasive power structure of dominant culture and its influence on perceptions of reality.

Target Population: This activity is appropriate for implementation with undergraduate students, graduate students, and adult learners who have foundation knowledge about the values and perspectives of American Indians and dominant cultures. The activity may also be adjusted for implementation with primary and secondary students. This activity is appropriate for all classrooms in the United States and may be of particular salience in areas where there is higher American Indian representation in the population.

Group Size: Because participants are divided into small groups of no more than four participants, this activity is most appropriate for implementation in small- to moderate-sized groups. The authors have facilitated this activity in groups as large as 30 participants.

Time Required: Ideally, this activity will be facilitated within at least a 1-hour class period as follows: instructions, group assignments, and distribution of stories (10 minutes); small-group discussion and drawing time (20 minutes); and discussion (30 minutes). If time is limited, the instructor may assign less time for drawing and/or discussion.

Setting: This activity can be completed in a standard academic classroom; however, participants will need to be able to shift seating arrangements and disperse throughout the classroom.

Materials: Instructors will need to download copies of accounts of the first Thanksgiving from both the Native American perspective (http://www.manataka.org/page269.html) and the dominant cultural perspective (http://www.apples4theteacher.com/holidays/thanksgiving/short-stories/). Instructors will need enough copies so that each small group has just one story. For example, if there are four small groups, the instructor will need two copies of the Native American story and two copies of the dominant cultural story. Also, the instructor will need one piece of poster board and a bucket of art materials (e.g., crayons, markers, and/or oil pastels) for each small group.

Instructions for Conducting Activity

Introduce the activity by explaining that the class will be exploring the first Thanksgiving; next, have the class divide into an even number of small groups of no more than four participants each. Distribute one poster board and set of art materials to each group. Next, pass out the Native American Thanksgiving story to half of the groups and the dominant culture's Thanksgiving story to the other half, without alerting the class to the fact that there are different versions of the stories. Keep discussion between groups to a minimum at this stage. Instruct the groups to find a place (e.g., hallway, floor, corner) in which they can discuss and illustrate their story. Allow groups to work simultaneously on illustrating the version of the story they were given for 20 minutes or more, depending on class period length. The instructor may wish to visit with groups at this time to answer questions without revealing activity goals.

As groups conclude their drawings, bring the class back together as a large group and ask one group from each story to volunteer to explain their illustration. Ask students to compare and contrast events, tone, and emotional content of each story. Ensure that all students are exposed to the Native American perspective of the story before proceeding with the discussion. Next, invite students to share reactions, thoughts, and feelings about this exercise. Encourage as many students as possible to share. In our experience, students will be surprised by the difference in the stories. For some students, this will be the first time they have heard the story told from the Wampanoag Indians' experience; hearing the story may invoke feelings of guilt, shock, anger at being lied to, sadness, or defensiveness. Some students may already have knowledge about discrepancies between accounts and act as process helpers with others.

As students process their reactions to the disparate accounts, ask students to consider how traditional American Indian cultural values (i.e., harmony, community, and cooperation) were demonstrated in each account. In a similar manner, ask students to identify how the Pilgrims' cultural and religious beliefs affected their perspective of the Native Americans.

At this point, use the following discussion questions to facilitate exploration:

1. Who has previously heard the Native American story? How did you come to know that version of the story?
2. For those who have only heard dominant culture's version of the Thanksgiving story, where did you learn it? Why do you think you only learned this version? How is this version of the story reflective of dominant cultural worldviews?
3. For those who are struggling to accept the Native American perspective as valid, please tell us a bit about your thoughts and feelings. What would it mean if we had undeniable proof that the story is 100% true? How might that understanding change your perspective of the Native American experience? The dominant cultural experience?
4. How might this process of distorting or silencing historical facts be present in other aspects of the Native American experience? Other minority groups' experiences?
5. Understanding that we can't change history, how can we use our new knowledge to facilitate a healthier and more balanced cultural perspective? (Note: Encourage students to consider concrete action steps, such as honoring experience by retelling the Native American version of the story on Thanksgiving Day or questioning other traditions or stories.)

6. How might acknowledgment of a more historically accurate version of Thanksgiving contribute to understanding and healing between dominant and minority groups in the United States?

Upon conclusion of the activity, help students explore how their feelings and perspectives did or did not change. Assist students to conceptualize key principles and terminology (e.g., oppression, assimilation, cultural values, ethnocentrism, dominant culture, power). If possible, conduct the activity as near to Thanksgiving Day as possible and ask students to reflect on this exercise over the holiday.

Handouts: Instructors can download handouts from http://www.manataka.org/page269.html and http://www.apples4theteacher.com/holidays/thanksgiving/short-stories

References

Reyhner, J. (2000). *Humility vs. self esteem: What do American Indian children need for academic success?* Retrieved November 14, 2007, from http://jan.ucc.nau.edu/~jar/

Additional Readings

Bates, S. (n.d.). *The real story of Thanksgiving*. Retrieved October 15, 2007, from http://www.manataka.org/page269.html

Bigelow, B., & Peterson, B. (1998). *Rethinking Columbus: The next 500 years* (2nd ed.). Milwaukee, WI: Rethinking Schools.

Garrett, M. T. (2006). When eagle speaks: Counseling Native Americans. In C. C. Lee (Ed.), *Multicultural issues in counseling: New approaches to diversity* (3rd ed., pp. 25–54). Alexandria, VA: American Counseling Association.

James, W. (1970). *The suppressed speech of Wamsutta (Frank B.) James, Wampanoag.* Retrieved January 5, 2009, from http://www.uaine.org/

Sue, D. W., & Sue, D. (2008). *Counseling the culturally diverse: Theory and practice* (5th ed.). New York, NY: Wiley.

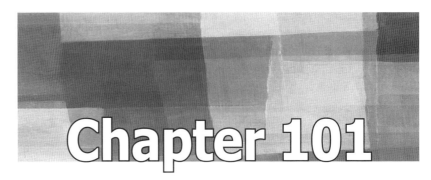

Chapter 101

Debunking the Myths of Age

David W. Hart

Topics: Cultural Identity Development
Culturally Skilled Counselor
Counseling Aging Clients

Purposes: The activity is designed to assist counseling students identify negative stereotypes propagated by the dominant culture within the United States about aging, and it provides empirical evidence that debunks specific myths of aging. The activity presents a holistic model for conceptualizing age in terms of success, health, and wellness. Participants are encouraged to explore their own perceptions of the aging process and identify areas for increased clinical competence in age-related issues. In addition, participants are challenged to expand their notion(s) of age to include the "successful ager"—a concept explored and defined as part of the activity.

Learning Objectives: As a result of this activity, participants will (a) develop an understanding of how negative perceptions and stereotypes of age may influence their interactions with aging clients, (b) develop a conceptualization of the aging process that includes empirically supported models of successful aging that contrast with conventional descriptions of aging, and (c) debunk dominant cultural myths regarding the aging process in general.

Target Population: Students enrolled in undergraduate and graduate programs in the human services, including counseling, education, nursing, kinesiology, and so forth, and mental health professionals with limited experience in working with older adult clients

Group Size: Group size can be anywhere between 15 and 50 participants.

Time Required: 75–90 minutes, depending on the size of the group

Setting: Classroom style (tables and chairs facing the front of the room), preferably with a circular or U-shaped seating set-up (tables and chairs arranged in a U-shape). Arrangements should have the ability to be reconfigured for small-group activity.

Materials: Flipchart or dry-erase board, markers, PowerPoint, sheets of paper for writing notes, and pens or pencils

Instructions for Conducting the Activity

1. Begin the activity by emphasizing the learning objectives (outlined in the PowerPoint presentation). The instructor will provide a professional context for students' increased awareness of cultural biases related to the aging process.

2. The instructor will explain to the group that a core objective of the activity is to genuinely and honestly explore negative stereotypes related to the aging process and develop alternative, positive perceptions that include successful aging. This task requires participants to openly share their personal and professional experiences in a safe environment. Accordingly, instructors are encouraged to discuss the importance of confidentiality and to define appropriate boundaries for effective group processes.

3. After describing the objectives of the activity and outlining group parameters, the instructor will break the large group into smaller groups of three to five, depending on the number of participants. Each group will select one member to take notes and one to report back to the large group. The instructor will provide paper and writing utensils if needed.

4. Give the groups 3–5 minutes per slide to collectively discuss the projected images. **The objective is to identify how the images resonate with group members, both individually and collectively**. Note-takers, in collaboration with the group, should detail the most salient parts of members' responses (i.e., a group member strongly relates to a picture of a woman with Alzheimer's disease as a result of a negative familial experience, which may manifest as a negative perception of the aging process in general). Individual members can choose to limit the detail and descriptiveness of their responses, but again they are encouraged to frankly share their reactions. This process should take about 30 minutes.

5. Once each small-group member has had a chance to comment on the images, small-group facilitators will direct the group to create two lists of adjectives, or descriptive sentences, describing the aging process: (a) a list that describes negative perceptions of aging and (b) a list that describes successful aging. This process should take about 10 minutes.

6. At this point, small-group facilitators will report back to the large group regarding the small groups' lists of adjectives describing the aging process. On the whiteboard or flipchart, the instructor will create two master lists, one of negative perceptions of aging and the other a list of descriptions of successful aging. Once the master lists are complete, the instructor will encourage students to describe how the activity, thus far, has assisted them in developing a broader understanding of the aging process and successful aging in general. This part of the activity should take 20–30 minutes.

7. After completion of Steps 1–6, instructors can return to the PowerPoint presentation, which includes examples of empirical studies that define and describe successful aging from multiple fields of study, including qualitative studies that explore older adults' definitions of successful aging. This part of the exercise should take 10–15 minutes.

8. Finally, instructors will request that students complete the "Debunking the Myths of Age" statement of goals—the final slide of the PowerPoint presentation. Instructors may decide to follow up with students within the large group to identify common goals and brainstorm additional resources for strengthening competencies in working with the older adult client. This part of the exercise should last 10–15 minutes.

Handout: Handout 101.1: Debunking the Myths of Age (PowerPoint Presentation)

References

Depp, C. A., & Jeste, D. V. (2006). The definition and predictors of successful aging: A comprehensive literature review. *American Journal of Geriatric Psychiatry, 14*(1), 6–20.

Rowe, J. W., & Kahn, R. L. (1998). *Successful aging*. New York, NY: Dell.

Vaillant, G. E. (2003). *Aging well: Surprising guideposts to a happier life from the landmark Harvard Study of Adult Development.* Boston, MA: Little Brown & Company

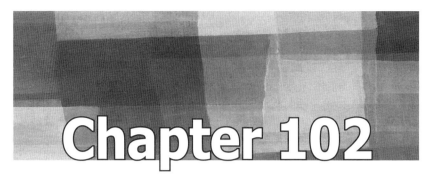

Chapter 102

Passing Strategies

Arpana G. Inman

Topics: Cultural Communication Styles
Cultural Identity Development
Oppression and Discrimination
Counseling Lesbian, Gay, Bisexual, Transgender (LGBT), and Other Sexual Minority Clients

Purposes: This activity aims to provide participants with opportunities to explore the struggles related to coming out. In particular, this activity will enhance one's understanding of passing strategies that may be used by sexual minority groups.

Learning Objectives: As a result of this activity, students will (a) have a better understanding of the concept of passing, in particular covering strategies; (b) gain knowledge about the challenges related to coming out; and (c) appreciate the privilege inherent in heterosexual identities.

Target Population: Beginning or advanced undergraduate master's- or doctoral-level students

Group Size: Any number

Time Required: 45 minutes (10 minutes for each role-play and 20–25 minutes for processing)

Setting: A regular class setting or a workshop

Materials: None

Instructions for Conducting Activity

Invite a male and a female student to engage in a couple of role-plays. Instructions for the first role-play: You are colleagues who have worked together for a while and know each other to some extent. Imagine you are back at work after a long weekend. In this role-play, you (female participant) are interested in finding out how your colleague spent his weekend. Both individuals are assumed to be in a relationship. Have the female participant ask specific questions related to how the colleague spent his weekend, who he spent it with, what kinds of activities he engaged in, and so forth. This role-play should reflect or mimic a typical conversation that two heterosexual individuals would engage in. After the couple has engaged in this dialogue, ask them to repeat this exact conversation (second role-play), but this time the male participant will not use any gender-specific pronouns in his responses. However, the female participant can continue to use such pronouns and engage in the dialogue as she did in the previous role-play.

Process questions include the following:

1. What was it like to engage in the role-play?
2. What were some challenges that you experienced in this dialogue?

3. What type of assumptions did you have entering this conversation?
4. How has this increased your awareness of the privilege you have as a heterosexual individual?

Additional Readings

Griffin, P. (1992). From hiding out to coming out: Empowering lesbian and gay educators. In K. Harbeck (Ed.), *Coming out of the classroom closet* (pp. 167–196). Binghamton, NY: Harrington Park Press.

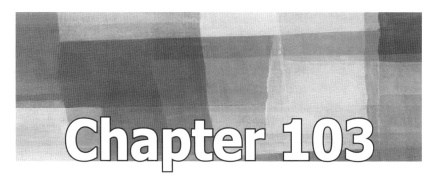

Chapter 103

Listening to the Narratives

William Maxon-Kann and Marty Jencius

Topics: Barriers to Effective Cross-Cultural Counseling
Cross-Cultural Family Counseling
Counseling Lesbian, Gay, Bisexual, Transgender (LGBT), and Other Sexual Minority Clients
Human Growth and Development

Purposes: The purpose of this activity is to assist learners in understanding and conceptualizing the perspectives, struggles, fulfillment, and experiences of transgender individuals.

Learning Objective: As a result of this experience, learners will gain awareness into the narratives and internal experiences of transgender individuals and family members or those who are associated with transgender individuals. Some of the areas of awareness will include the following:

- social and emotional stressors,
- experiences with discrimination or violence,
- family-related concerns and the impact of transgenderism on family, and
- the struggle experienced through gender-variant feelings.

Target Population: Individuals enrolled in graduate programs in multicultural counseling or individuals attending training on understanding and counseling the transgender population

Group Size: No more than 40 and no fewer than 5

Time Required: 30–45 minutes

Setting: Any room that allows for discussion. Seats can be in any arrangement that is appropriate and conducive to the atmosphere of the classroom and the needs of learners. The room should be small enough and have adequate acoustics so listeners are able to hear the narratives.

Materials: Pieces of paper at least 8″ × 11″ in size. Typed, large-font narratives of transgender individuals; their friends, family members, and associates; treatment providers; proponents and opponents of transgenderism; or those associated with transgender individuals—the narratives should be diverse (see Handout 103.1 for a sample narrative with instructions for participant). The narratives should be numbered so they can be read in a prearranged order determined by the instructor. The narratives should also have written instructions: learners should read the narrative, keep the narrative to themselves, and stand and read the narrative when called on by number to do so. The instructor should have enough narratives so that each learner attending, or who is willing to participate, has a narrative to read. The instructor can obtain narratives from books or articles on transgenderism (see examples in the References and Additional Readings sections) as well as from websites containing weblogs transcribed by transgender individuals and family members. A few examples of narratives that could be included in the exercise are included below.

An important aspect of exploring the transgender population is the variety of theories of "causes" of transgenderism that exist. After discussing the theories that exist, a learner could read the following narrative:

I do not care whether I was "born this way" or "became this way." The question of the "gay gene" or the "tranny brain" is a frightening way to destroy the brilliance of difference in the world, and the sooner we reject these ideas the better. (Lev, 2004, p. 131)

To help participants understand the struggle that often takes place in stages of transgender emergence and the perspective of the transgender person, a learner could read narratives such as the following:

As I became aware of how false my life had always been, it became harder and harder to live it. I became depressed at work and withdrawn at home. I began to feel anger at my body, which had started to disgust me. Sometimes I would roam the streets at night contemplating ways to end my life. (Lev, 2004, p. 237)

Our lives are proof that sex and gender are much more complex than a delivery room doctor's glance at genitals can determine, more variegated than pink or blue birth caps. (Fienberg, 1998, p. 5)

Instructions for Conducting Activity

1. Before the lecture begins, distribute narratives to all or selected learners, directing them to read the instructions and to add a voice, or a spirit, to the narrative or to act out the narrative.
2. Explain the use of narratives and the purpose of them for this exercise, including the necessity for the limited view of the narrative. This will help all participants who are not reading engage in actively listening to the narrative.
3. Begin the lecture/discussion.
4. After the participant reads the narrative, allow for a brief 5 seconds or so of silence.
5. If comments or responses take place spontaneously, facilitate that process.
6. Move on in the discussion of content, or encourage discussion of responses to the narrative by asking questions such as:
   a. Who might be saying this?
   b. What did you notice about the narrative?
   c. How did the narrative impact you?
   d. What emotions in the narrative did you hear?
7. The lecture/discussion proceeds until the next space for narrative.
8. Offer an opportunity for questions and for learners to process their experience.

Process Variations

- This exercise could also be applied to other cultural groups.
- The length of the overall exercise will vary depending on the size of the group, the number of narratives you have, the amount of reflection shared within the group, and the amount of lecture content. Time can be expanded or shortened, depending on learners' and instructor's needs.
- More narratives can be available if the instructor's goal is for each participant to read a narrative.
- The reading and processing of the narratives can be done without lecture content, focusing primarily on the experiential aspect.
- Learners could be broken into groups in which each group answers one of the questions above for each narrative.

Handout: Handout 103.1: Listening to Narratives

References

Feinberg, L. (1998). *Trans liberation: Beyond pink or blue*. Boston, MA: Beacon Press.

Lev, A. I. (2004). *Transgender emergence: Therapeutic guidelines for working with gender-variant people and their families*. New York, NY: Haworth Clinical Practice Press.

Additional Readings

Brown, M. L., & Rounsley, C. A. (1996). *True selves: Understanding transsexualism—For families, friends, coworkers, and helping professionals*. San Francisco, CA: Jossey Bass.

Girshick, L. B. (2008). *Transgender voices: Beyond women and men*. Lebanon, NH: University Press of New England.

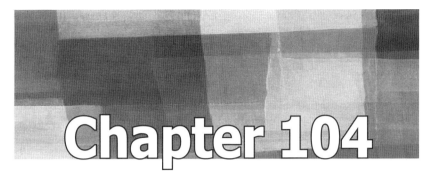

Chapter 104

A Few Hours in the Life . . .

Brigid M. Noonan

Topics: Barriers to Effective Cross-Cultural Counseling
Cultural Identity Development
Cross-Cultural Family Counseling
Counseling People With Disabilities
Career Development

Purposes: The purpose of this activity is to develop a better understanding of disability as it is viewed in different social and cultural contexts and to appreciate the relevance of this knowledge to current human rights issues.

Learning Objectives: As a result of this activity, students will develop analytical skills to understand the relationships between concerns of disability and the issues of other minority groups.

Target Population: Students enrolled in a graduate degree program in counselor education

Group Size: The activity begins with a class size of 20–30; however, final activity is done in pairs.

Time Required: Six weeks to interview an individual with a disability and write a paper; 60–90 minutes of class time to present the interview

Setting: Outside the classroom. Ideal space is in a quiet area.

Materials: Tape recorder, interview questions

Instructions for Conducting Activity

This activity takes place over the course of the semester, and students are paired with a student colleague. After students are introduced to disability-related information, they will interview an individual with a disability. Students will be provided with the interview questions, which will also be offered to the interviewee prior to the interview. Each pair will have the opportunity to interview the individual over the course of the activity. Once the interview has been conducted, the students will transcribe the interview.

Interview Questions

1. What is your disability? Is it congenital or acquired?
2. If acquired, at what age?
3. What was the adjustment process (if any) to your disability?
4. Can you talk about your experiences in school? Were there any incidents of discrimination or bias?

5. Can you talk about your career development? Were there any incidents of discrimination or bias?
6. How do you define *disability*? How has culture played a role in your disability identity?
7. What are some of the barriers that you have encountered (e.g., attitudinal, economic, architectural, sensory, cognitive)?
8. In terms of support (e.g., intrinsic and extrinsic), what has been your experience?
9. Can you talk about your family and how they did or did not support you?
10. Can you talk about other relationships and how those individual(s) did or did not support you?
11. What, if any, have been the greatest challenges to you and/or your family related to your disability?
12. If you could share information with a counselor-in-training, what would be the area(s) that you would like the counselor to know about individuals with disabilities?
13. Are there other areas or questions that we have not covered that you believe are important?

As a pair, they will then write their personal reaction to the experience. The students' focus needs to be on the strengths and limitations exhibited by the interviewee (e.g., focusing on verbal and nonverbal behaviors); how societal roles and expectations have played a part in this individual's experience; how the individual's experiences of discrimination (if any) have played a part in the individual's experience; any problems or challenges the students faced in conducting the interview; and, if the students were ever to be in a counseling relationship with a client who has a disability, how this experience would assist them in acquiring new skills.

Once the reaction paper is written, the students will visit with their interviewee and share their reactions. The pair should clarify any information that is pertinent to the assignment before handing in their paper and presenting it to the class.

Class time is allotted for students to present their interview and reactions regarding the experience.

Additional Readings

Dell Orto, A. E., & Power, P. W. (Eds.). (2007). *The psychological and social impact of illness and disability* (5th ed.). New York, NY: Springer.

Hockenberry, J. (1995). *Moving violations: War zones, wheelchairs and declarations of independence*. New York, NY: Hyperion.

Olkin, R. (1999). *What psychotherapists should know about disability*. New York, NY: Guilford Press.

Shapiro, J. (1994). *No pity: People with disabilities forging a new civil rights movement*. New York, NY: Three Rivers Press.

Additional Resources

Center for Independent Living
   http://www.cilberkeley.org/
Council for Disability Awareness
   http://www.disabilitycanhappen.org/
Federal government's disability-related information and resources
   http://www.disabilityinfo.gov/digov-public/public/DisplayPage.do?parentFolderId=500
National Council for Support of Disability Issues
   http://www.ncsd.org/
National Organization on Disability
   http://www.nod.org/
Office of Special Education and Rehabilitative Services
   http://www.ed.gov/about/offices/list/osers/osep/index.html
World Institute on Disability
   http://www.wid.org/

Lunch Time!

Derrick A. Paladino and Alicia M. Homrich

Topics: Definitions of Cultural Diversity
Cultural Identity Development
Culturally Skilled Counselor
Multiple Identities/Biracial, Multiracial

Purposes: The purpose of this activity is to assist learners to begin building understanding of and empathy for the unique experiences of multiple-heritage individuals in preparation for a discussion on the counseling implications for this clientele.

Learning Objectives: As a result of this activity, participants will better understand:

- some of the realities individuals of multiple heritage encounter in navigating racial and cultural identities in various contexts,
- the concept of "belonging everywhere and belonging nowhere" in the multiple-heritage population.
- how one's current level of identity development can facilitate gravitation toward one identity over another and the implications within a family, and
- potential difficulties individuals of multiple heritage may encounter in accepting an integrated identity (if chosen).

Target Population: Students enrolled in multicultural counseling courses and/or family counseling courses (as this can be adapted to discuss dynamics within interracial families) or participants in a workshop in which multiple-heritage or interracial family forms are addressed

Group Size: Groups of three, followed by a whole class discussion group

Time Required: 30 minutes

Setting: Classroom

Materials: (a) Handouts 105.1 and 105.2 or projection of images on a large screen (instructor can add criteria to "Yellow" and "Blue" columns of handouts if desired) and (b) dry-erase board for listing the participants' descriptions of inclusion criteria for the third lunch table ("Green").

Instructions for Conducting Activity

Part 1

1. Distribute Handout 105.1 or project on a large screen.
2. Inform participants that their racial or cultural background is "Green"—a combination of "Yellow" and "Blue."

3. Ask participants to make a personal decision about which lunch table they prefer to join based on the criteria listed in Handout 105.1.
4. Ask participants to think about what criteria led to their decision:
   a. What felt good about their choice?
   b. What felt uncomfortable about their choice?
   c. What were their affective and/or cognitive reactions to the experience of choosing a group?
   d. What was the decision process that led to their choice?
5. Request participants to divide into groups of three to discuss their choice and their experience in making their choice.
6. Ask triads to report their findings to the larger class group.
7. Initiate a discussion among the class about what they learned from the experience of looking through the eyes of a multiple-heritage individual:
   a. What kind of processes might a multiple-heritage individual go through in developing a cultural identity?
   b. How might an individual's identity development affect the decisions he or she makes about choosing a table? Alternatively, how might their choices about which groups they join affect their further identity development?
   c. What might a client decide about him- or herself in the context of evaluating a situation from a cultural inclusion perspective?
   d. What would this process be like for a child? An adolescent? An adult? An older adult? A man? A woman?
   e. How might the decision about which group to select change with the context? For example:
      (1) A college student choosing which student organization or racial/cultural group to join or affiliate with.
      (2) A teenager at an event where there is strong "in" group and "out" group pressure.
      (3) An elderly adult deciding what church to join in a new community.
      (4) A family making a decision about what neighborhood would be a good choice for re-location if each parent is from a group that is very different in appearance and customs from the neighborhood being considered.
      (5) A young couple who is trying to decide which heritage they want to socialize with in relation to their career choices.
      (6) A couple with children who are vocal about their strong cultural or ethnic identities as well as their prejudicial views about the heritage group of the other spouse.
      (7) A couple who is trying to decide which religion they would like to raise their children if each parent affiliates with a different religion.

Part 2

1. Distribute Handout 105.2 or project on a large screen.
2. Ask participants to look at the "Green" table on Handout 105.2 and (either individually, in triads, or as a large group) construct their own criteria for inclusion as a "Green" (as an individual with a multiple-heritage identity).
3. Write the inclusion criteria suggested by the participants on the whiteboard for the "Green" lunch table.
4. Ask participants how they might react as counselors to an individual of multiple heritage, based on the concepts illuminated by the discussion in Part 1.
   a. How would they assist a client navigating the challenges of a multiple-heritage identity?
   b. What dilemmas or decisions might they anticipate their clients encountering in making choices about participating in their social contexts, work settings, and community?
   c. What coping skills might an individual need to remain resilient in the face of the dilemmas and decisions identified in Part 1?

d. What problems might a family experience as a result of receiving social or familial pressure because of their multiple-heritage or interracial relationship status?

e. How would they help a client or family experiencing loyalty struggles because of the multiple heritages in their family of origin?

Handouts: Handout 105.1: Lunch Time! Part 1
                  Handout 105.2: Lunch Time! Part 2

Additional Readings

Fukuyama, M. A. (1999). Personal narrative: Growing up biracial. *Journal of Counseling & Development, 77*, 12–14.

Hardy, K. V., & Laszloffy, T. A. (1995). The cultural genogram: Key to training culturally competent family therapists. *Journal of Marital and Family Therapy, 21,* 227–237.

Henriksen, R. C., & Paladino, D. A. (Eds.). (2009). *Counseling multiple heritage individuals, couples, and families.* Alexandria, VA: American Counseling Association.

Jones, N. A., & Smith, A. M. (2001). The two or more races population: 2000: Census 2000 brief. *U.S. Census Bureau,* 1–10.

Laszloffy, T. A. (2005, March/April). Multiracial families. *Family Therapy Magazine,* 3843. Alexandria, VA: American Association for Marriage and Family Therapy.

Loving v. Virginia, 388 U.S. 1 (1967).

Poston, W. S. C. (1990). The biracial identity development model: A needed addition. *Journal of Counseling & Development, 69*, 152–155.

Root, M. P. P. (1996). *The multiracial experience: Racial borders as the new frontier.* Thousand Oaks, CA: Sage.

Root, M. P. P. (1999). The biracial baby boom: Understanding ecological constructions of racial identity in the 21st century. In R. H. Sheets, R. Hernandez, & E. R. Hollins (Eds.), *Racial and ethnic identity in school practices: Aspects of human development* (pp. 67–89). Mahwah, NJ: Erlbaum.

Root, M. P. P. (2001). *Love's revolution: Interracial marriage.* Philadelphia, PA: Temple University Press.

Stonequist, E. V. (1937). *The marginal man: A study in personality and culture conflict.* New York, NY: Russell & Russell.

Wehrly, B., Kenney, K. R., & Kenney, M. E. (1999). *Counseling multiracial families.* Thousand Oaks, CA: Sage.

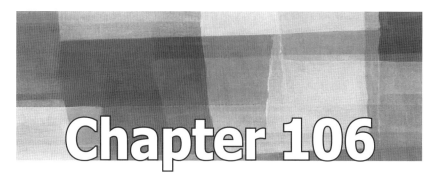

Aging Simulation Scavenger Hunt

Jacqueline Peila-Shuster, Nathalie Kees, Sharon K. Anderson,
Edward J. Brantmeier, and Antonette Aragon

Topics: Counseling Aging Clients
Human Growth and Development

Purposes: Rationale—The United States of America is undergoing a tremendous demographic shift. The number of Americans age 65 and over in 2000 was approximately 35 million, about one of every eight. It is projected that by 2030, about one in five Americans will be age 65 or older (He, Sengupta, Velkoff, & DeBarros, 2005). It's important to note that this demographic shift is not unique to the United States. According to the United Nations Department of Economic and Social Affairs, Population Division (2007), it is predicted that by 2050, 22% of the world population will be 60 years or older.

    The purpose of this activity is to provide an experience to increase awareness of some of the personal and societal difficulties an aging individual might face. This goal is accomplished by simulating the various sensory and motor losses that can commonly occur as we age.

Learning Objectives: As a result of this activity, participants will be able to (a) gain greater awareness of how sensory and motor losses associated with aging can cause difficulties for the aging individual; (b) develop a greater empathetic understanding of losses associated with aging and insights into how those losses, and society's reactions to them, may affect the elderly individual emotionally and psychosocially; and (c) identify ways that they can provide a more inclusive counseling environment that may mitigate these aging effects.

Target Population: Counseling (community, career) students and professionals; any human services students/professionals working with older adults

Group Size: 1–20 participants

Time Required: 60–90 minutes

Setting: Classroom, classroom building, and, if time allows, the entire campus

Materials: Elastic bandages (such as ACE bandages), foam rubber earplugs, glasses that have been slightly tinted yellow and have a small amount of petroleum jelly rubbed on lens exterior, cotton gloves, canes, walkers, and thin cotton bandages

Instructions for Conducting Activity

1. Have students put an elastic bandage around the ankle, knee, or elbow and a cotton bandage around a few of the finger joints to simulate stiffness of joints. Donning the glasses will simulate

decreased visual acuity as well as the yellowing of the lens (which filters out violet, green, and blue shades) that occurs with aging. The cotton gloves will provide lessened tactile acuity. The foam rubber earplugs will simulate hearing loss, and the canes and walkers will cause mobility impediments.

2. Give each student a list of activities they must complete (use regular-size font). These activities will need to be appropriate and tailored for the setting in which they will be done. The activities may include finding specific information or websites on a computer in a computer lab, climbing up and down stairs, asking for directions, maneuvering through cluttered areas, using an elevator, using the restroom, finding a specific book in the library or a specific office in the building, going where people are moving around, holding a conversation with someone, and so forth. A specific handout example is included (see Handout 106.1).

3. Follow up with process questions when students return.

Process Questions

- What were your experiences?
- What emotions were aroused during this activity?
- What new insights and empathy have you gained about the difficulties older adults may experience?
- How is this activity different from having an actual disability?
- How does mainstream society view aging and the losses that may occur with it? What strengths can be developed with aging, and how might these compensate or mitigate for losses?
- How can you apply this information to the counseling arena? Your office set up? Type and style of resources you provide? Personal issues older adults may face because of these difficulties? Societal barriers? What strengths from an elderly individual might you be able to draw upon? How can their experiences with loss be used as a strength? How might their experiences be different depending on their cultural background?

Follow-Up Integration

Have students write a 5-minute reflection paper about the insights they gained from this experience and the class discussion.

Handout: Handout 106.1: Aging Simulation Scavenger Hunt

References

He, W., Sengupta, M., Velkoff, V. A., & DeBarros, K. A. (2005). 65+ in the United States: 2005 [Electronic version]. *U.S. Census Bureau, Current Population Reports*. Washington, DC: U.S. Government Printing Office. Available at http://www.census.gov/prod/2006pubs/p23-209.pdf

United Nations Department of Economic and Social Affairs, Population Division. (2007). *World population ageing 2007*. Retrieved April 17, 2007, from http://www.un.org/esa/population/publications/WPA2007/ES-English.pdf

Additional Readings

Papalia, D. E., Sterns, H. L., Feldman, R. D., & Camp, C. J. (2007). *Adult development and aging* (3rd ed.). New York, NY: McGraw-Hill.

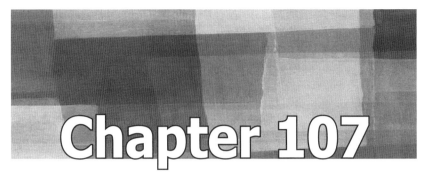

Chapter 107

Confronting Prejudice and Stereotypes: Working With Transgender Individuals

Varunee Faii Sangganjanavanich

Topics: Definitions of Cultural Diversity
Oppression and Discrimination
Professional Identity and Ethical Practice
Group Work

Purposes: This activity aims to provide participants with opportunities to examine their prejudice toward transgender individuals. This activity also improves participants' understanding about the prejudice and stereotypes that transgender individuals face; hence, participants develop and enhance empathy for this population.

Learning Objectives: As a result of this activity, participants will (a) have an opportunity to examine their prejudice toward transgender individuals, (b) be able to share and discuss their prejudice and stereotypes toward transgender individuals in a safe learning environment, and (c) develop strategies to enhance empathy for transgender individuals by confronting one's own prejudice toward this population.

Target Population: Students taking courses in counseling diverse populations, multicultural counseling, or psychology of prejudice

Group Size: 10–15 students

Time Required: 45 minutes

Setting: Regular classroom size. Sitting in a circle without tables is preferred.

Materials: Flipchart and marker

Instructions for Conducting Activity

First, the instructor invites students to go around the circle and share some stereotypes of transgender individuals as well some of their own perceptions or beliefs. Students are also asked to share the source of their information. Next, the instructor asks students to discuss how these stereotypes may prevent them from having empathy for transgender clients in counseling. Last, the instructor asks students to brainstorm strategies for developing empathy for transgender clients. The instructor then encourages students to discuss and reflect on this activity.

Throughout the discussion, the instructor is responsible for writing the students' contributions on the flipchart, including stereotypes, sources of stereotypes, obstacles to empathy, and strategies for developing empathy. During this activity, it is important for the instructor to create and maintain a nonjudgmental learning environment in order for students to feel secure in sharing and confronting their prejudice toward transgender individuals.

Additional Readings

Bieschke, K. J., Perez, R. M., & DeBord, K. A. (Eds.). (2007). *Handbook of counseling and psychotherapy with lesbian, gay, bisexual, and transgender clients (2nd ed.).* Washington, DC: American Psychological Association.

Dallas, D. (1998). *Current concepts in transgender identity.* New York, NY: Garland Press.

Jones, B. E., & Hill, M. J. (2002). *Mental health issues in lesbian, gay, bisexual, and transgender communities.* Washington, DC: American Psychiatric Publishing.

Lombardi, E. L., Wilchins, R. A., Priesing, D., & Malouf, D. (2001). Gender violence: Transgender experiences with violence and discrimination. *Journal of Homosexuality, 42,* 89–101.

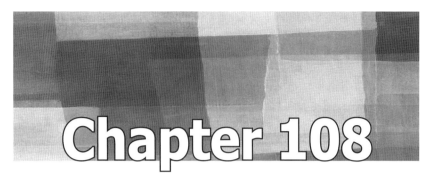

Chapter 108

Locating Yourself in the Story: Exploring the Therapeutic Impact on Elderly Sexuality

Angela Schubert

Topics: Culturally Skilled Counselor
Counseling Aging Clients

Purposes: The purpose of this activity is to provide participants with opportunities to explore the impact of their personal belief system and understanding of societal expectations on their ability to therapeutically establish an alliance with their elderly clients. This activity will promote self-introspection as a means to identify and demystify personal biases, opinions, and stereotypes toward elderly sexuality and sexual expression. This activity will also enhance the participants' awareness of the sexual continuum and how existential variables such as illness, disability, and death may affect the aging individual's level of sexual expression and interest.

Learning Objectives: As a result of this activity, participants will (a) enhance their awareness of personal biases and attitudes toward elderly sexuality; (b) examine how such biases and attitudes may affect the therapeutic alliance; and (c) conceptualize how certain variables such as age, illness, disability, and death may affect the level of interest and sexual freedom of aging individuals.

Target Population: Undergraduate and graduate students enrolled in counseling and mental health programs and practicing counselors. This activity is particularly effective for those individuals with limited knowledge and experience in working with older clients on the topic of sexuality.

Group Size: Group size can vary from 15–30 participants.

Time Required: 60 minutes; may vary depending on size.

Setting: U-shaped seating or roundtable seating is preferred. Seating will change to accommodate mini-group discussion.

Materials: Chalkboard or marker board, chalk or markers, colored sheets of paper, pens or pencils, pretest material (see Handout 108.1), scenario material (see Handout 108.2), and PowerPoint presentation (see Handout 108.3)

Instructions for Conducting Activity

1. Prior to class, the instructor will randomly tape five red sheets of paper underneath the seats of the classroom. Each sheet will contain a scenario relevant to the discussion on ageist sexuality. The instructor will address the red sheet scenario during the discussion portion of the activity.
2. Administer the pretest to participants (5 minutes).
3. Getting to know you: (5 minutes)—Ask participants to walk around and find a person whom they do not know in the group to talk to about the following:
   a. Their names.
   b. Their current position and some of their work experiences.
   c. Their reason for entering the program; academic and career expectations.
   d. Current feelings surrounding elderly sexuality.
   e. Write down one thing they could not live without.
4. Have participants move into small discussion groups of approximately 4–5. It might be helpful to assign roles to keep all participants involved (note taker(s), presenter, time keeper, and so forth).
5. Start PowerPoint presentation (20–25 minutes). The instructor will explain the objectives of the activity to the class, emphasizing the importance of honest reflection and expression of opinion as the main goal of the activity.
6. During the PowerPoint presentation, students will be asked to have ongoing mini-group discussions and will report findings throughout the presentation. (Please review PowerPoint and identify specified times for mini-group discussions.)
7. The mini-groups will discuss the topics and label findings under two categories: societal and personal. The discussion topics (as noted in the PowerPoint) are to:
   a. Identify stereotypes of elderly sexuality;
   b. Discuss the effects of stereotypes on elderly sexuality;
   c. Explore effects of aging on sexuality; and
   d. Discuss the impact of the therapeutic alliance on the elderly client's willingness to express self freely and honestly.

Throughout each topic, participants will be strongly encouraged to reflect on how such topics might affect them as sexual beings.

8. After the topics are covered, participants will then be asked to look under the seat for a red sheet of paper. The instructor will then engage the participants in a conversation about what it feels like to be separated from the other participants and to have their freedom hypothetically judged and restricted because of the scenario suggested on the red sheet (15–20 minutes).
9. The instructor will ask participants to reflect on the pretest and discuss feelings and attitudes that may have altered or stayed the same (10–15 minutes).

Handouts: Handout 108.1: Red Sheet Scenarios 1–5
Handout 108.2: Locating Yourself in the Story: Exploring the Therapeutic Impact on Elderly Sexuality—Pretest
Handout 108.3: Locating Yourself in the Story: Exploring the Therapeutic Impact on Elderly Sexuality (PowerPoint Presentation)

References

Lindau, S. T., Schumm, L. P., Laumann, E. O., Levinson, W., O'Muircheartaigh, C. A., & Waite, L. J. (2007). A study of sexuality and health among older adults in the United States. *New England Journal of Medicine, 8*(357), 762–774.

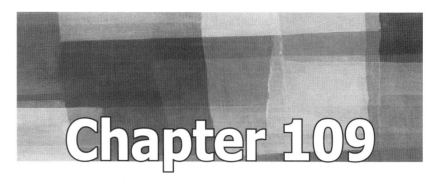

Chapter 109
Family Dinner and Photo

Mei Tang

Topics: Cultural Communication Styles
Dimensions of Worldviews
Cross-Cultural Family Counseling
Counseling Asian Americans
Creative Arts

Purposes: The purpose of this activity is to provide participants with opportunities to understand the important cultural values in Asian tradition that could potentially influence Asian American and Pacific Islanders' (AAPI's) thoughts, emotions, and behaviors. This activity also aims to help participants conceptualize culturally appropriate processes of counseling AAPI.

Learning Objectives: The learning objectives are (a) to enhance understanding of core cultural values held by AAPI and their influences on AAPI ways of interacting with others, (b) to understand family dynamics and interrelationship among family members of AAPI, and (c) to increase self-awareness of differences between one's own cultural background and AAPI's cultural background.

Target Population: This activity is designed for graduate students in counselor education programs and allied helping professionals training programs. This activity can also be used for continuing education training workshops.

Group Size: This activity can be completed in a small group of six to eight individuals, or it can be completed in a large class with a maximum of 30 persons.

Time Required: 30–40 minutes

Setting: A classroom or meeting room with 30-person capacity

Materials: Papers, pens, and index cards with titles of family members (quantity depends on number of participants)

Instructions for Conducting Activity

1. The instructor/leader first asks everyone to get a piece of paper and a pen ready.
2. The instructor/leader then asks the participants to write down as many English words describing the titles of family members and relatives as possible.
3. Let the participants count the number of words they have written down.

4. At this point, the instructor can ask the group who knows other languages than English. If someone in the group raises a hand, ask the student what languages he or she speaks and whether the list of words gets shorter or longer in that language.
5. Have the student explain why the list gets shorter or longer.

In fact, Chinese and most Asian languages have more words to describe family members and relatives than English does. On the other hand, in African languages, there are fewer words for family members.

The more words for family members in Chinese actually indicate a very specific relationship among family members and relatives. Such detailed and specific forms of addresses indicate an intricate relationship among family members that cannot be misunderstood. The specificity of the words to describe relationships also implies the kind of respect or authority you have for each other. The younger generations always have to reserve respect for the older generation. In English, cousins are not distinguished by either maternal or paternal side of the family, but in Chinese, there are 16 words to describe cousins, each specifically indicating this cousin's gender, age in comparison to yours, and whether the cousin is related to your mother's sister or brother or your father's sister or brother. In the Chinese tradition, the cousins from the father's brothers are considered just as your own siblings. Such elaborate ways of illustrating family members' relations also reflect the fact that traditional Chinese culture—and most Eastern Asian cultures—is relational; that is, the relationships among people guide how people treat each other but not necessarily the rules and laws. The nature and closeness of the relationship can often be determined by how people address each other. For instance, you would instruct your child to address acquaintances as "aunt" or "uncle" to show politeness, but if it is your friend, you would ask your child to call her or him "Aunt Zhang" or "Uncle Wang." Sometimes, people will tell their children that "Uncle Zhang" is "Uncle Third," meaning that he is truly part of the family because he is considered as the third brother of the family.

Ask the group members to randomly pick up an index card that contains titles of family members that are prepared for the class (see Handout 109.1). Then have them play the role of the family members on the index card they have picked as if they were at the family dinner table. The "family" now needs to seat themselves and serve the food. Do it as if they were in an AAPI family. After the eating is done, ask the group members to pose for a family photo.

Then have the group process the following questions: (a) Who is in charge? (b) Who has the most respect? (c) Who has the authority? (d) How is dinner served? (e) What is the behavior observed at the dinner table? and (f) what is the expected manner at the dinner table? After these questions have been processed, the group then shares their thoughts about the roles they played: (a) What rules did they follow to seat themselves for dinner? (b) What kind of values guided their decisions? and (c) How did they make such a choice? You may also want to observe the dynamics in this process, such as person in charge, flow of action, communications, interaction among the members, and so on. Then have the group discuss: If they posed for the photo as themselves, would the position/pose be different? Ask them the reasons of differences.

The purpose of the questions used in this activity is to process participants' awareness of their own cultural traditions and AAPI cultural traditions regarding family dynamics. Finally, ask the group to summarize what they have learned from this activity and how they will translate their learning to the next AAPI client they will encounter. Or, how would they conceptualize a former case with AAPI clients differently?

Handout: Handout 109.1: Family Dinner and Photo Activity

Additional Readings

Chiu, E. Y., & Lee, E. (2004). Cultural frameworks in assessment and psychotherapy with Asian Americans. In N. Charles (Ed.), *Cross-cultural psychotherapy: Toward a critical understanding of diverse clients* (pp. 205–229). Reno, NV: Bent Tree.

Markus, H. R., & Kitayama, S. (1991). Culture and the self: Implications for cognition, emotion, and motivation. *Psychological Review, 98,* 224–253.

Sandhu, D. S., Leung, A., & Tang, M. (2003). Counselling approaches with Asian Americans and Pacific Islanders. In F. D. Harper & J. McFadden (Eds.), *Culture and counselling: New approaches* (pp. 99–114). Boston, MA: Allyn & Bacon.

Takaki, R. (1998). *Strangers from a different shore: A history of Asian Americans* (Rev. ed.). Boston, MA: Little Brown and Company.

Zhou, M., & Xiong, Y. S. (2005). The multifaceted American experiences of the children of Asian immigrants: Lessons for segmented assimilation. *Ethnic and Racial Studies, 28*, 1119–1152.

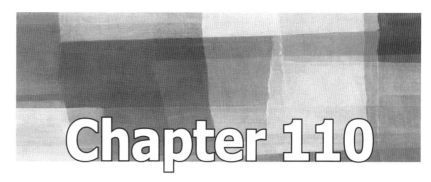

Chapter 110

Understanding and Resolving Conflicted Career Choices

Mei Tang

Topics: Four Forces in Counseling
Counseling Asian Americans
Career Development
Assessment

Purposes: The purpose of this activity is to provide participants opportunities to understand the factors in Asian American and Pacific Islanders' (AAPI's) values that could potentially influence their career choices. This activity also aims to help participants understand the career decision-making process of AAPI and to learn strategies that would help counselors work effectively with AAPI on career development issues.

Learning Objectives: The learning objectives are (a) to understand AAPI cultural values that influence their career choices, (b) to translate the understanding of Asian American cultural traditions to help AAPI in their career development issues, and (c) to learn about developing culturally appropriate strategies of career intervention.

Target Population: Graduate students in counselor training, professionals in other allied helping professions enrolled in training or educational programs, and school counselors and counselors in higher education institutions would benefit from this program.

Group Size: This activity can be completed in a small group with six to eight individuals who are identified as AAPI individuals or in graduate classes with 30 maximum students who are taking either a multicultural or a career development class.

Time Required: 30–40 minutes

Materials: Paper, pen, scissors, and markers. Depending on the number of participants, the quantity of the materials can range from 6 to 30.

Instructions for Conducting Activities

1. On a blank piece of paper, have the group members write down their ideal occupations. Then ask the participants to list the occupations of their current career choice. If the two sets of occupations are the same, ask the participants whether their parents have agreed with this choice.
2. Those folks who answer "yes" form a subgroup. Accordingly, ask those whose ideal occupations do not match their actual choices and those who haven't had approval from their parents to form another group.
3. In each group, the members will list the factors that influenced their actual occupational choices and how they achieved their decisions. Then ask the two groups to share their lists of factors.

4. Have the two groups compare their lists and find similarities and differences.

Researchers have found that parental expectation is a very important factor for Asian Americans in their career decision-making choices (e.g., Leong & Serifica, 1995; Tang, Fouad, & Smith, 1999). It should not be a surprise that family or parental influence will emerge as a factor on their list. The discrepancy between ideal and actual career choice might also be the result of parental insistence on a more practical occupational choice that would bring stability and security, compared with the occupation the participant wants to pursue that is interesting but less stable or secure.

- After the similarities and differences are discussed, have the group members write down the 10 most essential elements they want from their chosen occupations list.
- Then, have the group members cut the essential elements into small pieces. Use different colored markers to classify the values into three categories: (a) what I want, (b) what my parents want, and (c) what both my parents and I want.
- The next step is to put the previously identified influential factors into two piles: internal (out of my own interests/values, inspired by someone I admire, or understanding of the occupations) versus external (peer influence, parental influence, and so on).
- Now look at the essentials marked as "c" (i.e., what both my parents and I want) and the piles labeled "internal" for influential factors. Look at the career choices that were listed earlier for both ideal and actual category, and see if there is any one that fits both essentials marked as "c" and internal influential factors. Then go beyond the prewritten list and brainstorm for more occupational titles.
- The next step is to mix the two groups and reformulate two new groups. Have the groups then discuss the strategies that would help resolve the conflict between parental and individual choices. The purpose of mixing the groups is to let people see how others work on their career decision-making process and to share different perspectives among the group members.
- After the strategies are developed, the instructor/leader can facilitate a discussion on evaluating the likelihood of each strategy to be actually implemented by AAPI in the real world, based on the cultural relevance and appropriateness. The key issues are how to resolve parents' concerns about job security and financial rewards and how to make the parents and children understand each other's perspectives. Also discuss why it is not culturally appropriate to empower students to be independent in their decision making.

If this activity is being used with a graduate class, the instructor may modify the activity to let students complete the steps following the AAPI framework that they know. The other option is to split the class into half, with one group conducting the activity as if they were AAPI and other group doing the exercise as themselves. Then have the entire class discuss the similarities and differences.

References

Leong, F. T. L., & Serafica, F. C. (1995). Career development of Asian Americans: A research area in need of a good theory. In F. T. L. Leong (Ed.), *Career development and vocational behavior of racial and ethnic minorities* (pp. 67–102). Hillsdale, NJ: Erlbaum.

Tang, M., Fouad, N. A., & Smith, P. L. (1999). Asian Americans' career choices: A path model to examine the factors influencing choices. *Journal of Vocational Behavior, 54*, 142–157.

Additional Readings

Fouad, N. A., Kantamneni, N., Smothers, M. K., Chen, Y., Fitzpatrick, M., & Terry, S. (2008). Asian American career development: A qualitative analysis. *Journal of Vocational Behavior, 72*, 43–59.

Leong, F. T. L., & Gupta, A. (2007). Career development and vocational behaviors of Asian Americans. In F. T. L. Leong, A. Ebreo, L. Kinoshita, A. G. Inman, & L. H. Yang (Eds.), *Handbook of Asian American psychology* (pp. 159–178). Thousand Oaks: CA: Sage.

Louie, V. (2004). *Compelled to excel: Immigration, education, and opportunity among Chinese Americans*. Palo Alto, CA: Stanford University Press.

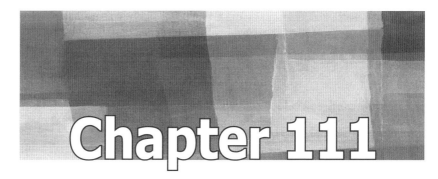

Chapter 111

What's in a Name:
Indians or Native Americans?

Anne M. Warren

Topics: Cultural Communication Styles
Cultural Identity Development
Culturally Skilled Counselor
Counseling Native Americans

Purposes: The purpose of this activity is to get participants interested in the use of terminology in cross-cultural counseling and to encourage students to reflect on their perceptions and experiences related to Native American culture.

Learning Objectives: As a result of this activity students will (a) have a better understanding of the terms *Native American* and *Indian*, (b) have an understanding that the Native American culture is not as overarching as the term implies, (c) have an understanding that each individual tribal entity is a culture, and (d) have an opportunity to explore terminology when identifying cultural groups.

Target Population: Undergraduate and graduate counseling, psychology, and social work students

Group Size: This exercise may accommodate 8–25 participants.

Time Required: 3 hours

Setting: Access to a library and the Internet

Materials: Student reading: *Cultural Identification*, library books, Internet.

Instructions for Conducting Activity

This experiential activity begins with students reading a short informational piece asking questions about how First Nation members prefer to be addressed (see Handout 111.1).

- Students are asked to form groups of four to six students to plan and execute a short research project in which they use available resources, such as a library and the Internet, to gain access to information regarding contemporary identification and self-identification of members of Native American culture. Any of the references for this activity or additional reading resources may be helpful in student's research.
- Students are given a time limit of 15 minutes for preliminary discussion and planning of the research phase.

- Students are given a time limit of 90 minutes for research.
- Students are given a time limit of 30 minutes for research compilation and discussion within the group, which should result in an outline of research findings offered to the class.
- Students are given a time limit of 45 minutes for general discussion that includes the whole class.

Request that students think about the following when coming to conclusions:

1. Why is what American Indians are called of importance to them?
   a. What cultural bias might be expressed through a cultural identifier/name?
   b. Why might the terms *Native American* or *Indian* be rejected by First Nation peoples?
2. Who are you within your personal cultural framework, and how does your personal cultural identity connect or diverge from your general cultural background?
   a. What are your personal cultural attitudes, and what is your personal cultural worldview?
   b. How might your personal cultural attitudes and your worldview differ from the personal cultural attitudes and personal worldview of members of a Native American culture?
3. What is your knowledge of human systems and concepts of cultural identity formation?
4. How might cultural beliefs and attitudes of a minority culture, such as Native Americans, reflect or diverge from the predominant North American culture?

Handout: Handout 111.1: Cultural Self-Identification

Additional Readings

Arden, H., & Wall, S. (1990). *Wisdomkeepers: Meetings with Native American spiritual elders.* Hillsboro, OR: Beyond Words.

Banks, J. A. (1997). *Teaching strategies for ethnic studies*. Boston, MA: Allyn & Bacon.

Barnes, B., Mitchell, M., & Thompson, J. (1984). *Traditional teachings.* Cornwall Island, Ontario, Canada: North American Indian Traveling College.

Beck, P. V., Walters, A. L., & Francisco, N. (1992). *The sacred: Ways of knowledge, sources of life.* Tsaile, AR: Navajo Community College Press.

Clifton, J. A. (1987). *The Potawatomi*. New York, NY: Chelsea House.

Duran, E. (2006). *Healing the soul wound.* New York, NY: Teachers College Press.

Fixico, D. L. (2003). *The American Indian mind in a linear world*. New York, NY: Routledge.

Graymount, B. (1988). *The Iroquois*. New York, NY: Chelsea House.

Hirchfelder, A., & Beamer, Y. (2000). *Native Americans today: Resources and activities for educators.* Englewood, CO: Libraries Unlimited.

Indian Country Today [Native American news source]. http://www.indiancountrytoday.com/

James, M. A. (1992). *The state of Native America: Genocide, colonization and resistance.* Boston, MA: South End Press.

Neihardt, J. G. (1972). *Black Elk speaks*. Lincoln, NE: University of Nebraska Press.

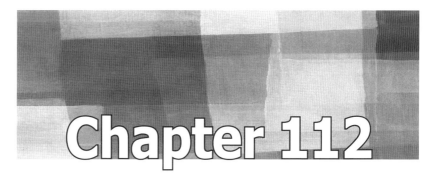

Chapter 112

Native American Ethics: Spirituality

Anne M. Warren

Topics: Cultural Communication Styles
Cultural Identity Development
Dimensions of Worldviews
Counseling Native Americans
Professional Identity and Ethical Practice
Spirituality
Creative Arts

Purposes: The purpose of this activity is to have students explore Native American cultural mores and spiritual beliefs and encourage students to reflect on their own spiritual beliefs and Native American spirituality and how they may differ.

Learning Objectives: As a result of this activity, students will (a) have a better understanding of Native American spiritual concepts, (b) analyze stereotypes about and misconceptions of Native American spiritual beliefs, (c) explore Native American cultural values, and (d) explore and compare Native American concepts with concepts of their own spiritual beliefs.

Target Population: Graduate and undergraduate psychology, counseling, social work, and art therapy core cultural studies class

Group Size: This exercise may accommodate 4–12 participants.

Time Required: 3 hours

Setting: Tables and chairs to accommodate a chair for each participant and generous tabletop space for each participant should be provided. Tables should be large enough to accommodate a working area of a square yard on the table surface for each participant, though smaller areas may be accommodated as necessary and students may be encouraged to work on the floor. The door to the room should be closed to define the therapeutic space. The room size should match the need; for instance, a gymnasium may seem intimidating in size and scale for working with small groups.

Materials:

- Student reading: Handout 112.1, "Native American Spiritual Beliefs";
- one cardboard circle for each student (12″, found in bulk through art supply stores);
- supplies to be shared: scissors; glue sticks and white school-type glue; glue gun and glue sticks; magazines and newspapers; drawing materials, such as markers, pastels, crayons, colored pencils, #2 pencils, and pens; various craft materials, such as ribbons, pieces of material, artificial flowers, glitter, beads, and buttons; acrylic and watercolor paints; and natural materials, such as pinecones, buckskin, stones, sticks, leaves.

Instructions for Conducting the Activity

- *Time allotted:* 5–10 minutes. This experiential activity begins with students reading a short informational written piece about Native American spiritual beliefs found in Native American proverbs (see Handout 112.1, "Native American Spiritual Beliefs").
- *Working time:* 90 minutes. Choosing one proverb from the handout, students are asked to work independently to create a collage in which they use available resources. The collage should reflect imagery that comes to mind when reading or hearing their chosen proverb and may incorporate elements from student's spiritual worldview that correspond or conflict with how they understand their chosen proverb.
- *Time:* 10 minutes. After the art-making process, have the class come together to form a circle. Within the circle, students will lay their collages on the floor. Students will take a few minutes to walk around the circle, looking at the images; next, those who wish to present their collage to the class and discuss it may do so.
- Each student may be given a time limit for discussion and presentation of 10–15 minutes. More or less time may be used by each student, depending on how many students participate.
- No idea is wrong; exploration is key.

When students are working, Native American drum or flute music should be played. Students may not chat while working so that they may focus on their process.

Request that students think about the following when coming to conclusions:

1. What are your personal spiritual beliefs?
2. What are your personal attitudes about spiritual beliefs that differ from your own, and what is your personal worldview of spiritual beliefs within cultures different from your own?
3. How do your personal spiritual attitudes and your personal worldview of spiritual beliefs influence how you interact with cultures different from your own, specifically your interaction with Native American culture?
4. What is your knowledge of human systems? Of cultural identity formation?

Handouts: Handout 112.1: Native American Spiritual Beliefs

References

Lombardi, F. G., & Lombardi, G. S. (1982). *Circle without end: A sourcebook of American Indian ethics.* Happy Camp, CA: Naturegraph.

Neihardt, J. G. (1970). *Black Elk speaks.* Lincoln, NE: University of Nebraska Press.

Additional Readings

Arden, H., & Wall, S. (1990). *Wisdomkeepers: Meetings with Native American spiritual elders.* Hillsboro, OR: Beyond Words.

Banks, J. A. (1997). *Teaching strategies for ethnic studies.* Boston, MA: Allyn & Bacon.

Barnes, B., Mitchell, M., & Thompson, J. (1984). *Traditional teachings.* Cornwall Island, Ontario, Canada: North American Indian Traveling College.

Beck, P. V., Walters, A. L., & Francisco, N. (1992). *The sacred: Ways of knowledge, sources of life.* Tsaile, AR: Navajo Community College Press.

Clifton, J. A. (1987). *The Potawatomi.* New York, NY: Chelsea House.

Duran, E. (2006). *Healing the soul wound.* New York, NY: Teachers College Press.

Fixico, D. L. (2003). *The American Indian mind in a linear world.* New York, NY: Routledge.

Graymount, B. (1988). *The Iroquois.* New York, NY: Chelsea House.

James, M. A. (1992). *The state of Native America: Genocide, colonization and resistance.* Boston, MA: South End Press.

Counseling Specific Cultural Groups

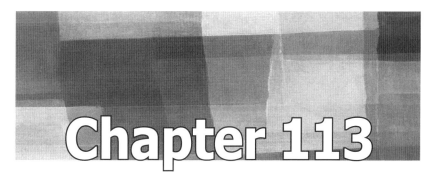

Chapter 113
Different Religious/Spiritual Cultural Experience

Mark C. Rehfuss and Agatha Parks-Savage

Topics: Introduction to Multicultural Counseling
Definitions of Cultural Diversity
Cultural Identity Development
Dimensions of Worldviews
Spirituality

Purposes: The purpose of this activity is to expose students to the diversity of religious and spiritual cultures that exist in their community. It will facilitate students' exploration of faith and culture and help them see how faith and culture can often affect the counselor relationship. In addition, the activity provides students with the experience of being a nonmajority member in this setting.

Learning Objectives: As a result of completing this activity, students will

- better understand the role of religion and spirituality in culture,
- demonstrate an ability to appreciate the similarities and differences of religious/spiritual cultural expression,
- reflect on how they felt and dealt with being a nonmajority member in this setting,
- interact with their peers and effectively process their diverse experiences, and
- transfer and directly apply what they have learned to their counseling practice.

Target Population: Master's- and doctoral-level counseling students

Group Size: Probably about 20–30 students. If there are more than 30 students, you need to break them into groups.

Time Required: Typically 4 hours for the immersion experience, which can be expanded based on goals; 6 hours for narrative paper and presentation prep; and 15 minutes for in-class presentation.

Setting: A field experience

Materials: A listing of religious, spiritual, and faith communities in the city and surrounding locations; a notebook or digital voice recorder may be needed for students to immediately make notes of their experiences; online discussion board and classroom technology resources for the presentation

Instructions for Conducting Activity

Advise students that they must complete the following five components of this assignment:

1. Submit a religious/faith/spiritual experience proposal to the professor. (3 points)
2. Participate in a different religious/faith/spiritual cultural experience.
3. Write an eight-page experiential paper (with research of faith beliefs or spiritual expression necessary) of your experience, submit it to the instructor, and post it to blackboard for your peers' review. Paper will be graded on criteria stated below. (25 points)
4. Make a response post to one paper posted on blackboard. (7 points)
5. Give a PowerPoint presentation (limited to five slides) relating your experience to the class. (15 points)

Proposal

You must get your topic approved by instructor prior to completing your experience. The proposal should be three sentences in length and should indicate how the experience will be significantly different from any previous religious/spiritual/faith cultural experiences that you have had.

Experience

You must seek out a religious/spiritual/faith cultural experience that is significantly different from previous religious/spiritual/faith cultural experiences that you have had in the past. This activity should include immersion into the religious experience of another faith and/or an experientially different occurrence of your own faith or spiritual culture. Preferably this experience would be going to another faith's worship service, such as prayers at a mosque, a celebration at a synagogue, a Hindi festival, a Buddhist temple, or the worship experience of another religion/spirituality/faith culture.

Experiences that are within your current religion/faith/spirituality must be significantly different in at least two components, such as ethnicity and worship style. An example would be going to a charismatic African American worship celebration if your faith experience is a noncharismatic, predominantly Caucasian church. So in this case, one different component is faith expression and one is ethnicity. On the other hand, the difference could be in terms of gender orientation, for example, attending a Universalist church where the majority of the congregation has a different sexual orientation than you.

By the deadline, you must submit a one-paragraph proposal for approval describing your planned immersion experience and noting why it is significantly different for you. Once your proposal is given approval, you must research the religion/spirituality/faith and make contact with someone from your desired setting to make sure you are sensitive to expectations that may surround your experience. This research will also facilitate the experience itself as you can verify where and when you should go. Once you have approval of the instructor and have made contact with the site, you may participate in the experience. This experience must take place by the seventh week of the semester in order for you to post your paper and make your presentation.

Reflection Paper

Your assignment is to write a maximum eight-page reflection paper sharing your experience. This paper should include the following components: how you identified the group; why you chose the group; when you participated in the experience; what it felt like to go there; who you interacted with; what the worship was like, noting similarities and differences both objectively and subjectively; and your personal reflections on the experience, also noting how someone from this faith might feel if they came and participated in your religious/spiritual/faith experiences. Include reflection on how you felt and dealt with being a nonmajority member in this setting. Also include a brief section on the core tenants of the religion/faith/culture. It is preferred that you find out about the core tenants of faith from the participants themselves (you can provide a pseudonym for an individual along with his or her actual title in the text), but you may also use other resources. Finally, you should express how you might transfer and directly apply what you have learned to your counseling practice.

The paper should not say something like, "They're not of my religion or faith so we had nothing in common." You have to look deeper than that. This paper should demonstrate both your personal experience and your ability to understand and learn from others. We are not looking for you to embrace the religion/faith you study but for you to demonstrate an ability to appreciate the similarities and differences of religious faith expression and to apply this learning to your practice. This should all be accomplished in a narrative experiential manner—no outlines or headings. The instructors should be able to sit down and read your paper like they were going through the experience with you—like you are relating your experience to us face-to-face. Obviously, this is a different kind of paper in that it is not primarily a research paper but an experientially based paper. You must address every issue that we have raised above and more if you so desire.

This paper will be posted to the Religious/Spirituality/Faith Cultural Experience discussion board on Blackboard by the deadline. The paper should not include a title page but should be in Word format, double-spaced, 12 point Times New Roman font, with one-inch margins all around. You should title the document after the group you observed and include your name in the header. References, if used, should be noted on a separate reference page.

Response Post

Each of you is to read one of your peer's papers and post a 250-word maximum discussion reaction/response by the deadline.

PowerPoint Presentation

The PowerPoint is limited to five slides in length. This is a presentation relating your religious/faith cultural experience to the class. It is a review of your paper and should include photos of your setting and, with their permission, those you interacted with. The length of this presentation to your peers must not exceed 10 minutes, with 5 minutes after for questions. Sign-up dates and times will be posted on Blackboard. PowerPoint must be e-mailed to instructor 3 days before your presentation date. References and additional readings sections should be formatted in American Psychological Association's (2010) *Publication Manual* style.

References

American Psychological Association. (2010). *Publication manual of the American Psychological Association* (6th ed.). Washington, DC: Author.

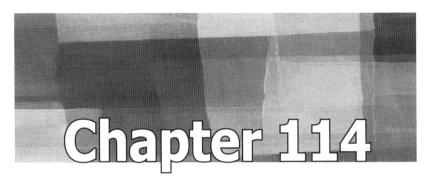

Chapter 114

The Road to "Here"— My Story in the United States

Anneliese A. Singh

Topics: Introduction to Multicultural Counseling
Definitions of Cultural Diversity
Cultural Identity Development
Oppression and Discrimination
Dimensions of Worldviews
Cross-Cultural Family Counseling
Counseling African Americans
Counseling Native Americans
Counseling Asian Americans
Counseling Hispanic/Latino Americans
Counseling European Americans

Purposes: The purpose of this activity is to allow students to identify the history of how they and/or their families arrived in the United States and to gain greater understanding of their own cultural background.

Learning Objectives: To meet the above purpose, students will achieve the following learning objectives in this activity: (a) describe the details of their immigration journey to the United States and/or indigenous history in the United States, (b) identify personal and collective stories of privilege and oppression issues based on their cultural background, (c) understand commonalities and differences between students' stories, and (d) identify areas of pride and/or challenges in one's cultural background.

Target Population: This activity is geared at students in an introductory multicultural counseling class.

Group Size: Ideally, this activity should be done with a class of 12–24 people in order to create an environment where each student has the time to share his or her story and receive feedback from fellow peers.

Time Required: 1–2 hours, depending on class size

Setting: Classroom

Materials: Magazines with images of individuals from diverse backgrounds; scissors; construction paper; tape, glue, markers, crayons, and small poster boards (one for each student)

Instructions for Conducting Activity

This activity includes four steps: (a) explaining the activity, (b) creating poster boards that document students' immigration and/or indigenous stories in the United States, (c) sharing students' poster boards; and (d) processing universal themes and differences across the stories. The details for each step are listed below.

Step One: Explaining the Activity

The instructor explains the purpose and goals of the activity (see above Purposes and Learning Objectives sections) and reminds the group of the importance of group confidentiality. A sample introduction may be as follows:

> In today's class, we will start off with a brief art activity in which you explore how you and your family arrived in the United States and/or had indigenous roots in this land. Our country has become a nation of immigrants for many reasons that we will learn about in this class, and people came here from all over the world. Everyone's story of how they came to the United States and/or have indigenous roots in this country is an important one. Today, we will use an art activity to depict these journeys, and we will call the activity "Road to Here: My Story in the United States." As you do this activity, think about the strengths and/or challenges you and your family have had along the way. You may realize quickly there are values associated with different parts of your cultural background, and you can depict those as well. Please feel free to use any of the art supplies here to make a poster depicting this journey. You may use a timeline and draw the major events or people in your story along a timeline, or you may prefer to cut out images from magazines to show the important parts of your immigration story. Remember there are no right or wrong ways to create art, and if you get stuck raise your hand and I can come and help you. We will take 15 minutes for this art activity.

The instructor may or may not choose to participate in the activity, depending on the size of the class. If there is a large class, the instructor may complete her or his art activity prior to class and briefly explain it during Step Three as a way to model the sharing of the activity with students.

Step Two: Creating Poster Boards

The ideal length of time for the students to create their poster boards is 15–20 minutes. The group facilitator may decide to lengthen or shorten the time for the art activity based on the number of students. It is helpful for the instructor to walk around the room and check in with members as they create their art, as they may need to be reminded of the purpose and directions for the activity. This is also an opportunity for the instructor to ask brief questions, such as, "When you think back on your story of how your family came to the United States and/or have indigenous roots here, what is the biggest event that stands out for you?" It is helpful to validate students' work, such as "I see you wrote down many of your strengths." It is also important to give students notice when there are 10 minutes and 5 minutes remaining for the art activity.

Step Three: Sharing Students' Poster Boards

At the end of the art activity, the instructor asks the students to share three things they learned about their strengths and/or challenges as they created their poster board. In order to ensure every student has time to share, it is helpful to ask people to go in order around the circle when they are sharing. After each student shares, the instructor may want to briefly ask students clarifying questions ("Could you let us know what you feel proud of in your story"), validate their stories ("That sounds like you felt good about that . . ."), and make statements linking the students' stories ("So, you can probably relate a lot to Sonali because your stories are similar") as they individually share in order to prepare for the next step. Step Three should take 30–35 minutes, depending on class size

Step Four: Processing Universal Themes Across the Stories

In the last step of this activity, the instructor will open up the sharing to the class, with processing questions linking commonalities among students' stories ("What were the major themes of all of the stories we heard today?") and identifying the differences between their stories ("What were the biggest differences between these stories?"). The goal of this step is to build a sense of universality and compassion among participants, creating space for students to build a sense of pride and understanding of their stories of immigration and/or indigenous history in the United States. It can be meaningful for the instructor to actively identify strengths and challenges in students' stories and coping resources they have developed because of their unique cultural backgrounds. At the end of the activity, it is helpful to have students do a check-out, where they list the main thing they learned in the activity and one important person in their lives with whom they might want to share this learning. This step should take 15–20 minutes, depending on class size.

Cautions

It is important to think about the students' emotional capacity and developmental level when introducing this activity to the classroom learning process, as this activity can bring up many emotions for students. If the class is shorter than 1–2 hours, facilitators can adapt the activity by having members complete the art activity at home. Because there are many different cultural values embedded in students' stories, it is also important to validate the diversity of values that students share in their art activity.

Additional Readings

Bode, J. (1999). *The colors of freedom: Immigrant stories*. New York, NY: Grolier. [For use with adolescents.]

Martin, D. A., & Schuck, P. H. (Eds.). (2005). *Immigration stories*. New York, NY: Foundation Press.

Zinn, H. (2003). *A people's history of the United States*. New York, NY: Harper Collins.

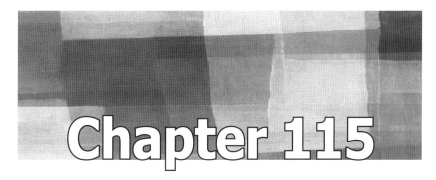

Chapter 115

Using *Real Women Have Curves* to Facilitate Cultural Perspective Taking

Casey A. Barrio Minton

Topics: Cultural Communication Styles
Cultural Identity Development
Cross-Cultural Family Counseling
Counseling Hispanic/Latino Americans
Gender Issues in Counseling
Multiple Identities/Biracial, Multiracial
Poverty, Social Class, and Socioeconomic Status
Use of Technology
Immigrant Experience

Real Women Have Curves (LaVoo, Brown, Lopez, & Cardoso, 2002) is a feature film in which Ana—an academically gifted, 18-year-old, first-generation Mexican American—experiences conflict with her more traditional, working-class parents. Instructors may use this film to facilitate understanding of Hispanic/ Latina/o Americans via experiential role-plays.

Purposes: The purpose of this activity is to assist students to develop multiple cultural explanations for behaviors and experiences sometimes encountered by Hispanic/Latina/o Americans. The activity also provides opportunities for participants to explore how identities intersect and to examine their own cultural assumptions and values.

Learning Objectives: As a result of this activity students will be able to (a) demonstrate culturally based explanations of behavior and experiences from the perspective of dominant European American culture and Latina/o cultures, (b) understand the impact of multiple identities and stages of identity development on one's own cultural experiences, (c) identify their own cultural assumptions and values, and (d) articulate implications for counseling.

Target Population: This activity is appropriate for implementation with master's- or doctoral-level student counselors who have foundation knowledge regarding elements of identity, cultural identity development models, and Latina/o cultural principles.

Group Size: This activity is appropriate for implementation in small- to moderate-sized groups, and the author has facilitated this activity in groups ranging in size from 12 to 30 participants. The activity may be carried out in several smaller groups; however, each group will benefit from the presence of a facilitator who can challenge participants to seek alternate perspectives in a respectful manner.

Time Required: Ideally, this activity will be facilitated within a 3-hour class period as follows: review Latina/o cultural principles (15 minutes), view *Real Women Have Curves* (LaVoo et al., 2002; 80 minutes), break (15 minutes), and role-play (60 minutes). If time is limited, the instructor may assign the video for viewing prior to class; however, a lapse between viewing the film and engaging in the activity tends to result in reduced immediacy during the experiential activity.

Setting: This activity can be completed in a standard academic classroom. Faculty members who have ready access to a live observation facility may wish to facilitate role-plays within the clinic setting.

Materials: Instructors will need a copy of *Real Women Have Curves* (LaVoo et al., 2002) and may wish to provide students with a copy of the viewing guide contained in Handout 115.1. Instructors may wish to use nametags or identifying props (e.g., book for Ana, apron for Carmen, and so forth) for each character.

Instructions for Conducting Activity

Open the class period by reviewing readings or lecture materials regarding Latina/o cultural principles. Next, prompt students to watch for these cultural principles in action, make note of identity variables at play for each character, and keep in touch with their reactions to each character. As students view the film, instructors may wish to observe student reactions for nonverbal indicators that a student is having a strong positive or negative reaction to a character. In my experience, students who are most expressive during the film tend to be excellent candidates for the participation in the experiential activity. As the movie ends, instruct students to take a short break; however, encourage students to save discussion of their reactions to the film for after the break.

Invite students to share just one thought or reaction regarding the movie. Respond using only reflections of content and feeling; refrain from challenging, reframing, or encouraging alternate explanations. Rather, encourage as many students as possible to share just one thought or reaction. In my experience, most students tend to have the strongest reaction to Carmen (Ana's mother), often describing her as cold, sabotaging, selfish, hypochondriac, and codependent and questioning why she cannot love or accept Ana. Other students tend to champion Ana's quest for independence, and some students may sadly recount their failed attempts to help Mexican American students "succeed." One or two students may note that they identify with the experience. Sometimes students do not share initial responses because they fear being seen as judgmental. If I sense hesitance, I may request participation from a student who exhibited strong nonverbal reactions during the film, or I may give permission to share responses by saying something like, "Am I the only one who felt very frustrated toward Mom?" If nearly all students seem to be taking a genuine, culturally sensitive perspective, commend students by noting that most groups have a great deal of difficulty understanding from multiple perspectives and note that you would like to take this understanding just one step further.

Instructors who identify a theme of responses based on the values and perspectives of dominant culture should reflect the theme to the class and remind students that not attending to these reactions could result in difficulty experiencing empathy. Frame the activity as an empathy-enhancing exercise, and ask for volunteers to come to the front of the room to represent Ana, Carmen, and Raul (Ana's father). Depending on time and class size, participants may also come forward to represent Abuelo, Mr. Guzman, Estela, and the women who work in Estela's shop. If you use numerous characters, provide participants with nametags or identifying props. One by one, prompt each character to share his or her perspective of the conflict. For example, "Dona Carmen, we would like to help you have a happy family. Please help us understand the problem." Insist students represent the character using first-person voice, and encourage audience members to assist participants when they become stuck. After each participant explains his or her perspective, ask an audience member to serve as that person's counselor by reflecting the content, feeling, and meaning communicated by the individual. Allow each dyad to role-play for

Counseling Specific Cultural Groups

several minutes. Because the individual who portrays Ana will likely have the easiest time accessing her experience, facilitators may need to redirect attention to other characters. If time allows, instructors can modify role-play to involve interaction among family members.

Upon conclusion of the activity, call on role-play participants, counselors, and audience members to share their experiences, and help students explore how their feelings and perspectives changed (or did not change) as they considered alternative explanations. Assist students to conceptualize key conflicts using cultural principles and terminology (e.g., *familismo*, *personalismo*, *machismo*, independence, individual achievement), elements of identity salient for each character, level/stage of identity development for each character, and counseling implications for Ana and Carmen. In closing, warn students regarding the dangers of overgeneralizing the conflict or Carmen's response to cultural stressors as representative of all Hispanic/Latina/o experiences.

Handout: Handout 115.1: *Real Women Have Curves* Viewing and Application Guide

References

LaVoo, G. (Producer/Writer), Brown, E. T. (Producer), Lopez, J. (Writer), & Cardoso, P. (Director). (2002). *Real women have curves* [Motion picture]. United States: HBO Films.

Additional Readings

Note: Nearly all multicultural counseling textbooks have at least one chapter dedicated to understanding and counseling Hispanic/Latina/o clients. Students should read relevant textbook chapters and review identity development models prior to class.

Constantine, M. G., Gloria, A. M., & Barón, A. (2006). Counseling Mexican American college students. In C. C. Lee (Ed.), *Multicultural issues in counseling: New approaches to diversity* (3rd ed., pp. 207–222). Alexandria, VA: American Counseling Association.

Lopez-Baez, S. I. (2006). Counseling Latinas: Culturally responsive interventions. In C. C. Lee (Ed.), *Multicultural issues in counseling: New approaches to diversity* (3rd ed., pp. 187–194). Alexandria, VA: American Counseling Association.

Miranda, A. O., Bilot, J. M., Peluso, R. R., Berman, K., & Van Meek, L. G. (2006). Latino families: The relevance of the connection among acculturation, family dynamics, and health for family counseling research and practice. *The Family Journal, 14,* 268–273.

Sue, D. W., & Sue, D. (2008). *Counseling the culturally diverse: Theory and practice* (5th ed.). New York, NY: Wiley.

Villalba, J. A., Jr. (2007). Culture-specific assets to consider when counseling Latino/a children and adolescents. *Journal of Multicultural Counseling, 35,* 15–25.

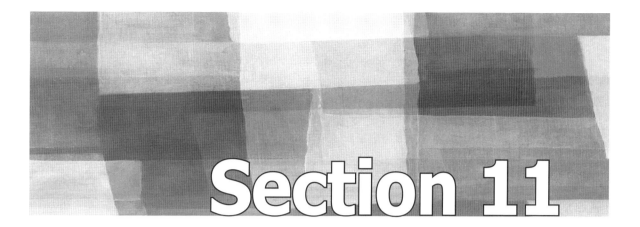

Section 11

Socioeconomic Status and Social Class

What does it mean to be a member of the working class, middle class, or wealthy social class? This section offers activities designed to help students explore terms and concepts related to socioeconomic status, class privilege, classism, and meritocracy. These activities also assist students in examining their own values, assumptions, and biases that they hold regarding social and economic class differences. These activities also encourage students' consideration of the ways in which socioeconomic class may affect both the therapeutic process and an individual's perceptions and usage of counseling services. A few of these activities contain creative arts as a teaching strategy.

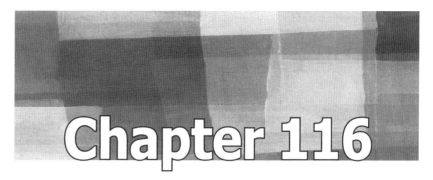

Chapter 116

Investigating Meritocracy: An Analysis of How All Children Are Not Part of the Meritocracy American Dream

Antonette Aragon,[1] Edward J. Brantmeier, Nathalie Kees, Jacqueline Peila-Shuster, and Sharon K. Anderson

Topics: Oppression and Discrimination
Counseling African Americans
Human Growth and Development
Poverty, Social Class, and Socioeconomic Status (SES)

Purposes: Rationale—Is America the land of limitless opportunity, where individual merit promotes hard work and getting ahead? Most people tend to believe this, and they approach the problem of inequality from a personal perspective rather than through its systemic manifestations. It is important to analyze critically the social, political, and economic structures that provide opportunity for some and disadvantage to others.

    The purpose of the activity is to provide an opportunity that allows students to experience privilege or disadvantage based on unequal social realities. This activity provides an analogy of how society is divided and is not a level playing field. Students may acknowledge how racism, classism, sexism, and ableism are promoted through inequity and systems of power. Furthermore, after students participate in this game, it is hoped they realize that individuals do not get ahead in life based on individual merit, such as possessing innate abilities, working hard, having the right attitude, and having high moral character and integrity. Instead, individuals are part of systems that inherently reward some and punish others. It is the examination of such systems that reveals how meritocracy becomes a myth in our society.

Learning Objectives: As a result of this activity, participants will be able to (a) deconstruct how society is not a level playing field; (b) critically examine how meritocracy is a myth in our society; and (c) reflect on power, privilege, and dominance in a broader U.S. society.

[1]*Author's note:* I was introduced to this activity by Dr. Deidre Magee of the University of Colorado in Denver and have adapted it here for working specifically with counselors-in-training. I'd like to extend a special thank you to Deidre Magee.

Target Population: Counselors, teachers, pre-service teachers, principals, and all students of education

Group Size: 10–70 participants

Time Required: 45–90 minutes

Setting: A large, open room is ideal to conduct this activity.

Materials: A number line in the shape of a square, with each side separated into sections of 10. One row of the number line is divided by 1–10, the next number line is divided by 11–20, the next is divided by 21–30, and the last is divided by 31–40 (please refer to Handout 116.1). In addition, six game pieces, such as pencil covers, are used; large foam dice are needed for students to roll and move around the number line. Finally, candy is provided at each corner of the number line: 10, 20, 30, and 40. Ask one person to help record comments made by participants so that the instructor can facilitate the game.

Instructions for Conducting Activity

1. Ask students: What is meritocracy? Record their answers on a whiteboard, chalkboard, or visible pad of large paper.
2. Have students count off by sixes (this is based on the number of game pieces that are used). Have each team take a game piece (the game pieces are different colors of pink, orange, lavender, purple, green, light blue). Have one person from each team roll the die to determine the order that the teams will participate in the game.
3. Have the number line set up in a large square with "10," "20," "30," and "40" representing the corners and candy on those corner numbers.
4. To start the game have the first team roll and ask that they move according to their roll, but stop them before they place their game piece on the number that they rolled and ask that they check the bottom of their piece.
5. Each game piece has a number written on the bottom of it, and the number determines if the team may move forward additionally or backward negatively. For instance, the game pieces will be marked with one of the following numbers: 0, +1, +2, +3, −1, or −2, and the team moves according to the roll of the die plus or minus the number written on their game piece.
6. Have the teams continue to roll the die and move around the number line according to the process outlined in Step 5.
7. When a team gets near candy, let them know that they get to take the candy if they land on a number that has candy on it.
8. Continue to play the game so that the teams progress around the number line.
9. As participants are playing, it becomes obvious that those teams with the positive numbers on their game pieces are progressing quite quickly around the number line, whereas the teams with the negative numbers are moving around the number line more slowly.
10. As the teams are playing, it is **crucial** to write down the statements they say both to their fellow teammates and to other teams—write these statements on a whiteboard or a large note pad that they may see after the game is completed. Such statements are important to reflect back on, and they reveal how students feel related to their random lot in the game. For instance, some teams may state, "It's not fair that we have to move back," or "We are so good because we move quickly," and so forth.
11. The game is completed after all of the teams have moved around the entire square of numbers to the number 40.
12. After all teams have made it to the number 40, let them know that you will read the comments they made while playing the game. Read their comments aloud and ask them to think about what the object of the game is.
13. Have a quick discussion to find out what they think the purpose of the game is and then ask that they sit down to debrief the game. Many of the students will state that the object of the game is to finish it and make it to the number 40. This is a great place to start the debriefing of the game.

Process Questions

After all statements have been read, reflect on the process and the formation of the game. Ask the following questions:

1. What does this say about counseling and education? Possible answers: We can't make assumptions; we need to be informed about our student and know our perspectives and their perspectives.
2. How did you end up getting your slot in the game? Possible answer: Chance, random roll of the die.
3. How did +3 feel? Possible answers: Successful; not really successful if they didn't get the candy, and this may show that teens from all walks of life feel similarly. A student may not feel like a winner because he or she didn't get any candy. Students may feel that the walk was boring and that they lacked motivation.
4. How can we look at the game pieces? Kindergartners walking into school—do they choose their status? They walk in based on chance. Are all children on equal footing? Can all children pull themselves up from their bootstraps? But that is what our macro culture says—is it a reality?
5. What is happening with the players? Possible answers: Some are trying to make it. Some felt "why try to do anything because I won't get any candy." How does this apply to students who give up? Relate the status of students to students in school: +3 may represent students in suburbia who are from higher SES; –2 students may represent urban/inner-city students or rural students—research says there are meth labs, lack of materials, lack of teachers in rural settings.
6. Why do children drop out? Possible answers: Family situations; no access to positive school experiences; there is no solid school guidance for students who are at-risk and they are not taught to plan for a more positive future; and at-risk or students of color may lack role models in their life. The path to get to 40 may be difficult and may feel overwhelming and unwelcoming, with many obstacles to get to the finish line. An example is when a student walks into an Advanced Placement classroom and the teacher asks her if she speaks English because she is Hispanic—what was the assumption and how does it impact a student?
7. Teachers in a school meeting were discussing how their students will not go to college, and one teacher said, "Well, they are not going to go to college, so why should we work so hard trying to get them there?" This shows assumptions and biases at work.

Interrogating Structural Racism, Classism, Sexism, and Ableism

1. How is this game an analogy that represents inequity in larger society?
2. How is the playing field unequal?
3. How do some teams gain, while others lose?
4. Discuss how a student's psyche is affected through poor self-esteem or low expectations—it may mean that students will not finish the journey around the track to 40.
5. How does this game mirror larger U.S. society?
6. How does this game represent inequities among race, class, ability, or gender?
7. How does this game represent larger social, political, economic, and environmental spheres?
8. How can we move toward more authentic racial equality and equity?
9. What is the role of counselors in contributing to that change process?
10. Summative question: How do you now examine meritocracy? Are all people created equally, and are we on an equal playing field? Is meritocracy a myth in our society?

Follow-Up Integration

After the processing questions, ask participants to return to their seats or classroom. Ask individual students to read and reflect on the following statistics:

The following stats are from Jackson-Leslie (1999):

*   The median annual income for Black men is $22,167 compared with $30,598 for White men.
*   White men hold 44.8% positions of administrative and managerial positions in banking.

- White men hold 51.6% positions in business services.
- White men hold 47.6% positions in communications.
- White men hold 74.6% positions in construction.
- White men hold 72% positions in utilities.
- White men hold 59% positions in transportation.
- White men hold 63% positions in manufacturing.
- White men hold 48% positions in public administration.
- White men lag behind in the lower paid positions of education, health, and social services, where White women are in the majority of the positions.
- Black men hold only 2.3% of executive administrative and management jobs in all private sector industries and only 3.9% of these positions in the public and private sectors combined.
- African American women hold 2.2% of the executive administrative and managerial jobs and 4.6% in public and private sector combined.

The following statistics are found in Douthat (2005):

- 1 in 2 will obtain a college degree from an elite college if she/he comes from a family with an annual income of $90,000 or more.
- 1 in 4 will obtain a college degree from an elite college if she/he comes from a family with an annual income of $61,000–$90,000.
- 1 in 10 will obtain a college degree from an elite college if she/he comes from a family with an annual income of $35,000–$61,000.
- 1 in 17 will obtain a college degree from an elite college if she/he comes from a family with an annual income less than $35,000.
- More low-income students enroll in college today compared with the 1970s, but they are less likely to graduate than their wealthier peers; of the American students coming from lower socio-economic backgrounds attending college, only about 6% obtain a college degree.
- What does this mean? Inequality of education breeds inequality of income and vice versa.
- African American men earn only $725 for every $1,000 earned by White men, and after 5 years of college an African American man earns $771.
- African American women and White women earn $907 for every $1,000 earned by White men, and after 5 years of college an African American woman earns $973.

The following quote is from Coleman (2003):

- "Applicant[s] [with] resumes with typically White names were 50% more likely to be called for an interview than were applicants with Black sounding names."

Overall Process Questions Based on the Above Statistics
- What do these statistics tell us?
- Why are the statistics above important related to counseling and education?
- What does this mean regarding societal inequities, racism, oppression, and how mainstream attitudes perceive this information?
- Are these statistics still valid today? Please investigate and report your answer in the next meeting.

Handout: Handout 116.1: Directions to the Game

References

Coleman, M. (2003). African American popular wisdom versus qualification question: Is affirmative action merit based? *Western Journal of Black Studies, 27*, 35–44.
Douthat, R. (2005, November). Does meritocracy work? *Atlantic Monthly,* 120–126.
Jackson-Leslie, L. (1999). Race, sex & meritocracy. *Black Scholar, 25,* 24–30.

Additional Readings

McNamee, S. J., & Miller, R. K., Jr. (2004). The meritocracy myth. *Sociation Today 2,* p. 14. Retrieved April 25, 2007, from http://www.ncsociology.org/sociationtoday/v21/merit.htm

Chapter 117

Self as a Socioeconomic Being

Devika Dibya Choudhuri

Topics: Introduction to Multicultural Counseling
Culturally Skilled Counselor
Poverty, Social Class, and Socioeconomic Status (SES)
Use of New Technology

Purposes: This activity is aimed at enhancing awareness of the dimensions of class as an identity that develops over a period of time and includes core beliefs about power, opportunity, money, values, and communication. It also allows students to self-reflect on the complexity of messages that they carry and perhaps carry out, bringing them into consciousness. Counseling students tend to join in the normative dominant cultural perspective of thinking of the United States as a classless society, or they naively accept demarcations of class as being simply about having money. Unlike awareness activities focusing on identities of race or sexual orientation, this activity allows students to enter into the activity with fewer separations and trepidations between them. The goal is for students to become better prepared for more in-depth discussions later.

Target Population: Counseling students in any cross-cultural or multicultural counseling course or in a personal growth workshop

Group Size: Can range from 8 to 30 participants. Higher numbers than that require more small-group work to ensure that all participants have time to share and process.

Time Required: 1 to 1.5 hours

Setting: Open seating that allows people to face each other in two concentric circles; some kind of surface to write on is necessary, so the seating can be chairs with desks attached or participants can use notepads.

Materials: Handout 117.1; board to write down group themes

Instructions for Conducting Activity

To begin, ask participants to call out the names of some of their favorite television shows and movies. Write them down on the board in a particular manner, grouping them without necessarily informing the participants of the order. The groupings should be based on the SES of the major characters in the show or movie: working class, middle class, and upper class. If there is a cross-over (for instance, *Pretty Woman*), note it silently and plan to discuss it later. If unsure about the show, ask the person to give a brief description of the show or movie. Typically, these days most shows will be framed in the middle class or upper class. Then ask participants about the class context of the shows and have them discuss the choices.

In the next phase, ask all participants to have some kind of writing instrument available. With participants who have visual disabilities, a partner may read the questions out to them. Participants sit in two concentric circles, with the outer circle facing in and the inner circle facing out. The handout with the questions is given out, and participants are instructed to read and make brief notes about their response to the first set of questions (4 minutes). They then share their responses and reflections with the person opposite them, who is instructed to listen intently. When everyone is done (about 6 minutes for each pair), the outer circle moves one over in seating so that they are now facing a different person opposite. They then are asked to respond to and share responses to the next set of questions. This process goes on until all sets of questions are completed and each participant has shared responses with six other participants. At this point, the outer circle makes room for the chairs of the inner circle, and participants merge into one large circle facing in toward each other.

The facilitator then directs a general discussion of the themes that came out, and individuals are encouraged to share their own responses (not the responses that were shared with them) and begin to make sense of the aspects of class that are often about values, access, opportunities, and communication. This is also a good time to share information about aspects of class mobility, such as the sense of being an imposter, fear of being found out, sense of not belonging, concealed hurt and shame, and so on.

Finally, if time permits, the facilitator can draw out the connections between one's own class identity and one's reactions to others; in the case of counseling students, have them think about clients they might find it difficult to work with. If time has run out, it is always an option to invite participants to journal on their reflections and further insights.

Handout: Handout 117.1: Self as a Socioeconomic Being

Additional Readings

Aldrich, N. W. (1988). *Old money: The mythology of America's upper class*. New York, NY: Knopf.

Allison, D. (1993). *Bastard out of Carolina*. New York, NY: Plume.

Alters, D. F. (2003). "We hardly watch that rude, crude show": Class and taste in *The Simpsons*. In C. A. Stabile & M. Harrison (Eds.), *Prime time animation: Television animation and American culture* (pp. 165–184). New York, NY: Routledge.

Argyle, M. (1994). *The psychology of social class*. New York, NY: Routledge.

Brooks, D. (2001). *Bobos in paradise: The new upper class and how they got there*. Clearwater, FL: Touchstone Books.

Butsch, R. (1995). Ralph, Fred, Archie and Homer: Why television keeps recreating the White male working-class buffoon. In G. Dines & J. M. Humez (Eds.), *Gender, race and class in media: A text-reader*. Thousand Oaks, CA: Sage.

Cole, H. (1999). *How to be: Contemporary etiquette for African Americans*. New York, NY: Simon & Schuster.

Constantine, M. (2001). Address racial, ethnic, gender, and social class issues in counselor training and practice. In D. Pope-Davis & H. K. Coleman (Eds.), *The intersection of race, class, and gender in multicultural counseling* (pp. 341–350). Thousand Oaks, CA: Sage.

DeMott, B. (1990). *The imperial middle: Why Americans can't think straight about class*. New York, NY: William Morrow & Company.

DeMott, B. (1996). *Created equal: Reading and writing about class in America*. New York, NY: Harper Collins.

De Santis, S. (1999). *Life on the line: One woman's tale of work, sweat, and survival*. New York, NY: Doubleday.

Ehrenreich, B. (2001). *Nickel and dimed: On (not) getting by in America*. New York, NY: Metropolitan.

Langston, D. (1992). Tired of playing monopoly? In M. L. Andersen & P. H. Collins (Eds.), *Race, class, and gender: An anthology* (pp. 110–120). Belmont, CA: Wadsworth.

Liu, W. M. (2001). Expanding our understanding of multiculturalism: Developing a social class worldview model. In D. Pope-Davis & H. K. Coleman (Eds.), *The intersection of race, class, and gender in multicultural counseling* (pp. 127–170). Thousand Oaks, CA: Sage.

Liu, W. M., Soleck, G., Hopps, J., Dunston, K., & Pickett, T., Jr. (2004). A new framework for understanding social class in counseling: The social class worldview model and modern classism theory. *Journal of Multicultural Counseling and Development, 34*, 95–122.

McClain, L. (1992). The middle-class Black's burden. In M. Andersen & P. H. Collins (Eds.), *Race, class and gender: An anthology* (pp. 120–122). Belmont, CA: Wadsworth.

Moon, D. G., & Rollison, G. L. (1998). Communication of classism. In M. L. Hecht (Ed.), *Communicating prejudice* (pp. 122–135). Thousand Oaks, CA: Sage

Russell, G. M. (1996). Internalized classism: The role of class in the development of self. *Women and Therapy, 18*, 59–71.

Shipler, D. (2004). *The working poor: Invisible in America*. New York, NY: Alfred Knopf.

Smith, L. (2008). Positioning classism within counseling psychology's social justice agenda. *Counseling Psychologist, 36*, 895–924.

Videos

Alvarez, L., & Kolker, A. (Producer/Director). (2001). *People like us: Social class in America* [Motion Picture]. United States: Center for New American Media.

Johnson, J. W. (Producer/Director). (2003). *Born rich*. [Motion picture]. United States: HBO.

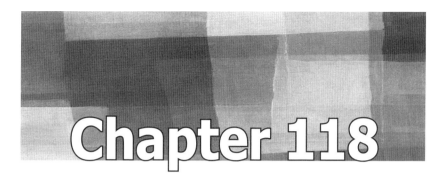

Chapter 118

My "Class" Photo:
Exploring Social Class Consciousness

Angela D. Coker

Topics: Introduction to Multicultural Counseling
Culturally Skilled Counselor
Professional Identity and Ethical Practice
Group Work
Multiple Identities/Biracial, Multiracial
Poverty, Social Class, and Socioeconomic Status (SES)

Purposes: The purposes of this activity are to (a) provide counselors-in-training with a reflective opportunity to explore their socioeconomic class consciousness, (b) explore the ways in which social class affects perceptions about self and others, and (c) explore how class consciousness may or may not affect an individual's help-seeking behaviors. This class activity is also intended to enhance student interaction and positive group dynamics.

Learning Objectives: As a result of this activity, students will

- gain greater awareness of SES as a social construct,
- understand how the social construction of class consciousness may impact our perceptions about self and others,
- understand the ways in which class as a social construct affects our interactions with each other,
- understand how perceived social class can influence client's perception about themselves in relation to the larger world, and
- understand how social class may influence an individual's use of counseling services.

Target Population: Students enrolled in introductory or advanced-level multicultural counseling courses

Group Size: Can vary, but ideal with 10–15 students in a class/group

Time Required: 1–2 hours

Setting: This activity can be conducted in any large-room setting. Chair seating should be arranged in a semicircle to allow group participants to have eye contact and interact with each other.

Materials: A computer and projector to show individual students' electronic photos. As a modification, students might elect to share an illustrative video clip.

Instructions for Conducting Activity

1. A week or so before you introduce this activity, assign students to read two required articles: Liu, Soleck, Hopps, Dunston, and Pickett (2004) and Constantine (2002). The instructor should dedicate adequate instructional time to discuss the two readings with students. Ask students to talk about their impressions and reflections regarding the content of the articles. During the next instructional session, invite students to bring to class a photo that depicts their perceived social class while they were growing up. Students may bring in photos showing a home, clothes that they wore, jewelry, items in a refrigerator, types of food they ate, or activities that they engaged in (e.g., working during the summer to pay for college, traveling overseas, photos of grandparents/parents). Each student will share his or her photo with the group. They should reflect on the following questions:
   a. What are the indicators in the photograph that depict your social class?
   b. What does class status mean to you?
   c. How did you (or your family of origin) discuss social class issues growing up?
   d. What kind of messages (direct or indirect) did you receive from other social groups growing up?
   e. How might the intersections of race, gender, sexual orientation, or other social identities influence your perception about your socioeconomic class?

2. Discussion: After each student has shared his or her photo, facilitate a general discussion using the following questions:
   a. In what ways, if any, did your socioeconomic class influence your help-seeking behaviors?
   b. How might our understanding of social class be instructive to us as counselors working with diverse socioeconomic groups?
   c. How would you evaluate your experience with this activity? What stands out in your exploration of socioeconomic class?

3. Wrap-up reflective summary: Go around the room and have all students share at least one or two things they have learned about social class consciousness as a result this activity.

References

Constantine, M. G. (2002). The intersection of race, ethnicity, gender, and social class in counseling: Examining selves in cultural contexts. *Journal of Multicultural Counseling and Development, 30*, 210–215.

Liu, W. M., Soleck, G., Hopps, J., Dunston, K., & Pickett, T., Jr. (2004). A new framework to understand social class in counseling: The social class worldview and modern classism theory. *Journal of Multicultural Counseling and Development, 32*, 95–122.

Additional Readings

American Psychological Association, Task Force on Socioeconomic Status. (2007). *Report of the APA Task Force on Socioeconomic Status.* Washington DC: American Psychological Association.

Cozzarelli, C., Wilkinson, A. V., & Tagler, M. J. (2001). Attitudes toward the poor and attributions for poverty. *Journal of Social Issues, 57*, 207–227.

Hollingshead, A. B., & Redlich, F. C. (1958). *Social class and mental illness: A community study*. New York, NY: Wiley.

Liu, W. M., Ali, S. R., Soleck, G., Hopps, J., Dunston, K., & Pickett, T., Jr. (2004). Using social class in counseling psychology research. *Journal of Counseling Psychology, 51*, 3–18.

Smith, L., Foley, P. E., & Chaney, M. P. (2008). Addressing classism, ableism, and heterosexism in counselor education. *Journal of Counseling & Development, 86,* 303–309.

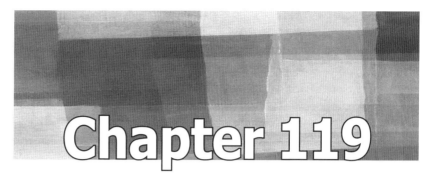

Chapter 119
The Working Poor Simulation Exercise

Brian Hutchison

Topics: Barriers to Effective Cross-Cultural Counseling
Oppression and Discrimination
Career Development
Poverty, Social Class, and Socioeconomic Status (SES)

Purposes: The purpose of this activity is to provide participants with the opportunity to explore the impact that working below or near the poverty line has on individual and family well-being, career development, and the interaction between the family and societal systems.

Learning Objectives: As a result of this activity, students will:

- have a better understanding of the impact that working in poverty has on family systems and career development,
- be able to identify potential stressors that are precipitated by poverty when working with clients from lower social classes, and
- be able to conceptualize the impact that (a) different systems and (b) differing access to social capital have on persons or families working in poverty.

Target Population: Counselor education master's and doctoral students; faculty and staff; late high school age students

Group Size: 8–24 participants

Time Required: 50–75 minutes

Setting: Any classroom with space for students to walk around (auditorium seating is not preferred)

Materials: One to two helpers (preferably from outside the class); kitchen timer for 5- and 7-minute alarms; complete set of game cards (see Handout 119.1); timesheet form (one per student; Handout 119.2); and one of the following for every two students: die, income and travel calculator form (Handout 119.3), and family financial ledger (Handout 119.4)

Instructions for Conducting Activity

Instructions for Moderators

The purpose of this exercise is to simulate some of the stress associated with raising a family while working in poverty. Family members are played by students. In this family, there is a goal of saving $30 during the next month for their eldest child's educational pursuit. There are several levels of stress you are administering during this game that represent potential events for these families, including the following:

1. Instructions are purposely vague and unwritten.
2. The exercise administrators are purposefully vague, arbitrary, and curt.
3. There is a time crunch because of a lack of resources and administrative obstacles.
4. Money is stretched tight.
5. Transportation is a real obstacle.
6. Chance plays a big role as to whether a family meets its goal.
7. Connections (with administrators) are a form of social capital; these can be present or not.

The outline of game play is as follows (see script in next section for further detail):

1. Exercise administrator checks in with the class regarding the potential for stress and frustration during the exercise.
2. Exercise administrator chooses one to four students to play the role of children (one or two if there are 15 students or less in class) and then has the remainder of the class get into dyads.
3. The exercise administrator reads the game-play script.
4. Round 1 lasts 5 minutes so that the family dyads can decide who will work, determine their hourly wage, and determine transportation. Child-care expenses are determined by the family's decision about work: If only one parent works, then there is no child-care expense, but if both work, then the expense is mandatory. There is a $20 penalty if they begin to fill out their standard budget ledger during this round.
   a. During this round, the exercise administrator instructs those playing child roles to divide up the dyads and randomly pass out one child card during each of four ensuing rounds. They should then try to convince the parent to get what they want from the card. The child may use reasoning such as, "I'll get made fun of," "If you love me you will let me," or "My friend Susie got this." Please remember they have to visit each family in 7 minutes!
   b. Rounds 2–5 each last 7 minutes and represent one week. Each family will receive an event card. They then fill out their timesheet for the week and stand in line for the time-card administrator and present their card in exchange for a signature (one worker cannot work more than 40 hours per week). After the time card is signed, they may fill out their standard budget ledger. They must also take the parental decision card whenever the child assigned to them approaches.
   c. Process discussion.

Game instructions are provided as a script in the following section. They are to be read aloud, not handed out. Most instructions in society are easily available via the Internet, something many low social class families may not have easy access to. The instructions are purposely vague and incomplete. It is up to the game administrators to fill in the gaps (possibly inconsistently).

The exercise administrator will have two sets of event cards. Blue cards are for families that drive a car. White cards are for families that take the bus. Have each family draw a card during each of the four weeks.

The event card is presented to the timecard administrator. This is the administrative step that must occur before the time-card administrator signs the time card for each worker. The time card must be signed by the time-card administrator before the amount the family earns is recorded in their ledger. The time-card administrator can take as long as he or she wishes to sign the cards, especially if the family is doing okay financially.

One to four of the students will play the role of children for all family dyads. The children walk around from family dyad to family dyad and ask each family to draw a parental decision card during each round of game play. Children happily accept when the card they administer is handled in their favor. They are encouraged to demand (as a child might) an explanation if it does not go the way they might wish.

The exercise administrator has total, and arbitrary if needed, control over the game. The administrator levies a monetary penalty for breaking any game rules. The goal of the game is for each family to save $30 by the end of game play. Compliance will be determined by their maintenance of the standard budget ledger.

It is important to practice this simulation once or twice before presenting it to a class or group to ensure smooth game play. If managed well, the results can be dynamic.

Script for Game Instructions (to Be Read by Proctor)

Before we begin, I would like to let you know that you may find this exercise to be frustrating and stressful. During game play if at any time you feel that you would not like to continue playing the game, please stop play. As the exercise administrator, I will be playing a role that may add to that stress but only for the duration of game play (33 minutes). Any questions before we begin?

I am here today to help you play a game. The game is a simulation of one that many in United States play every day. The game simulation and subsequent discussion will last approximately 60–75 minutes. While playing this game, you will each become a member of a low social class family that is attempting to make a better life for their children.

The younger of two children in this family is Juan(ita). Juan(ita) is 6 years old and attends half-day kindergarten in the local public school. Pat is the eldest child in the family and hopes to be the first in your family to attend college. Pat is 16 years old and hopes to take the first step toward this goal by taking the PSAT next month. Taking the test will cost $30, including transportation and lunch because it is on the other side of town.

The goal of this game is to save $30 for Pat to take the PSAT at the end of the month.

Some facts/assumptions:

- The current minimum wage in the United States is $7.25/hour.
- Postsecondary education is a person's best bet if he or she wishes to climb the social class ladder.

Game play will be divided into five rounds. (*Pass out "Income and Travel Calculator" form [Handout 119.3].*) The first round is 5 minutes long and will require you to do the following:

1. Decide who in your family will work. One or both of the adults in your family may work at a job that pays between $7.25 and $10.00 per hour. Each person who decides to work will determine your hourly wage by rolling a die and referring to the income and travel calculator form. Once game play begins, you will collect your paycheck from your job each week and then manage your budget. This form will assist you in determining your take-home pay and desired travel arrangements.
2. Using the income and travel calculator form, you will decide what type of transportation you will use to get to work each day.

The four remaining rounds will each last 7 minutes. These 7 minutes are the equivalent of one week in "real time." During each week, you will have four tasks you must complete or there will be a severe financial penalty. These tasks are as follows:

1. Get your timesheet signed to pay your bills for the week. You will receive your timesheet from the timesheet administrator in Round 1. In each round, you must receive an event card from me and present that to your timesheet administrator in exchange for a signed time sheet.
2. Decide what to do in response to your parental decision card (you will be provided a choice).
3. Respond to the event card (you have no choice about the action these cards direct you to take).
4. Reconcile your weekly family financial ledger form accurately.

Please note that there will be financial penalties for failing to complete any task. These will be assessed by the exercise administrator.

Now I will introduce you to the game participants.

I am the exercise administrator. (*You may want to have a lead and second exercise administrator for groups larger than 12.*) The exercise administrator is the overall game administrator. The administrator is there to answer any questions about the game. The administrator sets all rules for the game and makes judgments regarding participant questions, game play infractions, and supervision of the children and time-card administrator. The exercise administrator will also verify the financial ledger for each family when they deem appropriate. In addition, the exercise administrator will have families draw random event cards during each stage of the game. These cards will present the family with an unexpected event, either good or bad, that the family must incorporate into their strategy.

_____ (*insert name*) is the time card administrator. Each working family member must go to the time-card administrator to get his or her time card filled out and signed during each stage of the game or else they do not receive their paycheck.

(*Point to those playing the role of children.*) Children will be played by your classmates. Each one represents two children. Pat is 16 and wishes to go to college. Juan(ita) is 6 and attends half-day kindergarten in the local school district.

The children will be given parental decision cards for families to draw one from during each stage of the game. You may have to explain your decision to the child if he or she is unhappy with it.

Each of you is a parent in your family–Group members of two will take on the role of adults in their families. Each family has two children, one 16 and one 6. (We recognize the fact that many families have one adult in the household but have not included this in the simulation because it is our belief that learning in this exercise will be stimulated by small groups and shared experience.)

You will now receive your game materials. These include:

- your income and travel calculator form (*already handed out*),
- your standard family financial ledger form, and
- your die.

The game will begin when I announce it. The first period will end when the timer goes off, which will also be the beginning of the first week. The week ends when the timer goes off. (*Answer as few questions as possible before game play begins.*)

Process Discussion

- What was the experience like for you?
- How long did it take for you to figure out the system? What did you learn about this system? Did you ever talk to or rely on other families for help or support? How is this similar or dissimilar to the real system for families living in working poverty?
- How many in the room pay $600/month in rent? $160 for all utilities? $400 for food? Were these expenses over- or undervalued in this game? What type of living conditions would be available for a family of four at these prices?
- What type of child care would a child receive for $125 per week or $5.20/hour? How much time did you spend with your child? How might this be similar to real child care in families living in poverty? What impact does it have on child/career development?
- How difficult is it for families to not just survive, but thrive on a minimum wage income?
- What coping strategies would families have to develop to make it on this type of income? To thrive?
- Who might the proctor represent in the real world? Helpful aspects? Harmful aspects of the character?
- (*Must ask*): As a counselor, what might you keep in mind when working with lower social class clients? Behaviors? (*Probe for patience with tardiness, missed appointments, non-payment.*)

Handouts: Handout 119.1: Event Card List
Handout 119.2: Timesheet
Handout 119.3: Income and Travel Calculator
Handout 119.4: Family Financial Ledger for One Month

Socioeconomic Status and Social Class

Additional Readings

Blustein, D. L. (2007). *The psychology of working: A new perspective for career development, counseling, and public policy*. Mahwah, NJ: Erlbaum.

U.S. Department of Labor, Wage and Hour Division. (2009). *Compliance assistance—Fair Labor Standards Act (FLSA)*. Retrieved June 17, 2009, from http://www.dol.gov/esa/whd/flsa/

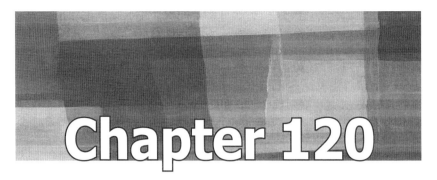

Chapter 120

Twenty Questions With a Twist: Uncovering Social Class Assumptions

Melissa Luke

Topics: Definitions of Cultural Diversity
Barriers to Effective Cross-Cultural Counseling
Human Growth and Development
Career Development
Poverty, Social Class, and Socioeconomic Status (SES)

Purposes: The purpose of this activity is to assist students in illuminating hidden assumptions about social class as related to occupation. The activity aims to facilitate an exploration of the ways in which values and beliefs can influence thoughts, feelings, and behavior.

Learning Objectives: As a result of this activity, students will

- be more aware of hidden assumptions related to social class and occupations, and
- have an increased understanding of how values and beliefs related to social class can influence observation and experience.

Target Population: This activity can be effective with students across a range of developmental levels, from beginning to more advanced. Because the activity can be modified to include participation roles for students who possess basic counseling skills, it can also accommodate a group of students with varying skills.

Group Size: This activity is effective across group size but is most effectively processed in groups of 20–25. The activity requires a minimum of three active participators but can be augmented to involve a maximum of six participators, with remaining students serving as the jury.

Time Required: This activity requires a minimum of 45–60 minutes in order to experience and fully process.

Setting: This activity can be used in a traditional classroom setting, with participating students seated in front of the student jury, who are seated in traditional rows. However, it is also effective in a setting where the jury is seated in a circle, surrounding the participating students. This activity requires three to six chairs for participating students, arranged according to Handout 120.1.

Materials: This activity requires no specific materials, other than the handouts.

Instructions for Conducting Activity

Students are told that they will be participating in a game of 20 questions (with a twist) and that everyone will have a role.

1. Student volunteers for three to six active participants are solicited.
2. The roles of all participants are explained to the entire class. (See Handout 120.2 for participant roles.)
3. A brief description of the following rules is given: This is a guessing game with a twist. It involves the use of two investigators, whose purpose is to help the jury to identify Subject's occupation. The investigators will alternate asking questions (10 each), but questions need to be answerable using yes or no, with no lying permitted. At the end of the game, the jury will guess the investigators' assumptions and beliefs.
4. The instructor organizes student participants' seating, distributes Handout 120.3 as needed, and then assists students to begin the activity.
5. If the optional roles are being used, the instructor may need to facilitate the timing/placement of students' interjected responses.
6. Once all 20 questions have been asked, the instructor queries the class, which is serving as the jury, about their guess as to the Subject's occupation. The investigators have an opportunity to offer their speculations as well.
7. The instructor then queries the jury about their guess as to the investigators' assumptions and beliefs. The Subject has an opportunity to offer his or her ideas as well.
8. The instructor elicits information regarding how and on what information all of these guesses were made. (See Handout 120.4 for potential prompts.)
9. The Subject reveals his or her occupation, and the investigators share their respective assumptions and beliefs.
10. Whether or not this information was accurately guessed, the instructor helps all students identify and explore the relationships between the assumptions and beliefs and the questions asked (behavior). (See Handout 120.4 for potential prompts.)
11. The Subject and the two investigators are asked to share their internal experiences as they took part in the activity.
12. The jury is invited to share some of their observations and experiences.
13. The instructor assists students in making connections between their experiential reactions within the activity with the assigned assumptions and beliefs and to others' behavior within the activity. (See Handout 120.4 for potential prompts.)
14. The instructor then reveals the final twist in sharing that the Subject's occupation was in fact a stripper, but that the Subject was a furniture stripper, removing paint and finishes from old dressers, tables, and chairs.
15. The instructor helps to process the students' reactions and assists them to identify the ways in which this twist changed their perceptions. In addition, the instructor helps students explore how any of what they discovered about themselves or others can be applied to other settings and contexts, including those that are counseling related. (See Handout 120.4 for potential prompts.)

Handouts: Handout 120.1: Suggested Seating Plan
Handout 120.2: Role Assignments
Handout 120.3: Identity Information
Handout 120.4: Processing Options

Additional Readings

Payne, R. K. (2001). *A framework for understanding poverty*. Highlands, TX: aha! Process, Inc.

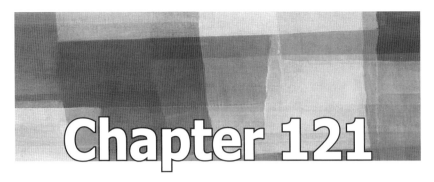

Chapter 121

Exploring Classism and the Effects of Socioeconomic Status Through the Use of Art Materials

Kate Davis Rogers

Topics: Oppression and Discrimination
Dimensions of Worldviews
Poverty, Social Class, and Socioeconomic Status (SES)
Creative Arts

Purposes: This activity aims to explore the effects of SES on the behavior of clients and therapists. By becoming a member of a particular social status, the student is allowed to explore his or her own biases of class and to watch the behaviors of other classmates as they take on roles of the lower, middle, or upper class. Information is given on the economic statistics of the world.

Learning Objectives: (a) To explore thoughts and feelings about different social classes and how they affect counselors in their practice, and (b) to increase awareness of the global nature of social classes and the students' privileges and responsibilities as people who belong to a particular class (lower, middle, or upper class).

Target Population: Graduate students but could be adapted for students from high school age and older

Group Size: 8–20 participants would be ideal.

Setting: A room large enough to hold four or five large tables and to provide enough space to have participants move around.

Materials: Newspapers, tape, markers, drawing paper, oil pastels, collage materials, chalk, and watercolors. Optional materials could include multicultural markers, different skin tone papers, and paper dolls with different skin tones.

Instructions for Conducting Activity

I have used this experiential exercise in five graduate-level art therapy classes to explore the various socioeconomic levels and participants' own biases toward lower, middle, and upper classes.

Classism is a relevant discussion at this time, given the economic troubles of the nation and the world. The possibility of people losing their economic status is higher than in the past several decades. There are also layers regarding what resources become available to the various groups, for instance, how many Whites, non-Hispanics, Hispanics, African Americans, and so forth are in the lower, middle, or upper class, and what kinds of education are various minority groups able to achieve. This information can be attained by going to www.census.gov.

The exercise is set up as a role-play. All students are assigned to a socioeconomic class as they enter the room. The students are not told what the experiential is until all students have arrived. The first two students are given upper-class status. The next students are assigned as the middle, and those arriving late are assigned to a lower class.

I chose the number to be assigned to each class status by referring to statistics given in the form of "if the world's population was only 100 people," which is listed on the website www.100people.org. Further statistics show that about 50% of the world's population lives on $1.00 to $2.00 a day. Therefore, I have assigned half of the participating students to the lower class. For instance, if there are 14 students, I assign 2 students to the upper class and 5 students to the middle class and 7 to the lower class. I do not share this information with the students in the beginning of the class.

The students are asked to make something that expresses their experience of culture. The lower class is given newspapers and tape and a few markers. The middle class is given several markers, drawing paper, oil pastels, and collage materials. The upper class is placed close to the cabinet with all of the art supplies and told that they may use any of the art materials available. In addition, they are given multicultural markers, papers of different skin tones, and the paper dolls of different skin tones.

The students begin to work. As the instructor, I sit back and let them start the process. After about 20 minutes, when I feel that the students are immersed in their roles, I begin to shake things up. I randomly pick students to become bankrupt and lower their status. I also randomly allow one person from the lower class to win the lottery. I have a person who graduated and was hired for a good job move to the middle class. I let the students pick numbers from a hat so that it is completely random and is not seen as a possibly biased decision of my own. I also suggest that they can apply for loans from another group if they want.

Responses From Students

Afterwards, I ask the class to discuss both their own internal process and what they observed in the group process. I point out my reasons for the predetermined number of participants in each group by supplying handouts showing the statistics. I explain that I had set up the tables for the middle and lower classes to be the same size and ask about spatial influences on the process. Did they feel overcrowded? Did they have adequate room in which to work?

The students have had various reactions to this process, although I have noticed some consistent results as well. The students assigned to the lower-class status tend to bond together quite quickly. In four out of the five groups, they have talked about stealing from the other groups, and in two groups the group members actually did steal from the upper-class group. In one class, the lower-class group worked out a way to create a diversion by one of the group members making loud random noises while another group member stole out of the art closet. She was actually able to do this without anyone in the room noticing what happened. The lower-class group has also tended to talk more crudely and about drugs, sex, and their oppression.

One student wrote, "Observing the change in others' attitudes and behaviors due to a superimposed fictional socioeconomic label was poignant if not unsettling. As a part of the lower class, I set out to steal supplies from the overabundant 'upper class.' When member of the upper class attempted to restrain and arrest me for my 'crime,' I could feel the depth of the disparity between us, even though these people— my classmates—were no different from me 10 minutes earlier. The end products spoke volumes about the creativity that can be accessed in the midst of poverty as well as the restrictive qualities that can emerge in the throes of overabundance. The strong feelings that emerged in all of us regardless of social economic status were externalized and complimented by equally strong imagery."

Another student stated, "As a member of the middle-class group with minimal resources, we were forced to really stretch. I think this yielded a more dynamic and creative product. Coming in really from middle-to-upper class backgrounds (as graduate students), we had to step outside of our box; instead of brand-name paint and brushes, we had to make art from newspaper and masking tape. It was a memorable experiential."

At the middle-class tables, the groups tend to be quiet and very cooperative with each other. They often plan out what they will do and then work independently and bring things together at the end. When I bankrupted one of their members, another member said she could crash on his couch until she got back on her feet. One member asked me very quietly if she really had to move to a lower class when she was bankrupted. The art pieces have tended to be focused on world peace and getting along with one another.

The upper class tends to feel isolated. A couple of different members attempted to talk to people in the lower class but were shut out by many of the members. One person when getting bankrupted hesitated in moving to the lower class and was rejected by the other members.

I point out to students that they are from an upper class because they have an educational level that many in the world will not achieve. One student wrote in her paper, titled "Who Wants to be a Millionaire?" the following: "There was a lot of resentment towards us millionaires. Would students remain contemptuous of people with power if they considered the power they have themselves?" Many students do not realize that they are very fortunate as graduate students. I point out how many groups do not have the resources to get through college and even to get to the graduate level. In fact, 1 in 100 people in the world has an education beyond high school. Through this exercise, students are able to increase their awareness of the privilege they have as graduate students."

The students in one of the upper-class groups decided to donate their extra supplies to the students in the lower class. The student reflected, "We were doing it (the donations) for ourselves, and they were totally unappreciative. The giving was patronizing and reflected on our own self-image, not what others truly needed. I can see how many Americans are shocked that international aid programs don't buy us international friendship. Also when we, the millionaires, decided to stop the lower-class member who was stealing from everyone else, I saw a strong parallel with the West's self-image as an international policeman, a view that contrasts so strongly with a world image of the West as a bully."

One way to help students get out of their roles at the end of this experiential is to have them walk around the room and reintroduce themselves to each other by their name. Even though these students know each other very well, I have sensed that they had become very involved in their roles. I wish I had done this experiment every time and strongly recommend it. Classism has lots of power attached to it and is often not addressed. I feel that the students need to remember that this was only a role-play and peers were only pretending.

Implications for the Counselor

When I have conducted this exercise, I have noticed that creativity has varied a little depending on what class level the participant was assigned to. I have been more impressed personally by the lower classes' art expressions then the upper classes'. However, students assigned to the middle and upper classes have all done the assignment and been cooperative. It was interesting to note that the students placed in the middle class seemed to be the most independent: Of all the groups, the middle class interacted the least with the other groups, and the students in the middle class were not even interested in interacting within their own group. The lower class seemed to have more camaraderie among its members.

In the real world, the lower class does not receive services and may be seen as unmotivated for change. Counselors may find they are having negative views of the lower class and perceive its values as distorted. For example, was even my own decision to reward the timely students flawed by allowing the first students to be the upper class? Was I using my own value system to select the members of the group? Will a client work harder because he or she arrives on time and sticks to the 50-minute hour?

According to research, middle-class clients are the clients most often seen in counseling. In the experiential exercises I have conducted, they were very compliant and did not seem to need much help in getting started with the assigned task; often they did not express any concerns until I approached them about changes because of the bankruptcy situation, making loans, and so forth. Are they easier because they have some resources? Did they feel certain complacency because of the resources?

Counselors are often faced with their own class status when working with clients of a higher status. Some of the upper-class clients will use their status as a defensive mechanism because they are able to say things such as, "I can own you." The fact a counselor needs to remember is that a client's problems are still the main focus; for instance, an addiction is still an addiction.

In the exercises I've conducted, I have found that those students playing the role of the upper class were very isolated. In another assignment, a student researched upper class people as a group and found that they were reluctant to seek out services because of their privacy needs and thoughts about needing to protect members of their family.

I would like to thank the students in all of my classes for their honesty and willingness to participate in the experiential. Your courage was always contagious. I would like to thank the following students for allowing me to reprint their thoughts and feelings regarding this experiential: Diane Barnes, Ginna Clark, Lisa Carey, and Kelsey Fagan.

Additional Readings

Sue, D. W., & Sue, D. (2008). *Counseling the culturally diverse: Theory and practice* (5th ed.). New York, NY: Wiley.

Author Index

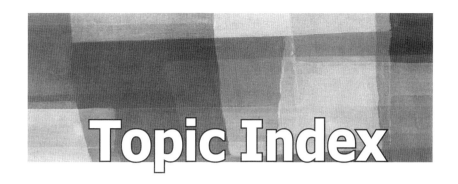

Topic Index